John Forster

Arrest of the five members by Charles the First

A chapter of English history rewritten

John Forster

Arrest of the five members by Charles the First
A chapter of English history rewritten

ISBN/EAN: 9783337204198

Printed in Europe, USA, Canada, Australia, Japan

Cover: Foto ©ninafisch / pixelio.de

More available books at **www.hansebooks.com**

ARREST

OF

THE FIVE MEMBERS BY CHARLES THE FIRST.

A CHAPTER OF ENGLISH HISTORY REWRITTEN.

BY JOHN FORSTER.

LONDON:
JOHN MURRAY, ALBEMARLE STREET.
1860.

[*The right of Tranſlation is reſerved.*]

CONTENTS.

I. INTRODUCTORY . . . . 1—10
PAGE

Text. An attempt fatal to its Author: Party mifreprefentations of it, 1. Not an ifolated Act. Dramatic correctnefs of the Eikon Bafilike. Authorities for this narrative, 2. MS. Illuftrations. Admiral Pennington, 3. Pennington appointed to fucceed Lord Northumberland. Captain Slingfby, brother of Strafford's Secretary: relates the Parliamentary news, *25th Nov.* (1641), 4. A night-long Debate. Sidney Bere, Under-Secretary of State: defcribes oppofition to printing the Remonftrance, 5. Fears of the wife. Narrow majorities in Houfe of Commons. Conflict continued, 6. Firft great Parliamentary divifions. Protefting with a difference, 7. Mr. Thomas Wifeman to Admiral Pennington, *2nd Dec.* (1641), 7, 8. Palmer's proteft and punifhment. Abfentees from the Houfes, 8. The majority of eleven. Never more heat in Parliament than now, *2nd Dec.* 1641. Minority fet up againft Majority, 9. Clofe of the firft ftruggle of Parliamentary party in England, 10.

Notes. Services to Englifh Hiftory rendered by Sir John Romilly. Clarendon's character of Pennington, 3.

II. THE KING'S RETURN FROM SCOTLAND . . 10—20

Text. Affertions of Clarendon, 10. The two attempts of the *3rd* and *4th January.* New State Appointments advifed by Lord Digby, 11. A queftion for enquiry. Sufpicions againft Falkland, Culpeper, and Hyde. Charges againft Pym and Hampden. The King's way of dealing with opponents, 12. Crufhing or conciliating, always too late, 13. Treafonable Correfpondence of Englifh members with Scotch Rebels. Clarendon's opinion of the five accufed, 14. Kimbolton a Scotch Commiffioner; narrowly watched by the Court. Lady Carlifle's intercourfe with both parties, 15. A dangerous mediator. Doubtful Services. Meetings in Pym's Lodgings, Chelfea, 16. Libels on Hampden. Avowed Rebels pardoned. Sufpected Rebels to be impeached, 17. The King's threats againft the popular Leaders. Treafons committed in Parliament. Coercing a minority put forth as breach of privilege, 18. Signs of danger abroad. *30th Nov.* 1641:

alleged conspiracy to get up charges of Treason, 19. Argument for giving weight to a minority. Alarms generally prevalent. Confidence of the King, 20.

Notes. Lord Digby's friendships, 11. Stratagem of winning by places. Offers to Pym. Their non-acceptance regretted by Hyde, 13. Secret Consultations. Kimbolton's ill company, 15.

§ III. FALSE RELIANCES . . . . . . 21—29.

Text. The Royalist party in the City. Banquet at Guildhall, 21. King's reception thereat. Lord Mayor Gourney made a Baronet. Welcome news for the King, 22. Speaker Lenthal alarmed: wishes to be relieved from Speakership, and to become again the meanest Subject of his Sovereign, 23. Speaker Lenthal to Secretary Nicholas, *3rd Dec.* 1641. Invokes the King's sacred mercy. Craves Mr. Secretary's help in lowest posture of obedience, 24. Expects ruin from continuing in the Chair of the House. A willing Dupe. Captain Slingsby to Admiral Pennington, *2nd Dec.* (1641), 25. Factious Citizens. Fears and misgivings of the best informed, 26. Slingsby's Alarm. Wealthy and discontented Citizens: coming in their coaches, 27. Unpopular acts of the Lord Mayor. Second thoughts of Speaker Lenthal, 28. An Under-Secretary's Prayer, 29.

Notes. Ovatio Carolina, 22. Clarendon's opinion of Lenthal, 23. The King and the two Houses. Citizens and M.P.'s. Sir Edward Dering, 26. Character of Sir Ed. Nicholas, 27. Speaker Lenthal to Secretary Nicholas, 28.

§ IV. FATAL MISTAKES . . . . . . 29—39

Text. Foolhardiness of the King. Removes the Guard from the Houses: Gives office to the Leaders of the Minority, 29. Assails Privilege, 30. Interferes with a Bill under discussion. Enforces Laws against Puritans. Remits Penalties against Roman Catholics. Partial execution of the Laws, 31. Resisted by the People, 32. A time for caution. Disastrous Resolve of the King. The Tower and its Governor, 33. Balfour removed. Lunsford appointed: his infamous character: his close friendship with Lord Digby, 34. Object in appointing him, 35. A man to execute anything: and keep the five members, once arrested, safe, 36. Evil forebodings of Sir Simonds D'Ewes. Address voted for Lunsford's Removal. Dismissal of Lord Newport. The Charge against him, 37. Proposal to seize hostages for the King's good Faith. The lie given to Lord Newport, *24th Dec.* The lie retracted, *29th Dec.* Warnings in the interval, 38. Sudden yielding of the King. Extraordinary determination taken, 39.

Contents.

Notes. Wifeman to Pennington, *2nd Dec.* (1641), 29. Under-Secretary Bere to Pennington, 25*th Nov.* and 9*th Dec.* 1641. Court Changes. Same to fame, 23*rd Dec*^r, 30. Slingfby to Pennington, 16*th Dec.* 1641. Attack upon Newgate. Reprievals of Popifh offenders, 32. Windebank's Crime and Efcape, 32, 33. Lunfford's Warrant, 34. Clarendon's account of the Appointment. Clouds of words. Digby the 'fcapegoat, 35. Lords who fided with majority in Commons. Duke of Richmond's fally, 26*th Jan.* (1641-2), 36.

§ V. PYM AND THE KING . . . . . . 39—60

Text. Popularity of the Leader of the Commons. Its caufes, 39. Pym imprifoned for his opinions in 1614. A Member of the Parliament of 1620. One of James the Firft's "Twelve Kings," 40. Rifes to the place of Leader, *April* 1640. Qualities and fervices which endeared him to the People. Clarendon's Tribute to his popularity, 41. Former intercourfe with the King. Negotiations again opened, 42. *King* Pym : fecret influence over King Charles, 44. Songs and Satires againft the Parliament, 45. Pym's Conftitutional opinions. Alternately held up for avoidance and for example. Characteriftics of his Oratory, 46. Chancellorfhip of Exchequer again offered to him. Pym lefs extreme than Hampden. The offer made too late, 47. Pym filent as to the King's propofal : rejefts it. Sir Edward Dering to Lady Dering, 13*th Jan.* 1641-2, defcribes Charles's overture to Pym, 48. Culpeper receives what Pym had declined, 1*ft Jan.* (1641-2), 49. Old Vane finally difmiffed, 50. Revenge for Strafford. Young Vane alfo difmiffed, 51. Captain Carterett. Young Vane fucceeded by a friend of Strafford. Captain Carterett to Pennington, 23*rd Dec.* 1641. Pym welcomes Old Vane into the popular Ranks, 52. Under-Secretary Bere to the Admiral, 23*rd Dec.* The Commons refent Young Vane's difmiffal. Previous offer to Pym and his Friends, *July* (1641), 53. Former attempt to give office to Leaders of the Commons. Not a mere expedient for faving Strafford : renewed after Strafford's execution. Hollis or Hampden named for Secretary of State, 15*th July* (1641), 54. Negotiations with popular Leaders kept open. Diftribution of offices fettled, 29*th July* (1641), 55. Preparation for the new Miniftry. Making provifion for the worft, 56. A fequel almoft too ftrange for belief. Prefent from the Admiral. Nicholas to Pennington, 29*th July* (1641), 57. Why Nicholas objefts to Ecclefiaftical Reform. King's propofed journey to Scotland : objefted to by the Commons. The new Miniftry expefted : Hampden, Pym, Hollis, and Lord Saye and Seale, 58. Nicholas about to retire : but does not retire. Why both attempts to conciliate popular Leaders failed. The rock

Contents.

they split against, 59. A warning for Pym to act upon. The warning taken, 60.

Notes. Sir R. Cotton's sufferings at seizure of his Library. The 1620 Parliament, 40. Why King's efforts to conciliate failed, 42. Royalist libellers of Pym. Doings when Pym was King. A proposed enactment, 43. Pym chides members for late attendance. Is happiest in Storms, 44. Pym and the "King's Daughter." Pym's Picture. Must avoid Heaven for fear of Bishops, 45. Pym's last resting-place, 46. Pym not adverse to the Church, but to Arminian practices, 47. Camden Society Books. Windebank to his Son, 17th Dec. 1641. Secret understanding with the Queen, 49. Windebank's grief at losing place. Same to his Son, 24th Dec. A fellow feeling, 50. Admiral Pennington looking for Young Vane's office. Captain Dowse to Pennington, 30th Dec., 51. Why Carterett was named Vice-Admiral by the Parliament, 52. Secretary Nicholas to Pennington, 54, 55. Sidney Bere to Pennington, 30th July, 1641. Notice to quit Whitehall. Proposed Viceroy during the King's absence. Consolations of a retiring official, 56.

§ VI. THE WESTMINSTER TUMULTS . . . . 60—67

Text. Publication of the Grand Remonstrance. A Fast Day, 22nd Dec. (1641), 60. How the King celebrated it. Discontented Holiday Crowds, 61. Sea and Land Storms. A religious war talked of. Lunsford's appointment cancelled. Too late. Memorable epithets first invented, 62. First blood shed in the Civil War, 64. Cause of sudden Assemblages in Westminster Hall, 65. Party statements. Who were the first Aggressors, 66. True beginning of the Civil War: in the attempt to destroy the Parliamentary Leaders, 66, 67.

Notes. Cavalier: Origin and Meaning of the Word. The King complains of its use. Roundhead, 63. William Lilly's evidence. The King's secret revealed. A Belief or Superstition. Character of Puritans, 64. What Lilly observed of the Tumults. A Parliament the People's only hope. Secret Counsels, 65.

§ VII. CITIZENS AND SOLDIERS IN THE HALL . . 67—81

Text. Monday 27th Dec. 1641. Severity of the Winter, 67. Tempest at Sea. Mr. Thomas Smith to Pennington, 30th Dec. At Whitehall Gate 29th Dec., 68. Exasperation of the People. Jesuitical Faction strong in the House. The Under Secretary to the Admiral, 30th Dec. Confusion and fears, 69. Lunsford knighted and pensioned upon his removal. Blood shed 27th Dec. Courtiers ordered to be armed, 70. Share in the tumults taken by Citizens and Apprentices,

70, 71. What Mr. Bramſton ſaw 27*th Dec.* Provocation to the People, 71. Soldier aſſailants. Volunteer Guard to the King. Clarendon's opinion of them, 72. Component elements of the Guard. The King's unſeaſonable acceptance of their Service. Citizens inſulted and aſſailed by them, 73. Cuts and flaſhes drawing blood. Plain meanings to Clarendon's ſpeech. Eager encouragement to attack on Citizens, 74. Abettors of the Outrage. Deſign in encouraging the Whitehall Deſperadoes: to draw together a ſtanding Guard, 75. Admiſſions by the King 9*th March* 1641-2. Witneſſes above ſuſpicion, 76. A mad Chriſtmas. Excuſes for the Whitehall Guard. Unpopularity of Sir John Biron. Citizens chaſed about the Hall by armed Soldiers, 77. Affray in the Abbey *Dec.* 28*th*. Unprovoked outrage by the Soldiers 29*th Dec.* Gentlemen armed crowding the Court: 500 volunteer Lawyers; 30*th Dec.* Charge againſt Lord Briſtol, 78. No blood ſhed by the Citizens. A fighting Archbiſhop, 79. Incitements to violence. Shops cloſed, and all men arming. Dangerous Beliefs, 80. A terrible reſponſibility, 81.

Notes. Fierce Froſt in Paris: Windebank to his Son, 67, 68. The Penſion and Knighthood to Lunſford, 70. Archbiſhop Williams, 71. Slingſby's Ship at Spithead. His brother's connection with Strafford, 76. His error relative to the Citizens, 77. Entry from D'Ewes's Journal, 79.

§ VIII. WHAT WAS PASSING IN THE HOUSE . . 81—88

Text. Firſt day of the tumults, 27*th Dec*ʳ, 81. Second day of the tumults, 28*th Dec.* Lord Newport's diſmiſſal debated. Oliver Cromwell ſpeaking, 82. Denounces the Earl of Briſtol. Denzil Hollis attacks Lord Digby. Lord Digby's complicity with attempts of 3*rd & 4th Jan*ʳ, 83. No acquittal of Lord Digby intended. Reſolution on his Impeachment. Long ſilences in the Houſe. Tueſday 28*th Dec*ʳ, 84. Wedneſday 29*th Dec.* Cromwell as to officering of the Army. Threats of French Interference to put down Engliſh Liberties, 85. Inſolence of a French Prieſt. Court Secrets known to the French. French Information, 86. Warning from a Priſoner in the Gate Houſe, 87. Priſon for Jeſuits and Recuſants. The danger known to Pym, 88.

Notes. State of D'Ewes's Journal in the Harleian MSS, 81. The Spaniſh Match, 82. Iriſh military appointments, 85. John Marſton to Lord Kimbolton: Nature of his Communication, 87. Attack on the Parliament expected, 88.

§ IX. THE BISHOPS SENT TO THE TOWER . . . 88—105

Text. Thurſday 30*th Dec*ʳ, 88. Meſſage from the Lords. Proteſtation of the Biſhops, 89. They retire from the Houſe: and proteſt againſt Proceedings in their abſence, 90, 91.

Contents.

Effect of Proteſt. An opportunity deſired by the King. "Mobs" for two days only. Amount of provocation given, 92. What the Biſhop of Norwich ſaw and heard. Fright given in the Houſe itſelf. Some Lords adviſing, 93. Lord Hertford alarms the Biſhops. Other Lords ſmiling. What paſſed at Williams's Lodgings. "Unfortunate" Accident, 94. Charles and his Lord Keeper at Whitehall. Accident or Deſign? A ſurpriſe for the Biſhops. What Cromwell thought of the Proteſtation, 95. The Biſhops characterized by Cromwell. General feeling at the time, 96. Clarendon's opinion as to Impeachment. Contemporary Accounts. Slingſby to Pennington, 97. His opinion of the Proteſtation: even Biſhops' friends averſe to it. Bere to Pennington, 30*th* *Dec*. Committal of the Biſhops, 98. "Our deplorable condition." Prays the great tempeſts have left the Admiral ſafe. Mr. Thomas Smith to Pennington, 30*th Dec*. Endeavour of Biſhops to undo what Long Parliament had done, and compel a diſſolution, 99. Williams compared to Achitophel. Complicity of Lords Briſtol and Digby. Real drift of the Proteſt. Prompt action of the Lords, 100. A conference. 30*th Dec*. 8 o'clock p.m. ten Biſhops ſent to the Tower, 101. Laud and Williams within the ſame walls at laſt. Door ſhut on perſecuted and perſecutor. Caricature of Williams as a Decoy Duck, 102. A witty conceit: Laud's enjoyment thereof. Perhaps his laſt gleam of mirth, 103. D'Ewes ſees the Biſhops' Bench turned into lumber. Is glad they no longer call themſelves "Lordſhips"; and would keep them where they are, 104. "Cloſe air" at Charing Croſs, 105.

Notes. What the mob did to Archbiſhop Williams. Evidence of Bramſton, Hyde, and Hacket, 89. Hacket's *Scrinia Reſerata* deſcribed. Uſeleſs Knowledge. Written during the Protectorate. Attack on Milton, 90. A ſchoolboy ſcribbler. Shakeſpeare not known. Praiſe of Jonſon, Chaucer, and Spenſer, 91. How the Proteſt was ſigned, 95. Caſe againſt the Biſhops. Themſelves to thank for their unpopularity. Their violence and paſſion 17*th June* 1641. A true prediction, 96. Great Storms raging on the coaſt, 99. Hacket's lament for the Biſhops. No love of Biſhops among the Lords, 101. Debate as to calling in Biſhops of Lichfield and Durham, 102. The two Archbiſhops exchange Civilities in the Tower. Caricature of Williams as Church Militant, 103. Diſadvantages of the Black Rod, 105.

§ X. SHADOWS OF THE COMING EVENT . . . 105—112

Text. Houſe of Commons *Dec*. 30*th* (1641), 105. Members delighted by the folly of the Biſhops, 105, 106. Members alarmed by a ſuggeſtion of Pym's. Objection made by D'Ewes, 106. A ſtrange motion expected: which follows accordingly,

Contents. xi

PAGE
106, 107. Pym's Speech. The remedy for danger. Neceffity for an immediate Guard, 107. The whole truth not told. Report of Pym's Speech by D'Ewes. A defign to be executed: Plot for deftroying the Houfe of Commons. Adjournment to Guildhall propofed, 108. D'Ewes oppofes departure to City. " Let us not be taken together." The defign near or diftant ? Friday 31*ft Dec.* (1641), 109. Demand for Guard under Lord Effex, 109, 110. No reply. Halberts meanwhile provided. Committee to receive reply. Saturday 1*ft Jan.* (1641-2), 110. A Council at Whitehall. Falkland and Culpeper fworn into their offices, 111. Confequences and refponfibilities incident to office at fuch a time, 111, 112.

Notes. Dates of New Appointments, 110, 111. Culpeper Chancellor of the Exchequer. Falkland Secretary of State, 111.

§ XI. THE IMPEACHMENT BEFORE THE LORDS . 112—118

Text. Monday 3*rd Jan.* 1641-2. King's meffage to Commons refufing Guard. Attorney-General delivers impeachment to the Lords. Introduced by Lord Keeper Littleton, 112. The Seven Articles of Treafon. i. General Charge. ii. Authorfhip of Remonftrance. iii. Tampering with the Army. iv. Invitations to the Scotch. v. Punifhment of protefting Minority. vi. Raifing Tumults. vii. Levying War, 113, 114. Agitation among the Lords. Immediate aftion taken. King's demand refufed. Agreement with Commons, 115. Lord Kimbolton repels the Charge. Lord Digby filent, 116. Failure in courage or good faith: Clarendon's charge againft him, 117. Digby affefts furprife: and fuddenly quits the Houfe, 117, 118.

Notes. MS. Articles of Treafon in State Paper Office, 114, 115. Date of tranfmiffion of Petition of both Houfes for Guard, 115. Charles's anfwer thereto. Not Lord Effex, but Lord Lindfay: the moft devoted of Royal Partizans, 116.

§ XII. THE IMPEACHMENT BEFORE THE COMMONS . 118—126

Text. D'Ewes in the Lower Houfe. Pym fpeaking to the King's refufal of a Guard. D'Ewes's hurried and unfinifhed Reports, 118. Suggeftion for a City Guard. Fragments of Pym's Speech. Pym and Hollis informed of outrage at their homes, 119. Their and Hampden's Papers feized by King's Warrant: Declared a breach of Privilege. Refiftance juftified. Refolution againft Seizure of Private Papers, 120. Violation of Law as well as Privilege. The new Minifters filent. Hyde abfent. No oppofition attempted. The King's Serjeant at the door of the Houfe, 121. Enters, without his Mace. Demands the five Accufed. No Debate. Compofure of the Houfe, 122. The Serjeant ordered to wait outfide. Deputation to carry Meffage to the King: The accufed will anfwer any *legal* Charge, 123. The Five Accufed

Contents.

ordered to attend daily. Refolution for Military Guard out of the City. Venn and Pennington fent to the Lord Mayor. Day declining, 124. Seals affixed by King's Warrant to be broken. King's Agents who feized Papers to be imprifoned, 125. Laft Act of the Houfe on 3rd Jan^r, 126.

Note. Sir Wm. Killigrew and the diamond hat-band and ring, 125.

§ XIII. WHAT FOLLOWED THE IMPEACHMENT . 126—129

Text. Interview with the King. A Promife for next day. Authority for Scene to be defcribed, 126. Admixture of true and falfe. View taken by Mr. Hallam: how far credible, 127. Did the King act apart from all advice? Were Attorney and Keeper wholly ignorant? What Strode thought of their participation, 128. Propofed attempt of the 4th not fecret to the laft. Difcuffed the previous night, 129.

Notes. Ill advifers. Mr. Hallam's view not confonant with character of the King, 127. Mr. Attorney's Excufes to the Houfe: difbelieved by Strode, 128. The Queen's Attorney put forward. "Shut the door," 129.

§ XIV. SCENE IN THE QUEEN'S APARTMENTS . . 129—139

Text. Ill Advifers, 129. Papifts and women. Statement of Madame de Motteville, 130. Warning to the Accufed from French Ambaffador. Effects of Queen's intermeddling. Her defigns fufpected by the Commons, 131. Sufpicions proved true. Clarendon explains her defire to have the Members impeached, 132. To fave herfelf from Impeachment. Lucy, Countefs of Carlifle: her daily intercourfe with Pym and Kimbolton after Strafford's death, 133. Retribution for betrayal of her friend: Betrays the Court to the Commons. Her conduct explained by her character, 134. Her brother Northumberland. Sir Philip Warwick's Scandal, 135. A fuggeftion more probable. Doctor Bates. Privy Counfellors faid to have advifed the King, 137. King and Queen on the night of the 3rd January: On the morning of the 4th. Lady Carlifle clofeted with the Queen, 138. The One hour. Queen betrays her Secret. Lady Carlifle betrays the Queen, 139.

Notes. Henrietta's conduct on the return from Scotland. May the Hiftorian, 130. Charles mifled, 131. Abftraction of the Crown Jewels, 132. A Courtier's view of the Impeachment and Arreft. Bufy Statefwoman become She-Saint, 135. No ground for Warwick's Libel. Pym's unpuritanic manners. "Roundhead" explained by Baxter, 136. "That roundheaded Man," 137.

§ XV. Council on the Night of the 3rd of January . . . . 139—154

Text. The night's debate: Who were prefent? 139. Teftimony of Sir Arthur Hafelrig. Gratitude to Lady Carlifle. Rage of the Queen. What Philofopher Hobbes fays, 140. Direction in which to look for motives and objects of attempt of *4th January.* Not fo rafh as fuppofed, 141. Pofition of the King after failure of attempt of the *3rd January.* Challenge taken up by the Commons. Difficulty of retreat. Alleged Evidence to fupport the Charge, 142. Falfe Step irretrievable within limits of Law. Nature of the act already committed. One way to recover ground, 143. Renewal of attempt with means to enforce it. Foiled only by Lady Carlifle's warning. Idea of refiftance infeparable from propofed attempt, 144. The King incapable of a wife fear. Iffue raifed, one of violence: reafon why Houfe withdrew its members, 145. Source of Queen's felf-reproach: not prevention of attempt, but interception of confequences. Previous preparations at Whitehall and in the City, 146. Evidence of Captain Langres. Affiftance fought from Inns of Court, 147. Killigrew fent round with Copy of Impeachment, 148. What the new Minifters thought of the guilt of the accufed, 149. Objection to arreft only after its failure. Hyde employed to juftify it. Mifreprefentation of the cafe, 150. No privilege claimed againft Treafon. Falfe Iffue raifed, 151. Indemnity from Treafon never claimed. Method of proceeding only objected to. Culpeper's confidence to Dering. Charles's truft in his new Counfellors, 152. Imputation againft Hyde and his friends. Believed to be "Contrivers" of the Arreft, 153. Their mode of objecting and denying: no evidence of "deteftation" of the Deed, but rather proof of indirect participation, 153, 154. Stake played for and loft, 154.

Notes. "Littel Vil Murry," 139. May, and Hobbes, as to a demand for names of King's Advifers, 141. What Hyde thought of the Arreft: and what he would have done himfelf, 142, 143. Whitelock's view. Extent of danger prevented by Lady Carlifle, 145. Inns of Court Volunteer Guard. A troubled midfummer: 1628. The country on the eve of Refiftance. Royal letter to Benchers of Gray's Inn, 147. Defire to have all citizens exercifed in arms. Defect to be fupplied, a want of difcipline. Law Students not to neglect Studies, but to occupy leifure and vacations, 148. What Falkland, Culpeper, and Hyde would have done with the Five Members: Seized them feparately, and fent each to a different prifon, 149. "Gentlenefs" of the King's attempt alleged by Clarendon. An act of favour, 150. Another fketch from fame hand. The King's ftyle of writing, 151.

Contents.

§ XVI. MIDNIGHT VISIT TO THE CITY . . . 154—160

Text. Secretary Nicholas confulting late with the King, 154. Provifion againft tumults next day, and againft demand of Commons for Guard, 154, 155. Order of Houfe for City Train Bands. Counter Warrant figned by the King. Grave Evidence againft the Court, 155. Order to Train Bands to fire on the Citizens: Intercepted, and not publifhed until now. Why not put in force. Reached the City too late, 156. Fortunate accident for the King. What might have been Hiftory. Copy of the Warrant. Reference to Five Members, 157. Train Bands called out for the King. All Gatherings of Citizens to difperfe: On refufal, to be fired upon. Letter of Nicholas's Agent, 158. Whitehall clocks behind time. Anticipated by deputation from Commons? Paft midnight at the Tower. Any further *private* Commands? 159. Inferences from Agent's Letter. Preparations for the morrow. Memorable day, 160.

Note. Interlineation by Secretary Nicholas, 158.

§ XVII. MORNING OF THE 4TH OF JANUARY . . 160—175

Text. Houfe of Commons: Falkland reports King's Meffage, 160. Motion as to King's tampering with Inns of Court. Four Members fent to the Four Inns. Grand Committee, 161. Pym replies to Articles of Treafon. Allufion to Strafford. Charge of bringing over the Army to Parliament: lefs treafonable than overawing Parliament by Army, 162. Comparifons invited. Avows publication of Remonftrance. Accepts the guilt and refponfibility. As to charge of levying arms againft King, 163. As to apprehending delinquents. Guilty of defending Chrift's doctrine, and orthodox Church government. Judgment defired from the Houfe. "Well moved." An ominous queftion, 164. Has not breach of privilege been committed? Hollis, Hafelrig, and Strode, defend themfelves. Strode's Speech. Hafelrig's: his reference to Scottifh Treafon, 165. Hampden fpeaks. Juftifies refiftance. Defines ill and difloyal, good and loyal fubjects. Unaccuftomed Emotion, 166. Where Hampden looked for true Religion. In the two Teftaments. The Proteftant Church true. Bible alone needful to Salvation. Traditions and fuperftitions devilifh. The Romifh Church falfe, 167. A Creed to live by and die for. Hampden's change of bearing. Secrets of his character revealed. Waiting his time. Charges by Hyde and D'Ewes, 168. "Serpentine fubtlety." Imperfect and prejudiced Judgments. What Hampden really was. Admiffions of Clarendon, 169. Higheft power of Statefmanfhip. A leader and governor of men, 170. Change in Pym as well as Hampden after accufation of Treafon, 170, 171. All thoughts of moderation

Contents.

gone. No compromife poffible. A memorable friendfhip. Remark to Hyde. Advantage of knowing one's friends, 171. Conference with the Lords demanded. Impeachment denounced as a fcandalous paper, 172. The Whitehall Guard an interruption to free debate. Compofednefs of the leaders of the Commons. Gatherings of armed Men near the Houfe, 173. Pym moves a deputation to City. Deputation departs. No man to know its errand. Alarm ftill increafing. Adjournment for an hour, 174.

Notes. The table at Whitehall for gentlemen of Inns of Court. A violent young lawyer, 161. What made Hampden's hurt mortal, 168. Clarendon's character of Hampden: Equal to anything, 170. Pym greateft in the Houfe, 171. Hampden and Pym as to "difcretion" of Mr. Hyde. "Snappifhnefs" of Mr. Hampden, 172. Bifhops in the Tower, 173, 174.

§ XVIII. BETRAYAL OF THE SECRET. . . . 175—179

Text. A momentous interval. Lady Carlifle betrays all to Pym. Private Meffage from Lord Effex. Houfe affembles: half-paft one, 175. Report from Inns of Court. Lincoln's Inn. King's meffage to be in readinefs this day: But as prompt in loyalty to Commons. Same from Gray's Inn, 176. From Inner Temple and from Middle Temple, 176, 177. The Houfe fatiffied. Armed Crowds gathering nearer. Re-entrance of the Five Members. The Secret difclofed to the Houfe, 177. Should the accufed retire or remain? A new Actor on the Scene. Lenthal announces King's approach, 178. Leave to Five Members to abfent themfelves. Away to the City by Water. Strode refifts, and is dragged out, 179.

Notes. Famous Entry in Commons' Journals, 177. Chronicler Heath, 178.

§ XIX. THE KING'S APPROACH TO THE HOUSE . 179—184

Text. The King's attendants, 179. As to their number and arms. Teftimony of Sir Ralph Verney: of Rufhworth: of Ludlow: of Thomas May, 180. Alfo of Mrs. Hutchinfon, and D'Ewes. Clarendon contradicts all: Relating what was "vifible to all," 181. Slingfby's account to Pennington, 6*th* *Jan*ʸ, 181, 182. Armed Guards at Whitehall. Terror and trouble of the Citizens, 182. Slingfby one of the King's companions. How "innocently" armed. Difmay at their approach. Shops fhut up. The King paffes through Weft-minfter Hall, 183. Lobby of Houfe of Commons fuddenly filled. Armed men ftill prefs from without. Charles enters the Houfe, where never King was but once, 184.

Notes. Reformadoes, 180. Slingfby defcribes Impeachment. Members fitting in Houfe notwithftanding, 182.

§ XX. THE HOUSE ENTERED BY THE KING . . 184—595

Text. Voice of Charles heard as he enters, 184. Armed followers vifible outfide. Door kept forcibly open. Captain Hide and Lord Roxborough, 185. Members rife and uncover. A crowd of bare faces. Charles turns to a well-known Seat. Miffes Mr. Pym. Paffes up to Speaker's Chair, clofe by D'Ewes's feat. Stands on ftep of Lenthal's chair, 186. Looks long before he fpeaks. Break in narrative of D'Ewes. One unmoved Spectator of the Scene. Young Mr. Rufhworth. His Report and Defcription fent for by the King. Important Corrections made therein, 187. Copy fo corrected in State Paper Office: A help to more vivid reproduction of the Scene. The King's Speech to the Houfe, 188. Expects Traitors to be delivered up to him, 189. Are the Five Members in the Houfe? No reply. Nothing will be well, until Accufed are furrendered. Muft have them. Painful hefitation and effort. Addition by D'Ewes, 190. Confirmation of Rufhworth. Enquiries for Pym and Hollis. Reply. Looking for them himfelf. Speaker Lenthal's Speech. No eyes or tongue but as the Houfe's Servant, 191. Extraordinary Speech for an Ordinary man. Another greater but like example. "Dreadful" Silence. The King confcious of his failure, 192. His birds flown. Protefts he never intended force. Means to maintain the conceffions he has made. Expects the Five will be fent to him. Declares their Treafon foul, 193. Leaves the Houfe: in anger, but not amid filence, 193, 194, 195. "Privilege! Privilege!" fhouted after him. Paffes out, through files of armed Adherents, 195.

Notes. Captain Hide: prominent in Weftminfter tumults: cafhiered and re-appointed, 185. Rufhworth's report of the Speech corrected by Charles, 188. Erafure by the King. Enquiry for Pym alfo erafed by King, 189. Charles the Firft's Speech at his Trial, 192. Slingfby's narrative of outrage. Silence of Houfe explained. Charles determined to have the Accufed. Houfe had fent to City for 4000 men. Shops all fhut. Bere to Pennington, 6*th Jan.* (1641-2), 194. Uncertainty as to flight of Members, 195.

§ XXI. IMPRESSION PRODUCED BY THE OUTRAGE . 195—204

Text. Proceedings in Houfe after King's departure. Speech of Hotham, 195. Cries for adjournment. Houfe rifes at 3.30 *p. m.* D'Ewes defcribes the King's defign: to have raifed a conflict in the Houfe. Details of the plot, 196. Armed defperadoes not to be reftrained. The King's perfon in danger. Strange deliverance. King's approach told to Fiennes, 197. Withdrawal of the members. Oppofition of Strode, 198, 199. Will feal his innocency with his blood. Sir Walter Earle pulls him out by the cloak. The

Contents.

PAGE

Accufed warned at dinner hour by Effex, 200. Unimpaffioned character of D'Ewes's teftimony. His fenfe of danger marked by execution of his Will : and fetting his houfe in order, 201. Ifolation of D'Ewes from mere party. His precifion and fobriety. Queftion of the King's conduct. Could have had but one purpofe, 202. Not the act but the failure unpardonable. Succefs narrowly miffed. Under-Secretary Bere's dread as to ultimate refult. Change muft be for the worfe. Rumours as to whereabouts of accufed, 203. Worfe ftorms on land than at fea. Circumftances well-known to Under-Secretary. His fears and forebodings, 204.

Notes. Abrupt entry in Journals of 4*th Jan.* (1641-2), 196. Identity of Strode with the earlier Strode difputed. Reply to objections made. Original impreffion ftrengthened, not weakened. Ages of the principal men of the Commons. Miftakes of Thomas May, 198. Contempt of Royalifts for Strode. Varieties of Royalift flander, 199. Queftion of accommodation with the King. Parliament men in peril, 201. An Invitation for Chriftmas declined, 204.

§ XXII. LORD DIGBY AND MR. HYDE . . . 204—218

Text. Violent and recklefs counfel. Carrying attempt to its iffue. Digby's propofal : to feize the Five Members dead or alive, 205. Mifchief let loofe by King's act. Rumours againft Briftol and Digby. Small comfort for the Admiral. Suffering on waters, fear on land, 206. Jacob and Efau. Two parties out of Houfe : but the leaders honeft, and only one party now in Houfe. Sole Rebels in England, 207. Open and fecret enemies. Caufe for this digreffion. Hyde the King's private advifer : fupplies fecret papers and information, 208. Playing double and falfe. Betrays the Commons to the King, 209. Complaint of the King againft Pym. Pym's rejoinder. Meffages fent before voted. Houfe warned againft treachery. Letter to Pym, 210. Able members informed againft. King's preparations. Parliament in danger. Charge aimed at Hyde, 211. Self-defence againft treachery. Hyde accufed of advifing Arreft : Suggeftion of his friends not to defend it, 212. Alleged fpeech upon Impeachment : Grofs mifreprefentation therein, 212, 213. Pretended occafion for Speech. Argument of Speech : no privilege for felony or treafon : undifputed by Pym and Hampden, 213. Imputation againft Leaders of the Commons. No proof exifting that the Speech was fpoken, 214. Hyde not in the Houfe, nor at Guildhall, or Grocers' Hall, 214, 215. No evidence that Hyde took part in debates on arreft, 215. Reafons for abfenting himfelf. His help more ufeful elfewhere. Appeal to force, 216. Impreffion to be made on the people, 218.

b

Contents.

Notes. Private meetings in Hyde's lodgings. Suspicions against him. Hyde shut up with Charles, 209. Inconsistency in Hyde's MS, 215. Hallam's view of Impeachment, 216. William Lilly as to arrest of Members. Cost the King his Crown. All confidence at an end. A dinner party on day of Arrest. Belief as to outrage intended. King's obstinacy, 217.

§ XXIII. SIR SIMONDS D'EWES AND SPEAKER LENTHAL 218—251

Text. Further pause in Narrative required. MS. Diary of D'Ewes, 218. Illustrations to be drawn from it. D'Ewes a reliable Witness. Not a thorough going party man, 219. Differences with Leaders. Epithets applied to popular Chiefs. Why more tolerant of Pym: Pym more tolerant of him, 220. Discussion upon Answers to a Message. Objection of Royalists: D'Ewes supports it. Is assailed by violent spirits, 221. Persists in spite of them. Receives encouragement. Pym's "discretion and modesty." Adopts the amendment, 222. Mr. Strode less civil: speaks thrice and gets laughed at, 222, 223. Good humour of the House. Moderation of D'Ewes, 223. Proposed censure of Sir Ralph Hopton. Pope soliciting help against English Parliament, 224. Hopton's offence: His expulsion moved, 225. D'Ewes's speech in mitigation. Interrupted by the hot spirits. Appeals to order. His suggestion adopted by House, 226. Makes similar objection to Hopton's: with better success. D'Ewes's love for moderate speech. Another Case for Censure, 227. Sir Edward Dering's published Speeches. D'Ewes's indignation thereat. Would have Dering expelled. Denounces his vainglorious Preface, 228. Dering's attack upon the House. Mr. O. C. libelled. Mr. Speaker compliments D'Ewes, 229. Objection to suppression of a Book: will raise its value from fourteen pence to fourteen shillings. Dering expelled, and his Book burnt, 229, 230. Suggestion from Mr. Oliver Cromwell: Will D'Ewes answer Dering? 230. D'Ewes declines: has better things to do. Might not Mr. Cromwell do it? Other proofs of D'Ewes's accuracy. Originality of his Journal, 231. Hollis would alter a message voted. Message already printed. Who copies nightly from Clerk's Journals? Falkland and two others, 232. But not D'Ewes: he reports "out of his head," never at second hand, 232, 233. Clerk Elsyng's Apologies. A delicate matter discussed. Note-taking inseparable from Speech-making. Relations of D'Ewes to Lenthal, 233. His authority in precedents: Critic and Patron of Mr. Speaker. Weaknesses of Lenthal. Self-surrender of his only claim to respect. A Witness against Scot the Regicide, 234. A Time-server always. Traits and incidents from D'Ewes's diary. Question of Privilege, 235. Haselrig and Lenthal.

Contents.

Attack on Mr. Speaker. D'Ewes rebukes Haselrig. Lenthal out of order, 236. Sugar duties' debate. Members entering juft before Queftion put. Not to withdraw. Extraordinary proceeding of Mr. Speaker. Lenthal again at fault, 237. An Honourable Member interrupted. Honourable Member retorts. Mr. Speaker fuccumbs. D'Ewes's indignation. Lenthal's deficiencies as Speaker, 238. A Letter from the King. D'Ewes the great authority as to Order: Compofer of difcords in debate. Heat of ancient Burgefs for Coventry, 239. Fierce and unparliamentary looks. D'Ewes's opinion thereon. Ancient member again. Vote for allegiance to Parliamentary General: difliked by D'Ewes, 240. Burgefs for Coventry required to fay *Aye*: fays *No*. Affailed by Mr. Speaker. Wifhes to fay *Aye*: but not permitted. Other members frightened, 241. Sir Peter Wentworth cannot truft the King. Chancellor of Exchequer's horror. Houfe overlooks this "folly." Old Sir Harry Vane. Startling Speeches. Sir John Northcote's avowal, 242. "Make the Prince our King." Old Vane declares for Militia and "new foundation," 243. Harry Killegrew's Speech. Novel Political Doctrine. Houfe laughs. Young Vane very ferious. Killegrew's apology. Pym refifts his expulfion, 244. An indifcreet friend. D'Ewes goes in fearch of Records. Expofes Cornifh ignorance. Is merciful in triumph, 245. Attempts to force early attendance. Alarming time when firft found neceffary. Tragi-comedy of the World, 246. Houfe in fadnefs: Suddenly moved to laughter. The Shilling Fine. A failure. Shilling Fine again propofed. D'Ewes oppofed to it, 247. Mr. Speaker late: rebuked: throws his fhilling on table: will not take it up again, 248. Ill refults of the Fine. Refufals to pay. Jack Hotham ordered to pay. Flings his fhilling on ground, 249. Beginning of the End. Call of Houfe attempted. Not forty members prefent, 250. A Stranger in the Houfe. How dealt with. Refumption of Narrative. Why interrupted, 251.

Notes. D'Ewes's detection of forged fignatures to a Royalift Petition, 219. Withdrawing for fupper, 223. King accufed of Popifh defigns. Too many grounds for fuch imputation. Englifh Politics at Rome. Letter to Hyde from brother-in-law, 224. The Pope's Nephew: Says he has not fomented Englifh troubles. His "intereft" in Pym and Hampden, 225. Remarkable entry in Journal. Generofity of Houfe to Strafford's fon, 227. Contraft to Lenthal, 234. Northumberland true to old friends. An example profitable to Kings, 235. D'Ewes avoids Chair of Committee, 239. Misfortune to Royal Standard, 240. Occafion of Northcote's Speech. Anecdote of Killegrew. Will "find" a good caufe, 243. A reprimand, 245.

Contents.

§ XXIV. APPEAL TO THE CITY . . . . 251—258

Text. Mr. Rushworth sent for by the King, 251. Report of his Majesty's Speech demanded. Mr. Rushworth's humble excuses. King's sharp rejoinder. Speech transcribed from Notes, in King's presence. Sent to press, 252. Proclamation against Five Members. Ports closed against their escape. Their place of refuge. City of London. Merchants' home as well as place of business, 253. Its palaces and privileges. Sources of its power, 254. Its complete and organized democracy. Its incredible enrichment by trade. Clarendon's lament, 255. City disaffected to Court. Well affected to Commons. Services in the War. Excitement on night of the Arrest, 256. " Cavaliers coming." Apprehended seizure of arms, 257. King's Message to the Lord Mayor. Warrants against accused, 258.

Notes. Lord Mayor's letter to Aldermen. Military organization of City. Instructions for Watch and Ward. Personal service required from Aldermen, 254. Fortifications of the City Walls, 255. Attacks on City in Royalist Satires, 256. City shops all shut. Rough draft of Royal Warrant. Ordnance safely disposed. Houses to be searched for muskets. Possessors of fire-arms to be examined, 257.

§ XXV. THE KING'S RECEPTION IN GUILDHALL . 258—263

Text. An important day for Charles I., 258. His last stake for good will of City. His confidence still unabated. Grounds for such false reliance. Present supporters and old traditions, 259. Reception on his way. Caution to be wary of Speech. Forced mildness. Captain Slingsby an eye and ear witness. " Privilege! Privilege!" "To your tents, O Israel!" 260. Arrival at Guildhall. King's Speech. Resolved to have the Five Members. Reliance on the City's good will. Will redress grievances and respect privileges: but must question Traitors, 261. Justifies Whitehall Guard. Offers to dine with liberal Sheriff. "Privileges of Parliament," and "God bless the King." Has any one anything to say? Yes: we vote you hear your Parliament, 262. No: that is not our vote. A bold fellow on a form. Rejoinder for him. "Trial —trial!" King dines with Sheriff. "Trial—trial!" 263.

Notes. King's Speech at Guildhall, 258. Assurances as to religion. Dinner at Sheriff's, 259.

§ XXVI. HUMILIATION AND REVENGE . . . 264—271

Text. Incidents of the return to Whitehall. Wiseman to Pennington, *6th Jan.* News of the Week, 264. Fears of Insurrection. Accused keeping out of way. Efforts to conciliate.

Contents. xxi

PAGE

Gentlenefs of King's voice. Firmnefs of his purpofe. Muft bring Traitors to Trial, 265. Dinner at Sheriff Garrett's. Shouts againſt the King. Glad to get home. Why Commons left Weſtminſter. Expectation of Bloodſhed. Doubts which party ſtrongeſt, 266. Retroſpect. More P.C.s made. God preferve His Majeſty! Meſſage from Mrs. Wifeman. A worfe trial for Charles. Vifit from Common Council, 267. Their advice: Confult with your Parliament: Leave Tower alone: Difperfe Whitehall Guard: Abandon Impeachment, 268. King's firſt act on return from City. New Proclamation againſt the Members! Rough Draft in King's hand. Kimbolton omitted. Inſtructions to Secretary Nicholas, 269. The guilty have efcaped. Injunction to feize them. Warning againſt harbouring them. The City threatened. Solely the King's act, 270. Hopelefs and recklefs perfiſtence. Repentance of Nicholas. Charles directs even Printing of Proclamation, 271.

Notes. Bere to Pennington: *6th Jan.* Cries in City, 264. Anecdote told by Slingfby, 268. King's inſtructions to Printer, 271.

§ XXVII. REASSEMBLING OF THE COMMONS . . 271—281

Text. Wedneſday *5th Jan.* 1641-2. Yeſterday's agitation not fubfided, 271. Watches fent out: 260 Members prefent: 90 of the King's party. Member for Colcheſter leads Debate. Grimſton's Speech. Its fcope and value, 272. Expofition of the Power of Parliament. Why fo awfully predominant? Becaufe it puniſhes evil doers: comforts the oppreſſed: and ſtrips the wicked of place, 273. Late outrage due to evil counfellors. Offences charged. Conduct in Parliament. Right to fpeak freely. Title not to have votes queſtioned: whether on Bills of Attainder or others: or in drawing up Remonſtrances, 274. Concluſion. Members accufed for conduct in Houfe: Lodgings entered and papers feized: a breach of privilege. Motion upon Grimſton's Speech. Oppofed by Hopton. Excufes for the King. Committee to prepare Refolution, 275. They retire: nothing to be done till their return. They return in a quarter of an hour: with a Refolution written before we met, 276. D'Ewes not in confidence of Leaders; but his account truſtworthy, 276, 277. Glyn's declaratory Refolution. Propofed Adjournment: Grand Committee to fit in the City. Warm Debate thereon. Sir Ralph Hopton, 277. Did not we give firſt provocation? And how gracious the King's Speech! Oppofes Committee and Adjournment. "Grand" Committee altered to "Select." Adjourn till tomorrow at 9 o'clock, 278. Divifion upon going into City, 170 againſt 86. Selection of the Committee. All who come to have voices, 279. Its duties. Comprifes feveral Royaliſts. Names on Committee. Hyde, St. John, and Cromwell abfent

Contents.

from it, 280. Motion by Lord Lifle. Irifh Affairs. Sharp Debate led by Fiennes. Meffage to Lords. Abrupt rifing of Houfe, 281.

Notes. Divifion as to Duke of Richmond. One of D'Ewes's "young" men, 279.

§ XXVIII. A SUDDEN PANIC . . . . . 281—289

Text. Armed men marching upon us. Sir John Clotworthy perfifts with Refolutions. Voted without being read. Diforderly Adjournment. Reafons for the fright, 282. Other Members to be accufed and feized. City only had prevented it. Alarm of the King. Change of purpofe. Refults of *4th Jan.* Darkeft Rumours thought true, 283. Scottifh "incident:" 284. Irifh rebellion: and army plot: King's fhare therein, 285, 286. Confequences of outrage worfe than itfelf. Belief obtained for groffeft Charges. Captain Carterett's fears. Mr. Wifeman's. Obedience poifoned, 287. Powers of the State in conflict. Specific caufes of Alarm. Digby's plan for fecuring Members. King withholds Confent. Clarendon's own plan: To feize and throw them into feparate Prifons, 288.

Notes. Offer of Montrofe to kill Argyle and Hamilton. Mr. Napier's difproof quite untenable. Text of Clarendon. Edition of 1826. Difclofed Author's plan. Hiftory compofed of two MSS. Secretary's tranfcript. Altered and corrupted by Author's Sons, 284. Reftorations. Scaffoldings of a book. Later and earlier Verfions of fame events. The Montrofe charge, the later Verfion. Intended fo to ftand. Impoffible not to print it: Reluctance of firft Editors, 285. Additions in 1826 not to be confufed with Reftorations, 285, 286. Two kinds: weight refpectively due to each. Montrofe charge intended. The King its authority. Why firft Verfion of it changed, 286.

§ XXIX. HOW HISTORY MAY BE WRITTEN . . 289—294

Text. Faithleffnefs of Clarendon. Unfafe guide. Comparifon with D'Ewes, Verney, and Rufhworth, 289. Statement by Clarendon. Alleged tone of Members' Friends, 290. Affected fears and griefs. Propofal to adjourn Parliament. King's wifh to get Parliament away from London. Appointment of Committee. Royalifts filent, 291. Three King's Advifers: too dejected to fpeak. Clarendon's Account fummed up. Five fpecific Statements, all untrue. Confronted with D'Ewes, Verney, and Rufhworth, 292. Never propofed to adjourn Parliament. Limit of ftay in City fpecified. Merchant Tailors' Hall not named. Royalifts not filent. Culpeper and Falkland on Committee, 293.

Notes. Verney's account of Sitting of 5th. Rufhworth's Account. Adjournment to City, 290.

Contents. xxiii

§ XXX. ADJOURNMENT AND SUSPENSE . . . 294—300

Text. Mafter-ftroke of meeting in the City. Neceffity of fufpending Weftminfter Sittings. Policy of appealing to Citizens. Alleged abfence of danger, 294. Fears pretended. to get help from "darling" City. But what fay private letters in State Paper Office? Serious alarm at Impeachment. Fate of Members in balance. Wifeman's view, 295. The Under Secretary's. Captain Carterett's, *7th Jan.* Gives no opinion, but ftates the faƈt. Vote of Houfe for the Accufed. Serjeant Dandie gone to feize them, 296. Attacked by the People. Obftinate refolve of the King. Thomas Smith to Pennington, *7th Jan.* Proteƈtion of Accufed againft King, 297. King will ufe force. City refolved to refift. "God help us!" Slingfby to Pennington, *6th Jan.* M.P.s difcourfing of adjournment to City. Many refufe to go, 298. Fear to be thought "Acceffories." Threats if Accufed not given up. Royalifts begin to favour Irifh. Pym's heavieft charge proved true, 299. Sympathy with Irifh Rebellion, 300.

Notes. Holborne's Argument, 299.

§ XXXI. COMMONS' COMMITTEE AT GUILDHALL . 300—316

Text. Thurfday morning, *6th Jan.* No exifting report of proceedings. Slight notices in Rufhworth and Verney, 300. Confufions of Clarendon. A regular record by D'Ewes. Where the Committee fat. Welcome of the Citizens. Military Guard in attendance, 301. City Hofpitalities. "Great cheer." Firft matter debated. Searching Lodgings and fealing up Papers. Iffuing illegal warrants, 302. Attorney-General's Proceedings firft queftioned. Motion to fend for Warrants. Refifted by D'Ewes. Speech by him, 303. Explains privileges againft arreft. Final, and temporary. Why fuch diftinƈtion. When the Houfe to judge as to faƈt and penalty, 304. When as to faƈt only. Otherwife Houfe might be thinned at pleafure. Yet Members guilty to be furrendered. Examples given. "Well moved," 305. Fair and juft temper of Committee. No defire to be irrefponfible, 306. D'Ewes refumes. As to cafes where Lords join. Privileges claimed by both Houfes. Impeachment by Lower Houfe: compels furrender of the perfon. Malice not prefumable, 307. Conclufion by D'Ewes. Loud acclamation. Glyn's Speech: aimed at fuch counfels as Hyde's. Private Informers of the King, 308. Spies in the Houfe. Manifeft breach of privilege. Glyn has taken leaderfhip. Chiefs under him, 309. D'Ewes's Argument on Privilege. A firm pofition. More than one queftion at iffue. Clarendon's evafion, 310. Not one, but many breaches of law. King powerlefs to arreft, 311. Each ftep an outrage. Subjeƈt may do what King cannot.

Contents.

PAGE

Shame of Attorney-General. Makes apology through a Friend, 312. Apology not believed. Mr. Strode's remark thereon. Debate as to warrants continued. Sound principles stated. No difference of opinion, 313. Dispute of D'Ewes with Wilde. Wrong issue suggested. Corrected by D'Ewes. Lords to issue Warrants. How to make a right thing wrong, 314. D'Ewes's victory over Wilde. Good sense of Committee. Resolutions voted. Against Warrants: against persons arresting under them. Young Vane rises, 315. Offers wise suggestion. Guard against claiming privilege for Crime. Subcommittee to draw proviso. Vane's clause voted and printed. Adjourn to Grocers' Hall, 316.

Notes. Why applaud D'Ewes and object to Hyde? 305, 306. Answer suggested. Doggrel " Five Members' March," 306. Just opinions as to Arrest. Smith to Pennington, 5th *Jan.* King not to accuse Subjects, 311. Discontent with the King, 312.

§ XXXII. FACTS AND FICTIONS . . . . 316—320

Text. Clarendon Fictions. Alleged restriction of Votes. Concurrent sittings of House. Hyde's asserted speech. Pretended references to House itself, 317. House confirming votes of Committee. All done during Five Members' Absence. Reply. Votes not so restricted. House itself not sitting. Hyde not Speaking, 318. No Short Sittings. Journals support D'Ewes. Evidence of published Declaration. As to Warrants: King powerless to issue them, 319. As to Arrest: King disabled from effecting it, 319, 320. As to claim of privilege: Not desired to bar a just charge. Readiness to bring guilty to Trial.

§ XXXIII. AGITATION IN THE CITY . . . 320—326

Text. Thursday night, 6th *Jan^r*, 320. Change in the People. Disposed to any undertaking, 321. Sudden alarm at Ludgate. Threatened attack on Coleman Street. The Digby Plot. Lunsford in it, 322. City in Arms. 140,000 men with weapons. Panic continues. Women in terror. Exertions of Lord Mayor, 323. Streets cleared., City again quiet. Thanks of Council to Lord Mayor, 324. Ill-timed defiance. Troop raised by Royalist Squire, 325. Tendency to undue fears, 326.

Notes. Evidence of Clarendon. Tribunes exalted. Court reduced. All slanders believed, 321. Speech of Stapleton. Lunsford's bragging, 322. Order from Council, Saturday 8th *Jan.* Members for City odious to Court. Swearing in of Falkland. Tumult of Thursday noticed. Its authors must be punished, 324. Certain persons (M.P.s) over earnest. Find out authors of Alarm. Give up their Names, 325.

Contents.

§ XXXIV. First Sitting at Grocers' Hall . 326—333

Text. Friday 7*th Jan.* Witneffes as to Outrage of 4*th.* Abftract of their Evidence, 326. Concerted plan. Signal to be given. Difappointment. Neceffity of forcing Commons to obey King. Signal only wanted. Forcibly keeping open door of Houfe, 327. Counting numbers. Ingenuous Confeffion. An important Witnefs: At Whitehall the previous Friday. What Lieut. Jenkin faid. Again at Whitehall on the 4*th.* Previous intelligence of King's defign, 328. Paffes over roof to efcape Crowds. Knew of coming trouble three weeks ago. Impreffion made on D'Ewes. Satiffied as to purpofe aimed at: to find excufe for armed conflict with Houfe. Moves and carries vote to that effect, 329. Sheriffs of London in attendance. Afked as to Warrants. One replies, the other refufes. Difference between Wilde and D'Ewes. Don't fhout "Aye" or "No," but reflect and confider, 330. Againft calling in Warrants. Difcreet tone as to the King. Refpect ftill due. Touch of humour. An ill choice, 331. Call in Sheriffs and difmifs them. Suggeftion adopted. Motion that Five Members attend Committee: difliked by D'Ewes: carried. King meets the challenge, 332. Frefh Proclamation againft accufed. Unwife courfe, 333.

§ XXXV. Second Sitting at Grocers' Hall. . 333—338

Text. Saturday 8*th Jan.* Reply of Houfe to King's Proclamation, 333. Open defiance of the Sovereign. Alarming News. Step taken thereon. Guard ordered for the Tower, 334. Selection of Commanding Officer: Major-General Skippon: character and fervices, 335. Named chief of City Militia. How Authority comes into being: attends upon Neceffity. Order for *poffe comitatus.* No fuch Guard needed, 336. Committee ignorant of their power. Triumph preparing. Members to be borne back by the People. Propofal of King to attend Committee. Its reception, 337. Due refpect to be paid. Way to be made for King and Nobles, 338.

Notes. Importance of the Tower. Security to Merchants. Pym's Great Speech to the Lords, 334. Effect of political troubles on trade. Defence of the Commons, 335. Skippon and his Soldiers. Liking for Short Speeches, 336.

§ XXXVI. Sunday the Ninth of January . . 338—339

Text. Vifitors in City Streets and Chapels. Strangers meeting as Friends. Petitioners for Pym, 338. Petitioners for Hampden. Savoury Difcourfes. 122nd Pfalm. Text preached from, 339.

Contents.

§ XXXVII. PREPARATIONS FOR THE TRIUMPH . 340—356

Text. Monday 10*th Jan.* Laſt Sitting in Grocers' Hall. Crowds aſſembled. Speeches of Glyn and Alderman Pennington. Suſpected tamperings at the Tower, 340. Evidence of danger. " Cavaliers." Sub-committee appointed, and Byron ſummoned. Motion againſt Killegrew and Fleming, 341. Moderation of Committee. Violent Language diſliked. Reſolutions modified and paſſed : Againſt agents on 3*rd* and 4*th*, 342. Againſt evil Counſellors : againſt Proclamations iſſued ; againſt warrants under King's hand, 343. Speech by Maynard : his fellowſhip with Glyn. Remembered at the Reſtoration, 344. His preſent view of Parliaments : their privileges : the attempted arreſt : and the unlawful ſeizures, 345. All public buſineſs in peril. "Well Moved." Lords and Biſhops uncontrolled. Men of Spirit diſabled, 346. Agitation outſide. Petition of Sailors. Services of Mariners accepted. To meet at 3 next morning : at the Hermitage, 347. The "Water rats." The Five Members approach. Enter and take ſeats. Greeting. Offers from the Common People, 348. Thanked by Committee. Offers from Southwark Trained Bands. Accepted and told to be in Arms, 349. Protection of Sub-Committee. Arrangements for Tueſday's Guard. Irrevocable Step. Raiſing troops without Commiſſion, 350. Reſolutions voted. 1*ſt* 2*nd* 3*rd* 4*th* 5*th*, 351. 6*th* to 12*th*, 352. Hampden Speaks. Will you receive my Conſtituents? 4000 from Bucks. Better go back? 353. No, we will hear them. War beginning. Hampden's attitude and bearing. Laſt acts of Committee, 354. Captain Hide diſabled. Refuſal to receive Sir John Byron's Meſſenger, 355. 3 p.m. 10*th Jan.* Committee cloſed, 356.

Notes. Verney's Notes, 343. Mr. Pepys's Political Rogues. Popular View of them, 344. D'Ewes more correct than Ruſhworth, 347. Harleian MSS, 349. Verney's Miſtakes. The Proteſtation, 351. What number from Bucks : Hyde, Dering, Ruſhworth, and D'Ewes, 353. Whitelock on ſame ſubject, 354. Hampden's ſhare in Bucks Petition. Falſe Charge. Captain Hide. New Lieutenant of the Tower, 355. Confeſſed uſurpations. Why neceſſary, 356.

§ XXXVIII. FLIGHT OF THE KING . . . . . 356—369

Text. 3 p.m. 10*th Jan*^{r}, propoſed Flight of King. Acts of Committee told to Charles, 356. His trouble and diſmay. Takes ſudden reſolve. Crowds for Hampden. For Pym, 357. Alarming defections, 358. "Water rats." Trained Bands. Triumph for " Traitors." Sudden ſenſe of Danger. Sir Edward Dering to his Wife. Commons going high. King's " terror." Pity for the King, 359. Noted vices leſs dangerous than ſecret. Reaſon for quitting London. Hope of support elsewhere. Project of the Queen. Vigilance of Commons, 360. Secret Service of Pennington. Conveys Queen to Holland. Under-Secretary Bere to the Admiral, 13*th Jan.* Reports King's flight. Essex and Holland, 361. Secretary Nicholas, 362. Small Work left for Under-Secretary. Grief of a Secretary of State's Wife. Lord Keeper offers to resign, 363. Royal Reverses, 364. Gloomy picture, 365. Slingsby to Pennington. Unexpected change of position. Officers following the King. Lunsford at Kingston, 366. "Drunken flourish." Suspicious Associations. Digby and Lunsford, 367. Rejected Plan against Five Members. Queen's reproach to King for its rejection. Charles I. quits London: never to return as King, 368. The Five placed on their "thrones," 369.

Notes. Popular Petition. Pym's support of Law. Author of the Long Parliament, 357. Attacks on Pym. "Not a Gentleman or Scholar." "Rogue and Rascal." "Penitent Traitor," 358. Refusals to accompany the King. Waiting on Committee. Final Desertions. Libel on Essex, Holland, Warwick, and Pym, 362. D'Ewes and Lord Holland. King's flight not temporary. Union in Houses, 363. Literary Entertainment. Letters not safe. Desolate Court at Windsor. Endymion Porter to his Wife: 14*th Jan.* Very old story, 364. Troubles of a Courtier. Fear of "Rabble." King and Queen lying with their Children. Desperate times. King's poverty. Slingsby and Pepys, 365. Captain Carterett, 366. Agreement in Houses. One exception. Faction subsiding, 367. Guizot's *Révolution d'Angleterre*, and English Translation of same, 368, 369.

§ XXXIX. RETURN OF THE FIVE MEMBERS . . 369—376

Text. Tuesday 11*th Jan.* March of City by Land. Guard by Water. Great Festival. No mere Holiday, 369. Soldiers' pikes and muskets: carrying printed Votes of Houses. Embarkation at "Three Cranes." Under-Secretary's Account, 370. Welcome at Westminster. Entrance into House. Pym thanks the City. Striking expressions used, 371. Impression made on Royalist Member. Would you be King Charles or King Pym? Letter of Sir Edward Dering. Guard against no Enemy. Members thought still in danger, 372. Why Bucks Men came. Thanks by Mr. Speaker. Speech by Goodwin, 373. Bucks Petition brought in. Its Guard of 6000. Crowd and pressure in Lobby. D'Ewes in Westminster Hall. "Little square banners," 374. Departure of King noted. Question by Culpeper. Question by Sir Henry Chomley. Answered by Denzil Hollis. Close of Narrative, 375. Questions not settled in one Generation. Struggle of Commons against Crown: why successful, 376.

Notes. What Clarendon faw, 370. Bere to Pennington, 13*th Jan*, 371. Bucks Petition to the Houfe. Views held by Hampden. Petition to King, 373. Other Counties petition the King, 374.

§ XL. Conclusion . . . . 376—387

Text. Arreft of Members a deliberate Act. How baffled. Only to be met one way, 376. The Civil War begun by it. Its connection with Remonftrance. Defign of Remonftrance. Object of Arreft: to make the Minority mafters of the Houfe. Improbable cafe, 377. Peculiar Opinions of King. Nullity of Statutes in bar of Prerogative. All recent Acts in peril. Affent under compulfion void. Dangerous Logic, 378. Pofition of Accufer to Accufed. Refufal to profecute or withdraw charge. "Vindication" of Pym. Why he changed his conduct after Arreft, 379. Parliament his only Refuge. Traitor or Minifter? King will do anything but withdraw charge. Will waive Impeachment: hopes Mr. Hampden is innocent: Will indict at Common Law, 380. Will abandon all proceedings: will give general Pardon: But nothing elfe. Attorney-General impeached and punifhed. King ftill immoveable. One of the Oxford propofitions, 381. The Earl and the King. Strong ground for difcontent: ftated by Whitelock, 382. Clarendon's defence of Charles. The truth mifftated: as a ground for affailing Commons. Doubtful affertion of Whitelock, 383. Probable effect of withdrawing charge. Effect of King's obftinate refufal. Perfiftence in the outrage. Interval for good Advice. Good Advifers provided, 384. Refult upon the King. Events between 4*th* and 9*th Jan.* 4*th* p.m. Proclamation againft Members. 5*th* a.m. King's Warrants and Vifits to Guildhall. 5*th* p.m. Second Proclamation, 385. 6*th* a.m. Serjeant fent to arreft. 7*th* a.m. Common Council Petition. 8*th* a.m. New Minifters at Council Board. Same day: Third Proclamation againft Members; and private order from Council Board, 386. No middle courfe poffible. Acceptance of iffue raifed. Civil War, 387.

Notes. Paper War. Blunt better than keen nib. Burleigh and Cecil. Too clever Clerk of Council, 382.

ARREST OF THE FIVE MEMBERS BY CHARLES THE FIRST.

A CHAPTER OF ENGLISH HISTORY REWRITTEN.

§ I. INTRODUCTORY.

ONE of the moſt fatal days in the life of Charles the Firſt is generally, and juſtly, accounted to have been that wherein he made the attempt to seize with his own hand upon five members of the Houſe of Commons ſitting in their places in Parliament, againſt whom, on the day preceding, he had exhibited in the Upper Houſe, through his Attorney-General, articles of impeachment for high treaſon. This incident, however, with its attendant circumſtances, having become, in common with the events immediately preceding it, the ſubject of Lord Clarendon's moſt elaborate, ingenious, and ſtudied miſrepreſentation, the true hiſtory of it remains to be elicited from truſtworthy, and as yet unpubliſhed, contemporary records.

An attempt fatal to its author:

Party miſrepreſentations of it:

It was certainly not the isolated act of rash imprudence and self-willed indiscretion which the champion of the party whom its failure most damaged very naturally desired that it should afterwards be considered. It was attended by too many incidents bespeaking a deliberate and settled purpose, and came in the sequence of events with which it too exactly corresponded, to permit us fairly so to consider it. The author of it, consistently enough, always himself resented that imputation; and it is with a strict dramatic propriety he is made, by the writer of the *Eikon Basilike*, to ascribe the act not to passion but to reason, to claim for it just motives and pregnant grounds, and to rescue it from the reproach of being wanting in the discreetness that the touchiness of the times required. It was most assuredly in only too perfect agreement with all that the King and the King's friends had been attempting since the day of Strafford's execution. The earlier period, with its close succession of agitating conflicts, has been retraced in an Essay describing the Debates on the Grand Remonstrance;* but some few gleanings in the field remain yet to be gathered, and will find here their proper place.

The authorities to be employed in the present narrative, all of them existing still in

---

* Forster's *Historical and Biographical Essays*, i. 1—175.

§ 1. *Introductory.*

manuscript, have not before been used in any
of the histories; and it may be premised, as to
several important illustrations of the time and
many new facts of much weight, derived from
contemporary correspondence in the State Paper
Office,* that among the letters to be earliest
quoted are several addressed to Admiral Sir
John Pennington, then commanding the fleet
in the Downs, by correspondents evidently able
and generally trustworthy, notwithstanding
strong Royalist leanings. Pennington† was a
favorite of the King's, and within a very few
weeks was to do him two memorable pieces of
service, by carrying across channel out of the
reach of Parliament not only Lord Digby,
but the Queen and the English crown jewels,

MS. Illustrations.

Admiral Pennington.

---

* Let me take the opportunity of saying, upon the threshold of this work, that it could not have been written without the facilities of access to the State Paper Office afforded by the kindness of Sir John Romilly, to whom I offer my warmest acknowledgments. Of the larger debt which all students of our history owe to the present Master of the Rolls, it would hardly be becoming to speak in this place; but it is due entirely to him that the noble stores of our State collections are now becoming accessible to all readers, and that in the double series of " *Calendars,*" and of " *Chronicles and Memorials,*" published by the Messrs. Longman under his direction, we have the promise of an ultimate contribution to our National History which Englishmen will be able to refer to with just pride, as unsurpassed for its variety and richness of materiel, and for the thoughtful consideration which, by the moderate price the volumes are issued at, has placed them within general reach.

Services to English History rendered by Sir John Romilly.

† Clarendon's *Hist.* ii. 277, 334-6, and iii. 98, 107. The historian says of Pennington that he was a very honest gentleman, and of unshaken truthfulness and integrity to the King; adding that he had a greater interest in the common seamen than any other person, having commanded them so many years.

to be employed abroad in raising materiel and means for the waging of civil war at home. A few months later, upon dismissal of Lord Northumberland, the King had secretly made Pennington Lord Admiral, but the appointment was superseded by Parliament. His present position in command of the home fleet rendered it extremely essential that he should be kept well-informed of events; and one of his captains, Robert Slingsby, brother of Strafford's friend and secretary, seems to have come to London mainly with this design.

Pennington appointed to succeed Lord Northumberland.

Captain Slingsby, brother of Strafford's secretary:

Writing on the day of his own and of the King's arrival there (the 25th of November), " from my lodging at a barber's house over " against the Rose Tavern, in Russell Street " in Covent Garden," Slingsby thus tells the Admiral the great parliamentary news:[*]

relates the Parliamentary news, 25th Nov. 1641.

" The business now in agitation is a Remon-
" strance to be published, wherein the state
" of this kingdom, before the Parliament, is
" sett down, and the Reformations since:
" all matters of state and government, since
" the King's coming to the crowne, being
" ript up: as some say, very much reflecting
" upon the King. On Monday last it was very
" hottly debated (in) the House, with greate
" opposition: some making protestations against

---

[*] MS. State Paper Office. Slingsby to Pennington, 25th Nov. 1641. I follow the ordinary mode of spelling the name, though the writer always subscribes himself "Slyngsbie."

§ 1. *Introductory.*

"it: it held almoſt all the night. At laſt being
"voted, it was carried for the Remonſtrance,
"by eleven voices: yett they have ſince fallen
"upon itt againe, and have mittigated ſome
"thinges which occaſioned greateſt oppoſition
"to it; yett doth it not paſſe freely them
"who befor oppugned it."

<small>A night-long debate.</small>

It was hardly ſurpriſing that it ſhould not, conſidering how much was at ſtake. Every inch of ground was conteſted. Alſo writing on the ſame 25th of November, Mr. Sidney Bere, who (having charge of the foreign diſpatches) had been in attendance on the King in Scotland, and who obtained employment as Under Secretary upon the appointment of Nicholas (on Monday the 29th November) as principal Secretary of State, makes ſimilar alluſion to the grand intelligence of the day, and in a tone which ſhows his nearer acquaintance not alone with public affairs, but with thoſe to whom their guidance was entruſted: "For
"the buſineſs of the Houſes of Parlᵗ. they
"have been in greate debates about a Remon-
"ſtrance, wᶜʰ the Houſe of Commons framed,
"ſhowing the grievances and abuſes of many
"yeares paſt: the conteſtation now is how to
"publiſh it, whether in print to the publick
"view, or by petition to his Majeſty. It was
"ſoe equally carried in a diviſion of opinions,
"that there were but 11 voices different:
"this day is a great day about it, but what yᵉ

<small>Sidney Bere, Under Secretary of State: deſcribes oppoſition to printing the Remonſtrance.</small>

Fears of the wife.

"event will be I shall not be able to write you by this ordinary. It seems there are great divisions betweene the two Houses, and even in the Commons House, wch if not suddenly reconciled may cause very great distractions amongst us. It's the fear of many wise and well-wishing men, who apprehend great distempers, wch I pray God to divert."*

So desperate was the struggle between forces not so unequally matched as historians have supposed; and the result thus far was, that the party which attempted a reaction in favor of the King had been defeated by this narrow majority. But other considerations still hung in the balance. It remained to be seen, on the one hand to what uses the victory would be turned, on the other what yet might be done to mitigate the consequences of defeat. While the struggle was at its height, Charles was on his way back from Scotland; having sent before him the most urgent injunctions that until his arrival at least the conflict was to be prolonged. Three days before he appeared at Whitehall the Remonstrance had been voted by its majority of eleven. Still there were questions to be raised in connection with it, and still, as we have seen, the contest was continued. Charles was hardly less eager that the terrible record of his past misgovernment

Narrow majorities in House of Commons.

Conflict continued.

* MS. State Paper Office. Sidney Bere to Admiral Pennington, 25th Nov. 1641.

should not be presented to him, than he had been that it should not be passed; and, after it was presented, it became the great object of himself and his friends to obstruct its publication.

On the 16th of December, Captain Slingsby writes to Admiral Pennington: "Yesterday "the House of Commons fell upon the Remon-"strance wch they had formerly presented to "the King with a petition; but had received "no answer. It was hotly debated, whether "it should be printed or nott: it helde them "very late in the nighte: at last being voted, "it was carried by many voices to be printed: "yett so as those were about a hundred wch did "protest against it, wth a caution if it were "not contrary to the orders of the House, "and desired their names might be printed wth "the Remonstrance: that caution was to "avoid the penaltie of Mr. Palmer, who was "before comitted for protesting against it. "It was after debated, whether to protest "against anything that is voted in the House, "be not contrary to the orders of the House: "and it is thought by some that some of the "protesters will be questioned for it."*

First great parliamentary divisions.

Protesting with a difference.

A fortnight before this date, another friend, Mr. Thomas Wiseman, a man of considerable wealth and influence, had written in similar

Mr. Thomas Wiseman to Admiral

---

* MS. State Paper Office. Slingsby to Pennington, 16th Dec. 1641.

<small>Pennington, 2nd Dec. 1641.</small> ſtrain to the Admiral of Palmer's impriſonment. He deſcribed, in a few lines which expreſs exactly the nature and weight of the offence Palmer had given, and which Clarendon has laboured ſo ingeniouſly to conceal, the act that brought with it the "penalty" referred <small>Palmer's proteſt and puniſhment.</small> to by Slingſby.* " Mr. Palmer, the lawyer, " was ſent three days agoe to the Tower, becauſe " hee was the firſt man that deſired to have " his Proteſtation entered Againſt the Remon- " ſtrance in the name of All The Reſt." In the ſame letter Mr. Wiſeman, adverting to matters connected with the Remonſtrance and making a curious miſtake as to the day of the great debate (which was Monday the 22nd, not Thurſday the 18th of November), gives us a glimpſe of the temperate hopes too ſanguinely expreſſed by the Admiral himſelf: " This " Parliament, as you obſerve, I hope may <small>Abſentees from the Houſes.</small> " prove more temperate; if ſoe bee all the " memb^{rs} of the Houſes were ſure mett " together: but I preſume they have already " don their worſt; the Remonſtrance being " finiſhed uppon Friday was ſennight, when " the Houſe of Comõns did ſit debating of " the matt^r therein contayned from three of " the clock in the afternoone on Thurſday till " Friday morning at three of the clock; and " beeing putt to the queſtione whether the " Remonſtrance ſhould procede or not, there

* See *Hiſt. and Biog. Eſſays*, i. 117-132.

"was 159 perſons for itt and 148 againſt it. The ma-
"And this very day it brought the King to jority of eleven.
"towne, it being preſented unto him wth a
"petition thereunto annexed yeaſterday at
"Hampton Courte: what the ſequel will bee
"of it, a little tyme and patienſe will inform
"us. But there was never more heate in both Never
"the Houſes then att preſent: God ſend them more heat in Parlia-
"better at unitie whereby we may enjoy fairer ment than now, 2nd
"hopes of peace and tranquillitie, and the Dec. 1641.
"King to ſhyne out wth as much brightneſs
"and ſplendor as heretofore he hath done." *

A hope, alas, with ſmall chance of realization after the vote of the 15th of December by which the Remonſtrance was placed in the hands of the people. But, diſcomfited in this direction alſo, a final ſtand was nevertheleſs to be made, and a final defeat to be encountered, upon the monſtrous aſſumption of a right in the Minority to enter formal Minority proteſt againſt the ſeries of votes it had itſelf ſet up againſt been ſuceſſively out-voted in reſiſting. That Majority. was on the 20th December: and within a fortnight after its date, as the ſucceſsful leaders ſat in their places in the Houſe (the interval having witneſſed a deſpairing effort, hitherto unknown and unſuſpected, to win over Pym to the Court by a large and lucrative employment), the attempt was made to ſeize them.

* MS State Paper Office. Wiſeman to Pennington, 2nd Dec. 1641.

Close of the first struggle of the Parliamentary Party in England.

Such were the ftages of a conflict, throughout very fteadily maintained, of which the object on one fide was to uphold, and on the other to overthrow, the legitimate action of the Houfe of Commons. Was it poffible that the long and hard fought battle fhould have had a more confiftent clofe? It began in a fecret project to overawe the Majority by bringing up the army to Weftminfter. It was continued through a fucceffion of organized efforts to defraud the Majority of its lawful powers by the pretence of unlawful conftraints. And it was to be ended, furely with no inappropriatenefs, after a fecret and fuccefflefs effort to bribe with place the moft diftinguifhed of the leaders of the Majority, by an attempt openly to ftrike them down. To what extent in this the King acted alone, or with the advice and countenance by which he had profited in every other ftage of the ftruggle, it will be one of the objects of this Effay to endeavour to develope.

§ II. THE KING'S RETURN FROM SCOTLAND.

Affertions of Clarendon.

IT is repeatedly afferted by Lord Clarendon that Lord Digby was Charles the Firft's only advifer in his refolve himfelf to effect the arreft of the five members; but in implying that the rafh act had the difapproval of the more legitimate advifers of the Sovereign, he nowhere afferts that the articles of impeachment, of which it was but the too hasty and violent assertion, were in their opinion unjust. It would be hazardous to affirm of the King's attempt of the 4th of January, that it was a more flagrant violation of law and privilege than his attempt by means of his Attorney-General on the previous day; yet, remembering that Falkland became a Privy Councillor only two days before, and five days later received the seals of a Secretary of State, that Culpeper sat as Chancellor of the Exchequer on the day Falkland was sworn of the Privy Council, and that Hyde had been offered concurrently the office of Solicitor General,—keeping in mind, moreover, that the person chiefly instrumental in bringing about all these promotions is admitted by Clarendon to have been Lord Digby himself,* —it would be still more difficult to believe that the act of the Attorney-General, and the pro-

The two attempts of the 3rd and 4th January.

New State appointments:

advised by Lord Digby.

---

* Clarendon expressly informs us (*Hist.* ii. 99, 100), "The Lord Digby was much trusted by the King, and he "was of great familiarity and friendship with the other three, "(Hyde, Culpeper, and Falkland), at least with two of them: "for he was not a man of that exactness as to be in the "entire confidence of the Lord Falkland, who looked upon "his infirmities with more severity than the other two did ". . . He was equal to a very good part in the greatest "affair, but the unfittest man alive to conduct it, having an "ambition and vanity superior to all his other parts, and a "confidence in himself, which sometimes intoxicated, and "transported, and exposed him . . . He had been instru- "mental in promoting the three persons above mentioned to "the King's favour; and had himself, in truth, so great an "esteem of them, that he did very frequently, upon con- "ference together, depart from his own inclinations and "opinions, and concurred in theirs."

Lord Digby's friendships.

Arrest of the Five Members.

A question for enquiry.

ceeding with which the King followed it up, with whatever feelings regarded after the event by these men, could have been taken in the first instance absolutely without their knowledge, or even their suspicion. There is ground for believing otherwise; and even if nothing more than a case of strong presumption be proved, it ought in the particular circumstances to tell

Suspicions against Falkland, Culpeper and Hyde.

heavily against them. That they were more than suspected at the time, Clarendon admits; and he adds that though such men as Hampden and Pym had a better opinion of his discretion than to believe he had himself any share in the advice of those proceedings, yet they were very willing that others should believe it.* Perhaps the real difficulty was, as the facts may tend to show, not to believe it.

Charges against Pym and Hampden.

The King had returned from Scotland, there cannot be a question, bent upon charging Pym and Hampden with treasonable correspondence during the Scotch Rebellion. Unfortunately

The King's way of dealing with opponents.

for Charles the First, it was almost always matter of doubt with him whether he should crush or cajole an antagonist; and such was his vice of temperament that whichever resolve he might finally take, was sure to be taken too late. He tried the one too late to destroy the league for the Covenant in Scotland, he tried the other too late to save

* *Life*, i. 103.

§ 11. *The King's Return from Scotland.*

the life of Strafford in England.* And now, even while bent upon fastening a charge of treason against the popular leaders, based upon the same transactions as those which suggested a similar charge at the eve of the Long Parliament, I shall be able to show that even now there again occurred to him, and again too late, that it might be possible to win by stratagem † what he could not but secretly distrust his power to win by force. Of course with the usual result. When a weak irresolution

<small>Crushing or conciliating, always too late.</small>

---

* Hear what is said by Clarendon : " If that stratagem " (though none of the best) of winning men by places had " been practised as soon as the resolution was taken at York " to call a parliament (in which, it was apparent, dangerous " attempts would be made, and that the court could not be " able to resist those attempts), and if Mr. Pym, Mr. " Hampden, and Mr. Hollis, had been then preferred with " Mr. Saint-John, before they were desperately embarked in ." their desperate designs, and had innocence enough about " them to trust the King, and be trusted by him, having yet " contracted no personal animosities against him ; it is very " possible that they might either have been made instruments " to have done good service, or at least been restrained from " endeavouring to subvert the royal building, for supporting " whereof they were placed as principal pillars." *Hist.* ii. 60. In another passage of his history (iv. 438-9), he tells us : " The King at one time intended to make Mr. Pym " Chancellor of the Exchequer, for which he received his " Majesty's promise, and made a return of a suitable profession " of his service and devotion: and thereupon, the other " being no secret, somewhat declined from that sharpness in " the House which was more popular than any man's." But again elsewhere he admits, still speaking of the proposal to give office to Pym and Hampden : " It is great " pity that it was not fully executed, that the King might "have had some able men to have advised or assisted him." i. 371.

† That, as has just been seen, is Clarendon's expression applied to the King's mode of procedure (ii. 60)—" the " stratagem of winning men by places." He had himself sufficient experience of it.

<small>Stratagem of winning men by places.

Offers to Pym.

Their non-acceptance regretted by Hyde.</small>

prevents a man from doing at the right time what is right, obstinacy (which is but another form of the same weakness and equally inaccessible to reason) will always confirm and make him obdurate in whatever he may have ultimately done wrong.

Treasonable correspondence of English members with Scotch rebels.

Ominous threatenings of that purpose of the King to revive the charge of treasonable correspondence with the Scotch against Hampden and Pym, had preceded his return from Scotland; and that it was known to those admitted to his confidence, no well-informed student of this period of history will be disposed to doubt. When Clarendon, therefore, speaking for himself and his friends as having with the greatest courage and alacrity opposed what he terms, "all the seditious practices" of the leaders of the Commons, proceeds to admit that they were far from thinking that the five

Clarendon's opinion of the five accused.

members were much wronged* by the accusation of treason; nay, that so visible in the House had been their extreme dishonest arts,† that nothing could have been laid to their charge incredible, only they thought it an unseasonable time to call them to account for it; and that, in regard to the choice of persons, it was indiscreet to have included Lord Kimbolton with the members of the Lower House,

---

* *Hist.* ii. 160.
† This word is incorrectly printed " acts " by Clarendon's editors.

§ II. *The King's Return from Scotland.*

—it would seem tolerably certain that he carries his affectation of ignorance somewhat too far.* Kimbolton was included notoriously because of his conduct in the previous year as one of the Commissioners "to arrange all causes of "dispute with Scotland," and because of the impossibility of stating the alleged case against Hampden or Pym without involving Kimbolton also.

<small>Kimbolton a Scotch Commissioner:</small>

There are several passages in Charles's secret correspondence with Secretary Nicholas, during his absence in Scotland, which show with what eager curiosity the doings of Kimbolton were watched at the time. Lady Carlisle, who, though still continuing her intercourse with the Court, appears undoubtedly after Strafford's death, for reasons hereafter to be noticed, to have given what help she could to the popular

<small>narrowly watched by the Court.</small>

<small>Lady Carlisle's intercourse with both parties.</small>

---

* "The purpose," says Clarendon (*Hist.* ii. 128, 129), "of
" accusing the members was only consulted between the
" King and Lord Digby; yet it was generally believed that
" the King's purpose of going to the House was communi-
" cated with William Murray of the Bedchamber, with
" whom the Lord Digby had great friendship; and that it
" was betrayed by him .... He [Lord Digby] was the
" only person who gave the counsel, named the persons, and
" particularly named the Lord Mandeville, against whom
" less could be said than against many others, and who was
" more generally beloved," &c. &c. And again he says,
(pp. 160, 161), when remarking that a fitter choice should
have been made of the persons for arrest—"There being
" many of the House of more mischievous inclinations, and
" designs against the King's person and the government, and
" more exposed to the public prejudice, than the Lord
" Mandeville Kimbolton was: who was a civil and well-
" natured man, and had rather kept ill company than drank
" deep of that infection and poison that had wrought upon
" many others."

<small>Secret consultations.</small>

<small>Kimbolton's ill company.</small>

leaders, is reprefented in one of Nicholas's letters (27 September, 1641), as having taken to the Queen a paper which it was much to the King's fervice to make public, and which fhe had obtained from Lord Mandeville.* (Lord Mandeville, or Kimbolton, I need hardly acquaint the reader, was the eldeft fon of the Earl of Manchefter, and had been called to the Upper Houfe in his father's barony of Montagu of Kimbolton.) The contents of that paper were fuch, however, that it became matter of doubt whether that which had appeared upon the furface of it fo defirable to be known in the King's intereft, was not in reality a matter much more effential to be known in the intereft of the King's opponents; and the conduct of Lady Carlifle foon confirmed the latter fuppofition. Nicholas himfelf makes no concealment of his doubts of Kimbolton. He is careful to tell the King, " I hear there are divers meetings at Chelfea, " at the Lord Mandeville's houfe, and elfe- " where" (Pym also had lodgings in Chelfea at this time) " by Pym and others, to confult " what is beft to be done at their next meeting " in Parliament."† Nor perhaps is it neceffary to add that the alleged notorious complicity of Hampden with the fo-called Scottifh treafon was the fubject of countlefs contem-

margin notes: A dangerous mediator. Doubtful fervices. Meetings in Pym's lodgings at Chelfea.

---

* *Evelyn Correfpondence*, iv. 75, ed. 1854.
† *Evelyn Cor.* iv. 76.

§ II. The King's Return from Scotland.

porary fongs and libels, which, contemptible and little credible as they generally are, will yet be found to reflect, in fome fhape or other, the party beliefs and hatreds of the day.

Libels on Hampden.

> Did I for this bring in the Scot
> (For 'tis no fecret now—the Plot
>   Was Say's and mine together) :
> Did I for this return again,
> And fpend a winter there in vain,
>   Again to invite them hither !

It was hardly attempted to be concealed, in fhort, from any of the King's friends, that his Majefty had taken advantage of his prefent vifit to Scotland to fatisfy himfelf of the fecret underftanding that had formerly exifted between the leaders of the army of the Covenant and the leaders of the Englifh Houfe of Commons ; and though even Royalifts might reafonably doubt whether fuch a charge could be made the bafis of impeachment againft fuf- pected rebels in England, after a grant to the avowed rebels in Scotland of an act of oblivion fo complete, that by the Crown's grace and favor Montrofe was now a Marquis, Argyle Scottifh Chancellor, and the little crooked Field-Marfhal of Balgony an Englifh Earl, yet the fact of fuch evidence exifting againft the Englifh members was freely fpoken of, and was the fubject of covert allufion in the correfpondence of Nicholas and the King.

Avowed rebels pardoned.

Sufpected rebels to be impeached.

" Some day they *may repent their feverity*.
" . . . I believe, before all be done, that they will

"not have such great cause of joy."* *"*You may see by this that all their designs hit not; and, I hope, before all be done that *they shall miss of more.*" † "Though I cannot return so soon as I could wish, yet I am confident that you will find *there was necessity for it, and I hope that many will miss of their ends.*"‡ These, and other similar expressions, show how strongly the conviction had taken possession of the King's mind, that he was bringing back with him to London the means of ridding himself effectually of the members of the House of Commons who were most obnoxious to him.

<small>The King's threats against the popular leaders.</small>

<small>Treasons committed in Parliament.</small>

On his return, indeed, he enlarged the scope of the accusation, so as to take in their conduct in parliament. To this the tone adopted by Hyde, Palmer, Culpeper, Falkland and their followers, in the Remonstrance debates, may be said to have urgently invited him; and he affected to believe, with them, that the minority had been so coerced in those momentous discussions as to have endangered the continued existence of parliamentary rights. But, irrespective of all this, the resolution to try an impeachment seems clearly to have been taken while he was yet in Edinburgh; and it was but the after suggestion of mingled

<small>Coercing a minority put forth as breach of privilege.</small>

---

* The King to Nicholas, 5th Oct. 1641. *Evelyn Cor.* iv. 78, 79.
† Same to same, 9th Oct. 1641. *Evelyn Cor.* iv. 80.
‡ Same to same, 12th Nov. 1641. *Evelyn Cor.* iv. 81.

§ II. *The King's Return from Scotland.*   19

fear, irresolution, and obstinacy, which induced him on the very eve of its trial, to attempt (as it will be shown shortly that he did attempt) to bribe over to his service the principal "traitor."

Nor have such indications been wanting, as the many curious details produced from the MS. Journal of D'Ewes during the progress of the Debates on the Remonstrance will have supplied, of a kind of consciousness on the part even of the members chiefly in danger, that some blow to be struck in secret might be preparing against them. We may there observe with what eager and prompt decision, when Mr. Waller threw out his ingenious parallel between Pym and Strafford, Pym met the challenge of his loyalty, and forced the House to a specific declaration upon it. The King had not been five days in London, after his arrival from Scotland, when the same leader of the Opposition had occasion to ask from his place, whether it did not become the representatives of the people to take serious note of the many signs around them of a conspiracy by some members of the Commons House to accuse other members of the same of treason? And when, on the 20th December, the question was independently discussed which had caused such agitation in the Debates of the Remonstrance, whether a minority in the Commons might not have the same liberty as in the

Signs of danger abroad.

30th Nov. 1641. *Alleged conspiracy to get up charges of treason.*

Argument for giving weight to a minority. Lords of protesting against the decisions of the majority, Mr. Holborne employed the significant argument that the absence of such a right, in the event of the majority having passed any measure carrying with it grave consequences, would involve as deeply in those consequences the resisting members of the minority, who might "lose their heads in the "crowd when there was nothing to show who "was innocent."* A vague feeling of individual insecurity, a shadowy sense of some possible impending danger, was now certainly *Alarms generally prevalent.* prevalent among members of the Houses in a manner not before known; and at the very hour when that remark was made by Holborne, D'Ewes, who had left to attend the King at Whitehall with an address, was with some alarm making a note for his Journal of the "confident and severe look" with which Charles, not deigning to receive the obeisances of honorable members, passed out through the midst of them.† It is a pity *Confidence of the King.* that confidence and severity should have been most the characteristics of this prince, at the very times when it most behoved him to distrust himself and conciliate others.

* See Sir Ralph Verney's *Notes of the Proceedings of the Long Parliament,* 135, 136; and the admirable note thereon of the editor, Mr. Bruce.
† Harleian MSS. 162 f, 265 a. See also my *Hist. & Biog. Essays,* i. 165.

§ III. False Reliances.

THE end to which matters were haftening had now become manifeft enough. Confident in his own fecret perfuafion that the means of vengeance were in his hand, and mifled by the accident of a Royalift Lord Mayor into believing alfo, in the teeth of every other indication to the contrary, that a ftrong Royalift party exifted in the City, the King's public conduct fince his return, under the further exafperation of the paffing, prefenting, and printing of the Remonftrance, and of the tone adopted by its authors in debate, had been a feries of acts that could have but one iffue. Before retracing them, let me fhow on what precarious foundations had been built the tone of confidence and defiance fo fuddenly and unadvifedly affumed. *The Royalift party in the City.*

The City entertainment provided by the enthufiaftic Firft Magiftrate had been arranged to take place on the day of Charles's arrival in his capital, and for the moment it fairly turned the heads of the King's friends as well as his own. Captain Slingfby informs his admiral that it was a magnificent reception, and that fince his coming to town he had been greatly pleafed to obferve a very great alteration of the affections of the City to what they had *Banquet at Guildhall:*

been when he went away.* Mr. Sidney Bere writes more cautiously, but remarks that all looked very "stately and well."† Mr. Thomas Wifeman protests that it was a reception and glorification of so much worth, as to be far beyond the precedent of any made to former Kings that history makes mention of; and that it had well suited with the goodness, sweetness, and meritorious virtue of so gracious a king as theirs was; adding, that his Majesty had "knighted in the field" the Lord Mayor and Recorder, and, to add more grace to so loyal a Chief Magistrate, had been pleased, the day after the banquet, to make him a Baronet.‡

King's reception thereat:

Lord Mayor Gourney made a Baronet.

But perhaps the most striking indication of all that now tended for the time completely to deceive and mislead the credulous King, was a letter dated the day after Mr. Wifeman's admiring effufion, which the new Secretary of State, to whom it was addreffed, muft with fome exultation have fubmitted to his mafter. It was from Lenthal, the Speaker of the Houfe of Commons. This weak and commonplace man, fo foon to be for ever affociated

Welcome news for the King.

---

* MS. State Paper Office. Capt. R. Slingfby to Admiral Sir John Pennington, 25 Nov. 1641.

† MS. State Paper Office. Sidney Bere to Admiral Pennington, 25 Nov. 1641.

‡ MS. State Paper Office. Wifeman to Pennington, 2d Dec. 1641. Court fcribes made the moft of it of courfe; and under the title of *Ovatio Carolina*, in *Somers's Tracts*, iv. 137, will be found a ludicroufly pompous account of the affair.

§ III. *False Reliances.*

in history with an apparently high-spirited assertion, in his own person, of the privilege and independence of the House of Commons, was now only eager to be quit of his employment, and proffer servile suit to the King. Clarendon truly characterises him as a man of a very narrow, timorous nature, and it seems probable that the fierce debates on the Remonstrance had thoroughly alarmed him.* With his opportunities of observation, he could hardly fail to have satisfied himself that a conflict of a yet more serious kind now impended between the King and the House, and this letter is decisive of his belief that the victory would be to the King. Nor was it possible that Charles himself should have drawn any other construction from it. In continuing to remain where he is, in the chair of the House of Commons, Lenthal sees only utter failure to his life, the ruin of his estate, and poverty for his children. He prays to be relieved from his too onerous dignity, and to become once more the meanest subject of a sovereign whom he professes to regard with abject veneration.

_{Speaker Lenthal alarmed:}

_{Wishes to be relieved from the Speakership:}

_{and to become again the meanest subject of his sovereign.}

---

* For illustrations of his character, and his sufferings at the hands of honorable and not respectful members, see my *Hist. & Biog. Essays*, i. 82-84. Another opportunity of adverting to the subject will occur in this narrative, but meanwhile I may add what is said, correctly enough, by Clarendon (*Hist*. i. 297). "In a word he was in all respects very unequal to the work; and not knowing how to preserve his own dignity, or to restrain the licence and exorbitance of others, his weakness contributed as much to the growing mischiefs as the malice of the principal contrivers." _{Clarendon as to Lenthal.}

Arrest of the Five Members.

Speaker Lenthal to Secretary Nicholas, 3rd Dec. 1641.

"Right Honorable and Moſt Noble S^r," runs this remarkable letter, written on the fourth day after the appointment of Nicholas as Secretary of State,* "The aſſurance of
"your noble favours imboldnes me to commit
"to your care the greateſt concernment y^t ever
"it befell me, the defyer beinge enforced by
"an unavoidable neceſſity. I have now in
"this imployment ſpent almoſt 14 months,
"wch hath foe exhauſted the labor of 25 yeares,

Invokes the King's ſacred mercy.

"that I am inforced to flye to y^e ſanctuary of
"his ſacred mercy. Could I ſuppoſe that my
"humble ſute (grounded on ye full expreſſion
"of duty and obedience) ſhould have other
"interpretation, or ſeeme unfitt in the deepe
"judgm^t of his Sacred Ma^{tye}, I ſhould then
"defyer my thoughts may periſh in their firſt
"conception, foe willinge am I to offer myſelfe
"and fortune a ſacrifice for his Royall Service:

Craves Mr. Secretary's help in loweſt poſture of obedience.

"but in that I hope it cannot, I moſt humbly
"defyer your honor on my behalfe (in y^e
"loweſt poſture of obedience), to crave of his
"Sacred Ma^{tye} his Royall Leave that I may uſe
"my beſt endeavour to the Houſe of Coṁons
"to be quitt of this imployment and to retyer
"backe to my former privat Life, that whilſt I
"have ſomme ability of body left, I may en-
"deavour that wthout wch I cannot but expect

---

* MS. State Paper Office. It is dated 3 December, 1641; and is addreſſed, "The Rt. Hon. Sir Edward Nicholas, Knt., "one of his Ma^{tys} Secretarys of State, Humbly preſent "theſ."

§ III. *False Reliances.*

"a ruine, and put a badge of extreame poverty
"uppon my children. The app^rhenfion of
"my fpeedy enfuing mifery, hath begot this
"moft humble regret, but ftill with that dew
"regard of my obedien^c and duty that noe
"earthly confideratiō fhall ever increafe the
"leafte of thoughts that may tend to the re-
"tardment of his Royall Commands. S^r, this
"being p^rfented to your honour^ble care, affures
"me of fuch a succefsful way as fhal be-
"comme the duty of me his meaneft fubject
"in all humilitie to befeech. Thus am I im-
"boldened humbly to declare the relation and
"defyers of your Honor's moft obedient fer-
"vant, WM. LENTHAL."

Expects ruin from continuing in the Chair of the Houfe.

To the King, fo willing to be duped, and exulting ftill in the belief that he had at laft won friends in the City all powerful, here might be ground hardly lefs for belief that in the Houfe of Commons his enemies were falling asunder. Charles clutched at it, and defperately held to it, with the impulfive weaknefs of his nature. But never was fuch a belief raifed on fuch bafelefs foundations.

A willing dupe.

Already, the very day before Lenthal's letter was written, a fufpicion that they were falfe reliances had occurred even to Captain Slingf-by. "Since the King's coming," he writes, "all thinges have not happned fo much to his "contentment as by his magnificent intertaine- "ment att his entrance was expected. . . .

Captain Slingfby to Admiral Pennington, 2nd Dec. 1641.

Factious Citizens.

"The factious Citizens begin to come again to the houses with their swordes by their sides, hundreds in companies; their pretences only against Episcopacie."* After a few days Sidney Bere, reflecting doubtless the temperate misgivings of his master the Secretary, writes *Fears and misgivings of the best informed.* of the fears and distractions increasing daily in London, and that such truly were not without cause, for that the existing contention in the House, and on points of so high nature, could not bring about less than confusion and combustion in the end, if God did not prevent it.† Nor from this date had a week passed

The King and the two Houses.

* MS. State Paper Office. Slingsby proceeds to say of the King: "The next day after his coming he was expected at the Parliament, but he went away to Hampton Court; he came again on Monday last and was expected on Tuesday at the House, but he went back the same night he came. Since that, a Petition hath been sent to him concerning the Remonstrance wch had formerly bren so much debate: and to desire the nomination of the greate officers as he had graunted to the Parliament in Scotland. This day the King came to London againe: at noone it was questioned whether he would go to the House or no, but I heare since he is gone." Of the factious Citizens he also further remarks in

Citizens and M.P.'s.

this letter: "One of the House was strictly examined by them of wch side he was, in such a manner that with goode wordes he was gladd to slippe from them: after he was gone some of them were heard to name him—saying it was such a one—the greatest enemye we have. He made complaints of it to the House. Yesterday a conference between the two Houses wherein this matter was ment^d and a declaration agreed to be sett out to prohibitt the like

Sir Edward Dering.

assemblys hereafter .... This day the House are upon Sir Edward Dering who it is thought will be called to the barre for something he hath spoke in the House."

† MS. State Paper Office. Sidney Bere to Admiral Pennington, 9th Dec. 1641. There is so pleasant a testimony in this letter to the character of Nicholas, not merely to his activity and industry, but to that sweetness of disposition and moderation of temper which is borne out by all that is

§ III. *False Reliances.*

before Captain Slingſby wrote with an alarm *Slingſby's*
which he hardly attempts to conceal, of the *alarm.*
diſplay of manifeſtations of feeling from the
City, of a far more deciſive and ſerious kind
than thoſe which ſo lately had ſtartled him.
Whereas it had been alleged that laſt week's *Wealthy*
"ſollicitation of the Parliament" had pro- *and diſ-*
contented
ceeded only from the ruder ſort of people, *citizens:*
now it was certain that " ſome of the
" better ſort of the ſame faction came in good
" numbers to the Houſe, accoutred in the beſt
" manner they could, and in coaches, to pre- *Come in*
" vent the aſperſion that was layed upon them *their*
coaches to
" that they were of the baſer ſort of people *the Houſe.*
" only which were that way affected." They
had come, moreover, not merely to petition
for the removal out of the Upper Houſe of the
popiſh Lords and Biſhops to whom excluſively

---

publicly known of him, that the paſſage is worth ſubjoining.
" By Mr. Valentine," he writes, " I acquainted you wth the
" remove of Sir Hen. Vane, and that I had made my way unto
" his Matie by the Murrayes, wch hath taken ſoe good effect
" that now I am with the Secretary Nicholas (the King
" having recommended me particularly); and he appearing *Character*
" moſt ready to accept me, mentioning with all the reſpect *of Sir Ed.*
" he bears unto you the affection you have always pleaſed to *Nicholas.*
" have for me, ſoe that I cannot faile of good uſage, and
" indeed his diſpoſition is ſoe ſweete that he is not capable of
" other. By this recommendation from his Ma^{ty} I gueſſe we
" ſhall not ſuddenlie have a ſecond Secretary, ſince all the
" Forraine diſpatches as well as Ireland are delivered into
" Mr. Secr^{ty} Nicholas, who noe doubt will acquit himſelfe
" well, being a man alſo very laborious and active, and in
" great fav^r with both their Maties." Nevertheleſs Mr. Bere
was wrong in his expectation : a ſecond Secretary, to replace
Vane, having already been ſelected in the perſon of Lord
Falkland.

Unpopular acts of the Lord Mayor.

they imputed the stoppage of those Acts which had passed the Lower for the settling of religion, but also to complain " of some ill-affected " persons in the Cittie that endeavoured to " hinder their petition, wherein my Lord " Mayor was comprehended, who the day " before had given order to all the constables " to raise their severall watches and be readie " in armes, which has been very ill resented " by the House."* So soon was the frail reed on which the King mainly relied, bending powerless under him.

Second thoughts of Speaker Lenthal.

Poor Lenthal himself seems to have had a safer second thought, and had hastened to crave from Mr. Secretary Nicholas, "if the other way did not take," no longer the royal influence to relieve him of Mr. Speaker's post, but the royal message customary in those times before Mr. Speaker's claim for a vote of money could be taken into consideration.† Shall we wonder that the Under Secre-

---

* MS. State Paper Office. Slingsby to Pennington, " aboard the Lyon in the Downes." The letter is dated by Slingsby himself " 16 January, 1641," but this is a manifest error for the " 16th December, 1641."

Speaker Lenthal to Secretary Nicholas.

† MS. State Paper Office. This second letter is well worth subjoining textually. " Right Honourable, May it please " your Honor," it runs, " If that other way doe not take, if " you may finde oportunity (without prejudice to your selfe) " let me entreat you to incline his Ma^{ty} to recomend me " to ye consideration of the House, by which meanes I may " hope of some satisfaction: but this is totally left to your " honor's considerati^{on} as oportunity offers, & y^r honor " thincke fitt in your owne judgment. Thus humbly cravinge " p^{r}don for this great p^{r}sumption I can safely say noe man " lives that is more
" Your honor's most humble servant,
W^M. LENTHAL."

tary, not many days later, is found writing to his friend the Admiral commanding in the Downs, " I pray God we find not that we " have flattered ourfelves with an imaginary " ftrength and partie in the citty and elfe- " where which will fall away if need fhould " be." * {.marginnote}An Under Secretary's prayer.

§ IV. Fatal Mistakes.

CHARLES neverthelefs continued to act as if that imaginary ftrength were folid and eternal. On any other affumption we fhould have to characterize as thofe of a madman the feries of his acts from the opening of December to Chriftmas Eve. He had removed the trainbands on guard at the two Houfes, and had fubftituted companies officered by himfelf. He had put forth a moft offenfive order on the fubject of religious worfhip. He had recaft the offices at Court, notorioufly that he might invite into his councils the leading opponents of the Great Remonftrance; † or {.marginnote}Foolhardinefs of the King. Removes the Guard from the Houfes: Gives office to leaders of the minority:

---

* MS. State Paper Office. Sidney Bere to Sir John Pennington.

† On the 2nd of December Mr. Thos. Wifeman thus writes (MS. State Paper Office), as his "affured and affectionate "friend to command," to Admiral Sir John Pennington: "My Lord of Holland, they fay, hath loft himfelf both "with the King and Queen; and for my part I believe it; "becaufe hee hath been obferved to hold councills and "confultations with the Lords in the abfence of the King "that have been againft Epifcopacie and the Booke of Common "Prayer: W^{ch} his Matie fince his cominge home hath "declaratively refolved to uphold, and with his lyfe to "mayntayne. It is noyfed there will bee fuddenly a greate {.marginnote}Wifeman to Pennington, 2nd Dec. 1641.

Arrest of the Five Members.

it might be with other hopes in that direction, secret as yet, or known to Pym alone.
He had assailed the privileges of the Commons

Assails privilege:

"remove at Court of cheiff offic^{rs}, and that Sir John Banks
"shall be Lord Treas^r. Mr. Nicleys [Nicholas] was on
"Monday last sworne Secretary of State and knighted; and
"my Lord Savill had the staff given him at Yorke of being
"Treas^r of the King's Houshold in Mr. Secret^y Ffane's
"place, who it is thought will not bee Secret^y long. He
"hath very ill lucke, to bee neither loved nor pittied of any
"man." Some few days before, Sidney Bere had written
(MS. 25th Nov.): "At Newcastle I understand Mr. Secretary
"Vane was commanded to deliver up his staffe of Treasur^r;
"wh^{ch} was confered att Yorke upon my Lord Savile: it is
"what was long spoken of & expected by him, and soe it
"will be noe greate newes to you. The place of Secretary he
"still keepes: wch if he continue, as I see no great appear-
"ance to the contrary, he will not much reflecte on the losse
"of the other." Seven days later, the Under Secretary wrote
again (MS. 9th Dec. 1641) to the Admiral: "The report
"goes strong with us that many great removes more shallbe,
"out of hand; what ground there is for it, I cannot tell, but
"thus the speech goes: Sir John Bankes to be Lo. Treas^t,
"Chamberlaine made Admirall, and Bristow Chamberlaine;
"Holland, Newport, and some say Hamilton, also to be
"displaced. In the mean time we have a Lo.-Steward wch is
"Duke of Richmond. And thus we have and shall have
"many changes and removes in Court. Sr Henry Vane the
"Yonger, its generally said, and believed, will loose his place.
"I writt you of it by my last; and mythinkes, if you have
"a thought that way, a timely office done by Mr. Secretary,
"who is soe much your friend, might be of good use."
Welcome to the Admiral, however, as the place of Treasurer
of the Navy would have been in quieter times, the troubled
reports of his correspondents appear to have decided him not
to apply for it. On the 23d Dec. the Under Secretary
writes (MS. State Paper Office), after mentioning the dissatisfaction of the Commons at the removal of Young Vane:
"Yet still, S^r W^m. Penningman [Pennyman] stands the man
"designed for it, though as yett nothing (to my best know-
"ledge) hath past to that purpose. But I easily assent to
"yor opinion that in such distempered tymes as these are,
"you have little desire to muster up friends for any employme^t
"of that nature, howsoever it were to be wished a place of
"that trust had a man of yor experience and worth—but I
"stirre noe further in it, since its not yor pleasure."

Under Secretary Bere to Pennington, 25th Nov. 1641.

Same to same, 9th Dec.

Court changes.

Same to same, 23rd Dec.

§ IV. *Fatal Mistakes.*

in a vital point, by an intemperate message of disapproval during their discussion of a bill for raising soldiers by impressment. He had rashly issued, on the very day after the citizens presented their petition against the Bishops, a proclamation commanding the severe execution of the statutes against all who should bring in question or impugn the book of Common Prayer. And while thus harsh in pressing, on the one hand, the law against Puritan opponents of the Church, he had the inconceivable folly to respite its operation, on the other, in favour of certain Roman Catholic priests who had incurred the wrath of the Commons and fallen under sentence of the courts, and whose lives lay justly forfeit.

_{Interferes with a bill under discussion:}

_{Enforces laws against Puritans:}

_{Remits penalties against Roman Catholics.}

What occurred thereupon would have daunted a sovereign of the Tudor line, but Charles the First had as little of the bold resolution as of the considerate fear which alone is truly valiant. At the same sessions when these priests were condemned to die, there had also been condemned to death several men for common offences. It was not supposed possible, after a reprieve had been sent to the Jesuit offenders, that their fellow-prisoners, condemned for offences held then to be comparatively venial, would be executed. An order for the execution was nevertheless received, and the agitation throughout the City was extreme. Monday the 13th December was

_{Partial execution of the laws.}

> appointed for the execution; but on the previous Sunday evening arms had been secretly conveyed into Newgate, and open resistance was made next day to the attempt to carry out the warrant. The resistance was overmastered that night, the wealthier citzens, however indignant at the King's interference, not choosing themselves to interfere against the law; and on the Tuesday the men were hanged.* The incident

Resisted by the people.

---

* I discover these curious facts in a letter which Captain Slingsby writes (MS. State Paper Office) to Pennington on the 16th of Dec. (the letter is dated by mistake the 16th Jan.). He mentions the City petition against the Bishops and their continued attempts to enforce the Liturgy, and proceeds: "The next day after the delivery of the petition the King "sett out a proclamation comaunding the severe execution of "the lawes against the contemners and oppugners of the "Comon Prayer Booke; and an other comaunding all men "whatsoever that had right to sitt in Parliament to repair "thither by the twelfth of Janu. These gave great distast to "that faction' of the Cittie that were the petitioners. There "was a very greate Sessions the last weeke, where there were "seven priests condemned but repreived by the Kinge: "many for other crimes: Munday last being appointed for "their execution. Some body had conveighed some armes "into Newgate to them the night before: so y^t they ceazed "upon the prison, and stood upon ther defense most part "of that day: but at night were overmastered and the next "day hanged . . . . the House is much distracted at the re- "prieve of the Priests, and att the forraigne Ambassadors for "medling in itt, especially at the Frenche, who did lay downe "some reasons wch did aggravate ther distast." Clarendon has not noticed this remarkable incident, nor is it mentioned in any of the histories, but in adverting to Secretary Windebank's flight he leaves us no room to doubt the view he was himself disposed to take of such a "suspending power" as Charles was practically exerting in these repreivals of popish offenders. "I could never yet learn," he says, speaking of the conduct of the leaders of the House, "the true reason "why they suffered Secretary Windebank to escape their "justice, against whom they had more pregnant testimony of "offences within the verge of the law than against any "person they have accused since this parliament, and of some

Slingsby to Pennington, 16th Dec. 1641.

Attack upon Newgate.

Repreivals of Popish offenders.

left such a sense rankling in the breasts of all ^{A time for}
classes of citizens, as the wisdom of the most ^{caution.}
powerful of princes might have feared; but
Charles the First only the more bethought him
how better to restrain and curb these factious
and rebellious citizens. And as, for other ^{Disastrous}
reasons, his mind had been brooding over a ^{resolve of the King.}
measure on which he had lately resolved, to
obtain more complete command of the Tower,
he selected this precise time to give effect to
an intention which was to carry with it the
most disastrous consequences.

The Tower commanded the City. It was ^{The Tower:}
the "Bridle" to the too restless citizens,
as the courtiers commonly called it;* and it
was essential not more to the safety of those
well affected to the House of Commons than
to the security of the House of Commons
itself, that its Governor should be a man in ^{and its Governor.}
whose good faith they had confidence. Sir

"that, it may be, might have proved capital, and so their
"appetite of blood might have been satisfied; for, besides
"his frequent letters of intercession in his own name, and ^{Winde-}
"signification of his Majesty's pleasure, on the behalf of ^{bank's}
"papists and priests, to the judges, and to other ministers of ^{crime and}
"justice, and protections granted by himself to priests that ^{escape.}
"nobody should molest them, he harboured some priests in
"his own house, knowing them to be such, which, by the
"statutes made in the 29th year of Queen Elizabeth, is made
"felony; and there were some warrants under his own hand
"for the release of priests out of Newgate who were actually
"attainted of treason, and condemned to be hanged, drawn,
"and quartered: which, by the strict letter of the statute, the
"lawyers said, would have been very penal to him."—*Hist.* i.
311-312.

* Clarendon, *Hist.* ii. 81.

Arrest of the Five Members.

Balfour removed.

William Balfour was such a man, as he had shown by his resolute refusal of enormous proffered bribes to connive at the escape of Strafford. But Balfour, the tried friend of the Parliament, was now suddenly removed from this all-important command, and it became known, on Christmas eve, that in his place there had been appointed a soldier of evil character and infamous name, whose only conceivable qualification could have been, that of presenting himself to the Court as a mere desperate tool for any kind of reckless service.*

Lunsford appointed:

His infamous character.

He was a man, says Sir Simonds D'Ewes, given to drinking, swearing, quarrelling, and other vices; much in debt, and very desperate.† More than ten years before the present date Lord Dorset had characterised him as a young outlaw who feared neither God nor man, and who took a glory to be esteemed rather a swaggering ruffian than the issue of an ancient and honest family. He belonged to the army of the North, and had been deeply involved in the plots for bringing it up to overawe the Parliament.

His close friendship with Lord Digby.

Clarendon cannot but admit that such was the confessed and notorious repute of Lunsford, who was nevertheless companion and friend to

Lunsford's warrant.

* The warrant of the appointment of "our trusty and "well-beloved servant Col. Thomas Lunsford," is in the State Paper Office. It is given "under our signet at our "Court at Whitehall the 22d Day of December 1641," and is addressed to Lords Manchester, Dorset, Dunsmore and Newburgh.   † *Harl. MSS.* 162, f. 272 *b*.

§ IV. *Fatal Mistakes.*

his excellent friend Lord Digby; and he explains with sufficient frankness, though after his usual fashion, the object of the King and Lord Digby in appointing him.* It was, that, having now some secret reason (which, he interposes but his editors omitted, "was not a "good one") to fill that place in the instant with a man who might be trusted, this man

_{Object in appointing him:}

---

* His account of Lunsford's appointment is indeed in every way highly characteristic. Sir William Balfour having, he says, had from the beginning of this parliament, "according to the natural custom of his country" (Balfour was a Scotchman, and by the prudence of Hyde's first editors these words are erased from all the ordinary editions), "forgot "all his obligations to the King ... there had been a "long resolution to remove him from that charge ... yet "there was neither notice or suspicion of it, till it was heard, "that Sir Thomas Lunsford was sworn Lieutenant of the "Tower; a man who, though of an ancient family in "Sussex, was of a very small and decayed fortune, and of no "good education; having been few years before compelled "to fly the kingdom, to avoid the hand of justice for some "riotous misdemeanour ... he was so little known, except "upon the disadvantage of an ill character, that, in the most "dutiful time, the promotion would have appeared very "ungrateful." And then follows one of those sentences of endless involution, and confusion of all relatives and antecedents, from which it is extremely difficult to elicit the precise meaning. He asserts that Lunsford's appointment was secretly the work of Lord Digby, who had meant to give it to his brother, "but *he* (the brother) being not at that time in town, "and *the other*" (strictly this ought to mean the king, but Lord Digby seems really meant) "having some secret "reason (which was not a good one)" the latter words also are erased from the ordinary editions—"to fill that place in "the instant with a man who might be trusted; *he* suddenly "resolved upon this gentleman, as one who would be faithful "to him for the obligation, and execute anything he should "desire or direct,"—hold fast the five members, for example, if he could once get them shut up in the Tower? But how monstrous the attempt of Clarendon to put up Digby in such a purpose as the 'scapegoat for the King—if (which perhaps is doubtful) the last quoted "*he*" must be taken to stand for Digby and not for the King himself.

_{Clarendon's account of the appointment. Clouds of words. Digby the 'scapegoat.}

Arrest of the Five Members.

A man to execute anything:
was suddenly resolved upon as one who would be faithful for this obligation, and execute anything that should be desired or directed. A laboured periphrasis, which Bishop Warburton puts into plain speech when he writes upon the margin of the page containing it, that the

and keep the five members, once arrested, safe.
object was "to keep the five members safe whom it was determined to arrest." "So as now," writes D'Ewes, in that entry of his Journal of the 24th of December which reports the discussion upon Lunsford's character, preserves the angry speeches respecting him of the members for York, Middlesex, and Essex (Sir William Alison, Sir Gilbert Gerrard, and Sir William Masham), sets down the King's proclamation confirming the appointment, and laments over the vote of the Lords declining to join the Commons in prayers that it should be cancelled,* "So as now all things

Lords who sided with majority in Commons.
* The minority of twenty-two peers who protested against this too scrupulous objection to interfere with the King's prerogative of placing or displacing his officers, gives us the names of the leading members of the popular party in the Upper House. They were the Earls of Northumberland, Essex, Pembroke, Bedford, Warwick, Bolingbroke, Newport, Suffolk, Carlisle, Holland, Clare, and Stamford, and the Lords Say and Seale (old Subtlety as he was called), Wharton, St. John, Spencer, North, Kimbolton, Brooke, Grey de Werk, Robartes, and Howard de Escricke. It may be worth adding that, a very few weeks later, upon the incident of the 26th

Duke of Richmond's sally: 26th Jan. 1641-2.
Jan. 1641-2, when the Duke of Richmond perpetrated his famous sally of proposing to evade the Militia bill, sent up from the Commons, by adjourning for six months, twenty-four Peers entered a protest against the vote requiring the Duke to make submission and ask pardon, as "not a "sufficient punishment for words of that daingerous conse-"quence." On this occasion seventeen of the foregoing

§ IV. *Fatal Mistakes.*

"haften apace to confufion and calamity; "from which I fcarce fee any poffibility in "human reafon for this poor Church and "Kingdom to be delivered. My hope only "is in the goodnefs of that God who hath "feveral times during this parliament already "been feen in the Mount, and delivered us "beyond the expectations of ourfelves and of "our enemies, from the jaws of deftruction."*

Evil forebodings of Sir Simon D'Ewes.

An addrefs for Lunfford's removal was that day voted in the Lower Houfe without a diffentient voice; and the Conftable of the Tower, the Earl of Newport, was requefted for the prefent to take command of the place and to lodge therein.

Addrefs voted for Lunfford's removal.

The defire of the Houfe was conveyed to Lord Newport by Sir Thomas Barrington and Mr. Henry Marten, who were informed thereupon that he was no longer Conftable. The King had fuddenly difmiffed him for an alleged difloyal fpeech during the royal abfence in Scotland. The incident further fhows in what direction all was now rapidly tending. The charge againft Lord Newport was that on the occafion of a meeting held at Kenfington, at which Pym and Lord Kimbolton were prefent, as well

Difmiffal of Lord Newport.

The charge againft him:

---

names reappeared, with omiffion of thofe of Lords Newport, Carlifle, Clare, Say and Seale, and North, but with addition of thofe of the Earls of Lincoln and Leicefter, of Vifcount Conway, and of Lords Chandois, Hundfdon, Paget, and Willoughby de Parham. See Sir Ralph Verney's *Notes*, p. 149.   * *Harl. MSS.* 162, f. 278 *b*.

A proposal to seize hostages for the King's good faith. as Nathaniel Fiennes, his father Lord Say and Seale (old Subtlety), Lord Wharton, Lord Dungarvon, and Sir John Clotworthy, upon some discourse of an apprehended design to overawe the Parliament by means of the army of the North, the Earl had remarked, "If there be such a plot, yet "here are his wife and children,"* meaning that these might be seized as hostages. Taxed with the words by the King himself, Lord Newport indignantly denied them: upon which, with insulting addition, the question was re-

The lie given to Lord Newport, 24th Dec. peated: "You can tell me nothing more than "I know already; therefore consider well "what you answer." Lord Newport answered with vehement repetition of his denial; and the King, contemptuously professing sorrow for his Lordship's memory, intimated that he was no longer Constable of the Tower, and turned upon his heel. That was on the afternoon of Friday the 24th December. On Wednesday the 29th the King informed the House of

The lie retracted, Dec. 29th. Lords that he had never believed the charge against the Earl, and desired it to be withdrawn.

Such was the wonderful, the almost incredible levity of Charles the First, in matters of *Warnings in the interval.* accusation the most grave. Between that 24th and 29th of December the aspect of

* See *Commons Journals* (Tuesday 28th December), ii. 359.

affairs had grown more serious, frequent gatherings together of large numbers of the people had increased, discontent took a threatening aspect, and on the eve of the most desperate resolution of his life, his wavering irresolute temper seemed to have yielded suddenly. The withdrawal of the charge against Lord Newport was one indication; but another, much more remarkable, and hitherto unsuspected by any historian, is now to be disclosed. *Sudden yielding of the King.*

Extraordinary determination taken.

§ V. PYM AND THE KING.

Beyond all question the most popular man in England at this time was Pym. The attempts made upon his life during the debates on the Remonstrance, and above all the victory obtained in that struggle, had raised him even higher than during the memorable conflict with Strafford. It was not simply that ne was the foremost man in the Parliament by which so much had been achieved for the people, or that its very existence was in some measure due to him, but also that he alone represented in his person the parliaments of former years, and those usages and precedents, become since the very bulwarks of freedom, which had only then been won by the hard and desperate endurance, the long imprisonments, not seldom the deaths, of the great men of the past. In him the people still saw the Cokes, the Eliots, the Sir *Popularity of the leader of the Commons.*

Its causes.

Arreſt of the Five Members.

Pym imprisoned for his opinions in 1614.

A member of the Parliament of 1620.

One of James the Firſt's "twelve "kings:"

Robert Cottons,* remembered and honored as the earlieſt martyrs of the Stuart Kings. He had himſelf been the inmate of a ſtate priſon, as the reward for his conduct as a repreſentative of the people, now nearly eight-and-twenty years ago. He had been a leading member in that wiſe and noble aſſembly which met in 1620, and aboliſhed the infamous monopolies at that time eating out the heart of the kingdom.† He was one of the twelve who carried their famous declaration to King James at Newmarket, when the quick-witted ſhrewd old monarch called out, "Chairs! "chairs! here be twal kynges comin!" In all the ſubſequent parliaments of that and the ſucceeding reign he had played a diſtinguiſhed part; and when, after intermiſſion of thoſe conventions for twelve years, they met once more in April 1640, and men gazed upon each other looking who ſhould begin, much

Antiquary Cotton's ſufferings at ſeizure of his library.

* On pretence of a charge that he had furniſhed precedents to Selden and Eliot, Sir Robert Cotton's noble library was ſeized and held by the King, and unable to ſurvive its loſs the great ſcholar died. "When," ſays D'Ewes, "I went "ſeveral times to viſit and comfort him in the year 1630, he "would tell me they had broken his heart that had locked up "his library from him . . . He was ſo outworn within a "few months, with anguiſh and grief, as his face, which had "formerly been ruddy and well colored, was wholly changed "into a grim and blackiſh paleneſs, near to the reſemblance "and hue of a dead viſage." A few months afterward he was dead.

† "A parliament" it is well ſaid by the leading liberal ſtateſman of our time, "to which every Engliſhman ought "to look back with reverence." Lord John Ruſſell's *Eſſay on the Hiſtory of the Engliſh Government and Conſtitution, p.* 50.

§ v. *Pym and the King.*

the greater part, as Clarendon says, having never before sat in Parliament, there quietly arose to his place at their head the man above all others qualified by experience, by eloquence, and by courage to lead the English people. It was then that Pym's extreme influence struck root, and his name became a word familiar over England. This was he who, in that brief Parliament so fatally dissolved, had told the wonderful story of their wrongs, which was all it bequeathed to the suffering millions. This was he who chiefly had wrested from the Court its assent to the greater and stronger Parliament, from which at last redress was come. This was he who, on the issue of the writs for that memorable assembly, had with Hampden ridden England through, to urge upon all its inhabitants their duties and their right, to choose honestly and petition freely. This finally was he who since had broken down for ever the tyranny of Strafford and of Laud, and who now had published to the world the Great Remonstrance. Shall we wonder if every nook and corner of the kingdom were pervaded with his influence and renown, and that, so identified with the past, on him it might almost seem exclusively to rest what the future was to bring. "I think Mr. Pym was at this time," says Clarendon, "the most popular man, and "the most able to do hurt, that hath lived in "any time."

Rises to the place of Leader: April, 1640.

Qualities and services which endeared him to the people.

Clarendon's tribute to Pym's popularity.

Arrest of the Five Members.

<small>Former intercourse with the King.</small>   Already once the King had turned to him in a terrible extremity. When the scheme was on foot to save the life of Strafford he had offered Pym the Chancellorship of the Exchequer. Clarendon, who states the matter not unfairly, says the offer came too late, for that Pym and his friends could not then permit the Earl to live; and he regrets its failure on the ground that it would have given the King some able men to advise and assist him.* Strange and startling as it seems, amid the events I am here describing, the King appears to have now again, even with what he afterwards alleged to be the proof of treason in his hand, opened a negotiation with the parliamentary leader for acceptance of the same office. The details I have not been able to ascertain,

<small>Negotiations again opened.</small>

<small>Why the King's efforts to conciliate failed.</small>   * There is much beside said by Clarendon on this head, which, though coloured of course by his peculiar manner and tone, throws light upon the real causes of the failure of every effort at accomodation: " But the rule the King gave " himself (very reasonable at another time) that they should " first do service and compass this or that thing for him, " before they should receive favour, was then very unseason- " able; since, besides that they could not in truth do him that " service without the qualification, it could not be expected " they would desert that side, by the power of which they " were sure to make themselves considerable, without an " unquestionable mark of interest in the other, by which they " were to keep up their power and reputation. And so, " whilst the King expected they should manifest their inclina- " tions to his service by their temper and moderation in those " proceedings that most offended him, and they endeavoured, " by doing all the hurt they could, to make evident the power " they had to do him good, he grew so far disobliged and " provoked that he could not in honour gratify them, and " they so obnoxious and guilty that they could not think " themselves secure in his favour." *Hist.* ii. 61.

§ v. *Pym and the King.*

beyond the fact that the offer was made to Pym alone.   King Pym* the people

> * The reader may perhaps be amused by one or two Royalist examples of the use the Royalist libellers made of this epithet.   As thus:
>
>
>
> Your ferious subtilty is grown fo grave,
> We dare not tell you how much power you have.
> At least you dare not hear us. How you frown
> If we but fay, King Pym wears Charles's crown !
>   *   *   *
>   Well, we vow
> Not to act anything you difallow :
> We will not dare at your ftrange votes to jeer
> Nor perfonate King Pym with his ftate-flear!
>   *The Players' Petition.*
>
>
>
> Or again : from *Pym's Anarchy*:
>
>
>
> Afk me no more why Strafford's dead,
> And why we aimed fo at his head ?
> Faith, all the anfwer I can give,
> 'Tis thought he was too wife to live !
> * * * *
> Afk me no more why in this age
> I fing fo fharp without a cage . . . .
> This anfwer I in brief do fing ;
> All things were thus when Pym was King.
>
>
> *Royalist libellers of Pym.*
> *Things done when Pym was King.*
>
> Or, from the *New Diurnall*:
>
>
>
> And yet their Rebellion fo neatly they trim
> They fight for the King, but they mean for King Pym.
>
>
>
> Or, from that Epigram upon *The Parliament's Beliefs* which fhows how far fuch libellers could go :
>
>
>
> Is there no God ? let's put it to a vote.
> Is there no Church ? fome fools fay fo by rote.
> Is there no King, but Pym, for to affent
> What fhall be done by Act of Parliament ?
> No God, no Church, no King—then all were well
> If they could but enact there were no Hell.
>
>
> *A propofed enactment.*
>
> Or, from the *Cavalier's Prayer*:
>
>
>
> Lawn fleeves and furplices muft go down,
> For why, King Pym doth fway the crown—
> But all *are* Bifhops that wear a Black Gown,
>   Which nobody can deny.
>
>
>
> Or, finally (for fuch illuftrations might be indefinitely prolonged), from the libel of which the opening lines alfo

Arrest of the Five Members.

King Pym: called him; and the incident, one of the last before the country separated into two hostile camps, and hardly credible if simply related as from King to subject, might indeed rather seem to express the relation of sovereign to sovereign. But Charles had always, as will sufficiently be seen throughout this narrative, a feeling towards the great leader of the opposition against him, which appeared strangely to fluctuate between desire and dread. In the correspondence between himself and his Queen, Pym's name is that which most

Secret influence over King Charles. frequently occurs, whether the design be to inveigle and snare, or more openly to denounce, the most powerful of the parliamentary leaders;* and even in the Royalist songs against the popular tribune there is that which expresses, though very often in most extrava-

curiously reflect Pym's continuous and zealous efforts to enforce that early and full attendance at the House in which so many members of even the popular party were so frequently remiss:

Chides the members for late attendance.
Truth! I could chide you Friends! why how so late?
My watch speaks eight and not one pin o th' state
This day undone! Can such remissnesse fit
Your active spirits, or my more Hellish wit?
The sun each step he mounts to Heaven's crown,
Whilst Pym commands, should see a kingdome down.
 * * *
Thus whilom seated was Great James's Heir
Just as you see me now, i' th' Kingdom's Chair.
 * * *

Happiest in storms.
Calmes proper are for guiltlesse sons of Peace,
Our vessels bear out best in stormy seas.
Charles must not reign secure whilst reigns a Pym:
The sun, if it rise with us, must set with him.

Pym's Juncto, 1640.

* See my *Hist. & Biog. Essays*, i. 19.

gant forms, a something that yet involves him more closely with the King than is attempted against any other of the zealous and active men upon whom those reckless libellers emptied most eagerly their ribaldry and scorn.*

<small>Songs and Satires against the Parliament.</small>

* For one instance take the following: selected from many of a similar character:

(*The Humble Petition of the House of Commons*).

Next, for the State, we think it fit
That Mr. Pym should govern it,
   He's very poor:
The money that's for Ireland writ,
Faith, let them have the Devil a bit,
   We'll ask no more.

(*The King's Answer to the Humble Petition*).

When you no more shall dare hereafter
A needlesse thing which gains much laughter,
   Granted before;
When Pym is sent Ireland to slaughter
And ne'er more hopes to marry my daughter,
   You'll ask no more.

<small>Pym and the "King's daughter."</small>

To this I may add some lines UPON MR. PYM'S PICTURE, which through all their violent abuse yet express a kind of awe and terror at the man's predominance and power.

Reader, behold the counterfeit of him
Who now controuls the Land—Almighty Pym!
A man whom even the Devil to fear begins,
And dares not trust him with successlesse sins.
A man who now is wading through the Flood
Of reverend Laud's and noble Strafford's blood,
To strike so high as to put Bishops down
And in the Mitre to controul the Crown.

<small>Pym's picture.</small>

The wretch hath mighty thoughts, and entertains
Some glorious mischief in his active brains,
Where now he's plotting to make England such
As may outvie the villany of the Dutch:
He dares not go to Heaven, 'cause he doth feare
To meet (and not pull down) the Bishops there!

<small>Must avoid Heaven for fear of Bishops.</small>

Is it not strange that in that shuttle head
Three kingdomes' ruines should be buried?

Pym's constitutional opinions.

Remarkable in every respect indeed was the mingled influence exerted by this famous member of the Commons over the Sovereign whose destiny he so largely controlled, and who never seems to have raised against him the hand to strike but with a misgiving that paralysed its aim, and soon or late brought himself into the suppliant posture to which he would have reduced his adversary. Still Pym is ever the person singled out for notice by Charles, and still the evil and the good alternate. Again and again,

Alternately held up for avoidance and for example.

during the paper war which attended the events I am relating, and ushered in the more terrible war, Charles is found recurring to his speeches for causes of indignant protest, of expostulation, of reproach; but the day as surely comes later in the struggle, when Pym is lying in his grave in Westminster Abbey,* when his place is occupied by sterner and less scrupulous men, and when the poor King is fain to ransack the

Characteristics of his oratory.

very speeches in which once he found nothing but rebellion, for maxims of constitutional lore, for just expositions of the monarchy, for counsels to respect the law. These, the most

> Is it not strange there should be hatch'd a Plot
> Which should outdoe the Treason of the Scot,
> And even the malice of a Puritan?
>
> Reader behold, and hate the poysonous man!
> The Picture's like him: yet 'tis very fit
> He adde one likeness more—that's—*Hang,* like it!

Pym's last resting-place.

* " Mr. Pym was buried with wonderful pomp and magnificence in the place where the bones of our English kings and princes are committed to their rest."—Clarendon, *Hist.* iv. 441.

§ v.   *Pym and the King.*   47

ftriking qualities of the orator, and from which Chancel-
even Charles could not turn away altogether lorſhip of Exchequer
unheeding, may indeed have had fome influence again offered
thus early in bringing about a renewal of the to Pym.
offer of the Chancellorſhip of the Exchequer.
Clarendon evidently thought fo.   He does
not refer to it in exprefs terms; but he helps
materially to explain it when he intimates that
even Hampden's acceffion, after his return from
Scotland, to what was called the root and branch
party in the State, had not entirely carried Pym Pym lefs
along with it;* that the member for Tavif- extreme than
tock had no infuperable diflike to the conftitu- Hampden.
tion of the Englifh Church, apart from Laud's
grofs and cruel adminiftration of it; and that
in confenting to let Pym fave the Monarchy,
Epifcopacy alfo might be faved.   Be this as it
may, the offer came too late.   In the authority The offer
from which my information is derived, there made too late.
is nothing to explain the circumftances of it,
and I cannot difcover that Pym himfelf made

* " Mr. Pym was not of thofe furious refolutions againſt Pym not
" the Church as the other leading men were, and wholly adverfe to
" devoted to the Earl of Bedford, who had nothing of that the
" fpirit."—*Hiſt.* i. 323.   " In the Houfe of Commons, though Church:
" of the chief leaders Nathaniel Fiennes and young Sir
" Harry Vane, and fhortly after Mr. Hampden (who had
" not before owned it), were believed to be for root and
" branch; which grew fhortly after a common expreffion,
" and difcovery of the feveral tempers; yet Mr. Pym was not
" of that mind, nor Mr. Hollis." *Ib.* i. 410.   " Mr. Pym was
" concerned and paffionate in the jealoufies of religion, and
" much troubled with the countenance which had been given But to
" to thofe opinions that had been imputed to Arminius. . . . Arminian
" yet himfelf profeffed to be very entire to the doctrine and practices.
' difcipline of the Church of England."—*Ib.* iv. 437.
'

Pym silent afterwards the remotest allusion to it. It is hardly likely indeed that any such reference from him would have been compatible with the terms on which it was submitted, with the respect still necessarily paid to Charles, or with the safety of his own position among the extreme members of the Commons. But Pym must well have known his danger in declining the offer, and that it thickened the royal snares which already were spread around him.

as to the King's offer:

Rejects it. The fact is at any rate indisputable, that such an offer was specifically made and rejected. It rests on the authority of the member for Kent, Sir Edward Dering, whose services to the Court in the debates on the Grand Remonstrance had won him recent and grateful acceptance there; and whose colleague in the representation of the county, Sir John Culpeper, received the office on Pym declining it. In a private letter to Lady Dering, written early in January, containing other evidence of his favor at Court and with the Queen, he tells her: " The King is too flexible and too good-natured; for within two howers, and a greate deale lesse, before he made Culpeper Chancellor of the Exchequer, he had sente a messenger to bring Pym unto him, and wold have given him that place."* Cul-

Sir Edward Dering to Lady Dering, 13th Jan. 1641-2:

Describes Charles's overture to Pym.

---

* Since this letter was obligingly communicated to me, it has been, with many other very interesting papers from the Surrenden manuscripts, placed for publication in the hands of the Camden Society by the Rev. Lambert Larking, and

§ v.   *Pym and the King.*   49

peper's patent is not dated until the 7th of January, but the office had been given to him several days before, and he had taken his seat at the Council Board on New Year's Day. The exact period of the offer to Pym can only now be guessed at, but we may narrow it within the limits of the last half of December.

Thofe days had feen feveral changes. The feals, which Windebank had voided by his ignominious flight, were given to Nicholas.*

_{Culpeper receives what Pym had declined, 1st January, 1641-2.}

the volume, already announced for publication under Mr. Camden Larking's editorship, will rank appropriately with the many other rare and important illustrations of this great period of our history in which the Camden Collection of books is peculiarly rich.

   * I have found in the State Paper Office, and cannot refift quoting, a letter written by Windebank from Paris (whither he had fucceeded in making good his flight), upon hearing that Nicholas had been appointed Secretary in his place. It exhibits the meanness of the man's nature; but more than this, it shows in my judgment plainly enough, that parliament was thoroughly justified in having charged the Ex-Secretary as accomplice with the Queen in private and illegal practices to favour the Roman Catholic religion. The letter is addreffed to his fon and dated the 27th (or in the English ftyle the 17th Dec.), 1641. "Tom," it begins, "your letters . . . . .
" were very wellcum both for the greate honor they brought
" me from the Queene's Ma: & the good news of your health
" and of the reft of myne in thofe partes. I do forbear to
" prefent my moft humble thankes myfelfe to Her M: for
" the fame reafon that She in Her wifdom did not think fitt
" to venter a lett^r to me : Yet yo^u muft not fail to paffe that
" office in all humility for me, acquainting Her M: withall
" that I never was in a condition that more required her
" comfort and gracious affiftance than now that I finde, by
" the difpofing of the place I had the Honor to holde neere
" His M:, no hope left to ferve my Royall Mafter againe,
" wch really is the greateft corofive to my harte that can be.
" I do acknowledge it is no more than I had reafon to
" expect, & I thank God I have had time to be prepared for
" it. Neverthelesse now it is come I cannot be fo ftupid as
" not to be fensible of that wch ruines me and my pofterity,

_{Society books.}

_{Windebank to his fon, 17th Dec. 1641.}

_{Secret understanding with the Queen.}

E

Old Vane finally dismissed.

The Court exodus of Old Vane, whose staff of the Treasurer of the Household had been taken from him at Newcastle to be at York bestowed on Lord Savile, was now completed by the demand that he should deliver up the seals of Secretary, designed for Falkland.* The old

Grief at losing place.

"nor so iniurious to myne owne harte to think that after so many years painfull & faithfull services to both their M M: I have deserved it. My hope is that His M. hath done it to preserve me from a greater blow (though truly for my own particular & setting aside the interests of you & the rest of my poor children a greater cold not falle upon me) & that knowing my entire affections to his person & service most farr from the least guilte of any intention to offend, will in His Princely Goodnesse & His owne best tyme vouchsafe me & myne reliefe. In the meantime I shall esteem this & (if occasion serve) my deerest harte bloud a blessed sacrifice, if they may contribut any thing to the redresse of His M: affaires, hoping that this shall serve for satisfaction & expiation (even in the opinion of the most severe) for any offence taken against me; and so the displeasure of the time relente and go no farther, but that I may be permitted to retourne to myne own poor nest in the Country to end my dayes there in peace." Equally characteristic is the conclusion. The Queen in her secret communication had asked Windebank to attend the French court for her, and to this he pleads unfitness, by reason of the state of his mind, adding: "Besides I acknowledge I am not yet in case to appear in publique, nor can for the pres^t wynne so much upon my self to looke upon a foraine Prince wth any contentment, being deprived of the blessed & gracious aspect of my Master."

Windebank to his son, 24th Dec.

A fellow-feeling.

* Poor Windebank upon this writes to Son Tom from Paris $\frac{14^{th}\ D^{er}}{24^{th}\ J^{a}}$} 1641-2, taking the strictly economical view of Vane's dismissal, "The newes of the removall of Sir Henry Vane from the place of Secretary is very strange heere, and truly my owne condition makes me sensible of his, wch considering his great burden of children is very comiserable. But wthall I am infinitly comforted wth that of the D. of Richmond wch is one of the noblest things the K: hath don of many yeares & of singular consequence to his service. If I durst, I would wish yo^u to congratulat with His Gr: in all humbleness from me." It is quite in character that Windebank should consider the appointment

man's disgrace was but part of the punishment <small>Revenge for Strafford.</small> over which Charles had brooded ever since Strafford's trial, which but for his weakness and isolation he would then have inflicted, and which now he thought himself strong enough to inflict, not simply on Vane himself but on his son. Young Vane, who held the office of joint Treasurer of the Navy with Sir William <small>Young Vane also dismissed.</small> Russell, was ordered suddenly to send in his accounts preparatory to the issue of a new patent without his name.* We learn this from the letter of another correspondent of Pennington's, Captain Carterett, a man of

of an amiable young Duke to an office in the Household as the noblest and wisest act of his glorious master.

* Admiral Pennington's desire (already adverted to) to have had this office for himself, seems to have been generally understood by his friends; and upon the fact of Young Vane's dismissal being first known, Capt. Dowse, ignorant of the Admiral's intimation to the Under Secretary that he did not wish the matter pressed for the present, went and asked the office from the Lord Admiral, the Earl of Northumberland. His note (in the State Paper Office) proves that the gift of the office to Strafford's friend Pennyman was the King's personal act. "Noble Sir," he writes from York House on Dec. the 30th, "Upon the first notice of Sir Henry Vane his "being discharged of the Treasurer's place of the Navy I "did (as I have written to you before) repaire to my Lord to "desire his Lo^p to remember your name to the King, if his "Ma^{ty} did put by Sir Henry Vane. My Lord told me then "that Sr Henry Vane was not absolutely dismissed until his "accounts were perfected for the whole yeare." A second time he waited on the Earl; but "My Lord told me then "that the King had bestowed the place upon Sir William "Pennyman, but if he could doe you any service in it, he "would doe it. Soe wishing you a Merry Christmas I rest "&c." So long previously as the 16th December Capt. Slingsby had written decisively to the Admiral "Sir Henry "Vane the Younger is dismist of his Treasurership of the "Navy, and Sir William Pennyman in his place." <small>Admiral Pennington looking for Young Vane's Office. Captain Dowse to Pennington, 30th Dec.</small>

Captain Carterett.

great worth and diſtinction, who held the office of Comptroller of the Navy, and was, ſays Clarendon, of great eminency and reputation in naval command.* Charles had alſo further reſolved, to expreſs more plainly the ill-adviſed challenge he was thus flinging down to the Houſe of Commons, to beſtow the office on Strafford's agent and follower, Sir William Pennyman. "This much I knowe," writes Captain Carterett on the 23rd December, to the Admiral of the fleet in the Downs,† "that the attorney hath a warrant for to prepaire a bill for the drawinge a patente for Sʳ William Ruſſell alone, his joyned patente with Sʳ Hen. Vane being recalled in, wᶜʰ the Parliament doth take ſomething ill. For it ſeemes that Sʳ Henʸ Vane the Younger is much eſteemed in the Houſe of Commons: but I doe not heare the licke of his father, but rather that hee hath loſt the good oppinion of both ſides." It might be ſo, but not in that hour of Court disfavor would Pym have it thought ſo by the Court. He welcomed into the popular ranks the old ſervant of the King by adding his name to the ſelect committee for Iriſh

Young Vane ſucceeded by a friend of Strafford.

Captain Carterett to Pennington, 23rd Dec. 1641.

Pym welcomes Old Vane into the popular ranks.

---

* See *Hiſt.* iii. 115. Carterett's intereſt and reputation in the navy, according to the hiſtorian, was ſo great, and his diligence and dexterity in command ſo eminent, that the Parliament, in a criſis of much difficulty, notwithſtanding his Royaliſt opinions, named him for their Vice-Admiral.

† MS. State Paper Office. Carterett to Pennington, 23rd Dec. 1641.

§ v.   *Pym and the King.*

affairs; and on the same 23rd of December, when Carterett so wrote to his Admiral, Under Secretary Sidney Bere, employed with Nicholas at Whitehall, was writing thus to the same correspondent:* " I can now give you this " certainty, that a warrant hath passed for the " outing young Sʳ Hen. Vane, and on the con- " trary an order is made in the Lower House " for to consider of some meanes and wayes " whereby to preserve him in; so that it is " likely there will bee greate debate and con- " testation about this businesse." It became, in fact, a new cause of quarrel between the Commons and the King, and the conduct of Pym in regard to it seems to show that the startling overture so suddenly made to himself must already have been made and rejected. *[margin: The Under-Secretary to the Admiral, 23rd Dec. The Commons resent Young Vane's dismissal.]*

Upon the probable motives, as well for that overture itself as for its rejection, though it has been seen that nothing can with certainty be stated, it will yet be not inappropriate to add such suggestion here towards an explanation of both, as will fairly arise out of a careful con- sideration of circumstances attending not only the attempt involved in the present instance, but the similar attempt which preceded it, to obtain for the King the service of some of the chiefs who led the opposition against him. But for this it will be necessary to go back to a period *[margin: Previous offer to Pym and his friends: July, 1641.]*

---

* MS. State Paper Office. Sidney Bere to Pennington, 23rd Dec. 1641.

of nearly four months before the opening of my narrative.

Former attempt to give office to leaders of the Commons:

Clarendon leaves it to be inferred that the negotiation by which office was placed at the difposal of the Parliamentary leaders during the proceedings againft Strafford, had for its fole object the hope of faving by fuch means the life of that great minifter; and that when this failed, and Strafford's head had fallen, no attempt was made to renew the propofal. This however is not the fact. Within two months of the execution, Secretary Nicholas, in the fame letter in which he communicates to Admiral Pennington the vote by which the Commons had fentenced Lord Digby's publifhed fpeech on Strafford's attainder to be burnt, and had declared Lord Digby himfelf to be for the future unfit to hold place or receive employment under the King, adds this remarkable poftfcript: "The Lord Digby was by "his Matie defigned to have gonne Lord "Ambaffador into Fraunce as foone as the "Earl of Lecefter fhould returne thence, but "(it is thought) the Parliament will difable "him for any fuch imployment. The fpeech "is that Mr. Hollis or Mr. John Hampden "fhalbe Secretary of State, but the Lord "Mandeville doth now againe put hard for "that place."*

Not a mere expedient for faving Strafford:

Renewed after Strafford's execution.

Hollis or Hampden named for Secretary of State, 15 July, 1641.

Secretary Nicholas

* State Paper Office. The letter is addreffed "To my "much efteemed friend Sir John Pennington, Knight, Ad-

§ V.   *Pym and the King.*

From this it is clear (for no one had such sources of information as Nicholas) that, notwithstanding the execution of Strafford and Digby's disqualification for office, the King had still a purpose of his own in keeping open the negotiation for receiving into his counsels the men who had struck so heavily against his dead minister and his living friend. The letter of Nicholas is dated on the 15th of July, and until the close of that month, indeed as long as the King remained in London, the best informed of Charles's own officers of state continued to expect the change. In less than a fortnight Nicholas wrote again as if all doubts and disputes as to the particular distribution of offices had been settled. Lord Mandeville and Hampden had in the interval withdrawn their claims to the principal Secretaryship of State in favour of Denzil Hollis, while Hampden was to take the Chancellorship of the Duchy, Lord Saye and Seale to be Lord Treasurer, and the Chancellorship of the Exchequer to be, as in all the previous proposed arrangements, committed to Pym. Nor is it Nicholas alone who thus, up to the 29th July, believes that

Negotiations with popular leaders kept open.

Distribution of offices settled, 29th July, 1641.

"miral of His Maties Fleete imployed for garde of the Narrow "Seas, aborde His Maties ship the St. André, nowe riding in "the Downes or thereaboutes. Leave this with the Post of "Sandwich to be conveyed." The existence of this letter was known to Lady Theresa Lewis. See her very interesting book in illustration of the portraits in the Clarendon Gallery, *Lives of the Friends and Contemporaries of Lord Chancellor Clarendon*, ii. 442.

to Penington.

<small>Preparation for the new ministry.</small> these men are about to assume the great offices of state. Even the smaller clerks and secretaries serving under him are making preparations against the expected loss of their employments; and Mr. Sidney Bere writes to tell <small>Making provision for the worst.</small> Admiral Pennington, on the very eve of the King's departure to Scotland, that he hopes he has made provision against the worst.*

<small>Sidney Bere to Admiral Pennington, 30th July, 1641.</small> * I subjoin some curious passages from this letter, which is also in the State Paper Office (MS. Sidney Bere to Admiral Pennington, 30th July, 1641, Whitehall). Bere's employment at this earlier time was in connection with the Foreign Office, to which he had been recommended by a previous engagement as Secretary with Sir Balthazar Gerbier. "I must needs," he writes to the Admiral, "take y‘ occasion of this enclosed "wch was left att my chamber, to tell you, that the noise of "remove of officers increases still, and some thinke wee shall not "escape wth less than the losse of Secretarys, wch I begin to "feare much by many signes. One, & truly a noble one, is this, <small>Notice to quit Whitehall.</small> "that Mr. Trea^r asked me this day how farre my graunt was "advanced, I told him ready for the Kinge's hand tomorrow; "he bid me to hasten it all I could, for a reason he knew, w^{ch} "you may easily guesse carryes noe good interpretation. I "am glad Mr. Murray is ingaged, who, should any such thinge "happen soe suddenly, will wthout doubt make good what "he hath undertaken, & I am confident both he and Mr. "Trea^r will recommend me to ye successor. But for all these "doubts and surmises we prepare still for ye Scotch journey, "& horses goe before on Monday. Wee follow on Friday <small>Proposed Viceroy during the King's absence.</small> "nexte, and ye King on ye 9th which is Munday. The Par"liam^t its said will move for a longer stay, but the King is "resolved. A whisper goes the Houses will stand for a Lo. "Lieut. in his absence w^h power to passe bills: what that "proposition will produce in his resolution to graunt or deny, "goe or stay, we shall shortly see: but every one is full of "expectations what every grand councill should produce in "the change of officers. Come the worst, if this graunt "passe, I have something to trust to ag^t I am old, and till then, "I hope w^h God's blessing, the countenance of my friends, <small>Consolations of a retiring official.</small> "& my own industry, to passe well enogh. I have not soe "ill spent this time, but I have pursed up for a yeare's sub"sistence and more, in wch time many changes will happen. "Thus I take all att the worst on the first alarum, but I hope

§ v.   *Pym and the King.*

Yet so strange does it seem that purposes involving a complete change in the greatest employments of the State should have been entertained up to the very eve of the King's departure for Scotland, that they then should suddenly and silently have been dropped, and that the King's letters to Nicholas from Edinburgh should as suddenly be filled with covert threats against the men chosen so recently for the highest dignities he had it in his power to bestow, that credit may hardly be claimed for such a statement without production of the actual evidence. The second letter of Nicholas, also in the State Paper Office, begins with acknowledgment of a welcome present of four Guinea-birds, which the Admiral had sent for Mrs. Nicholas, " whereby you have made " her a proude woman, and she desires me to " present to you her affectionate thankes for " that great raritie." He then describes the appointment of Lord Essex to be General of the Forces on this side Trent; speaks of Lord Pembroke as bearing the loss of his employment with much patience and discretion; and makes frank allusion to the eccle-

A sequel almost too strange for belief.

Present from the Admiral.

Nicholas to Pennington, 29 July, 1641.

" there is noe cause, but that we shall rubb out yett this Sum-
" mer at the least." It is very remarkable to observe from this
letter that at no time do the popular leaders, even when their
immediate induction into the great offices was looked upon as
certain, appear to have taken the pressure of Parliament from
off the King. The proposal of a Viceroy or Regent was singularly distasteful to him, and the dispute as to the proper time of
his quitting London was vehemently maintained even to
within a few hours of his departure. See my *Essays*, i. 13.

> fiaftical reforms in progrefs, and the abufes they are levelled at. "The acte againft Bish^pps, "Deanes, & Chappters, is not as yett paft the "Comons Houfe of P^t, and I hope never will: "for iff it shall, my father and myselfe shall "by the change of our Landlordes lose 1500l. "in the value of our eftates. But I hope the "Parl^t will not holde it wife to punifhe the "Tenants for ye Landlord's faulttes. The "Comons are much troubled that the Kinge "will goe on Monday come fennight (as hee "has declared openlie) towards Scotland. "They have had a conference with ye Lords "ab^t prefenting to his Maj^ty fome reafons ag^t "his Maj^ty's goinge untill the armie be difbanded, w^ch, if there were money readie, "woulde not bee this fortnight. It is heere "faid that wee shall shortly before the Kinge's "departure have a greate change & addition "of officers ab^t Co^te, as that the Ld Saye "shall be made Ld Treas^r, the Ld Newburg "Mafter of the Wardes, Mr. Jo. Hampden "Ch^r of ye Dutchy, Mr. Pym Cha^r of the "Excheq^r, Mr. Denzill Hollis Principall Secr^y "of State; and that ye Earl of Bath and L^d "Brooke shall be sworne of his Ma^sty moft "hon^ble Privy Counfell."* He adds fome

Why Nicholas objects to Ecclefiaftical Reform.

King's propofed journey to Scotland:

Objected to by the Commons.

The new miniftry expected: Hampden, Pym, Hollis, and Lord Saye and Seale.

---

* This letter (alfo in the State Paper Office, and dated 29th July, 1641) is addreffed like the former, with this addition: "Leave this with the foote poft of Sand^wch in "Philpot Lane att ye figne of ye Sand^wch Armes to be "conveyed."

particulars as to the army plot, the examinations as to which were then in procefs of being taken; and he clofes by faying that he propofes himfelf, God willing, to retire on the next following Saturday to his houfe in the country, to live quietly there if he can; and that howfoever the world goes, the Admiral fhall be fure always to find that he is ftill conftantly and firmly his faithful and affectionate friend. *Nicholas about to retire:*

But of courfe Nicholas did *not* retire into the country, nor did the parliamentary leaders make their entrance into Whitehall. Not lefs myfterious in its origin and fate than the later attempt to obtain Pym's folitary fervice, it feems impoffible to review the circumftances attending this earlier effort to place both him and his friends in power, without arriving at the only folution which either feems capable of receiving. Neither, it muft have been fufpected or difcovered, was really or fincerely intended by the perfon who alone could give effect to it. Both were wrecked by the utter diftruft and difbelief which the King in all his dealings had infpired. In making again the overture fingly to Pym, there can be little queftion that Charles had the idea in his mind, as already hinted, that by fome artifice or trick, fome juggling and playing with the cards, Epifcopacy, even in its laft extremity of danger, was to be refcued ftill by bringing over the only popular leader not committed to *But does not retire. Why both attempts to conciliate popular leaders failed. The rock they fplit againft.*

A warning for Pym to act upon: root and branch. But the fate of the earlier negotiation, which I have thus been able to retrace, opened also, as the later had been, at the very moment when Lord Digby had been singled out for royal favour, was doubt-
The warning taken. less the sufficient warning on which Pym wisely acted. We need not look for his motives further a-field. The calm refusal with which the proffered place was put aside, and the dignified silence preserved in relation to it, may thus alike receive their satisfactory solution.

§ VI. THE WESTMINSTER TUMULTS.

Publication of the Grand Remonstrance. ON the third day after the Grand Remonstrance, printed by order of the House, had begun to circulate among the people, the observance of a day of Fast and Humiliation had been appointed. The circumstance is referred to by the Under-Secretary, with whose letter, already quoted in the preceding section, as with a similar communication from Captain Carterett, there also went to the Admiral a copy of the published Remonstrance. "The Remonstrance is
" likewise come out," he writes, " which I now
" send herewith, and leave unto your readinge to
" judge of it. This is all I can say more for
" the present save that yesterday the fast was
A Fast Day, 22nd Dec. 1641: " observed through London and the Court,
" and is to-day in Westminster. Indeed, there
" needs some extraordinary devotion to divert
" the many troubles and distractions this State

"is threatened withal, wch if God doe not of his mercy turne awaye, it's much to be feared will very shortly fall upon us: Soe that I cannot wonder to reade y^or compassionate sense thereof, but doe joyne wth you that it's a time wherein he that hath leaste to doe may thinke himself the happiest."* The King, as we have seen, had celebrated the fast at Court by signing on that day, the 22nd December, the warrant for appointment of the dissolute Lunfford to one of the places of greatest trust in his dominions. We have seen also the tumult it provoked in the House of Commons, and this had now reacted on the people out of doors. It was the time of Christmas holidays, when unusual numbers were in London, daily thronging the streets; and such and so alarming were the manifestations of popular discontent, that within three days after the letters just quoted we find another of Pennington's correspondents, and a high civil functionary, writing to him in a strain that might well shake the nerves of the gallant seaman far more than those terrible gales then sweeping the coast during which his ships had well-nigh foundered in the Downs. "But though," writes Mr. Thomas Smith, a man highly esteemed and holding important office in the Admiralty, to his loving

How the King celebrated it.

Discontented holiday crowds.

---

* MS. State Paper Office. Sidney Bere to Pennington, 23rd Dec.

and much honored friend, "the ftormes are efcaped at fea, they are not fo on fhoare. For here we have fuch jealoufies, and difcontents are dayly rayfed by the malignant party between the King and his people, that there talks now of nothing but drawing of fwords and a war between the Proteftants and Papifts. W^ch God forbid! for though we may know the beginning, noe man can the end and confequences of an inteftine warre."*

Sea and land ftorms.

A religious war talked of.

On the evening of the day when that letter was written, the King found it abfolutely neceffary (upon a reprefentation perfonally made to him the previous night at Whitehall by the Lord Mayor, a member of his own party) to cancel Lunfford's appointment; but fwiftly as the ill-advifed act was fo recalled, it was yet recalled too late. It was too late to prevent the tumults and difturbances of that and the following day. In thofe tumults, duly recorded, but not fairly or juftly difcriminated, in the hiftories, were firft heard the memorable epithets of Roundhead and Cavalier: two words deftined to become as famous as thofe other two of Whig and Tory, which, invented feven-and-thirty years later, ufed alfo as terms of reproach,† and bandied about from fide to

Lunfford's appointment cancelled.

Too late.

Memorable epithets firft invented.

---

* MS. State Paper Office. Thomas Smith to Pennington, 23rd Dec.
† That the word *Cavalier*, not neceffarily a term of re-

side, like these, amid tumultuous assemblages of English citizens,* became in like manner

proach (Shakespeare certainly does not so employ it when he speaks of the gay and gallant English eager for French invasion—

> For who is he . . . that will not follow
> These cull'd and choice-drawn Cavaliers to France?)

Cavalier: origin and meaning of the word:

was unquestionably used in that sense on the occasion of these tumults (probably to connect its French origin with the un-English character of the defenders of the Queen and her French papist adherents to whom it was chiefly applied), appears from the fact that it is bandied about in declarations alternately issued on the eve of the war by the Parliament and the King, the latter speaking of it more than once as a word much in disfavour. And, after the standard on either side was unfurled, nay, when the battle of Edgehill had been fought, Charles elaborately accuses his antagonists, "pretenders to peace " and charity " he calls them, of a hateful attempt " to render " all persons of honour, courage, and reputation, odious to " the common people under the style of Cavaliers, insomuch " as the highways and villages have not been safe for gentle- " men to pass through without violence or affront." Even in the very earliest popular songs on the King's side the word has not the place it afterwards assumed, and one meets with Royalist poets of a comparatively sober vein

The King complains of its use.

> " Who neither love for fashion nor for fear,
> As far from Roundhead as from Cavalier."

D'Ewes's earliest uses of the word in his MS. Journal I find under dates of Monday 10th January and Friday March 4th, 1641-2, and Friday 3rd June 1642. In the first he is speaking of parties who had been seen suspiciously entering the Tower; in the second, of the Cavaliers at Whitehall who wounded the Citizens; and in the last, of the King's party in Yorkshire. Of the word Roundhead, on the other hand, and the mixed fear and hatred it represented and provoked, decidedly the most characteristic example is furnished by the ever quaint and entertaining Bishop Hacket, who (*Scrinia Reserata*, ii. 207) tells a story of a certain worthy and honest Vicar of Hampshire who always (in such manner as to evade the notice of one section of his hearers while he secretly pleased the other) changed one word in the last verse of the Te Deum—O Lord in thee have I trusted, *let me never be a Round-head!*

Roundhead.

* See my *Hist. & Biog. Essays* ii. 6 (under Essay on De Foe).

the indelible distinction of the two great parties in English history.* The first blood shed in the great civil war had flowed on that 27th of December, several citizens having been wounded and Sir Richard Wiseman slain.

First blood shed in the Civil War.

* There is a curious and characteristic passage by William Lilly (*Monarchy or no Monarchy in England*, part ii. ed. 1651), referring to these tumults, of which he was himself an eye-witness, and deserving more attention than it has received. He is speaking of the King: "Fearing the worst, as himself "pretended (from the tumultuous assemblages of Citizens), he "had a Court of Guard, before Whitehall, of the Train "Bands; he had also many dissolute gentlemen, and some "very civil, that kept within Whitehall with their swords by "their sides, to be ready upon any sudden occasion. Verily "men's fears now began to be great; and it was by many "perceived, that the King began to swell with anger against "the proceedings of Parliament, and to intend a war against "them: some speeches dropt from him to that purpose. It "happened one day, as some of the ruder sort of Citizens "came by Whitehall, one busy Citizen must needs cry 'No "Bishops.' Some of the gentlemen issued out of Whitehall, "either to correct the saucinefs of the fool in words, if they "would serve; else, it seems, with blows. What passed on "either side in words, none but themselves knew. The "Citizen, being more tongue than soldier, was wounded, and "I have heard, died of his wounds received at that time. It "hath been affirmed by very many, that in, or hearunto, that "place where this fellow was hurt and wounded, the late King's "head was cut-off, the Scaffold standing just over that place. "These people, or Citizens, who used thus to flock unto "Westminster, were, most of them, men of mean, or a middle "quality . . . and yet most of them were either such as had "public spirits, or lived a more religious life than the vulgar, "and were usually called Puritans, and had suffered under the "tyranny of the Bishops. In the general they were very "honest men and well meaning: some particular fools, or "others, perhaps, now and then, got in amongst them, greatly "to the disadvantage of the more sober. They were modest "in their apparel, but not in their language; they had the "hair of their heads very few of them longer than their ears; "whereupon it came to pass that those who usually with their "cries attended at Westminster, were by a nick name called "Round-heads. The Courtiers again, having long hair and "locks, and always swordes, at last were called by these men

William Lilly's evidence.

The King's secret revealed.

A belief or superstition.

Character of Puritans.

§ VI.   *The Westminster Tumults.*

The Lords had at first declined to join the Commons in petitioning for Lunsford's removal, and it was the excitement consequent upon this refusal, first known by the published protest of twenty-two peers headed by names in such popular esteem as those of Bedford, Northumberland, Pembroke, and Essex, which led to the assemblages that met suddenly together, in large numbers certainly but unprovided with arms, in Westminster Hall and outside the door of the House of Lords.* It has been, notwithstanding an admission to the contrary

[margin: Cause of sudden assemblages in Westminster Hall.]

" Cavaliers; and so &c. &c. few of the vulgar knowing the
" sense of the word Cavalier. To speak freely and ingenuously,
" what I then observed of the City Tumults was this: First,
" the sufferings of the Citizens who were anything well
" devoted, had, during all this King's reign, been such and so
" great (being harrowed or abused, continually, either by the
" High Commission Court or the Star Chamber), that, as men
" in whose breasts the spirit of Liberty had some place, they
" were even glad to vent out their sighs and sufferings in this
" rather tumultuous than civil manner: being assured that if
" ever this parliament had been dissolved, they must have been
" racked, whipt, and stript by the... Clergy, and other extrava-
" gant courses: and for any amendment which they might
" expect from the King, they too well knew his temper ; that
" though in a time of parliament he often promised to
" redress any grievances, yet the best friend he hath cannot
" produce any one act of good for his subjects done by him
" in the vacancy of a parliament. The losers usually have
" leave to speak, and so had the Citizens. All this Xmas
" 1641, there was nothing but private whisperings in Court,
" and secret counsels held by the Queen and her party, with
" whom the King sate in council very late many nights.
" What was the particular result of these clandestine consulta-
" tions, it will presently appear." In these last few words he
alludes of course to the impending attempt to arrest the
members.

[margin: What Lilly observed of the tumults. A Parliament the People's only hope. Secret counsels.]

* " The tumults," says Nalson, the most unscrupulous of Royalist partizans, " began upon this little clash of the two " Houses, the Lords refusing to join with the Commons to " petition out Lunsford."—*Collections*, ii. 781.

F

to be quoted shortly even from Clarendon himself,* uniformly asserted by Royalist writers since, and with such confident pertinacity that less partial writers have been overborne by it, that these gatherings of the people were accompanied by violence, that the Citizens were the aggressors, and that swords were drawn at last on the other side only in self-defence. The point is an important one to place beyond further question, because here, and not in any dispute as to whom the powers of the militia should reside with, really began the Civil War. Elaborately to argue upon this or that claim of right, whether to the militia or to any other power of the State, in the position to which the incidents now under discussion were about swiftly to bring the opposing parties, is to be at infinite pains to throw words into the air. Both King and Parliament were soon to ascertain that peace was no longer possible; and it was but the prelude of fence to the sharper conflict, the understood pause for collection of strength on either side, when the war of words about the militia began. In the chapter of history I have here undertaken to rewrite lies the true settlement of the doubt as to who began the Civil War; and in these Westminster tumults, which were the prologue of the tragedy, it will not be difficult to show, on the unquestion-

Party statements.

Who were the first aggressors.

True beginning of the Civil War:

---
* *Hist.* ii. 92.

able evidence now to be produced, not merely that the bloodshed was exclusively the act of the King's friends and dependants, and that the natural alarm it created was made the excuse for other and more deliberately planned violence against the people, but that all this was unavoidably a portion of that design against the Parliament for which the time had prematurely been supposed to be ripe, and which had for its first and immediate object the destruction of the leaders of the House of Commons. *[in the attempt to destroy the Parliamentary leaders.]*

§ VII. CITIZENS AND SOLDIERS IN THE HALL.

THE old year had now only five days to run, and was fast departing amid incidents that only too fitly ushered in its dark and gloomy successor. On this eve of the first year of the Great Civil War, the physical and the moral atmosphere alike seemed charged with storm. So severe a season had not been known for many winters;* and while each day, and hour *[Monday, 27th Dec. 1641.]* *[Severity of the winter.]*

---

* It extended to Paris, from which city Windebank, writing to his son in London on the $\frac{10\text{th Jan.}}{31\text{st Dec.}}$ 1641-2, speaks of the extraordinary storms that were prevalent, and of "the very "fierce frost methinks much exceeding those in England." I am tempted to add a further portion of the letter, which is every way characteristic of the weak and poor-spirited writer, to whom a leading share in the government of England had been unreservedly committed in the most difficult and dangerous crisis of her story. He is telling his son of his intense wish to return to England. "Wherein, methinks, I sh^d not "longer be impedimented now that I am out of danger to *[Fierce frost in Paris.]*

of the day, brought its grief or terror to unprejudiced watchers of events, it was in the midſt of a tempeſt that ſwept the Engliſh coaſt with almoſt unparalleled violence that the Admiral in the Downs continued to receive the letters which happily have preſerved for us, in fair and unexaggerated language, an impartial teſtimony of eye-witneſſes to events very memorable in our hiſtory.

<small>Tempeſt at ſea.</small>

"Concerning the ſtate of our affaires here," wrote Mr. Thomas Smith, already named as a friend of Sir John Pennington, and who held confidential office under the Earl of Northumberland, with whom he had rooms at York Houſe, "they are not ſoe well as I could wiſh, for wee "are in dayly fears of uproares and diford^{rs}. "The 'Prentices and our Souldiers have lately "had ſome bickerings wherein many of the "'prentices were wounded, and loſt their hats "and cloakes. This was don yeſterday at "Whitehall Gate, as the 'prentices were coming "from demanding an anſwer of their petition "lately exhibited to the Parliam^t houſe. The "ſould^{rs} continue in greate numbers in White-

<small>Mr. Thos. Smith to Pennington, 30th Dec.</small>

<small>At Whitehall Gate, 29th Dec.</small>

<small>Windebank to his ſon.</small>
" retourne any more to buſineſſe. This I deſire you to ſollicit
" & purſue wth all earneſtneſs if yo ſhall find it ſafe to ſtir in
" it, that I may ſee myne own dear country, & poor neſt
" again, and ſom ende of my wanderinges and greate ſuffer-
" ings, wch if the world did rightly conſider, I am confident
" they wold be ſenſible of my condition, & the moſt rigorous
" & hard-harted wold thinke I have been abundantly puniſhed
" already for anything that I have donne. But God's will be
" donne, and whatſoever you ſhall negotiate herein muſt be
" with entire & all humble ſubmiſſion to His Ma^{ty}."

"hall. These woundes of the 'prentices have
"soe exasperated them, that it is feared they
"will be at Whitehall this day to the number
"of ten thousand; whereupon the souldiers
"have increased their number, built up a
"Court of Guard w^{th}out the Gate, and have
"called down the millitary company to their
"assistance: and what will be the event, God
"knows. Neither do the Houses and King
"agree so well as I could wishe. The Jesuiti-
"call Faction, according to their wounted
"custome, fomenting still jealousies between
"the King and his people, and the Bishops
"continually concurring with the Popish Lords
"against the passing any good bills sent from
"the House of Commons thither." *

Exasperation of the people.

A Jesuitical Faction strong in the House.

Under Secretary Sidney Bere, also writing on the same day (the 30th of December) to his friend commanding in the narrow seas, is more specific as to the causes of the prevailing excitement: "Since the Hol-
"lidays began," he writes, "here have
"been such rude assemblies and multitudes
"of the baser sort of people, that everyday
"threatened a desperate confusion. Nor are
"we yet free of those feares. The first pre-
"tended cause of this was the making of
"Collonel Lunsford Lieut^t of the Tower.
"Which begat soe generall a murmure and

The Under Secretary to the Admiral, 30th Dec.

Confusion and fears.

---

* MS. State Paper Office. Smith to Admiral Pennington, 30 Dec. 1641. And, under same date, the letter which follows: Bere to Pennington.

"discontent that his Matie was pleased to
remove him after two or three dayes possession and to putt Sir John Biron in his
place; having made the other a knight and
as I am told given him 500lb. a year pension.* But the people, not being as it
seemes sufficiently perswaded of this remove,
on Monday [the 27th] continuing their
insolencies, and meeting this Lunsford at
Westminster, they fell to blowes, in wch disorder divers were lightly hurt, but without
further danger; and one of their chiefe
leaders there was Sr Richard Wiseman, who
was alsoe hurt. In fine these distempers
have soe increased by such little skirmishes, that now the traynebands" [of
Middlesex] "keepe watch everywhere: all the
courtiers commanded to weare swords: and
a Corps-de-Gard House built up within the
railes by Whitehall. All which fills every one
wth feares and apprehensions of greater evils."

margin: Lunsford knighted and pensioned upon his removal.

margin: Bloodshed 27th Dec.

margin: Courtiers ordered to be armed.

Such fears and apprehensions might well
exist, but from which quarter came the graver
threatenings of storm? On one side were
citizens and apprentices, at first altogether unarmed, irritating doubtless as all crowds are,

margin: Share in the tumults

---

* This fact is now for the first time known. Of its correct-
ness there can hardly be a doubt, for no man was in so good a
position for obtaining reliable information as the Under
Secretary. The same fact is moreover confirmed and repeated
in a letter, also in the State Paper Office, dated the 29th Dec.
1641, from Capt. Carterett to Admiral Pennington.

margin: The pension and knighthood to Lunsford.

§ VII. *Citizens and Soldiers in the Hall.* 71

but wreaking no mischief worse than a crumpled cloak or band, a torn gown, an impertinent word, or an inconvenient hustling and pressure. An eyewitness of the assault on the Archbishop of York, referred to always as the incident most provocative of what followed, has described it for us. " I was witness," says Mr. Bramston,* the son of the Chief Justice of the Queen's Bench, and at this time an intimate associate of Mr. Hyde, " to a lane " made in both the Palace Yards, and no man " could pass but whom the rabble gave leave " to, crying *A Good Lord!* or *A Good Man!* " *Let him pass!* I did see the Bishop of " Lincoln's gown† torne as he passed from the " stair-head into the entry that leads to the " Lords' House." And as Mr. Bramston saw we may still for ourselves see, vividly enough, those troublesome citizen-quidnuncs, those idle varlet-apprentices, and with the help of what the Under Secretary tells us, can imagine the reception they were likely to give to Lunsford, insolent with favors so heaped upon him even in that hour of his dismissal, as to afford but a new and exasperating instance of a popular concession haughtily unmade in the very act of making it. But, such being on one side the

taken by Citizens and Apprentices.

What Mr. Bramston saw, 27th Dec.

Provocation to the people.

---

* In his *Autobiography*, published by the Camden Society, p. 82.

† Williams, Bishop of Lincoln, had so recently become Archbishop of York that Bramston calls him by his more familiar title.

Arrest of the Five Members.

The soldier assailants.

case, bad and vexatious enough, what presents itself to us on the other? A set of fierce soldier adventurers, not only men of completely desperate fortune, but all of them under the ban of the majority of the House of Commons, yet offered and accepted with their riotous and reckless followers as a Court of Guard to their sovereign, entertained and feasted at the very gate of his palace, and enlisted under a condition of service which even Clarendon thought "unseasonable," seeing that it began not in any needful defence of the King, but in a needless shedding of the blood of his subjects.

Volunteer Guard to the King:

It would not be easy to select a passage more characteristic of the historian than that in which he speaks of this Whitehall Guard, and of the disastrous service in which they were employed. He cannot deny that their entertainment by Charles was an act of gross indiscretion, and he is obliged to confess that they first drew their swords upon the people. But

Clarendon's opinion of them.

the form in which he gives utterance to such all-important admissions against the party for whom he holds his brief, is the most singular manifestation conceivable of the degree to which a partizan writer may permit himself to become unconscious of the plain effect and meaning of the language he employs. He begins by saying* that all the while the King had been at Whitehall, besides his ordinary

---

* *Hist.* ii. 92, 94.

§ VII.   *Citizens and Soldiers in the Hall.*

retinue, and menial servants, he had kept in close attendance upon him a considerable number of officers of the late disbanded army, who were soliciting their remainder of pay from the two Houses which was secured to them by Act of Parliament, and were expecting some farther employment in the war with Ireland; and that these not very scrupulous gentlemen, upon observation and view of what he calls the insolence of the tumults, and the danger that they might possibly bring to the Court, offered themselves for a Guard to his Majesty's person, and were with more formality and ceremony entertained by him, than, upon a just computation of all distempers, was by many conceived seasonable. And then he goes on to say that "from these officers,— "warm with indignation at the insolences of "that vile rabble which every day passed by "the Court,—there proceeded, first, words of "great contempt, and then, those words com- "monly finding a return of equal scorn, blows "were fastened upon some of the most prag- "matical of the crew." In plain language, the provocation both of words and blows came first from the Whitehall desperadoes. Their advocate continues: "This was looked "upon by the House of Commons like a "levying of war by the King, and much "pity expressed by them that the poor people "should be so used who came to them with

Component elements of the Guard:

The King's unseasonable acceptance of their service:

Citizens insulted and assailed by them.

"petitions"—to go to the House of Commons with petitions was in reality the tumult and insolence complained of—"for some few of "them had received some cuts and slashes that "had drawn blood; and that made a great "argument for reinforcing their numbers. "And from these contestations the two terms of "Roundhead and Cavalier grew to be received "in discourse, and were afterwards continued "for the most succinct distinction of affections "throughout the quarrel: they who were "looked upon as servants to the King being "thus called Cavaliers, and the others of the "rabble contemned and despised under the "name of Roundheads."

<small>Cuts and slashes drawing blood.</small>

To put all this into plain speech is to say that, at a time when above all others it behoved the King to be wary of unduly exciting jealousies and suspicions, he accepted from a band of reckless and desperate soldiers of fortune a proffered personal devotion which was to display itself in the most active hate of a particular section of his people. Nor was it dry acceptance only, but eager encouragement, that Charles extended to them. While these men so insulted the Citizens, upon whom they fastened blows, and upon whom they drew their swords, they were the guests of the King in his own palace, entertained and fed at his expense. And whether those of the assailed were few or many, who, in the nicely-

<small>Plain meanings to Clarendon's speech.</small>

<small>Eager encouragement to attack on Citizens.</small>

chosen phrase of Hyde, "received some cuts *Abettors* "and flashes that had drawn blood," neither *of the outrage.* exaggerates nor diminishes the crime. The fact undeniably remains, as admitted by Clarendon, and (in a passage which will shortly be quoted) confirmed by Rushworth; and to it is to be added the further not less significant circumstance, that when that famous Declaration of both Houses was presented to the King at Newmarket in the early days of March, to which, as Lord Holland read it, Charles spared no epithet of anger or scorn (*that's false! that's a lye!* broke from him at its several averments), he heard in silence those portions of it which charged him with *Design in* having enlisted in an unusual manner, and put *encouraging the* into regular pay under the command of colonels, *Whitehall* this Whitehall Guard; with having feasted *desperadoes:* and caroused them at the palace in a manner altogether unaccustomed; with having endeavoured to engage the gentlemen of the Inns of Court to co-operate with them; and with having for his manifest design in all this, "a "perpetual guard" such as the laws did not *To draw* warrant.* In his own formal answer, indeed, *together a standing* published on the 9th March, he substantially *Guard.* admits the allegations made. "Why the lifting," he says, "of so many officers, and entertaining "them at Whitehall, should be misconstrued, "we much marvel, when it is notoriously

---

* *Rushworth*, III. vol. i. 529.

Admissions by the King: 9th March, 1642.

"known the tumults at Westminster were "so great, and their demeanour so scan- "dalous and seditious, that we had good cause "to suppose our own person, and those of our "wife and children, to be in apparent danger; "and therefore we had great reason to appoint "a Guard about us, and to accept the dutiful "tender of the services of any of our loving "subjects."*

Witnesses above suspicion.

Let me upon this subject add to the evidence already quoted, that of another witness equally above suspicion; whose discontent at this time with the House of Commons† would have ill disposed him to sympathy with any but its most bitter assailants; and who distinctly tells us, not merely that Lunsford and his friends, with drawn swords, charged upon the Citizens and "chased" them round the Hall, but that small parties of some fifteen or sixteen officers of the army had fallen upon crowds of unoffending civilians, and left forty or fifty of them wounded.

---

* *Rushworth*, III. vol. i. 536, 537.

Slingsby's ship at Spithead, 25th Nov.

† On the 25th Nov. 1641, Captain Slingsby had thus written (MS. State Paper Office): "On Saturday morning last I "brought the Happie Entrance to the Spitthead, where, having "a pilott aboard, but the wind still Northerly that she was not "like suddenly to gett into the harbour, I came away to "London. She is presently to be made ready again to go "for Ireland, Captain Owen in her: some of the Parliament "as I hear having made some scruples concerning my fitnesse "for that imployment, in respect of my brother's neare relation "to my Lord of Strafford: yett I find no alteration in my "Lord's [Northumberland] countenance towards me, as he "sayth it will not prejudice me for other employments."

His brother's connection with Strafford.

§ VII. *Citizens and Soldiers in the Hall.*

"I cannot fay," writes Slingfby, already
defcribed as the brother of Strafford's Secre-
tary,* "we have had a merry Chriftmas,
"but the maddeft one that ever I faw. The
"prentices and bafer fort of citizens, faylors,
"and water men, in greate numbers everie day
"at Weftminfter, armed with fwords, † hal-
"berds, clubbs, wch hath made the King keep
"a ftronge Guard about Whitehall, of the
"Trayned Bands without, and of gentlemen
"and officers of the army within. The King
"had upon Chriftmas Eve putt Coll. Lunfford
"in to be Lieutenant of the Tower, wch was
"fo much refented by the Comons and by the
"Cittie, that the Sunday after he difplaced
"him again, and putt in Sir John Biron, who
"is little better accepted than the other.
"Lunfford being on Monday laft in the Hall,
"with about a dozen other gentlemen, he was
"affronted by fome of the citizens whereof the
"hall was full; and fo they drew their fwords,
"chafing the citizens about the Hall, and fo
"made their way through them wch were in
"ye Pallace Yard and in Kinges Street, till
"they came to Whitehall. The Archbifhop
"of Yorke was beaten by the 'prentices the

A mad Chriftmas.

Excufes for the Whitehall Guard.

Unpopularity of Sir John Biron.

Citizens chafed about the Hall by armed foldiers.

---

* MS. State Paper Office. "R^t Slyngfbie to the hon^ble Sir
"John Pennington Knt. Admirall of his Maties Fleete for
"guard of the narrow feas:" 30th Dec. 1641.

† This is a mere carelefs affertion, as is proved by the
paffages immediately following it, which fhow that the Citizens
could not have been armed.

"same day, as he was going into the Parlia-
"ment. The next day they assaulted the
"Abbey to pull down the organs and the altar"
(there had been recent order for peculiar
ceremonies and observances at the altar), "but

Affray in the Abbey, Dec. 28th.
"it was defended by the Archbishop of Yorke
"his servants, with some other gentlemen that
"came to them: divers of the citizens hurtt
"but not killed: amongst them that were
"hurtt, one knight, Sir Richard Wiseman,
"who is their cheife leader. Yesterday about
"fifteen or sixteen officers of the army stand-

Unprovoked outrage by the soldiers, 29th Dec.
"ing at the court gate, took a slight occasion
"to fall upon them, and hurt about forty or
"fifty of them: they in all their skirmishes
"have avoided thrusting, because they would
"not kill them. I never saw the Court so full
"of gentlemen. Every one comes thither with

Gentlemen armed crowding the court. 500 volunteer Lawyers: 30th Dec.
"their swordes. This day 500 gentlemen of
"the Innes of Court, came to offer their ser-
"vices to the King. The officers of the army
"since these tumults have watcht and kept a
"Court of Guard in the Presence Chamber, and
"are entertained upon the King's charge. A
"company of soldiers are put into the Abbey
"for defence of it. The House of Commons
"have drawn up a charge, and sent it up against

Charge against Lord Bristol.
"my Lord of Bristol: the same that he was
"long since accused of and acquitted by the
"first Parliament of the King."

It has been seen, as described by an actual

§ VII. *Citizens and Soldiers in the Hall.*

eye-witnefs, what was the nature of the fo-called
"beating" of the Archbifhop of York referred
to in this letter; and it is hardly neceffary to
direct attention to the fact that all the real hurts
defcribed in the various accounts are exclufively
thofe inflicted on, and in no fingle inftance by,
civilians. No mention occurs anywhere of a No blood
wound, however flight, inflicted by an apprentice fhed by the Citi-
or citizen. But we get fome clue to the means zens.
ufed to irritate the mob into violence, by what
was complained of in the Houfe of Commons
on the morning after the Archbifhop's gown
was fo rudely handled in Weftminfter Hall.
Going from the Houfe to his lodging, an
Honorable Member, "as he paffed thro' the
"churchyard, found there a guard of foldiers;
"and inquiring of them by whofe command
"they were there, they anfwered by the Arch- A fighting Arch-
"bifhop of Yorke's:" whereupon, after fharp bifhop.
difcuffion, the Houfe generally declared it to
be a grave mifdemeanor that guards fhould fo
be fet about without due authority, to the terror
and affright of the people.* Certainly a torn

---

* Nalfon's *Collections* ii. 793. I add a remarkable paffage
from D'Ewes MS. Journal of little more than a fortnight's Entry
later date, which may help to fhow that the incidents now from
under notice, and the principal actors in them, had a clofe and D'Ewes's
ominous connection with the attempt fo foon to be made by Journal.
the king. "Mr. Miles Corbet made a relation touching one
"Mr. Pemberton, who was examined when the Committee
"fat in Guildhall, before Mr. Edward Wright an Alderman
"of London, and was fent by him to one of the Counters:
"that he had confeffed that he was one of them that had
"come hither with the king on Tuefday, Jan. 4, and that he
"commanded 40 men at the Abbey of Weftminfter that

gown hardly juftified preparations fo formidable, and the reader may perhaps fee in the incident a fufficing explanation for what Captain Slingfby defcribes as occurring on "the next day."

Incitements to violence.

In brief, each hour now brought its alarm, and figns and portents of approaching calamity were everywhere abroad. The clofe of Captain Slingfby's letter leaves us no room to doubt the definite and dangerous impreffion already produced upon himfelf. "The cittizens," he fays, "for the moft part fhutt up their fhoppes, and "all gentlemen provide themfelves with armes "as in time of open hoftillities. Both factions "talke very bigge, and itt is a wonder there is "noe more blood yett fpilt, feeing how earneft "both fides are. There is no doubt but if "the King doe not comply with the Commons "in all thinges they defire, a fudden civill "warr muft enfue; wch everie day we fee "approaches fooner." Dangerous in its growth fuch a belief as this could not fail to be. It narrowed the grounds of agreement left, fhut out all hope in which ultimate fafety lay, and brought nearer the dreaded calamity by making the mere thought of it more familiar. If fuch men as Slingfby reafoned that civil war was unavoidable, it was but natural that the recklefs men of his party fhould act

Shops clofed, and all men arming.

Dangerous beliefs.

" evening when Sir Richard Wifeman was hurt [to death]." —*Harl. MSS.* 16, f. 331 a, 336 a.

§ VIII. *What was passing in the House.*

as if civil war were come. It is at least certain that in such a state of feeling and apprehension, so widely spread, a terrible responsibility attended any act which should carry with it a sudden and violent increase of the prevailing excitements; nor, were its consequences ever so appalling, might its author with any justice claim exemption from the charge of having deliberately intended to produce them.

A terrible responsibility.

§ VIII. WHAT WAS PASSING IN THE HOUSE.

RESORTING, for information of what was meanwhile passing in the House, to the manuscript Journal of D'Ewes,* we find the details of Captain Slingsby's letter in all respects confirmed. On the first day of the tumults, D'Ewes makes a brief and hurried note of what was passing in the House; and the abrupt, unfinished sentence, more strikingly than any elaborate detail, depicts the prevailing agitation. The sitting was only prolonged to receive evidence that " the quarrel in Westminster " Hall began from some soldiers or gentlemen

First day of the Tumults, 27th Dec.

---

* Brit. Mus. *Harleian MSS.* 162-166. This most curious and valuable record, as I have stated in a former work, is contained in five several volumes, to which correct reference is often extremely difficult; the same period occupying more than one volume, and it being frequently necessary to examine all the volumes in searching for the completed record of one particular debate. The state of the writing, too, with its blotted and often hopelessly involved interlineations, interposes frequent obstruction. My references have, however, been made with much care; and, where not minutely exact, will always be found within one or two folios of the precise place sought.

State of D'Ewes's Journal in the Harleian MSS.

G

"who first offered violence to the citizens,"* and that Colonel Lunfford was one of those whose swords had flashed in the faces of unarmed men. Next day, however, Tuesday the 28th December, the day following that on which Lunfford had so led the assault on the crowd in Westminster Hall, D'Ewes was again at his post, and found Cromwell speaking on Lord Newport's dismissal from the constableship of the Tower.

Second day of the Tumults, 28th Dec.

The honorable member for Cambridge seldom failed to give a practical bearing and purpose to any debate he engaged in, and now he was employing the Newport affair to bring the House back to consideration of the point, not whether such idle words as the King imputed had been spoken,† but whether treasonable advice had at any time been given, and by whom, for bringing up the army to overawe the deliberations of that House. Cromwell, as we have seen Captain Slingsby inform his Admiral, distinctly pointed to my Lord of Bristol, Lord Digby's father; and, reviving an old to couple with it a new charge, arraigned him not merely as having notoriously counselled the Sovereign in former years, for worldly and prudential reasons, to become Roman Catholic,‡ but as having, in regard to

Lord Newport's dismissal debated.

Oliver Cromwell speaking:

---

* *Harleian MSS.* 162, f. 287 b.
† See ante, p. 38.
‡ When they were together in Spain, upon that mad freak of the Spanish Match which carried with it several very grave con-

the matter of bringing up the Northern force, distinctly advised his Majesty, in language confessed by himself, to " put the army in a " posture." Fit, then, said Cromwell, that this House desire the Lords to join with us in moving his Majesty that such a person as this Earl of Bristol be removed from his councils. For what room was there to doubt that a more than ordinary meaning lay beneath the words so used? The due posture of the army at that time, added Cromwell, with the homely force and vigour that characterised all his speeches, was *the posture of lying still*, and that posture the said army was already in.* Denzil Hollis followed up this attack on Lord Bristol by some telling blows against his son, Lord Digby, who had declared only the previous day, in a speech which Hollis justly characterised as the most dangerous and pernicious that could be spoken by a subject, that this was not a free Parliament.†

Denounces the Earl of Bristol.

Denzil Hollis attacks Lord Digby.

And here let me interpose, that though the accused members always maintained that the King acted on other than a single person's advice in his great outrage against them, it is hardly necessary also to say that they needed nothing to assure them of Lord Digby's thorough complicity. It may be well to premise,

Lord Digby's complicity with attempts of 3rd and 4th Jan.

sequences. Perhaps the best account of it can be gathered from Howell's *Letters*.
* *Harleian MSS*. 162, f. 288 a.
† *Ib.* f. 291 a, b.

however, that in whatever is further to be said having a tendency to involve others, no acquittal of Lord Digby is intended. His share was open and avowed, at any rate after the event; and when on the 19th February 1641-2, the House (overruling a recommendation from the committee to whom the matter had been referred, and of which Sir John Evelyn was chairman, for a bill of attainder) resolved to impeach him, one of the resolutions on which they proceeded was " That hee was an " adviser of the articles ag* the five members, " and of the King's coming to the House of " Commons."* Other notices and indications of the suspicion in which both Digby and his father were justly held will hereafter appear also in many private letters.

marginalia: No acquittal of Lord Digby intended.

marginalia: Resolution on his impeachment.

A considerable pause ensued in the House after Cromwell had spoken, and in the course of his entry in this day's Journal, D'Ewes has thrice to remark that there followed " a long silence." The shadow of events of which no man could forecast the course or see the end, had by this time fallen upon the most voluble debaters; and only the few resolute men who held together and led the majority, proof alike against the temptations of the Court and the impatience of the People, kept their courage and resolves unshaken.

marginalia: Long silences in the House:

marginalia: Tuesday 28th.

The next day passed more quietly. For

---

* Verney's *Notes*, 157.

though a grofs outrage was fuddenly committed by a party of foldiers upon a number of citizens paffing Whitehall after having carried up a petition to the Houfe of Commons,* means had been taken by the popular leaders to prevent the recurrence of the crowds of the two previous days; and the only threatening appearances in the ftreets were from flowly increafing groups of diffolute armed men, filently gathering to the new Guard at Whitehall. Still the greateft fears and doubts prevailed, and while Cromwell was addreffing the Houfe upon the neceffity of having the army, efpecially in Ireland, officered by men in whom the people's reprefentatives had confidence, a man named Rowley was brought to the bar to give evidence of certain matters by which a worthy member had been not a little alarmed. "De-"pofed by Rowley," fays D'Ewes, "that he "heard a French papift fay to another in "Cheapfide on Monday laft that he under-"ftood there were hurly-burleys at Weft-"minfter, and that if there fhould fall out any "hurly-burleys here, there fhould soon come "fifteen thoufand French out of France upon "our backs."† The Houfe took no action upon

<small>Wednefday the 29th Dec.

Cromwell as to officering of the army.

Threats of French interference to put down Englifh liberties</small>

---

* *Ante*, 68 and 78.
† D'Ewes MS. Journal: Wednefday, 29 December, 1641. The Member for Cambridge complained loudly on this occafion that no place had yet been found among the Irifh Military appointments for Captain Owen O'Connel.

this, any more than upon a report subsequently brought in by Sir Arthur Haselrig to the effect that a French priest had said he hoped ere long to see half-a-dozen parliament men hanged. It is nevertheless not undeserving of remark, that it was mainly from French persons that every ascertained or distinct warning was obtained, before the event, of the outrage about to be committed. Madame de Motteville, and the people about the Queen, undoubtedly knew it; the French ambassador, Montreuil, took credit to himself afterwards for having secretly sent notice to the leaders of the House; it was from a French officer, on the day of the attempt, that the intelligence was obtained which certainly prevented bloodshed; it was, as we shall find stated by D'Ewes, from a "noble person who wishes well to this "nation"* (in other words most probably Montreuil, whose credit, hitherto impugned, the remark may re-establish), that the French officer in question, Captain Langres, was enabled to do that service; and, the same authority will tell us, it was by a member of the King's new guard, a Frenchman named Fleury, that Captain Langres was informed, three weeks before the more special warning on which he acted, that great troubles were hatching.

Insolence of a French priest.

Court secrets known to the French.

French information.

From one of our own countrymen, indeed,

* *Harleian MSS.* 162 f. 310 b.

§ VIII.   *What was passing in the House.*   87

an Englishman still famous for his imagination
and wit, a warning reached Lord Kimbolton
the day before the arrest : when Marston the
dramatist, then laid by the heels in the Gate-
House, had written to him of a danger to
himself and the Parliament which it concerned
him at once to know ; which admitted of no
delay, inasmuch as no one could tell how soon
it might be too late ; and which, not more for
his own than the Parliament's sake, he was on
no account to slight, as thinking it of mean
consequence.* But, of all the debtors' prisons,

*Warning
from a pri-
soner in
the Gate-
House.*

---

* I subjoin this letter, found by Mr. Cunningham among
other papers of the time at Kimbolton Castle, and first printed
by Mr. Collier in his edition of Shakespeare (1858, i. 179).
It is undated, but that "this present Monday" was Monday
the 3rd January 1641-2, is rendered in my judgment absolutely certain by the circumstances. Whether, indeed, the
writer was the poet Marston I was disposed to doubt until I
was favored with a communication from Mr. Beedham of
Kimbolton, to whom my best thanks are due. "To the
" Right Honorable the Lord Kimbolton these. My Lord,—
" Though my owne miseries press me hard to sollicite your
" Honours Compassion, yet that you may be assured how much
" I am vnseduc't from my former temper, I shall now dis-
" serue my selfe (though my condicōn be very calamitous)
" to serue your Honour, and yᵉ Parliamᵗ, in a matter of no
" meane concernmᵗ : The errand I send this paper on to your
" Lordˡᵖ is to offer to your Honour a discovery of no meane
" consequence, wᶜʰ I beseech your Honor not to slight before
" you know it ; for when you do, I am sure you will not ;
" to wᶜʰ purpose I humbly beg that your Honor will send
" som such trusty and rationall messinger to me, whose
" relacōn to your Honour may be heere vnknowne, and yᵗ
" the same messinger may bring me som assurance yᵗ I shall
" be concealed in yᵉ business ; My Lord, I hope you will not
" delay, for I cannot tell how soone, it may be to late : For
" yᵉ future I beseech your Honor to esteeme me a most fayth-
" full seruant to your Honor and yᵉ Parliamᵗ, from wᶜʰ nothing
" shall euer dissoblige Your most humble seruant, JOHN
" MARSTON.—From the Gate-Howse this present Monday."

*John
Marston to
Lord Kimbol-
ton :
Has a dis-
covery to
make, im-
portant to
his Lord-
ship and
to Parlia-
ment.*

the Gate-House was that to which all men under remand or examination from the Council-table, and eminently all Jesuit priests and recusants, were incessantly committed; and that Marston had derived his information from some one connected with the French fathers and confessors about the Queen, I entertain no doubt whatever. Other circumstances render it as little doubtful that the contemplated impeachment had been secretly talked about for some days, and that hints and cautions had been permitted to escape. It will shortly be seen what good grounds D'Ewes gives us for believing, that Pym himself knew at least enough of the intention to hazard the impeachment to put him warily on his guard as against a particular impending danger, at least four days before the attempt of which it has been the custom of all historians to write as having entered into the mind of the King only the moment before its execution.*

Prison for Jesuits and recusants.

The danger known to Pym.

§ IX. THE BISHOPS SENT TO THE TOWER.

Thursday 30th Dec.

THURSDAY, the 30th December, was now

---

* See also my *Hist. and Biog. Essays*, i. 135, *note*, for singular intimations, in the reasons presented to the Lords for the claim of the Houses to be guarded by the trainbands they had selected, that Pym knew the possible danger they had most cause to dread. He there speaks of the "surprizing of the persons of divers members of the Scottish parliam^t;" says that whisperings had gone abroad of "the like being intended ag^t divers persons of both Houses here;" and broadly states in his conclusion that there was "just cause to apprehend some wicked and mischievous practice still in hand to interrupt the peaceable proceedings of this parliament."

Attack on Parliament expected, 30th Nov. 1641.

come, and hardly had the Lower House assembled, when an urgent message from the Lords, touching matters of dangerous consequence, called them to conference. The Bishops in a body had sent to the Lords, through the King, that ill-advised Protestation which was the fruitful source of so much subsequent mischief, stating that such had been the tumults in Westminster for the last three days, and so obstructed and menaced had they been in the attempt to take their seats,* that they did not

Message from the Lords.

Protestation of the Bishops.

---

* I have already quoted the account of the assault on the Archbishop given by the son of the Chief Justice of the Queen's Bench, a great friend of Mr. Hyde's, who saw Williams's gown torn, and was witness to all that led to what Clarendon describes as the irrepressible rage, and the ill-advised protestation, of the too fiery Archbishop. Hyde himself also relates the incident (*Hist.* ii. 113), declaring in his exaggerated way that Williams's "robes" were "torn "from his back;" with the addition, which his friend Bramston carefully avoids making, and for which there is no proof, that the Bishop's " person was assaulted." I must add the account of the same disturbances from another eye-witness, Williams's quaint and admiring biographer, Hacket (*Scrinia Reserata*, ed. 1693, part ii. 177-179), who attended Williams at the time, and who, notwithstanding all his fanciful superfluity of phrase, rather confirms Bramston than Hyde: "There had been an unruly " and obstreperous concourse of the people in the Earl of " Strafford's case; but a sedition broke forth about Xmas " that was ten times more mad .... The King came to " the House of Commons, to demand five of their members " to justice, upon impeachment of treason. His Majesty, it " seems, was too forward to threaten such persons with the " sword of justice, when he wanted the buckler of safety ... " I am sure the King suffered extremely for their sakes: all " sectaries and desperate varlets in city and suburbs flocked by " thousands to the Parliament .... Let the five members " be as honest as they would make them, I am certain " these were traitors that begirt the King's House where his " person was, with hostility by land and water ... every " day making battery on all the Bishops as they came to " Parliament, forcing their coaches back, tearing their gar-

What the mob did to Archbishop Williams.

Evidence of Bramston, Hyde, and Hacket.

They mean again to sit or vote until effectually
retire from
the House: secured by his Majesty from the repetition

> "ments, menacing if they came any more." (Given with all
> the intercalated quotations and illustrations of the original,
> the foregoing passage would have filled several pages). It is
> now many years since I called attention to Hacket's work, in
> the hope that it might find some learned society not indisposed
> to give a modern and accessible form to so genuine a Curiosity
> of Literature. It may be doubted if the language contains
> such another product of a busy, garrulous, fertile, fanciful,
> not very useful, but prodigiously stored memory and brain.
> Every folio page of it (and it contains nearly 600 of the
> closest print) bristles with Greek and Latin quotations, applied
> with a rich and ready resource that is fairly astonishing. It is
> nothing to say that Seneca could not be too heavy nor Plautus
> too light for him, for he has all the classics from Homer down-
> wards at his fingers' ends; and it is really little short of appalling
> to observe to what a small practical use it is possible to turn
> such a vast amount of the kind of learning still prized in our
> schools and colleges as beyond every other in importance.
> Witty conceits and well-chosen poetry; admiring excerpts
> out of Chaucer, Spenser, and Ben Jonson; metaphors and
> figures out of all departments of knowledge; apophthegms of
> the study and the field; quips of the nursery; and the blackest-
> lettered lore of the Fathers of the Church; are heaped up in
> extravagant profusion. Too learned Hacket! When he wrote
> this book (he finished it in 1657, though it was not published
> till 1693), it behoved him to keep wary watch over his public
> sayings in his Rectory of Cheam; and his *Scrinia Reserata*
> was the only escape he had for all that accumulated mass of
> useless knowledge. Cromwell was then our English Sovereign,
> the "jetting" up and down, as Hacket phrases it, in all his glory,
> and nobody had courage enough to "strike him to the heart
> "and expire upon the murderer." Nay, there was one man
> who had what he terms the incredible effrontery to defend
> and champion the murderer, and, "petty school-boy scribbler"
> as he was, to engage in controversy with—"O what a miracle
> "of judgment and learning!—Salmasius!" Yes, even with
> the "matchless Salmasius, with the prince of the learned men
> "of his age," did "so base an adversary—O horrid!"—dare
> to measure himself, as that "blackmouth'd Zoilus" Milton!
> "Get thee behind me, Milton," exclaims Hacket, foaming
> over at the very mention of the name. He is "that serpent
> "Milton:" he is "a Shimei," "a dead dog," "a canker-
> "worm;" his spirit is "venomous" and his breath that of a
> "viper." This, to be sure, was while Europe rang from side
> to side with the *Letter to Salmasius*, and ten years before

Hacket's
Scrinia
Reserata
described.

Useless
know-
ledge.

Written
during the
Protecto-
rate.

Attack on
Milton:

§ IX. *The Bishops sent to the Tower.*

of such affronts, indignities, and dangers: and Protest against
wherefore did they then and therein protest proceed-
against all laws, orders, votes, resolutions, and ings in
determinations, as in themselves null and of absence.
no effect, "which in their absence, since the
"27th of this instant month of December 1641,
"have already passed; as likewise against all
"such as shall hereafter pass during the time
"of their forced and violent absence." The
design of this daring act, and the object of
Archbishop Williams, its real author, have
been remarked upon by the present writer in a

---

the publication of *Paradise Lost*, which Hacket (who died
Bishop of Lichfield and Coventry) survived three years; but
it seems probable, by the allusion to petty schoolboy scribbling, A school-
that he at least knew of the *Minor* and *Juvenile Poems*, boy
though I think it more than probable, if he had read them, scribbler!
that even the controversy with Salmasius would hardly have
thrown him into such transports of unmitigated abuse. For
Hacket really appears to have had some judgment in poetry.
He knew nothing about Shakespeare, but neither did anybody Shake-
else, though the four greatest works of human genius, Hamlet, speare
Lear, Macbeth, and Othello, had all been written within not
the century, and Hacket had himself arrived at man's estate known.
before the Tempest was played, and the wand of the magi-
cian broken. Still, he carefully avoids the admiration, then so
common, of the second rate fantastical school; and he declares
Ben Jonson, whom he calls "our laureat poet," and "our Praise of
"master poet," to be "the best of our poets of this century." Jonson,
Chaucer with him is "noble Chaucer;" and little short of Chaucer,
the rapturous are his allusions to "our divine poet Mr. and Spen-
"Spenser," to "our arch poet Spenser," to "our most ser.
"laureat poet Spenser," to "Mr. Spenser's divine wit," and
to "Mr. Spenser's moral poem," on which he largely draws
for illustrations and comparisons. One rather grieves to think
that even if Mr. B. Simmons should happen to have sent
to the good old Bishop in 1667 the new epic poem he had
published, he is less likely to have read beyond the author's
name on the title page than to have thereupon instantly thrust
it aside with another "Get thee behind me, Milton!"

former work.* Its immediate effect was thoroughly to excite both Houses into at once disabling its abettors from such power of further mischief as, if the Protest had been admitted, or even passed in mere silence and contempt, they might thereafter have exerted fatally. Carry such a protest but into its next stage, and what was known to be the most cherished hope of the King, that he might be able one day to revoke, on the ground that Parliament had not been free, all the popular concessions of the past momentous year, was open to him at any time as not distant or impossible.

Effect of Protest.

An opportunity desired by the King.

Whatever the view taken of the nature or extent of the tumults, no contemporary witness has ventured to state that they were such as to provoke an act like this. The gatherings in the Hall, and at the entrance to the House of Lords, were limited to the Monday and Tuesday, the 27th and 28th; and while the tumults of those days were at their height, we have evidence of what was suffered by the chief complainant himself, the author of the Protestation, from the only person who says expressly that what he sets down he saw. Archbishop Williams had his gown torn as he passed into the House. But beyond that insult, witnessed by Mr. Bramston, there is no

"Mobs" for two days only.

The amount of provocation given.

---

* *Hist. and Biog. Essays,* i. 262, 268: "The Civil Wars and Cromwell."

§ IX.   *The Bishops sent to the Tower.*

evidence of any kind on record of a special hurt or injury received by any of them. The utmost that is alleged by the only member of the Episcopal party who has himself described the occurrences, is that the rabble came by thousands to the House, filled the outer rooms, and abused them as they passed in, crying, *No Bishops! no Bishops!* * On the other hand there seems to me sufficient testimony that pains had been taken, by members of their own House, to put the Bishops generally into that sort of needless fright which might induce them readily to fall in with such a Protestation. One of the most famous among them, the pious and learned Hall, Bishop of Norwich and author of the *Satires*, has informed us † that as they were all sitting together in the afternoon of the 28th, it grew to be torchlight, and Lord Hertford, who had lately received his marquisate and other special favors from the King, went up to the form on which they sat, told them they were in great danger, and advised them to take some course for their own safety. "What is it?" they cried. "What should we do?" Whereupon the Marquis (with difficulty holding his countenance, it may be imagined, while he did so) counselled them to continue in the Parliament House *all that night*. "Because

What the Bishop of Norwich saw and heard.

Fright given in the House itself.

Some Lords advising:

---

* Hall's *Works*, i. xliv.
† In his Hard Measure: *Works*, i. xlv. ed. Oxford, 1837.

Lord Hertford alarms the Bishops:

"(faith he) these people vow they will watch you at your going out, and will search every coach for you with torches, so as you cannot escape." At this some of them rose, and earnestly desired of their Lordships that for the present ("for all the danger," interposes the Bishop, "was at the rising of the House") some care might be taken for their safety. Then proceeds Bishop Hall very innocently: "*The motion was received by some Lords with a smile:* and some other Lords, as the Earl of Manchester, undertook the protection of the Archbishop of York and his company (whose shelter I went under) to their lodgings." At the same time the good Bishop frankly adds that those who cared to stay long enough, got safely home without help of any kind.

Other Lords smiling.

What passed at Williams's lodgings.

In Williams's lodgings, doubtless, the Protestation was that night mooted; and thither next day, at the invitation of Williams,* repaired no less than ten other right reverend Lords. "Where," says Clarendon, "immediately having pen and ink ready," the paper was drawn up, signed by all present, and addressed to the King for presentation to the Lords; and away with it went Williams next morning to Whitehall. There, by an accident which Clarendon calls "unfortunate," not only the King, but his Lord Keeper, at the very

"Unfortunate" accident.

* Clarendon, *Hist.* ii. 113; Bishop Hall, *Works*, i. xlvi.

moment "happened" to be; and Charles no sooner received the Proteſt, than, "caſting his "eye perfunctorily upon it," he gave it to Littleton, and, one hour later, the aſſembled Lords were with much amazement liſtening to it.* In this there may have been nothing but an "accident," as Clarendon alleges; although, from the firſt note of alarm given by Lord Hertford, it looks, all of it, extremely like a ſettled and planned deſign.

But the hands that aimed were leſs ſtrong than thoſe that received the blow, and the recoil was inſtant and fatal. In "half-an-"hour" † from the time when the Commons were informed of the outrage propoſed to be committed on the liberties of Parliament, the impeachment was ſent up againſt its authors. Biſhop Hall ſays that though they had ſigned the Proteſt, they intended ſtill to have had ſome further conſultation about it; when, before they had time even to ſuppoſe that it could have paſſed out of Williams's hands, they were all kneeling as accuſed traitors at the Bar of the Lords. Cromwell had been active in this prompt retribution; and long years afterwards, when addreſſing the laſt Parliament of his Protectorate, he exulted in the part he

marginalia: Charles and his Lord-Keeper at White-hall.

Accident or deſign?

A ſurpriſe for the Biſhops.

What Cromwell thought of the Proteſtation.

---

* *Hiſt.* ii. 114. Hall's account ſlightly differs in ſtating that though they all heard the Proteſt read at Williams's lodgings, it was afterwards ſent for their ſignatures to their own ſeveral places of abode.—*Works*, i. xlvi.

† *Hiſt.* ii. 118.

had so taken against men who would needs have it that no laws made in *their* absence should be good, and so, without injury to others, cut themselves off! Men, pursued Cromwell, in his rough grand way, that were truly of an Episcopal spirit; men indeed that knew not God; that knew not how to account upon the works of God, how to measure them out; but would trouble nations for an interest that was but mixed at the best, iron and clay like the feet of Nebuchadnezzar's image!*

Nor in this did Protector Oliver go beyond what undoubtedly had been the feeling at the time. So generally adverse did opinion run against the ill-advised act, that even Clarendon cannot find it in his heart to spare any expression of contempt for the silliness and folly of so many Bishops, during a storm which had carried

<small>The Bishops characterized by Cromwell.</small>

<small>General feeling at the time.</small>

<small>Case against the Bishops.</small>

<small>Themselves to thank for their unpopularity.</small>

<small>Their violence and passion, 17th June 1641.</small>

<small>A true prediction.</small>

* This is not the place for any detailed statement of the case against the Bishops, which was a very strong one; or of the causes, which were many and great, that had led to their extraordinary unpopularity at this time. Suffice it to say that they had themselves mainly to thank for it, and that the tumults of which they now complained were but what their own friends, arguing from the violence and passion displayed by them, had expected and predicted in the preceding summer. On the 17th June 1641, Sidney Bere had thus written to Pennington (MS. St. P. O.): "Fears & suspitions amongst "us are soe great that I feare nothing lesse than that we shall "yett fall into a confusion, wch God forbid. The businels of "the Bishopps wilbe of dangerous consequence, they being "violent and passionate in their owne defence, & having in- "gaged (as it were) the Lords by their late votes in their "favo^r, to the maintenance of their cause, whereas the Com- "mons seeme as resolute to passe the bill for their utter extir- "pation, and soe transmitt it to the Lords according to y^e "custome, & then it may justly be feared the Citty will "prove as turbulent as they were on Strafford's cause."

§ IX.   *The Bishops sent to the Tower.*   97

away card and compass, and sent the best pilot to his prayers, severing from the good ship and trusting themselves to such a cockboat as Williams! But, quite as strongly as his dislike of the mischievous Protestation, the danger and scandal of which he cannot pretend to conceal, his objection to the punishment that so promptly followed it is put prominently forward; and he affects to think that posterity will hold it for incredible that Parliament should so have outraged public decency, as to affix to such an offence as a simple protest a penalty so outrageously disproportioned as that of treason. But as usual this is a gross misrepresentation of the facts, as well as of the sentiments of the time, even as they are yet discoverable among those least friendly to the two Houses; and the entire untrustworthiness of the author of such statements is never fully manifest, until we are able to place them side by side with contemporary notices of the same occurrences, set down with no other object than upon the instant to reflect and convey, without concealment of the passions or bias of each writer, the living opinions and emotions of the hour. *Clarendon's opinion as to Impeachment. Contemporary accounts.*

Captain Slingsby does not affect to be any great politician, but even as he hastily wrote to Pennington, in the afternoon of the very day of this memorable incident, he makes its gravity and danger very conspicuous through his few confused sentences describing it. "This *Slingsby to Pennington, 30th Dec.*

"day," he writes, "the Bishopps have made a
"Protestation against the proceedings of this
"Parliament, declaring it no free parliament.

His opinion of the Protestation:

"This makes a great stirre here. The favourers
"of them thinke it don to soone. The other
"side do seeme now to rejoyce that it is don,
"having thereby excluded themselves from
"it."* He means that the act was at once
seen to exclude its authors from ever
resuming their seats in Parliament, which, indeed, was all the Commons had in view in
bringing against them a charge of treason; and

Even Bishops' friends adverse to it.

that even those friends of the King who were
favourable to so bold an assault on the very
existence of the Parliament, felt that it had
been done prematurely. In the same spirit, on

Under Secretary Bere to Pennington, 30th Dec.

the same day, writes Under Secretary Bere:
"This day there hath been great debatinge
"in ye houses, and is still, but I cannot stay
"soe long to heare the issue, leaste I loose the
"comodity of this ordinary. Only thus much
"is even now brought for newes—that the
"Bishopps having protested against all the
"Acts made this Parliament against them,

Committal of the Bishops.

"twelve of them are now committed, and
"two others sent for whereof York is one.
"But the particulars hereof I will not asseure,
"being but even now brought unto me; but
"something there is wch by my next you shall

* MS. State Paper Office. Slingsby to Pennington, 30th Dec.

"have more particularly: onlie thus much to lett you see into what a deplorable condition we are falling. I pray God blesse his Matie in his royall person and councills, that wee may once see a peaceable and quiett time againe. I wish you, S^r, a happy new yeare, and I pray God the great tempests have left you in health and saftie."* To which may be added the still stronger testimony of a third correspondent, equally anxious to keep the Admiral, amid those tempests at sea, quickly and surely informed of the worse storm raging on the land. "The last plott of the Bishopps," writes Mr. Thomas Smith to "his very lovinge friend," on the afternoon of the day when the Protest was made, "hath beene their indeavour to make this Parliam^t no parliament, and so to overthrowe all actes past, and to cause a dissolution of it for the present: wch hath been so strongly followed by ye Popish party, that it was faine to be putt to the vote, and the protesting lords carryed itt to bee a free and perfect Parliam^t as ever any was before. This did soe gawle the Bishopps that they made their Protestačon ag^t the

Our deplorable condition.

Prays that the great tempests have left the Admiral safe.

Mr. Thomas Smith to Pennington, 30th Dec.

Endeavour of Popish Bishops to undo what the Long Parliament had done, and compel a dissolution.

* MS. State Paper Office. Sidney Bere to Admiral Pennington, 30th Dec. 1641. An illustration occurs in the same letter of the violence of the storms then raging on the coast. "The Post of Sandwich tells me that ye last weeke "when he came awaye, your boats could not come ashoare." "We heare," writes Slingsby, in a letter of an earlier date, "of the disaster lately hapened to the Roebucke; and have "been very sensible of the extreame tempestuous weather you "have had so long together."

Great storms raging on the coast.

"freedom of y" vote and y" Parliam', and in their Protestaćon have inserted such speeches as have brought y'" w"'in y" compasse of treason, and thus the Counsell of Acittaphill is turn'd into foolishnesse. The Earl of Bristoll and his sonne have been cheife concurrents with them, in this and other evill councells, for which they have been impeacht and branded in y" House of Comons."*

Williams compared to Achitophel.

Complicity of Lords Bristol and Digby.

The writer of that letter, as already stated, was high in the employment and confidence of Lord Northumberland, and his account, hasty and confused as it is, expresses more accurately than any other not only the real drift of the Protest to effect for the King an "overthrow of all acts past," and render unavoidable a dissolution, but the prompt proceeding by which, under the lead of the Earl, a majority in the House of Lords at once met and baffled the intrigue of Archbishop Williams. For once, indeed, as soon as the first division had been taken, the Lords acted quite as eagerly as the Commons, and quite as eagerly and promptly as the King in sending up the Protestation. Within half an hour after it was presented, it was voted a breach of the fun-

Real drift of the Protest.

Prompt action of the Lords.

---

* MS. State Paper Office. Mr. Thomas Smith, from York House (the Admiralty), to "His very loving Friend Sir John "Pennington, knt. Admiral of His Maties Fleete at Sea on "Board His Maties Ship the Lyon at the Downes." 30 Dec. 1641.

§ IX. *The Bishops sent to the Tower.*

damental privileges and being of Parliaments; upon the instant, after conference between the Houses,* Glyn was sent up from the Commons to impeach the Bishops for an endeavour to subvert the very existence of Parliaments, and therein the fundamental laws of the realm; and by eight o'clock that winter night, ten out of the twelve were committed to the Tower,† and the other two, by reason of their great age (" and indeed of the worthy " parts of one of them, the learned Bishop of

A conference.

30th Dec. 8 o'clock p m. ten Bishops sent to the Tower.

---

* See *Commons Journals*, ii. 362, 363.

† " In all the extremity of frost," says Bishop Hall (*Works*, i. xlv.), "at eight o'clock in the dark evening, we were voted to "the Tower." And listen to the good indignant Hacket. (*Scrinia Reserata*, ii. 179): " Hear and admire, ye Ages to come, what " became of this Protestation, drawn up by as many Bishops as " have often made a whole provincial council. They were all " called by the temporal Lords to the bar, and from the bar " sent away to the Tower. Nonne fuit satius tristes formidinis " iras, Atque superba pati fastidia? A rude world when it " was safer to do a wrong than to complain of it. The people " commit the trespass, and the sufferers are punish'd for their " fault. Ἀν μάγειρος ἁμαρτάνοι, αὐλήτης παρ' ἡμῖν τύπτεται. " *Athen.* lib. 9. A proverb agreeing to the drunken feasts of " the Greeks: If the cook dress the meat ill, the minstrils " are beaten. That day it broke forth, that the largest part " of the Lords were fermentated with an anti-episcopal " sourness. If they had loved that order, they would never " have doomed them to a prison, and late at night, in bitter " frost and snow, upon no other charge, but that they " presented their mind in a most humble paper to go abroad " in safety. Ubi amor condimentum inerit quidvis placiturum " spero, Plaut. *in Casin.* Love hath a most gentle hand, " when it comes to touch where it loves. Here was no sign " of any filial respect to their spiritual fathers. Nothing was " offer'd to the peers, but the substance was reason, the style " lowly, the practice ancient; yet upon their pleasure, without " debate of the cause, the Bishops are pack'd away the same " night to keep their Christmas in durance and sorrow: And " when this was blown abroad, O how the Trunck-men of " the Uproar did fleer, and make merry with it !"

Hacket's Lament for the Bishops.

No love of Bishops among the Lords.

"Durham,") to the cuſtody of the Black Rod.*

And ſo that bitter night of froſt and ſnow, the 30th December 1641, ſaw the two Archbiſhops, York and Canterbury, whoſe unſeemly perſonal conflicts had been the ſcandal of the town for years, lodged at laſt together within the ſame priſon walls. Heretofore it had ſeemed impoſſible but that the downfal of the one muſt involve the well-doing of the other. During Laud's long aſcendancy, and under his inceſſant perſecution, Williams had been an inmate ſucceſſively of the Gatehouſe, the Fleet, and the Tower; nor could the doors of the grim ſtate fortreſs be ſaid to have fairly opened for him until they had cloſed upon Laud himſelf. But now, after brief exulting triumph over his ancient adverſary, thoſe gates are open for him again; and into them re-enter the Biſhop of Lincoln, elevated meanwhile into Archbiſhop of York, leading with him nine other Right Reverend priſoners. Who could wonder that the wits made merry at it? They deviſed a picture, ſays Dr. Peter Heylin, in which my Lord of York was reſembled to the Decoy Duck (alluding to the

margin notes: Laud and Williams within the ſame walls at laſt. The door ſhut on perſecuted and perſecutor. Caricature of Williams as a Decoy Duck:

---

* And ſee *Harleian* MSS. 163, ff. 410 a—414 b. At a ſubſequent part of the proceedings in the Impeachment, according to D'Ewes, "Mr. H. Bellaſis moved that the Biſhops of "Lichfield and Durham were at the door. Debate if they "ſhould come within the bar, and ſit on chairs or ſtools by "reaſon of their great age: but reſolved that they come in "ſingly and ſpeak at the bar."

§ IX. *The Bishops sent to the Tower.*

Decoys in Lincolnshire where he had been
bishop), restored to liberty on design that he
might bring more company with him at his
coming back : the device representing the conceit, and that not unhappily. "Certain I am,"
adds the ingenious biographer of the rival
prelate, "that *our* Archbishop, in the midst
"of those sorrows, seemed much pleased with
"the fancy, whether out of his great love to
"wit, or some other self-satisfaction which he
"found therein, is beyond my knowledge."*
Poor old Laud! One need not grudge him
that ray of mirth which was probably the last
that glimmered feebly upon him between
Strafford's scaffold and his own.

It may well be supposed that D'Ewes, ardent
puritan as he was, underwent no great anguish

A witty conceit:

Laud's enjoyment thereof:

Perhaps his last gleam of mirth.

---

* Nor is this the only caricature of Williams which Heylin
with infinite unction describes. Relating (*Life of Laud*, p.
461) the committal of the Bishops to the Tower, he proceeds: "*Our* Archbishop had now more neighbours than he
"desired, but not more company than before, it being
"prudently ordered amongst themselves, that none of them
"should bestow any visits on him, for fear of giving some
"advantage to their common enemy; as if they had been
"hatching some conspiracy against the publick. But they
"refrained not on either side from sending messages of love
"and consolation unto one another; those mutual civilities
"being almost every day performed betwixt the two Archbishops also, though very much differing both in their
"counsels and affections in the times foregoing. The Archbishop of York was now so much declined in favour, that
"he stood in as bad termes with the common people as the
"other did; and his picture was cut in brass, attired in his
"episcopal robes, with his square cap upon his head, and
"bandileers about his neck, shouldering a musket upon one of
"his shoulders in one hand, and a rest in the other."

The two Archbishops exchange civilities in the Tower.

Caricature of Williams as Church Militant.

of mind at the ſtroke which had fallen on the Biſhops. Looking in at the Upper Houſe ſhortly after to hear a ſentence pronounced, he ſaw without any kind of emotion that the epiſcopal bench had been turned into lumber. "There was but a thin Houſe of Lords, and "on the right ſide thereof a great emptineſs ; "the two forms on which the Biſhops uſed to "ſit being thruſt up cloſe againſt the wall."*
On a ſubſequent occaſion, however, he gives a reaſon which ſounds rather oddly to us now for regarding with equanimity the continued incarceration of the prelates. "The "Speaker," he ſays (in his Journal of the 21ſt March, 1641-2), "delivered in a petition "from the 12 Biſhops. I ſaid I was glad "to ſee they had omitted their ſtyle of Lord "Biſhop; for I heard from ſome that ſaw "ſome of them in the Tower but laſt Saturday "calling to one another by the title of Lord-"ſhip, whereas by the fundamental laws and "ancient conſtitution of the kingdom, their "ſtyle is, 'Your Paternity' or 'Fatherhood.' "As for enlarging them, I will ſay nothing, "becauſe I think they follow their function "of preaching better than they did before "they came in, and are likewiſe lodged in a "good air: but for Durham and Lichfield, "I deſire they may be enlarged for their "humble ſubmiſſion. They are lodged in a

margin: D'Ewes ſees the Biſhops' Bench turned into lumber.

margin: Is glad they no longer call themſelves "Lordſhips:"

margin: and would keep them where they are.

* *Journal; Harl. MSS. 163, f. 459 a.*

§ x. *Shadows of the Coming Event.*

"clofe air, namely, in the houfe of Mr. "Clofe
"Maxwell, ufher of the black rod, near air" at Charing
"Charing Crofs."* D'Ewes can hardly have Crofs.
meant that the air was clofe at Charing Crofs,
but rather, we may prefume, that Mr. Maxwell's houfe afforded, for the clofe keeping of a prifoner of ftate, lefs roomy and airy as well as much more coftly accommodation, than might be found in the buildings of the Tower.†

§ X. SHADOWS OF THE COMING EVENT.

OTHER incidents, more exciting even than the impeachment of the whole epifcopal bench, Houfe of Commons, were meanwhile helping to make more memor- Dec. 30th, able this laft day but one of a moft eventful 1641. year, and D'Ewes enables us for the firft time to retrace them. "The Conference," he fays, "being ended, we returned to the Houfe, moft Members "men expreffing a great deal of alacrity of delighted by the "fpirit for this indifcreet and unadvifed act of folly of

---

* *Harleian MSS.* 163, f. 433 a.

† Bifhop Hall confirms this view, telling us how much fubfequent reafon he had to congratulate himfelf that the courtefy of the Black Rod, which at firft he had much defired, had not been extended to himfelf. "Only two of our number Difadvan-
"had the favour of the Black Rod, by reafon of their age; tages of
"which, though defired by a noble Lord on my behalf" (Hall the Black
was in his 68th year) "would not be yielded. Wherein Rod.
"I acknowledge and blefs the gracious providence of my
"God: for had I been gratified, I had been undone both in
"body and purfe; the rooms being ftrait, and the expenfes
"beyond the reach of my eftate." *Works,* i. xlvi.

"the Bishops."* It was such alacrity of spirit as lighted up the gloomy features of St. John when he felt that all must be worse before it could be better. But it was quickly dispelled in the present case by the unusual gravity and seriousness with which Pym, after report made of the Conference, moved unexpectedly that the door of the House might be shut, and that none might go out. Others, carrying further the fears of their grave leader, would have had it ordered also that the outward room might be cleared, and that none might go into the Committee Chamber. But at this Sir Simonds arose. "Thinking it," he says, "too great a restraint, upon any reason "whatever, I moved that I did very well allow "that the door should be shut, but to restrain "our going into the Committee Chamber "there was no need, seeing we intended to "clear the outward room, where there would "be none left but the officers and ministers of "the House, whom I conceived we might "trust to." D'Ewes's suggestion was admitted to be reasonable, and was adopted; but the Speaker made a point at the same time of desiring that nobody who went into the said Committee Chamber should speak to anybody out at the window, or throw out unto them any paper writing. "I expected," D'Ewes adds, "some strange motion upon this secret

* *Harleian MSS.* 162, f. 294 b.

§ x.   *Shadows of the Coming Event.*   107

"fecluding and clofe reftraining of ourfelves; <small>which follows accordingly.</small>
"and it followed accordingly."*

What Pym proceeded to fay had fomething in it beyond that mere general fenfe of danger, which, from his knowledge of the King's character, he muft have known to be incident to his own refufal of the offer that had been fo recently made to him. His remarks, as briefly reported by D'Ewes, can hardly fail to be regarded as evidence of fome knowledge, on his part, of the attempt fo foon to be made. He is <small>Pym's speech.</small> miftaken as to time, the danger being lefs immediate; he underftates it as to perfons, the peril ftretching to the Houfe generally through individuals firft to be affailed; but in defiring to obtain from the majority a prompt and decifive action upon their claim to a fufficient Guard or Protection to be chofen by themfelves, which was ftill in difpute with the King, he <small>The remedy for danger.</small> had, while neceffarily perhaps leaving unrevealed the entire extent of the danger known to him, with great fagacity at once addreffed himfelf to the remedy that alone could fully meet the danger, whatever it might be. His object was to induce the Houfe to invite a Guard of Citizens to their protection without <small>Neceffity for an immediate Guard.</small> another day's delay; but he fpoke evidently under fome reftraint, and the reception given to what he faid would feem to indicate that he had taken but few into his confidence as to

* *Harl. MSS.* 162, f. 295 a.

the particulars which rendered him fo urgent. Altogether, indeed, it is evident enough that, through the interval which had yet to pafs, before the King's attempt was made, Pym was driven to concealments and half-confidences which circumftances rendered unavoidable ; and there is little reafon to doubt that from thofe who had fecretly opened with him the negotiations for that acceptance of office which would have been his ruin, he had derived, under the fame feal of fecrecy, knowledge which proved directly inftrumental to his fafety and that of his friends.

The whole truth not told.

Report of Pym's Speech by D'Ewes.

The precife words of D'Ewes are thefe: "Mr. Pym moved that there being a defign "to be executed this day upon the Houfe of "Commons, we might fend inftantly to the city "of London. That there was a plot for the "deftroying of the Houfe of Commons this "day. That we fhould therefore defire them "to come down with the Train Bands for our "affiftance." At which D'Ewes confeffes he was very much troubled, becaufe he feared that the remedy propofed would be as dangerous as the pretended defign. "Some few," he adds, "feconded Mr. Pym's motion, but more op-"pofed it; and fome wifhed that we might "adjourn ourfelves to Guildhall." D'Ewes fpoke on that queftion, remarking, in oppo-fition to Pym, that if all the grounds of fufpicion were that fome officers of the late

A defign to be executed:

A plot for de-ftroying the Houfe of Com-mons.

Adjourn-ment to Guildhall propofed.

§ x. *Shadows of the Coming Event.*

army had been carousing at Whitehall the previous day, or that the King had drawn together a Guard, he did not think these sufficient to justify departure to the city. He added a suggestion oddly characteristic of himself, that if Mr. Pym had more certain grounds for the causes of fear alleged, he knew of no such present preventive than that "we should "adjourn ourselves till three of the clock, "that so we may not be taken altogether."* As for the proceeding into the city, he quoted a saying of the Recorder, that the citizens are not all the sons of one mother, nor of one mind; and it was not well that the House should place absolute faith even in London citizens. The words which closed his speech are all of it that he has further left on record. He wished to learn what the design was to which Mr. Pym had alluded, and whether it were near or distant.

[margin: D'Ewes opposes departure to City. "Let us not be taken together." The design near or distant?]

Pym made no reply to this appeal, and the result of the day's debate is not known. But it is probable, from what occurred next day, that the middle course was adopted of a renewed appeal to the King.

On Friday the 31st December, Denzil Hollis delivered verbally to Charles the First, in the name of the Commons of England, their earnest desire for a Guard out of the City under command of the Earl of Essex. The

[margin: Friday, 31st Dec. 1641. Demand for Guard]

---

* *Harleian MSS.* 162, f 295 b.

King, whose object now was to gain time however brief, declined to receive this verbal message, and required it in writing. It was immediately drawn up and presented the same day; and we learn that the Commons, receiving no immediate answer, committed it to three of their members, Pye, Glynn, and Wheeler, justices of peace for Westminster, to set, in convenient places for the safeguard of the House, good watches sufficiently armed. They further ordered that Halberts should be provided, and brought into the House, for their own better security; which was done accordingly to the number of twenty, "and the said Halberts " stood in the House for a considerable time " afterwards." Reluctantly was consent then given* to adjournment over even the old recognised holiday of New Year's Day, and not without the naming of a Committee to receive the King's answer if it should meanwhile be vouchsafed.

That answer, however, the King had resolved to accompany by another document that should be the most characteristic comment it was capable of receiving, and both were withheld until the morning of the following Monday. For the intervening Saturday he had other engagements.† On that day, the

under Lord Essex:

No reply.

Halberts meanwhile provided.

Committee to receive reply.

Saturday 1st Jan. 1641—2.

Dates of

---

* After a remarkable speech by Pym at conference with the Lords: see *Parl. Hist.* Ed. 1762, x. 151-5.

† The Council Register supplies important dates. On the 1st January 1641-2, the subjoined entry appears.

§ x. *Shadows of the Coming Event.* 111

first of the ill-omened year when his standard was finally unfurled against the most earnest and conscientious of his subjects, he sat with his ministers in Whitehall; and, the great Leader of the Long Parliament having refused his proffered bribe, those two members of the Long Parliament who at its opening had with the greatest vehemence denounced the crimes of his misgovernment took places at the Board. Lord Falkland was sworn of his Majesty's most honorable Privy Council, and seven days later received the seals of a Secretary of State; and Sir John Culpeper having been also duly sworn, order was given for preparation of his patent as Chancellor of the Exchequer. It was made out "for life:" the King vainly hoping by such unconstitutional expedients to bar the power of the Commons to effect a removal of his Councillors. Whether or not Culpeper and Falkland had cognizance of the first official act that was to follow their

A Council at Whitehall.

Falkland and Culpeper sworn into their offices.

Consequences and responsibilities

"This day Lucius Viscount Falkland was sworne of his Ma⁺ˢ Most Hon⁺ᵇˡᵉ Privy Counsell, by his Ma⁺ˢ Command sitting in Counsell, tooke his place and signed with the other Lords."
   A similar entry of the same date has relation to Culpeper, and order is given for his admission "into the place of his Ma⁺ˢ Under Treasurer and Chancellor of his Excheq⁺:" but the patent securing him the office for life (he held it for little more than a year, it being then given to Hyde) is not dated until the 6th of January. Two days later we have the following entry:
   "This day, his Ma⁺ᵗⁱᵉ present in Counsell, and by his Royall Command, the Lord Visc⁺ Falkland was sworne one of his Ma⁺ˢ Principall Secretaries of State."

appointments.

Culpeper Chancellor of Exchequer.

Falkland Secretary of State.

acceptance of office, it cannot be doubted that they accepted it at too critical a time, and amid public excitements and diffenfions of too high and dangerous a nature, not to imply alfo a deliberate and fettled acceptance of all the confequences it might carry with it.

incident to Office at fuch a time.

§ XI. THE IMPEACHMENT BEFORE THE LORDS.

THE day had at length arrived when the danger fo long believed to be impending was to take definite fhape. Early in the morning of Monday the 3rd of January, while the Lower Houfe were moodily liftening to the King's meffage refufing them the military Guard they had afked for under Effex's command, but promifing, with what muft have founded as contemptuous irony, to be himfelf their protector, Mr. Attorney-General Herbert, who was no longer a member of the Commons but had taken his feat with the Lords under his writ of fummons as Affiftant, was delivering at the clerk's table of the Upper Houfe the fubftance of another Royal Meffage, accufing of high treafon five members of the Commons and one of the Lords. Every circumftance of mere form was obferved in the accufation; and Mr. Attorney had not left his feat on the Judges' woolfack until Lord-Keeper Littleton, as the mouthpiece of the King, had duly referred to

Monday 3rd Jan. 1641-2.

King's meffage to Commons refufing Guard.

Attorney-General delivers impeachment to the Lords.

Introduced by Lord-Keeper Littleton.

§ XI. *The Impeachment before the Lords.*   113

the public bufinefs which his officer was there to difcharge. It is not unimportant to obferve this, feeing that both thefe dignitaries of State fought afterwards to put off from themfelves upon the Sovereign the refponfibility which the act had made their own.

The articles of treafon were feven in number, and were read from a paper which Sir Edward Herbert afterwards, in defending himfelf, faid that he had received directly from the King. Whether the formal and ftrictly legal wording and expreffion of the articles had been received alfo directly from the King, he omitted to fay. The firft article charged the accufed generally with the attempt to fubvert the Government and fundamental laws, and to place in fubjects an arbitrary and tyrannical power. The fecond, aimed againft their authorfhip of the Remonftrance, attributed to them the traitorous endeavour, by many foul afperfions upon his Majefty and his Government, to alienate the affections of the people, and to make his Majefty odious to them. The third charged them with having endeavoured to draw the King's late army to fide with them in their traitorous defigns. The fourth, directed againft alleged communications with the Scottifh Rebels, imputed to them the traitorous invitation and encouragement to a foreign power to invade his Majefty's kingdom of England. The fifth, adopting

The Seven Articles of Treafon.

i. General charge.

ii. Authorfhip of Remonftrance.

iii. Tampering with the army.

iv. Invitations to the Scotch.

I

v. the language of the Minority of the Commons when the demand to record a proteſt againſt the paſſing of the Remonſtrance was refuſed, accuſed them of having traitorouſly endeavoured to ſubvert the rights and very being of parliaments. The ſixth accuſed them of having actually raiſed and countenanced tumults againſt his Majeſty. And by the ſeventh, having reference to the armed Guard which they had perſiſted in voting for protection of the Houſe, they were ſaid to have traitorouſly conſpired to levy, and actually to have levied, war againſt the King. A manuſcript copy of the charge, endorſed in the handwriting of Secretary Nicholas as "articles of treaſon "againſt Mr. Pym and the reſt," exiſts in the State Paper Office, and is printed below.*

Puniſhment of Proteſting Minority.

Raiſing tumults.

Levying war.

MS. Articles of Treaſon in State Paper Office.

* " Articles of High Treaſon and other high miſdemeanors " agᵗ the Lord Kerñolton, Mr. John Pym, Mr. John Hampden, " Mr. Denzil Hollis, Sir Arthʳ Haſlericke, and Mr. Willᵐ " Strode.

" 1. That they have traytorouſly endeavʳᵈ to ſubvert the fundamentall Lawes and Govⁿᵗ of the Kingdome of England, to deprive yᵉ king of his royale power, & to place in ſubjects an arbitrary & tyrannicall power over the lives, libertyes, & eſtates of his Majᵗˢ lovinge people.

" 2. That they have traytorouſly endeavᵈ by many fowle aſperſions upon his Maᵗⁱᵉ & his Governᵗ, to alienate the affections of his people, & to make his Maᵗⁱᵉ odious unto them.

" 3. That they have endeavᵈ to drawe his Maᵗˢ late armye to diſobedience to his Maᵗⁱᵉˢ corñands, & to ſyde with them in their traytorous deſignes.

" 4. That they have traytorouſly invited and incouraged a forreigne power to invade his Maᵗⁱᵉˢ kingdome of England.

" 5. That they have traytorouſly endeavᵈ to ſubvert the rights & very being of Parlamᵗˢ.

§ XI. *The Impeachment before the Lords.* 115

While the articles were publicly read, the trouble and agitation were extreme. Their Lordships, to use the expression of Clarendon, were "appalled." He is hardly justified, however, when he somewhat spitefully adds that they took time till the next day to consider of it, that they might see how their Masters the Commons would behave themselves. Waiving altogether the King's requirement through his Attorney-General for immediate possession of the persons of the accused, and for a committee to take evidence on the charges, the Lords at once raised the question of the regularity of the accusation itself, and referred it to a certain number of their members to produce precedents and records. They sent an immediate message to the other House and named members for a Conference. On the previous day, as on a day preceding, they had declined the urgent instance of the Commons to join with them in demanding a Guard under an officer of their own selection; but now they intimated their readiness to join in that demand.*

Agitation among the Lords.

Immediate action taken.

King's demand refused.

Agreement with Commons.

" 6. That for the compleating of their traytorous designs, they have endeav^d as farr as in them lay by force & terror to compell the Parlam^t to joyne with them in theire traytorous Designs, and to that end have actually raysed & countenanced tumults ag^t ye King and Parlam^t.

" 7. That they have traytorously conspired to levie & actually have levyed warr ag^t the King."

* The petition of both Houses was transmitted on the evening of the 3rd, but the reply, suspended by the exciting events which immediately followed, was not handed in until after the King had left London never to return, and the Houses had provided their own Guards. The original MS.

Arrest of the Five Members.

Lord Kimbolton repels the charge.

The feeling displayed was altogether such, indeed, that though the peer included in the articles of impeachment, Lord Kimbolton, was not only present, but upon the instant arose, repelled the charge, and challenged public enquiry into it, no one was so hardy as to press for his commitment. The person sitting next to Kimbolton while the Attorney-General read the articles, was Lord Digby,

Lord Digby silent:

who alone, according to Clarendon, knew of the King's intention, and had promised to move the commitment (after the precedent in the case of Strafford) as soon as the accusation

Charles's answer to petition for Guard.

of this reply still exists in the State Paper Office, dated the 3rd, and wholly in the handwriting of the King. It shows what his determination had been to fight out the matter to the last, and the secret reliance he still placed, notwithstanding the Citizen assemblages and tumults at Westminster, on the power of the Lord Mayor within the City to promote and support his service. It is endorsed "Answer for a Guard," and runs thus:

Not Lord Essex, but Lord Lindsay:

"We having considered the Petition of bothe houses of
" Parlament concerning a Guard, doe give this answer; that
" we will (to secure there feares) command the L. Mayor of
" London to apoint 200 men out of the Trained Bands of the
" Citie (such as he will be answerable for to us) to wait on
" the Houses of Par: that is to say, a Hundred on each
" House, & to bee commanded by the E: of Lindsay: it being
" most proper to him, as' being L: Great Chamberlaine; who
" by his place hath a particular charg: of ye Houses of
" Parliam^t, and of whose integritie, courage, & sufficiencie,
" none can dout."

The most devoted of Royal partizans.

The amount of sincerity involved in this proposal may be measured by the fact, that the Hereditary Great Chamberlain, being its author's most devoted adherent, was the man who within two or three weeks after signing the celebrated Belief that Charles had no intention to declare war against his subjects, actually took command of the troops levied for that purpose, and immediately after fell bravely fighting for his master as Commander-in-chief of the Royalist forces at Edgehill.

§ XI. *The Impeachment before the Lords.*

should be made.* Whether the warning sent this day by Marston† had already reached Lord Kimbolton, we have no means of knowing; but it seems probable that it had, and that his prepared and resolute aspect took Digby by surprise. It is quite clear, from a subsequent passage in Clarendon's History, that the author believed his friend to have failed either in courage or good faith.‡ Not to have moved at once the commitment " as soon as the At-" torney-General had accused Kimbolton," he made a distinct charge against Digby, on the ground that if he had done so, he would pro- bably " have raised a very hot dispute in the " House, where many would have joined with " him." I do not think it unjust to Lord Clarendon to say, that we may infer from this passage what his own feeling was. Yet between the proceeding by Attorney, and the King's personal interference, the difference was not very great.

Failure in courage or good faith:

Clarendon's charge against him.

For the moment, there is little doubt, even Digby's reckless audacity would appear to have failed him. Seeing the temper of the House, he not only sat silent, but affected the utmost surprise and perplexity as Mr. Attorney proceeded; and at the close, whispering in Lord Kimbolton's ear with great seeming agitation that the King was very mischievously advised,

Digby affects surprise:

---

* Clarendon, *Hist.* ii. 125.   † See ante, 86-88.
‡ *Hist.* ii. 128.

that it should go hard but he would discover his adviser, and that he would at once go to him to prevent further mischief, he rapidly quitted the House.*

<small>and suddenly quits the House.</small>

§ XII. THE IMPEACHMENT BEFORE THE COMMONS.

<small>D'Ewes in the Lower House.</small>

D'EWES meanwhile was busy in the Lower House with his pen and ink, in his usual place by the Speaker's chair, "on the lowermost "form close by the south end of the clerk's "table;" but his pen moved less regularly than was its wont, and there is scarcely a single sentence in this particular day's entry that is not left half-finished. As he entered the House he had observed groups and crowds of officers and others scattered about here and there, in the lobbies and outside passages, in a manner not usual; but he took his seat without suspicion of what was passing in the Lords, and found Pym speaking to the Answer made by his Majesty to the desire of the House for a Guard of their own choosing, and making report as to those very incidents, of a threatening and unusual kind, which had attracted his own attention outside. Soon the agitation prevailing communicated itself to the learned member for Sudbury, and we can but follow in unfinished and somewhat incoherent lines the course of the speech, at the close of which

<small>Pym speaking to the King's refusal of a Guard.</small>

<small>D'Ewes's hurried and unfinished reports.</small>

<small>* Clarendon, Hist. ii. p. 128.</small>

§ XII.   *The Impeachment before the Commons.*   119

Pym moved and carried a suggestion by way of request to the authorities of the City, that they would permit companies of trained bands to attend as a Guard upon the Houses at Westminster, and that they would set strong defences and watches about the City streets and walls. *Suggestion for a City Guard.*

One or two of the sentences still traceable in D'Ewes's note-book may show the tone Pym spoke in. "The Great Counsel of the Kingdom should sit as a free Counsel . . . No force about them without consent . . . Not only a Guard of soldiers but many Officers in Whitehall . . . Divers desperate and loose persons are lifted and combined together under pretext to do his Majesty service. . . . One Mr. Buckle had said the Earl of Strafford's death must be avenged, and the house of Commons were a company of giddy-brained fellows." After Pym ceased, Nathaniel Fiennes brought forward, by way of report, some other facts exhibiting the disloyal conduct of the Digbys to the House; but his relation was brought suddenly to a close. Pym and Denzil Hollis were called to the door upon urgent messages by their servants, and members, in much excitement, began talking to each other at the same moment of what was passing in the Lords. Then Pym returned to his place, and Nathaniel Fiennes closed his report. *Fragments of Pym's speech.*   *Pym and Hollis informed of outrage at their homes:*

"Mr. Fiennes's relation was scarce made," says D'Ewes, "when the whole House, *at least*

"*the most of us*, were much amazed with
"Mr. Pym's information, who showed that
"his trunks, study, and chamber, and also
"those of Mr. Denzil Hollis, and Mr. Hamp-
"den, were sealed up by some sent from
"his Majesty." This the House proceeded
to declare a grave breach of privilege; and it
was further ordered, without debate, and with
wise and well-timed reference to the solemn
Protestation which every member had signed
on the eve of Strafford's execution in behalf of
the rights of Parliament, that if any person
whatsoever, without first acquainting the House
therewith and receiving from it due and necessary instruction, should offer to arrest or detain
the person of any member, it was lawful for
such member to stand upon his guard of defence, and to make resistance according to the
Protestation taken to defend the privileges of
Parliament. D'Ewes adds, that " though pri-
" vate intimation was now given to us that the
" King's Attorney had in his Majesty's name
" in the Lords' House accused the said mem-
" bers, and some others of our House of high
" treason, yet we accounted it a breach of
" privilege that their papers, &c. should be
" sealed up before their crime was made known
" to this House." *

A breach of privilege had indeed been committed. Fifty voices arose with that of the

* *Harleian MSS.*, 162, ff. 300 b, 302 a.

§ XII. *The Impeachment before the Commons.* 121

learned master of precedents at once to declare it so. It was not simply that the privileges of Parliament had been outraged in the form and manner of the proceeding, but that the most ordinary safeguards of law, to which the meanest citizen had to look for his daily and hourly protection, had been deliberately violated and put aside. The new Chancellor of the Exchequer, Culpeper, was present; and with Lord Falkland, the new Privy Councillor, occupied for the first time the official seats on the right of the Speaker's chair: but not a word against the resolution now moved was uttered by either. Hyde was not in the House, and it will appear hereafter to be a fact of some significance that no proof is discoverable of his presence during any of these debates. *Violation of law as well as privilege.* *The new ministers silent.* *Hyde absent.*

The declaration of breach of privilege, and the order for resistance, having passed by acclamation, a Committee of conference was appointed to carry them to the Lords; the managers named being Glyn, the member for Westminster and one of the leading lawyers on the popular side, Nathaniel Fiennes, and Sir Philip Stapleton. These had answered to their names, and were about to proceed to the Lords, when it was announced that Mr. Francis, King's Serjeant-at-Arms, was at the door of the Commons, having the mace in his hand, and bearing command to deliver from his Majesty *No opposition attempted.* *The King's Serjeant at the door of the House:*

a meſſage to Mr. Speaker. But, even in that hour of ſupreme excitement, the leaders of the Houſe forgot nothing that was due to its power and pre-eminence within its own walls. Mr. Francis was not permitted to enter until he had laid aſide his mace. Diveſted of that ſymbol of authority he advanced to the Bar, and amid profound ſilence ſaid that he had been commanded by the King's Majeſty, his maſter, upon his allegiance that he ſhould repair to the Houſe of Commons where Mr. Speaker was, and there to require of Mr. Speaker five gentlemen, members of the Houſe of Commons; and thoſe gentlemen being delivered, he was commanded to arreſt them in his Majeſty's name of High Treaſon. "Their names," he added, "are Denzil Hollis, Sir Arthur Haſlerig, "John Pym, John Hampden, and William "Strode."

Enters, without his mace.

Demands the Five Accuſed.

No Debate.

No debate followed. The temper of the Houſe had been too decidedly ſhown to render ſafe any attempt to contravene it; and a ſort of ſettled and ſtern compoſure, contraſting ſtrangely with the agitation that prevailed while yet the threatened blow had not fallen, appears in all the proceedings that immediately followed. The full knowledge of the worſt, or what too haſtily was taken for the worſt, brought with it all that upon the inſtant became neceſſary to ſecure—what now was

Compoſure of the Houſe.

§ XII. *The Impeachment before the Commons.* 123

directly in peril—even the very exiftence of
Parliament and parliamentary power.

Mr. Francis was directed to wait outfide *The Ser-*
the door until the pleafure of the Houfe *jeant or-*
fhould be communicated to him. A meffage *wait out-*
to the King was then ordered, not to be carried *fide.*
by Mr. Francis, but by four of their own members, of whom two, being his Majefty's Privy
Councillors, might haply ferve to remind
him, that, even from his chofen and felected
Minifters, an allegiance was due within thofe
walls from which no power or prerogative
claiming above the law could abfolve them.
As the fworn fervants, not of the King, but of *Deputa-*
the Commons of England, Culpeper and Faulk- *carry mef-*
land were required to accompany Sir John *fage to the*
Hotham and Sir Philip Stapleton, when the *King:*
clofe of the conference with the Lords fhould
have releafed Sir Philip. They were to inform
the King that his meffage, being matter of
great confequence, and concerning the privilege
of all the Commons of England, would be
taken into ferious confideration by the Houfe,
which in all humility and duty would attend *the ac-*
his Majefty with an anfwer with as much fpeed *cufed will*
as the greatnefs of the bufinefs would permit, *legal*
and that the faid accufed members in the *charge.*
meantime fhould be ready to anfwer any *legal*
charge made againft them.

The five members were then feparately addreffed by Mr. Speaker, who enjoined them, one

The Five Accused ordered to attend daily.

by one, to attend *de die in diem* in that House until further direction, such attendance to be specially entered upon the Journals.* Of the matter charged in the articles of treason no notice now was taken. An order was simply made that the House should sit next morning at ten o'clock, as a Grand Committee, to consider the message of the King. But what this meant was well understood, and that the members were then to be heard in reply to their accuser.

Resolution for Military Guard out of City.

The act which followed proved to be one of the most important of all. The resolution for a Guard of the trained bands of the City, moved and carried by Pym at the opening of the sitting, was turned into an order of the House and committed to the care of Alderman

Venn and Pennington sent to the Lord Mayor.

Pennington and Captain Venn, members for London, who were directed immediately to repair thither and demand of the Chief Magistrate and Authorities therein, in compliance with such order, a Military Guard for protection of the House. The charge was promptly executed; in what circumstances, and with what effect, will hereafter be seen.

Day declining.

All this had been done with marked deliberation, and the day was far advanced. The conference with the Lords as to breach of privilege had been brought to a close, and the Upper House had joined with the Lower in

---

* Where it yet stands, *C. J.* ii. 368.

§ XII. *The Impeachment before the Commons.*

declaring against the outrage committed by the act of sealing up the trunks, papers, and doors, in the private houses of the accused. Then an order passed the House, giving power to its Serjeant-at-Arms to break open those seals, and to Mr. Speaker's warrant to take into custody the persons by whom they were attached. Sir William Fleming and Sir William Killigrew,* it had now been ascertained, were the King's principal agents; and, a warrant for their apprehension having been issued, Sir William Fleming and the persons who had acted under his direction were conveyed that night to the custody of the Serjeant-at-Arms. Sir William Killigrew was not to be found. Seals affixed by King's warrant to be broken.

King's agents who seized papers to be imprisoned.

Of the acts and proceedings of this memorable day, which before midnight were in print and circulated throughout the City, that was

---

* These were men reckless and needy, hangers-on of the court, and of broken fortunes. Among more important documents in the State Paper Office there remains a note of this Sir William Killigrew's dated eighteen months before this time, which shows, not merely the straits he was in for money (common enough then for the best men about the Court), but the discreditable ways and means he resorted to for getting it. "Knowe all men," it runs, "that I, Sʳ Wᵐ Killigrew " of London Knᵗ have borrowed of Mastʳ Robert Longe of " London Esqʳ a diamond hatband and one table diamond " ringe, wʰ I the said Sʳ Wᵐ Killigrew have pawned unto " Capt. Peeter (who dwelleth at Mˢᵗʳ Southe's the cutlar " in the Strand) for one hundred pounds; the which I doe " binde myselfe my heires and executors to redeeme and to " restore unto Mastʳ Longe in or before Michaelmas Terme " next: in witness whereof I have hereunto sett my hand,
"London: June 22ᵈ, 1640. Wᵢˡˡ Killigrew."
Endorsed: "Sir Wᵐ Killigrew's note for the Diamond " Hatt Band and Ring." Sir William Killigrew: and the diamond hatband and ring.

the last but one. The last was to send out intimation to the King's Serjeant-at-Arms and Meſſenger, Mr. Francis, "who attended "all this while at the door of the Houſe of "Commons," that the anſwer to the King would be borne by members of their own.

Laſt act of the Houſe on 3rd Jan.

§ XIII. WHAT FOLLOWED THE IMPEACHMENT.

It was night before Falkland, Culpeper, Stapleton and Hotham were admitted to audience at Whitehall, and very ſtrange the interview muſt have been. Charles appears to have addreſſed himſelf ſolely to Falkland. Haſtily, when the meſſage had been delivered, he aſked whether any reply was expected, and, in the ſame breath, before Falkland could anſwer, ſaid that the Houſe ſhould have his reply as ſoon as it aſſembled next morning, and that meanwhile it was to take his aſſurance that what had been done was done by his direction. It is juſt poſſible that Charles's intention, when he ſaid this, may have been to ſend ſuch reply; but if ſo, it did not ſurvive the ſcene which is alleged to have been acted in thoſe royal apartments not many hours after the four members quitted them.*

Interview with the King.

A promiſe for next day.

The anecdote reſts on the authority of a manuſcript note publiſhed by the hiſtorian Echard, which had been left by Sir William Coke of Norfolk to Mr. Archetil Grey, the

Authority for ſcene to be deſcribed.

* Echard's *Hiſtory* (ed. 1720), p. 520.

§ XIII. *What followed the Impeachment.*

brother of Lord Grey of Groby; and though Admixture of true and false.
it certainly seems dated some hours too soon
even for the occurrence it professes to relate,
and should be read very guardedly, there
is room to suspect that it possesses a considerable substratum of truth, for the understanding of which the reader will be better
prepared if certain preliminary circumstances
and considerations are submitted to him.
Upon the entire statement of the facts he will
have to judge, how far the proceedings which View taken by Mr. Hallam:
already have been described are likely, in all the
startling and dangerous circumstances of the
time, to have been taken, as Mr. Hallam
seems to suppose, by the King acting singly
and apart, not merely from his authorized
advisers and from all his Privy Council,* but
from the new adherents of his person and
recipients of his favour, won to him by the
Great Remonstrance. He will have to deter- How far credible.
mine how far it is credible, that a design of
such magnitude as the impeachment of leading
members of the Commons, of which before
the event rumours and alarms had gone forth

---

* Hallam's words are (*Const. Hist.* ii. 125, ed. 1855) that
"the King was guided by bad private advice, and cared not
"to let any of his Privy Council know his intentions lest he
"should encounter opposition." This surmise may be correct,
but the King's character and history cannot be said to support
it. The life of Strafford offers incessant proof that Charles
took strange pleasure in resisting the advice of men most
attached to him, and in whom he had reason to place the
greatest confidence. All the most serious acts of his own life
were done in the very teeth of the most prudent counsellors
who remained with him. Ill advisers: Mr. Hallam's view not consonant with character of the King.

Arrest of the Five Members.

<small>Did the King act apart from all advice?</small> in many quarters; for which the late lawless levy of a Court of Guard at Whitehall was now loudly afferted to have been the preparation; which, to every one in the King's confidence, was beyond all question known to be a <small>Were the Attorney and Keeper wholly ignorant?</small> design not now for the first time entertained; and which required the aid of the keeper of his conscience, and the first law officer of his crown, to carry through its very first stage; had yet been imparted to no member of his Council when from his own hand the Attorney-General Herbert received the written articles <small>What Strode thought of their participation.</small> of treason, and from his own lips the Lord Keeper Littleton took the message to the Lords. When Littleton and Herbert afterwards afferted so much, Strode, one of the accused, publicly avowed his disbelief.* But

---

* This incident took place on the 12th February, when the conduct of Sir Edward Herbert (who had sat for Old Sarum: there were ten other Herberts in this Parliament) was under discussion. D'Ewes tells us (*Harl. MSS.* 162, ff. 377 b, 385 a): " Mr. Pierrpoint said that the Lord Keeper had told " him that after his Maj^y had shown the articles to the <small>Mr. Attorney's excuses to the House.</small> " Attorney (impeaching Pym, &c.) he did to his uttermost " power advise his Ma^y not to prefer them; but the King " commanding him to do it, he came to the Lords House " to perform the same, but was so troubled in mind when " he came there, that he did adventure to return back " to his Maj^y, and did humbly and earnestly advise " him the second time not to prefer the same, but then " receiving his Maj^{ties} absolute and peremptory command " to do it, he performed it accordingly. Mr. Strode said <small>Disbelieved by Strode.</small> " he believed that Mr. Attor^y did not only contrive the " fame, but knew of the design itself also, for he was a man " of great parts and well skilled in state matters, and was very " violent both on Monday and Tuesday Jany 3 and 4." All things considered, Strode's suggestion was at least a pardonable one; and the reader will shortly have an opportunity of testing

such a question cannot even be raised upon the more daring act which was to be done on the succeeding day. There is not a shadow of pretence for the assertion, that the King had kept secret to the last hour the purpose to which effect was now to be given. It was most certainly discussed on this preceding night, and on the morning of the day itself; nor is there any doubt as to some at least of those who were present at the ill-judged and ill-fated Council.

Proposed attempt of the 4th not secret to the last.

Discussed the previous night.

§ XIV. SCENE IN THE QUEEN'S APARTMENTS.

WHITELOCK, who had fair opportunities of information both at the time of the occurrence and afterwards, says in his *Memorials* that " the " Papists, by the means and influence of the

Ill advisers:

---

the credibility of the Lord Keeper's and Attorney General's statement by comparing it with accounts of the transaction under the King's own hand. A few days before the present debate (Saturday, 29 Jan.) an effort had been made by the Court party to acquit Herbert by putting off upon " Peter " Baal, Esq. of the Middle Temple, being the Queen's " attorney " (this is the " Ball " of the not very comprehensible paper memorandum in Sir Ralph Verney's *Notes*, p. 150) the act of having drawn the articles of treason. D'Ewes enables me to state this; and as the close of his Journal on that day is characteristic of the usage of the time, and of the unruly practices of honorable members, I subjoin it: " Several committees " went out between 12 & 1, and many members, about one half " in the House, went out to dinner. Divers called to keep " the doors shut, which made me to move—not to disturb the " service of the House by calling out 'Shut the door,' but " that we might again renew the ancient order of Parliament, " and, seeing the days were growing longer, fit to a later " period in the afternoon."—*Harl. MSS.* 162. f. 359 b.

The Queen's Attorney put forward.

"Shut the Door."

Arrest of the Five Members.

Papists and women.
"Queen, as was supposed, persuaded the King the next day in the morning to come himself to the House of Commons;" and he adds, as an accredited rumour of the time, that it was the women's counsel and irritation of Charles, telling him that if he were King of England he would not suffer himself to be baffled about these persons, which provoked him to go to the House himself, and fetch them out.* Madame de Motteville states distinctly in her *Memoirs* that the Queen had told her of a project to strike terror into the Parliament, and seize again the power that had been wrested from them; and, in another passage, she says more plainly that the King returned from the great dinner which had been given him in the City on his arrival from Scotland,† so elated by the cheering and applause

Statement of Madame de Motteville.

---

* *Memorials,* i. 154. (ed. 1853).

† Ante, 21, 22. Without placing anything of an implicit reliance on what is said by the Queen's chamber-woman, her position at the time yet fairly entitles her to be heard. "She" (the Queen) "was ever diligent," says Madame de Motteville, "in gaining partizans to her husband, and won over the Lord Mayor. On the King's return from Scotland she went to meet him and to apprise him of the compliant disposition of his subjects. The royal family were received in London with great marks of loyalty, & the King resolved to take advantage of this state of things, to seize the leaders of the House of Commons. He entrusted his plan to few but the Queen." A more trustworthy witness to the disastrous effects of that unfortunate City dinner is the historian May: "Who would not in probability have judged," he says (*Hist.* lib. 2, cap. 2, 18-19), "that the forementioned costly and splendid entertainment which the City of London gave to the King, would have exceedingly endeared them unto him, and produced no effects but of love & concord? Yet accidentally it proved otherwise. For many people, ill affected to the Parliament, gave it out in ordinary dis-

Henrietta's conduct on the return from Scotland.

May the historian.

§ XIV. *Scene in the Queen's Apartments.* 131

of the Citizens, that he determined to avail himſelf of the ſuppoſed popularity implied in it, to ſeize the "leaders" in Parliament. Monte- reuil, the French Ambaſſador, ſubſequently claimed the credit to himſelf of having given timely notice to the leaders (" J'avois prévenu " mes amis, et ils ſ'étoient mis en ſûreté ") to provide for their ſafety ; and even if the faƈt of his having done ſo were doubtful, he would hardly have ventured to claim the credit unleſs it were notorious that he had the opportunity. Finally, it only needs to advert, in proof of the notorious complicity of the Queen's party in the deſign, to the ſubſequent ſtate paper of the Commons in which they denounce " the in- " fluence which the prieſts and Jeſuits had " upon the affeƈtions and counſels of the " Queen, and the admiſſion of her Majeſty to " intermeddle with the great affairs of ſtate."*

Warning to the accuſed from French Ambaſſador.

Effeƈts of Queen's intermeddling.

The leaders of the Commons had indeed good reaſon to ſuſpeƈt her Majeſty. Not many months before this date, when their interference had arreſted her announced journey to Spa, they were foully aſſailed by the Royaliſts upon the ground that they had covered her with

Her deſigns ſuſpeƈted by the Commons : Charles miſled.

" courſe (non ignota loquor, it is a known truth) that the
" City were weary of the Parliament's tedious proceedings,
" & would be ready to join with the King againſt them.
" Whether it begat the ſame opinion in the King or not, I
" cannot tell; but certainly ſome conceived ſo, by aƈtions
" which immediately followed."

* Remonſtrance from Grocers' Hall Committee. See Clarendon's *Hiſt.* ii. 185.

K 2

disloyal suspicions, nor had scrupled to discover,
in a simple excursion for health and pleasure,
treasonable motives, and even a possible design
upon the property of the Crown. Yet not a
great many days after the events now described,
Suspicions every one of those suspicions was proved* to
proved true. have been well-founded ; and when at length it
was known that she had managed to quit
England upon the enterprize of raising foreign
arms for the King, carrying with her to this
end not only her own and the King's jewels,
but the jewels of the Crown,† the regret might
well be felt, even by moderate men, that the
patriots had not put their old misgivings into
force. Conscious of her own intentions, this
was doubtless what she had herself most dreaded;
Clarendon and Clarendon explains the eager violence with
explains her desire which she threw herself into the King's project
to have the of impeaching the members, by the terror she
members im- entertained of their impeaching herself. " That
peached: " which wrought so much upon the Queen's
" fears," he says,‡ " besides the general obser-
" vation how the King was betrayed, and how
" his rights and power were every day wrested

Abstrac- * See *Nalson*, ii. 391, for indication that the Commons
tion of the suspected the design against the Jewels as early as July 1641.
Crown † Whitelock's *Memorials* (ed. 1853), i. 159; and see
jewels. Hallam, *Const. Hist*. ii. 139. Mr. Hallam is infinitely moderate and cautious in dealing with these passages of our history,
but he admits, in a note to the passage just referred to, that
the Queen's intended journey to Spa in July 1641, which
was given up at the remonstrance of Parliament, was highly
suspicious.
‡ *Hist*. ii. 231.

§ XIV. Scene in the Queen's Apartments.

" from him, was an advertisement that she
" had received of a design in the prevalent
" party to have accused her Majesty of high
" treason; of which, without doubt, there had
" been some discourse in their most private To save
" cabals, and, I am persuaded, was imparted herself
" to her upon design, and by connivance (for from impeach-
" there were some incorporated into that ment.
" faction who exactly knew her nature, pas-
" sions, and infirmities), that the disdain of it
" might transport her to somewhat which
" might give them advantage. And shortly
" after that discovery to her Majesty, those
" persons before mentioned were accused of
" high treason."

The person here more particularly pointed Lucy,
at as having played out, apparently on both Countess of Carlisle.
sides, the double intrigue of friend and of
betrayer, was undoubtedly Lady Carlisle, now
in daily intercourse with Pym and Lord Kim- Her daily
bolton, and herself a chief actor also in the intercourse
scene about to be related. Without raising with Pym
the question whether it might not have been and Kimbolton:
even with herself for "messenger" that the
Queen and King had lately made the overture
to Pym which was meant to ensnare him
from his party, it does not admit of controversy that this strong-willed woman, by far the
most generous and the most constant of all
the friends of Strafford, and for that reason after
still in acceptance and reputation at Court, Strafford's death.

had been, ever fince the King's furrender of his great Minifter, deep in the fecret counfels and confidence of Pym and his friends, and had done them moſt material ſervices. Cla-rendon's firſt editors fuppreffed the paffage in which he dwells explicitly on the evil fhe wrought againſt her quafi-friends at Court: but it may properly here be reproduced. The hiftorian is clofing a fort of fumming up of the adverfe circumſtances with which Charles the Firſt at this time had to contend. "And laſtly, " which, it may be, made all the reſt worſe, the " Countefs of Carlifle, who was moſt obliged " and truſted by the Queen, and had been for " her eminent and conftant affection to the " Earl of Strafford admitted to all the con-" fultations which were for his prefervation, " and privy to all the refentments had been " on his behalf, and fo could not but remember " many fharp fayings uttered in that time, was " become a confidant in thofe counfels, and " difcovered whatfoever fhe had been trufted " with."* So did Clarendon, out of his fimple obfervation and knowledge of humanity, and without reproach to the Countefs for fo avenging a bitter wrong, fufficiently explain, as it feems to me, the fudden tranffer of Lady Carlifle's allegiance from Strafford's falſe friends to his open enemies. In that way,

Sidenotes: Retribution for betrayal of her friends: Betrays the Court to the Commons: Her conduct explained by her character.

* Clarendon, *Hift.* ii. 603-604.

§ XIV. *Scene in the Queen's Apartments.* 135

not unnaturally, might so vehement and impetuous a spirit resent his betrayal; it is to be remembered also that her brother, the Earl of Northumberland, had by this time, after a far less constant and generous devotion to Strafford, changed sides from the Court to the Parliament; and there is certainly not the shadow of a ground for the imputation which so many grave historians have since repeated on the authority of a jesting remark by Sir Philip Warwick,* that this mature lady of

<small>Her brother Northumberland.

Sir Philip Warwick's scandal.</small>

---

* The passage is worth quoting as written by one who passed much time in very intimate personal attendance on the King, because the only regret expressed in it with regard to the attempt of the 4th January is that it was made too late: " In Scotland having learnt the confederacies against him, " and the intelligence some of our great members had held " with the ambassadors of foreign princes, particularly the " French, and somewhat of the depth of their designs, he was " forced to resolve to accuse some members of both Houses " of treason; but too late, God knows: enough to show, " that when Princes will long put off their dangers by " unreasonable concessions, they do not divert their hazard, " but run into it. And now tho' he resolves to proceed " against these members by a due processe in law, & accuse " them first in the Lords house by his Attorney Generall, " and then in the House of Commons by himselfe (both " Houses having ever allowed that no priviledge of parlia- " ment could by any single member of either House be pre- " tended unto in the case of treason, felony, or breach of " peace), yet his coming to the Lower House being betrayed " by that busy statefwoman the Countess of Carlisle (who had " now changed her gallant from Strafford to Mr. Pym, " and was become such a she-Saint that she frequented their " sermons and took notes), he lost the opportunity of seizing " their persons " &c. &c. *Memoires* (ed. 1702), p. 204. While I am bound to state my conviction that the imputation which would give to Lady Carlisle the great Puritan leader for her gallant, is without a shadow of other testimony to support it, I need not conceal the fact that the Royalist libellers kept a well supplied armoury of weapons of this kind, which any

<small>A Courtier's view of the Impeachment and arrest.

Busy statefwoman the she-saint.</small>

more than forty years of age, who had been twenty years a wife* and five a widow, had now

No ground for Warwick's libel.
Royalist writer was sure to find always ready to his hand. Pym's free living and gallantries were an untiring theme. From the *New Diurnall,* or from *The Senſe of the Houſe,* or from *Reaſons againſt Accommodation,* I could furniſh abundant inſtances, but they are not always quotable. One of the more ſcholarly of theſe reckleſs penmen had invented even a Latin ſong which went by Pym's name, and ſupplied material for infinite libels by way of anſwer.

> I wonder one ſo old, ſo grave,
> Should yet ſuch youth, ſuch lightneſſe have.
> * * * *
> Thou mayſt as ſoon turn Turk as king;
> And that, oh that's the tempting thing—
> That thou mayſt glut thine appetite
> With a ſeraglio of delight!

Pym's unpuritanic manners.
Occaſionally, however, even a Royaliſt libeller is under ſome influence which gives him pauſe in his career of ſlander, and his charge againſt the great leader reſolves itſelf, at ſuch times, into what may poſſibly have originated the whole of this fruitful theme of unſcrupulous wit—Pym's free unpuritanical manners, and flowing courteſy to women, repeatedly noticed by contemporaries. Take an example from *Lines to a Lady:*

> Then go, fair lady, follow him;
> Fear no trumpet, fear no drum,
> Fair women may prevail with Pym,
> And one ſweet ſmile when there you come
> Will quickly ſtrike the Speaker dumb.

"Roundhead" explained by Baxter.
Let me add that when Baxter, in a well-known paſſage of his *Narrative* (p. 34), repreſents the Queen, in Pym's preſence, aſking who that round-headed man was (which, by the way, ſhe is not at all likely to have done, for there is ample evidence that his perſon was well-known both to Queen and King long before the Strafford trial), the reader muſt yet not ſuppoſe her to have meant by the phraſe that he was what is called cloſe-cut or crop-eared. In that ſenſe it would not be more applicable to Pym and Hampden than to Hopton and Rupert. The remark of Baxter may be given for its illuſtra-

---

* She was married to Lord Hay, afterwards Earl of Carliſle, in the autumn of 1617.

XIV. *Scene in the Queen's Apartments.*

changed her "gallant" from Strafford to Pym. One of the King's phyſicians, Doctor Bates, in his *Riſe and Progreſs of the Troubles*, is not difpoſed to be more complimentary to her than Sir Philip was; but at leaſt he keeps more within the probabilities when he aſcribes her conduct to a willingneſs now to ſet off her wit, as formerly ſhe had done her beauty, the gifts of different ages, amongſt the Parliament men. This writer, a partizan of Charles the Firſt, though he did not decline, during the Protectorate, to preſcribe for Cromwell, alſo diſtinctly declares, in that portion of his *Elenchus Motuum* which was written and printed before the Reſtoration, 'that it was "by the advice of ſome of his Privy Council "who were themſelves members of the "Houſe,"* that the King, finding the Commons reſolute not to deliver up their members on legal charge, went himſelf the next morning to arreſt them.

A ſuggeſtion more probable.

Doctor Bates.

Privy Councillors ſaid to have adviſed the King.

Of a different complexion from his ſtatement, though not neceſſarily at variance with it, is the ſcene that waits to be deſcribed from Coke's Manuſcript, preſerved by Archetil

---

tion of the ſubject treated ante, 63. He is ſpeaking of the word *Roundhead*. "The original of which name is not certainly "known. Some ſay it was becauſe the Puritans then com- "monly wore ſhort hair, and the King's party long hair; "ſome ſay it was becauſe the Queen at Strafford's trial aſked "who that round-headed man was, meaning Pym, becauſe he "ſpake ſo ſtrongly." "*That round-headed man.*"

* Ed. 1685; p. 34.

Grey. A long and very paſſionate debate had paſſed in the royal chamber on the night of the fruitleſs attempt of the Attorney-General, the Queen taking prominent part therein; and it had ended, according to this account, in the ſettled reſolve that Charles would himſelf demand the members next morning. But his heart failed him when the morning came. He went to the Queen's apartments early, and, finding Lady Carliſle with her, took her Majeſty into her cloſet, and there, having put to her all the hazards of the attempt, and all its poſſible conſequences, declared that he muſt abandon it. Whereat the Queen, no longer able to contain her paſſion, violently burſt out, "Allez, poltron! Go, pull theſe "rogues out by the ears, ou ne me revoyez "jamais!" Without replying the King left the room. The anecdote is certainly not in any reſpect reliable, if accepted ſtrictly in this form; but it ſeems to favor the ſuppoſition of ſome admixture of truth in it, though miſdated as well as miſſtated, that Madame de Motteville ſhould unconſciouſly have given us in her Memoirs a ſort of ſequel to it. She deſcribes the Queen, while waiting in her cloſet with vehement expectation, rejoined by Lady Carliſle. In a previous paſſage ſhe had dwelt upon Charles's leave-taking hardly an hour before, not in ſilence indeed, as Coke reports, but with a haſty promiſe to Henrietta that if she found one hour elapse without hearing ill news of him, she would see him, when he returned, master of his kingdom. With impatient dread she had since passed that interval of suspense, and now, on Lady Carlisle's sudden entrance, thinking the hour was past and the stroke made not missed, she exclaimed to her friend, "Rejoice! for I hope that the King is now master in his States, and that Pym and his confederates are in custody." She had told the triumph of her hate too early to prevent Lady Carlisle from making it the triumph of her own. Within an hour from that time, adds Madame de Motteville, Pym knew what was to be done that day.

The one hour.

Queen betrays her secret.

Lady Carlisle betrays the Queen.

§ xv. Council of the Night of the 3rd of January.

The nature of the debate of the preceding night, the number who were present at it, and the character of those who took active part in it, remain still matters of doubt to us. Was it a meeting of the King and Queen with the Queen's friends only, with Lord Digby, the French Ambassador, and William Murray* of the Bed-Chamber, as Clarendon would have us believe; or was it one at which, or immediately preceding which, the King had consulted with those of his Privy Council who

The night's debate:

Who were present?

---

* "Littel Vil Murry," as the Queen calls him in her letters.

were alfo members of the Houfe of Commons, in other words with Sir Edward Nicholas, Culpeper, and Falkland, as Doctor Bates diftinctly avers? When Sir Arthur Hafelrig, himfelf one of the accufed, recalled the circumftances fixteen years later, in one of the Parliaments of the Protectorate, it is remarkable that in what he faid, after expreffing his thanks to God that through the timely notice given by the kindnefs of that great lady, the Lady Carlifle, bloodfhed had been prevented, he feems at once both to confirm the fubftance of Sir William Coke's ftory, and to make it much more probable by changing the time alleged for it, while he leaves it compatible with either fuppofition as to the character of the previous night's meeting. On the King's "return," he faid, " the " Queen raged and gave him an unhandfome " name, poltroon, for that he did not take " others out; and certain, if he had, they " would have been killed at the door."* On the other hand, when Hobbes fpeaks, in his *Behemoth*, of the long fubfequent altercations between the Parliament and the King, and fays that the perfiftent demand of the Houfe of Commons, that the King fhould declare who were the perfons that advifed him to go, as he did, to the Parliament Houfe to apprehend them, had for it no other motive than

* Burton's *Diary of the Parliaments of Cromwell*, iii. 93. Hafelrig's fpeech was delivered on the 7th February, 1658-9.

§ XV.   *Council of the Night of 3rd January.*

"to stick upon his Majesty the dishonour of deserting his friends and betraying them to his enemies,"* he distinctly sanctions the assertion of Bates that the act was neither unpremeditated by the King nor unadvised by his counsellors.†

Perhaps the question, which must after all be left to a careful and impartial judgment upon the attendant circumstances, may receive its not least important illustration from considering all that was involved in that chance of a fatal issue, with such emphasis referred to by Haselrig. The turning point of the case is probably there; and in what the undertaking included beyond its ostensible pretences, its real key or solution may be found. It is usual to treat the attempt which the King was now about to make, as an act of rashness far transcending in its danger that which already through his Attorney General he had made, and far surpassing in its folly all his other acts of state since his return; as an undertaking which he never could have dared to submit to any of his advisers, and

marginal notes: Direction in which to look for motives and objects of attempt of 4th January.

Not so rash as supposed.

---

* The truth was, as the historian May has pointed out (lib. 2, cap. 2, p. 25), that in this demand the House was thoroughly justified and perfectly regular; "the law in two "several statutes providing that if in time of Parliament the "King accuse a member of the same of what crime soever, "he ought to signify to the Parliament who were the "informers."

† Hobbes in the same tone and spirit adds: "The King "waved the prosecution of the 5 members, but denied to "make known to them the names of those who had advised "him to come in person to the House of Commons to "demand them."

marginal notes: Demand for names of King's advisers.

an adventure which necessarily he must have undertaken, if at all, on his undivided responsibility. But does this view take sufficiently into account the antecedent circumstances, the challenge flung down to the Houses, the continued exasperation of the Citizens, and the position in which, amid a population already so dangerously excited, the failure of the first day's enterprise had left the King? There are occasions when what would ordinarily be the madness of despair becomes a courage only equal to the occasion. All the dangers involved in a deliberate attack on the privileges of the House of Commons, and the persons of its leaders, had now been incurred. The challenge thrown down had been promptly taken up, and from it, to a vision less narrow and obstinate than the King's, there might well seem no possible retreat, consistent with dignity or safety. Let it be assumed, as an act of justice to Charles the First, that he honestly believed himself to be in possession of evidence, which, before such a tribunal as might be obtained to try them, would bring the accused members certainly within the penalties of treason. Hyde professes that he had no doubt of it; and neither, it is probable, had Culpeper or Falkland.* But, on the other hand, the reso-

Position of the King after failure of attempt of the 3rd January.

Challenge taken up by the Commons.

Difficulty of retreat.

Alleged evidence to support the charge.

---

* He is speaking, in another passage, of the fears entertained by himself and them that the attempted arrest might prove a disadvantage to the King's affairs. "Not that they "thought the gentlemen accused, less guilty; for their

§ xv.   *Council of the Night of 3rd January.*   143

lute determination of the House to protect its members interposed an insuperable difficulty, and at once made painfully apparent that a false step had been taken. This, if at all to be retrieved, it was now not possible to retrieve by any proceeding within the limits of the law. Five Commoners had been accused of treason before a tribunal which had not the shadow of a jurisdiction to try them; and the forms of the grand jury, which for centuries had shielded and protected the English subject, had given place to a lawless exercise of the most hateful of all the processes of law and of prerogative, an Attorney-General's Ex-officio upon the information of the King. Could anything now suggested to meet such a crisis be in effect worse, whether by failure or success, than what had thus directly occasioned it?

<small>False step irretrievable within limits of law.</small>

<small>Nature of the act already committed.</small>

These were the circumstances in which, on the night of the 3rd of January, we must assume the idea to have been started, that,

<small>One way to recover ground;</small>

"extreme dishonest arts in the House were so visible, that
"nothing could have been laid to their charge incredible:
"but the going through with it was a matter of so great
"difficulty and concernment, that every circumstance ought
"to have been fully deliberated, and the several parts dis-
"pensed into such hands, as would not have shaken in the
"execution. . . . . If the choice had been better made,
"and the several persons first apprehended, & put into dis-
"tinct close custodies, that neither anybody else should have
"heard from them, nor they one from another, all which
"had not been very difficult, the high spirit of both Houses
"might possibly have been so dejected, that they might have
"been treated withal." *Hist.* ii. 183-4.

<small>What Clarendon thought of the King's proceeding.</small>

<small>What he would have done himself.</small>

strong in the justice of a case to which the subtleties and niceties of law were no longer applicable, the King should go with the armed attendants of his new Court of Guard (provided for that special occasion, men afterwards said) to the House next morning, and himself demand the members to be given up to him. Objection might be made that this would be but the repetition, in an exaggerated form, of what had failed that day: but the obvious answer, that, in the event of such resistance being repeated, means of counter-resistance were provided, gives its distinctive character to what the King now designed. If bloodshed followed upon violence, the responsibility would rest with those who provoked it: nor is it possible to doubt, that, but for Lady Carlisle's interference, such must have been the issue raised. The whole of the occurrences of the past three weeks had gone altogether in the same direction; and we have seen that merely on the view of what was passing from day to day, a terror and foreboding of calamity was in the hearts of the most moderate men. It was hardly a time when even the thought of such an act as the King was about to undertake could have arisen, unaccompanied by the prevision of some consequences sure to follow, of which the weight or levity would wholly turn upon the degree of confidence or fear already inspired by the conduct of the people. But when

§ XV.   *Council of the Night of 3rd January.*   145

fear was wisdom, Charles the First had no fear. We shall find that he still to this hour, and beyond it, blindly relied on the City as under the control of its loyal Chief Magistrate. He confessed afterwards his mistake in having been induced to believe that the House of Commons had now ceased to be popular. Armed bravos and soldiers of fortune had unpunished drawn their swords on the people, and "chafed" and hunted them in the public ways. And why not complete, at the House itself, what in the streets had been thus begun? *The King incapable of a wise fear.*

The change of position taken up by the accused members on the second day, bears out this view of the case, and sanctions the belief that the issue sought to be raised was, and could be, no other than one of violence.* The House of Commons withdrew its members at the approach of the King, not because it feared the King more than it feared his Attorney-General or his Serjeant-at-Arms, but because of the danger of a collision with *The issue raised, one of violence: reason why the House withdrew its members.*

---

* Whitelock says (*Memorials* i. 153): "And divers "imagined that if the five members had not received a secret "notice from a great court lady, their friend (who overheard "some discourse of this intended action, and thereof gave "timely notice to those gentlemen) whereby they got out of "the House just before the King came: otherwise, it was "believed, that if the King had found them there, and called "in his Guards to have seized them, the members of the "House would have endeavoured the defence of them, which "might have proved a very unhappy and sad business; and "so it did, notwithstanding that was prevented. This sudden "action being the first visible & apparent ground of the "ensuing troubles."   *Whitelock's view: Extent of danger prevented by Lady Carlisle.*

L

the armed men who accompanied him. Attention has not been sufficiently fixed on this part of the case. Madame de Motteville tells us that the Queen never ceased to reproach herself to the last day of her life, for having casually disclosed what led to the removal of the members from the House. To have prevented, not the King's attempt, but the possibility of violence and bloodshed in giving effect to it, was to her the most bitter reproach. "Never did he treat me for a "moment," she exclaimed, "with less kind-"ness than before it happened, though I had "ruined him." She had ruined him, because unconsciously she had caused the betrayal of his plan for disabling or striking down his enemies, in the House where they had mortally assailed him by upholding the liberties of his people.

Source of Queen's self-reproach:

not prevention of attempt, but interception of consequences.

There is no injustice to the King in the views here expressed. The injustice is in treating his scheme as a braggart display of force it was never designed to use. The preparations for it were all too deliberately made to render credible any such belief. It was afterwards clearly proved, and admitted by Charles, that on this 3rd of January means had been taken to fortify Whitehall with a considerable access of arms and ammunition. What was hoped, and desperately planned, to have been done in the City, will shortly be revealed upon

Previous preparations:

At Whitehall;

and in the City.

§ xv. *Council of the Night of 3rd January.*

evidence beyond cavil or dispute. So far back as the previous Friday the 31st of December, as will appear hereafter from what D'Ewes reveals to us of evidence given by Captain Langres, orders had been sent to the officer in command of the Court of Guard at Whitehall to obey "one Sir William Fleming." On this very night while the subject was yet in debate, means had been taken to obtain assistance from the gentlemen of the Inns of Court, who could themselves furnish at that time an important military guard, and whom we have already seen eager, during the Westminster Hall tumults, to proffer for the King's protection a band of 500 men.* Sir William Killigrew had been

Side notes: Evidence of Captain Langres. Assistance sought from Inns of Court.

---

* Ante, 78. I have found curious evidence existing in the State Paper Office of the anxiety of the Court to render this force efficient and to secure its services in case of need. It is a Royal letter to the Benchers of Gray's Inn touching the exercise of arms, and is dated at that striking period preceding the dissolution of the Third Parliament, when, to most thinking men, the hope of any final settlement without ultimate appeal to arms must first have begun to appear desperate. No one who examines the State papers of this time in our National Repository, still untouched by the historian, can fail to be struck by the change of tone and attitude taken by the people. Thus early the country was on the point of rebellion. Only faith in the leaders of the House of Commons kept it still. Even in a thing which till then had been a mere matter of course— the bringing of State prisoners from the Tower to the Courts —days, times, and modes of conveyance had to be selected with the nicest care for avoidance of popular tumults; and whether Eliot and Selden were to be brought by water or by land, on particular occasions, was matter of anxious deliberation between the Governor of the Tower and the Law Officers of the Crown. The paper to which I have referred, and which has never been printed, is worth subjoining in detail. Apart from its special historical significance, there may be found in it at the present time an interest which makes appeal, yet nearer and closer, to that spirit which supplies in all ages a

Side notes: Inns of Court Volunteer Guard. A troubled time. Midsummer, 1828: the country on eve of resistance. Royal letter to Benchers of Gray's Inn.

Killigrew sent round with copy of Impeachment. sent round to each of the Four Inns with copies of the articles of treason, and with summons from his Majesty in each case to be in waiting the next morning at Whitehall. A similar course had been taken also with the Guard at the Palace.

country's only efficient safeguard,—the patriotic ardour, the disciplined valour, and the skill in arms of her sons.

"Trusty and Well Beloved Wee Greet you well. Con-
"sidering that these times are full of action and danger, true
"religion being now assaulted in all parts of Christendome,
Desire to have all citizens exercised in arms. "our purpose is to employ our best care to make all our
"subjects well prepared by the exercise of armes to defend
"the truth and our Kingdomes, and to maintaine the safetie
"and honour of Our Nation; and because the voluntary
"example of the gentlemen of the Innes of Court will much
"conduce to that good end, Wee therefore will and require
"you that you doe in our name recommend vnto them the
"exercise of Archerie and Armes, inciting and incourageing
"them at theire times of recreation to employ themselves
"therein, and especially in horsemanshipp, a commendable
"and noble exercise and most necessarie in all occasions of
"Warr wherein other Nations have gott the advantage of
Defect to be supplied, a want of discipline. "Us. Our greatest defect is want of discipline and Knowledge
"therein: by occasion thereof the greatest disorder and con-
"fusion doe usually happen in armes. But Wee doe usually
"referr it to every gentleman to exercise, either on horse or
"foot, what armes shall best sort with his owne disposition;
"and Wee will extend our Royall grace and furtherance by
"all fitt waies and meanes to all such as shall manifest their
"forwardnes in that worke, which will be an honour to
"your Societyes and a worthie example to our Subjects.
Law students not to neglect studies, but to occupy leisure and vacations. "Our meaning is, not that any the Students of our Lawes
"should by this occasion neglect their studies, but that they
"should change their former exercises in time of Vacancie
"and recreations into the most usefull actions for the
"common good and defence of religion, our Royall person,
"themselves, and our countrye. And Wee will that you shall
"cause these Our Letters to be openly read unto the
"Gentlemen of the Societie, declaring unto them that Our
"care shall be duely to encourage and advance all such as
"shall well deserve either by their Studdies or the com-
"mendable Actions Wee now commend unto them. Given
"under our Signet at our Pallace at Westminster the 28 of
"June on the 4th Yeare of our Raigne."

§ xv. *Council of the Night of 3rd January.*

Still, even assuming the matter to have been so presented to the new Secretary of State and the two Privy Councillors most recently sworn to advise the King, and most deeply interested in providing for his ultimate safety by the advice they gave, all must yet be conjecture as to the probable course they took. But it is impossible to exclude from consideration the fact, which Clarendon repeatedly admits, that they agreed thoroughly with the King as to the guilt of the accused, and never placed on higher grounds than those of "con-" "venience" and expediency their objection to the attempted arrest.* We are to remember also that the objection was not publicly ex-

{margin: What the new Ministers thought of the guilt of the accused.}

---

* In the very passage where he ventures on the strongest expression of doubt and apprehension as to the course taken by the King (remarking that he and his friends, between grief and anger, were confounded with the consideration of what had been done and what was like to follow), he nevertheless thus continues: "They were far from thinking that "the accused members had received much wrong; yet they "thought it an unseasonable time to call them to account for "it. That if anything had been to be done of that kind, "there should have been a better choice of the persons, there "being many of the House of more mischievous inclinations "and designs against the King's person and the Government, "and were more exposed to the public prejudice, than the "Lord Mandeville Kimbolton was . . . Then Sir Arthur "Haselrig and Mr. Strode were persons of so low an account "and esteem . . . that they gained credit and authority by "being joined with the rest, who had indeed a great "influence. However, if there was a resolution to proceed "against those men, it would have been much better to have "caused them to have been all severally arrested, and sent "to the Tower, or to other prisons, which might have been "very easily done before suspected, than to send in that "manner to the Houses with that formality which would be "liable to so many exceptions."

{margin: What Falkland, Culpeper, and Hyde would have done with the Five Members: Seized them separately, and sent each to a different prison.}

pressed until after the attempt had issued in complete disaster; that it was then accompanied by other statements too grossly at variance with the known facts not necessarily to subject it to grave suspicion; and that the very person on whose single assurance posterity has been content to believe it, is the same whose pen was employed by the King to justify the very act objected to. Within a few days after its occurrence, Hyde, replying in the name of Charles to the City petition, vindicates it as "a gentle" proceeding against men who had been accused on the clearest grounds of high treason; for that, in such a case, as it was notorious that no privilege of Parliament could extend to treason, felony, or breach of the peace, and as, in despite thereof,* the House

marginalia: Objection to arrest only after its failure. Hyde employed to justify it. Misrepresentation of the case.

---

* The answer to the City petition will be found in *Hist.* ii. 149. "For his going to the House of Commons, when "his attendants were no otherwise armed than as gentle- "men with swords, he was persuaded, that if they knew "the clear grounds upon which those persons stood ac- "cused of high treason, and [what would be proved against "them, with which they should be in due time acquainted, "and considered the gentle way he took for their appre- "hension (which he preferred before any course of violence, "though that way had been very justifiable; since it was "notoriously known that no privilege of parliament can "extend to treason, felony, or breach of the peace), they "would believe his going thither was an act of grace and "favour to that House, and the most peaceable way of having "that necessary service performed; there being such orders "made for the resistance of what authority soever for their "apprehension." It is difficult to steer through the involutions of these sentences, but to discover their drift is not difficult. Somewhat later, when it had ceased to be safe to urge the guilt of treason against the accused as entirely clear and capable of proof, quite another colour was sought to be

marginalia: "Gentleness" of King's attempt alleged by Clarendon. An act of favour.

§ xv. *Council of the Night of 3rd January.*

of Commons had made order for resistance of the apprehension of their members against all authority whatsoever, "any course of violence had been very justifiable."

Let me add that when Clarendon, speaking in his proper person,* repeats this argument, and states that the leaders claimed immunity against even regular proceedings upon the charge of treason, he practises largely indeed upon the carelessness or credulity of his readers. "For if," he says, "the judges had been compelled to deliver their opinions in point of law, which they ought to have been, they could not have avoided the declaring that by the known law, which had been confessed in all times and ages, no privilege of Parliament could extend in the case of treason; but that every Parliament-man was then in the condition of every other subject, and to be proceeded against accordingly."

margin: No privilege claimed against treason.

margin: False issue raised.

---

given to the fatal act. "We put on," Charles is made to say, (Husband, *Coll.* 246) "a sudden resolution to try whether our own presence, and a clear discovery of our intentions, which haply might not have been so well understood, could remove their doubts, and prevent those inconveniences which seemed to have been threatened; and thereupon we resolved to go in our own person to our House of Commons, which we discovered not till the very minute we were going, the bare doing of which we did not then conceive could have been thought a breach of privilege," &c. &c. William Lily, characterising Charles the First's style, describes exactly that of Clarendon: "He would write his mind singularly well, and in good language and style; only he loved long parentheses." It is scarcely necessary to add, that, in the style of instances just quoted at least, the parentheses are Clarendon's. —See *Life*, 130-133.   * *Hist.* ii. 193.

margin: Another sketch from same hand.

margin: The King's writing.

Indemnity from treason never claimed: He knew perfectly well, when he wrote this passage, that the House of Commons had solemnly disclaimed the views and pretensions here attributed to them; and that the real point, from which he always studiously manages to carry off the attention of his readers, turns upon the breach of privilege and gross breach of all *Method of* common as well as constitutional law, involved, *proceeding only objected to.* not in charging members of Parliament with treason, but in the mode adopted to give effect to such a charge.

It is surely no very harsh assumption, seeing how soon these arguments were resorted to in vindication, that some such arguments might also have been debated on the memorable night of the 3rd of January, when it is known that Falkland and Culpeper were certainly with the King; when they had been sworn so recently of his Council; and when the question was no longer whether the rash attempt should be made, but whether it should be wholly abandoned by abandonment of all *Culpeper's confidence to Dering:* further authority. That Sir Edward Dering had derived from the new Chancellor of the Exchequer, Sir John Culpeper, his colleague in the representation of Kent, the information that shortly before the Chancellorship was conferred upon himself it had been offered *Charles's trust in his new counsellors.* to Pym, seems hardly to admit of doubt; and the mere fact of the new ministers possessing this information, carries other presumptions with it inconsistent with the notion that they had failed as yet to obtain the real confidence of the King. Such most certainly was not the impression at the time. When Clarendon complains that himself, Falkland, and Culpeper, could not avoid being looked upon as the authors of those counsels to which they were so absolute strangers, and which they so perfectly "detested;" when he expresses his vexation that they continued to be pointed at as the "contrivers;" he at least exhibits what was a prevailing belief, and one which a partizan and servant of the King, in a grave account of the period, has distinctly sanctioned. When, on the other hand, in almost the same page of his History, Clarendon declares that "the three persons," Falkland, Culpeper, and himself, believed in the guilt of the accused, and only thought it would have been far better to have caused them to have been all severally arrested and sent to the Tower or to other prisons (which, he adds, if every circumstance had been fully deliberated, and the several parts distributed among such hands as would not have shaken in the execution, might have been very easily done), he supplies us with the means of testing, by a very accurate measure, the nature and amount of "detestation" with which the King's act had inspired these counsellors of the King. Let Falkland and Culpeper have all the advantage derivable from

Imputation against Hyde and his friends.

Believed to be "contrivers" of the arrest.

Their mode of objecting and denying:

no evidence of "detestation" of the deed:

having shared, at one and the same time, the deteftation at the ill-doing of it by the King, and the eagernefs to have had opportunity of doing it better themfelves. The prefent writer at leaft is convinced that if thefe men were not direct, they were indirect, parties to the deed that now waited to be done. If it failed, the King's cafe could not be more defperate than already it was become. If it fucceeded, and the leaders of the Majority in the Houfe of Commons were ftruck down, intimidation might be left to do its work upon their followers, the Minority which had rallied againft the Remonftrance might be gathered and reinforced under lefs troublefome leaders, and the Englifh people be led back into bondage by the very power which had effected their deliverance.

but rather proof of indirect participation.

Stake played for and loft.

§ XVI. Midnight Visit to the City.

Secretary Nicholas confulting late with the King.

One remarkable incident remains to be defcribed, which a document in the State Paper Office enables me to eftablifh, and which will probably be accepted for irrefragable proof that at leaft the King was in confultation with one of his principal Secretaries of State, Sir Edward Nicholas, late in the night of this 3rd January; and that the object of their deliberation muft have been, beyond all poffible queftion, to provide againft popular

Provifion againft tumults next day ;

§ XVI. *Midnight Visit to the City.*

tumults which there was special reason to look for on the following day, and to neutralize any measures taken by the House of Commons for defence against further and forcible aggression. To what extent the argument in the foregoing section receives confirmation from such an occurrence, every reader will be able to judge for himself, and will be better able to judge correctly when all its curious circumstances are told.

and against demand of Commons for Guard.

It has been seen that one of the last acts of the Commons before they broke up their sitting after the articles of impeachment were presented, was to send Pennington and Ven into the City with a request for a Guard out of the Trained Bands under the immediate order of the Chief Magistrate. Upon this being made known to the King, he thought himself strong enough to defeat it by a counter warrant to the Lord Mayor, and this was directed to be prepared accordingly. The rough draft of the warrant remains still among the Papers of the State. It is in the handwriting of Under Secretary Bere, and is corrected by Secretary Nicholas himself, sufficing proof of its authenticity. Such proof, indeed, it needed, for it is in its terms very damnatory evidence against the King and the King's counsellors. It is an instruction to the Chief Magistrate of London, not merely to refuse to the Commons the Guard they had desired, but in its place to

Order of House for City Train Bands.

Counter-warrant signed by the King.

Grave evidence against the Court.

enroll such a Guard for the royal service, with order for its immediate employment in suppressing and dispersing all tumults, disorders, and assemblages of the people in the streets of the City; and with express instruction to it, in case persons so assembling should refuse to retire to their houses peaceably, to fire upon them with loaded bullets.

Order to Train Bands to fire on the Citizens.

Happily for the King, this royal warrant remained *brutum fulmen*, and sees the light first in these pages; for, had the attempt been made to enforce it, London would in all probability have witnessed such a scene as must then have changed the entire subsequent course and aim of our English Revolution. Nor is the cause which interposed itself to prevent the attempt the least striking part of the story. Near the paper as it lies in our National Collection remains also the letter of the agent employed by Secretary Nicholas to carry it to Sir Richard Gourney. His instructions appear to have been to hasten with it into the City, to see the Lord Mayor, to urge upon him the necessity of immediately calling the Sheriffs to council (one of whom was known to be as strongly royalist as Gourney himself), to open and read it in their presence, and to give directions then and there for carrying it into effect. But the night was farther advanced than in the haste and eagerness had been supposed. The clocks at Whitehall had not kept good time.

Intercepted and not published until now.

Why not put in force.

Reached the City too late.

§ XVI. *Midnight Visit to the City.*

Mr. Latche the meſſenger found the Chief Magiſtrate in bed, and Ven and Pennington had been beforehand with him. In a word the project had failed, happily for all involved in it, moſt happily for the King. It is diſcovered only now, when two centuries have paſſed away, as one of the ſecrets of what might have been hiſtory, that late in the night of the 3rd of January, 1641-2, Charles the Firſt, in deliberation with his principal Secretary of State, had provided, in a certain and too probable contingency, itſelf the reſult of an excitement he was himſelf creating, for the firing with powder and bullet upon aſſemblages of his unarmed ſubjects in the ſtreets of the City of London.

Fortunate accident for the King.

What might have been hiſtory.

Thus ran the warrant: " To the Lord
" Maior of London. Right truſty and well-
" beloved Counſ^r. Wee underſtand that
" the House of Comons hath ſent to have
" Guard of the trained Bands of that O^r
" Citty. Foraſmuch as ſome of wch ſaid
" Houſe are lately accuſed of high treaſon,
" Our will and command is that you take
" eſpeciall care that none of Our trained bands
" be raiſed wthout ſpeciall warrant from us,
" and wee ſhall take in O^r royall care that
" nothing ſhall be don to the prejudice or
" diſturbance of O^r ſaid Citty, [wch we ſhall
" be as vigilant to keepe in quietnes as others
" are to engage & put into tumult and

Copy of the warrant.

Reference to Five Members.

"disorder *]: But in case you shall find any great numbers of people to assemble together in a tumultuary & disorderly manner w^{th}in O^r said Citty or the liberties thereof, Our will and command is that you then cause soe many of O^r trained bands to be raised as you shall thinke fitt, well armed and provided, and that you give order to suppresse all such tumults and disorders, and if they shall find resistance, and that the persons soe assembled shall refuse to retire to their houses peaceably, or to render y^mselves into the handes of justice, that then, for the better keeping of the peace, and preventing of further mischeefes, you command the Cap^{ts}, Officers, and Souldiers of our said trained bands, by shooting with bullets, or otherwayes, to suppresse those tumults, & destroy such of them as shall persist in their tumultuous wayes and disorders: For which this shall be yor warrant. Given, &c. 3rd Jan. 1641."

marginalia: Train Bands called out for the King. All gatherings of Citizens to disperse: On refusal to be fired upon.

And thus runs the letter which announced to Secretary Nicholas the failure of a mission which so temperate and discreet a minister must in his heart have wholly disapproved. It is addressed "To the Rt. Honorable Sir Edward Nicholas, Kn^{t.} Principal Secretary to his Matie att Court. Present these:" and is endorsed in cipher by Sir Edward himself.

marginalia: Letter of Nicholas's agent.

---

* The words in Brackets are interlined in the handwriting of Nicholas.

§ XVI. *Midnight Visit to the City.*

"Right Honorable,

"The Clocks att Whitehall laſt night went
"to late. The nighte was further ſpent than
"they ſhewed. My Lo. Major was in his
"bedd before I came thither. Yet I ſpake
"wth him & delivered the Letter: this
"morning he will call the ſheriffs to him &
"open it. This encloſed is a copie of the
"Order of the Houſe wch was brought unto
"him by Alderman Pennington and Captn
"Venn, who did much enlarge themſelves in
"diſcourſe thereupon, intimating great feares,
"but kept themſelves in ſuch generall termes,
"as the Order is, that their meanings were not
"eaſilie to be known. I was till One of the
"clock aboute the Tower, and found all
"places very well guarded, & the tumultuous
"rout diſperſed. If the King upon ſight of
"this Order ſhall direct anything otherwiſe
"than laſt night, my man ſhall attend to
"receive y^or comaunds & bring it *privatly*
"to me. In the meanetime I ſhall this morn-
"ing purſue yeſterday nighte's direction, and
"then attend you wth an Account of my pro-
"ceedings who ſhall and [ever] remaine

"Y^r humble ſervant

"*Strand 4th Jan.* 1641."   "JOHN LATCHE."

*[Side notes: Whitehall clocks behind the time. Anticipated by deputation from Commons. Paſt midnight at the Tower. Any further *private* commands?]*

Doubtleſs much was left unſaid in that letter, but what is ſaid leaves it ſufficiently clear that the members for London had in-

Inferences from agent's letter.

spired the Lord Mayor with a salutary general fear, which they were careful not to weaken by a too great explicitness. So the Court emissary was fain to betake himself to the Tower, to see at least that the Guards were all duly set and maintained about the great fortress. But why all this mystery and anxiety, why these untimely visits and alarms, if there were not expected to arise upon that January midnight a morning fraught with issues for good or ill of an unusual and important nature?

Preparations for the morrow.

Memorable day.

Nor did it indeed fall short of such expectation. As much as any day in the long course of our varied and noble history, did this memorable day of the 4th of January, 1641-2, contribute to turn the balance of events in favor of popular freedom.

§ XVII. Morning of the 4th of January.

House of Commons: Falkland reports King's message.

It was early in the morning when D'Ewes entered the House; but Lord Falkland had already reported the King's reply to their message of the preceding night, to the effect that he would send an answer that morning before the House was set. Still the answer was delayed, and, shortly after, D'Ewes took his seat. Mr. Alexander Rigby, the member for Wigan, a lawyer of Gray's Inn who afterwards sat upon the trial of the King, then rose and

§ XVII. *Morning of the 4th of January.*

made some significant comments on his Majesty's promised answer, in connection with certain messages which he alleged to have been sent round to the Inns of Court on the previous night, with copies of the articles of impeachment, and with injunctions to the gentlemen there "to be in "readiness this day to attend at Whitehall, "and to be ready at an hour's warning to "defend his Majesty's person." * . Mr. Rigby closed with a motion, which was adopted, that four members of that House, also members of the Inns, should on the instant proceed thither, and ascertain the facts by personal inquiry.

Motion as to King's tampering with Inns of Court.

Four members sent to the Four Inns.

Then, pursuant to the Order of the previous day, the House turned itself into a Grand Committee; and Pym, with the articles of treason in his hand, arose. He read the charges

Grand Committee.

---

* Harl. MSS. 162, f. 304 b. Ludlow has a characteristic anecdote and illustration in his *Memoirs*, (i. 21-22): "The "King, finding that nothing less would satisfy the Parl^t than "a thorow correction of what was amiss, & full security of "their rights from any violation for the future, considered "how to put a stop to their Proceedings: & to that end "encouraged a great number of loose debauched fellows "about the town to repair to Whitehall, where a constant "table was provided for their entertainment. Many gentle- "men of the Inns of Court were tamper'd with to assist him "in his design, and things brought to that pass that one of "them said publicly in my hearing—'What! shall we "'suffer these fellows at Westminster to domineer thus? "'Let us go into the country, and bring up our tenants to "'pull them out.' Which words not being able to bear, "I questioned him for them; and he, either out of fear of "the public justice, or of my resentment, came to me the "next morning, and asked pardon for the same: which, by "reason of his youth & want of experience, I passed by."

The table at Whitehall for gentlemen of Inns of Court.

A violent young lawyer.

M

successively, admitting frankly that they established treason if proved: but he so repeated them, to that eager and excited audience, as with the highest art of the orator to strike heavily against the Court itself with the very weapons aimed at the accused. "True, Mr. "Speaker," he said, "this present Parliament "hath adjudged it treason to endeavour to "subvert the fundamental laws of the land." No one could mistake that allusion. "Sir, "it hath likewise been voted high treason to "attempt to introduce into this kingdom a "form of government arbitrary and tyrannical." In what particular series of acts of State and of Council, such attempt consisted, the Remonstrance had lately spread and diffused all over the land. "Sir," he added, pausing at the third article which charged upon them the attempt to win over the King's Northern army to themselves, and so pointedly rewording it as to bring plainly before the House the recent proved conspiracy of the King's servants to overawe the deliberations of Parliament by means of that very army, "Sir, it is un- "doubtedly treason to raise an army to com- "pel any Parliament to make and enact laws "without their free votes and willing pro- "ceedings therein." A cry of stern satisfaction broke forth, as the orator so proceeded through each of the charges of treason.

Then, still earnestly declaring that each, if

[marginal notes:]
Pym replies to articles of treason.
Allusion to Strafford.
Charge of bringing over the army to the Parliament:
Less treasonable than overawing Parliament by army.

§ XVII.   *Morning of the 4th of January.*   163

established, might well justify the last penalties of its high offence, with a singular vividness he confronted it with the comment of the particular conduct in Parliament to which alone, in his own case, it could possibly apply. With severe simplicity he confined himself to the parallel in each instance, and he employed not an unnecessary phrase or word. Thus, as to the second article, he said, that if by free vote to join with the Parliament in publishing a Remonstrance against delinquents in the State; against incendiaries between his Majesty and his kingdom; against ill-counsellors, who labored to avert his Majesty's affection from Parliament; and against ill-affected Bishops for their innovations in religion, their oppression of painful, learned, and godly ministers, their vexatious suits in their unjust courts, their cruel sentences of pillory and mutilation, their great fines, banishments, and perpetual imprisonments—if *that* were to cast aspersions upon his Majesty and his government, and to alienate the hearts of his loyal subjects, good Protestants and well-affected in religion, from their due obedience to his Royal Majesty, then did he avow himself guilty of that article. If it were to levy arms against the King, he continued, to consent by vote with the Parliament to raise a Guard of Trained Bands to secure and defend the persons of the members thereof, being environed and beset with many

[sidenotes: Comparisons invited. Avows publication of Remonstrance. Accepts the guilt and responsibility. As to charge of levying arms against King.]

dangers, then was he guilty alſo of that act of treaſon. And further, if it were to be a traitor, to agree with the chief Council of the State in apprehending and attaching as delinquents ſuch perſons as they knew to be diſaffected to the King's crown and dignity, to his wife and great Council of Parliament, to the pure and ſimple doctrine of Chriſt, to the true and orthodox government of the Church of England as eſtabliſhed and confirmed by many Acts of Parliament in the reigns of Henry, Edward, and Elizabeth Tudor, and of King James of bleſſed memory, in that reſpect alſo he avowed himſelf to be guilty.

Apprehending delinquents.

Guilty of defending Chriſt's doctrine and orthodox church government.

Then, in concluſion, having thus ſeparately contraſted, under the ſeven ſeveral heads of treaſon, his actions with the accuſations againſt him, Pym craved of the Houſe that it ſhould further weigh both reſpectively in the even ſcales of its wiſdom, and he doubted not of being found altogether clear of the crimes laid to his charge. He was reſuming his ſeat amid loud ſhouts of "Well moved," "Well moved," when he ſtopped a moment, again advanced towards the Clerk's table, and, while a ſudden ſilence fell upon the Houſe, humbly craved Mr. Speaker's further patience to offer to his conſideration, whether to exhibit articles of treaſon by his Majeſty's own hands in that Houſe agreed with the rights and privileges thereof; and whether for an armed Guard to

Judgment deſired from the Houſe.

" Well moved."

A further and ominous queſtion.

§ XVII.   *Morning of the 4th of January.*   165

beset the doors of the House during such Has not breach of privilege been committed?
accusation of any of the members thereof,
were not a grave breach of the privilege of
Parliament? The last question had a pregnant
meaning on the morning of this eventful day,
but its full significance was still to come.

 Upon Pym resuming his seat, Hollis, Hasel- Hollis, Haselrig, and Strode defend themselves.
rig, and Strode rose afterwards in succession,
and in the brief phrase of D'Ewes, "protested
"their innocency." Strode further declared
his belief that the Impeachment was not
directed against them upon any supposition of Strode's speech.
their being really guilty of the matters charged,
but merely to compel their absence from debate; and he warned the House, that if,
under pretence of trial, they were to be arrested
and taken thence, they would never be proceeded against legally, but be simply by force
cut off. Haselrig alone expressly avowed Haselrig's speech.
that he was conscious of that part of the
charge on which the King solely relied for
any vestige of evidence in proof of it. After
declaring that anything in the nature of a
hostile attack aimed against the privileges of
Parliament, constituted one of the worst kinds
of treason, or of attempts to subvert the funda-
mental laws, he averred that his acts, and those Haselrig's reference to Scottish treason.
of the gentlemen with him, *particularly with
reference to Scotland*, had been in perfect accordance, upon every occasion, with votes and
resolutions of that House; and that the charge

of promoting tumults and infurrection was utterly groundlefs.

Hampden fpeaks. Hampden next arofe. His fpeech was more ftriking; it was indeed fingularly impreffive; and in the fragment afcertainable yet of what actually was faid by the member for Bucks, there is affuredly nothing that in any way confirms or countenances thofe manifeft interpolations in the publifhed fpeech attributed to him which led Mr. Southey to characterize it as an *Juftifies refiftance.* avowal of flavifh obedience! It might, on the contrary, almoft feem as though his tone were exprefsly affumed to render impoffible any fuch imputation. As if, in a fingle fentence, he would anticipate and overthrow the whole miferable doctrine of Sir Robert Filmer and his followers, Hampden at once declared to the Houfe, on rifing, that he underftood it to be *Ill and difloyal, good and loyal, fubjects.* the fign of an ill and a difloyal fubject, if a man fhould yield obedience to the commands of a King when thefe were againft the true religion and againft the ancient and fundamental laws of the land; whereas a good and a loyal fubject was he, who, to a King commanding anything againft God's true worfhip and religion, or againft the ancient laws, denied obedience. One feems to hear that calm, clear *Unaccuftomed emotion.* voice, troubled and fhaken with a paffion to which it was unaccuftomed, in this plain affertion of the doctrine of Refiftance.

But what, then, was the true religion? I

§ XVII. *Morning of the 4th of January.*

find it, said Hampden, in my Bible. "By
"searching the sacred writings of the New
"and Old Testament, we may prove whether
"our religion be of God or no, and by look-
"ing in that glass discern whether we are in
"the right way or no. In these two Testa-
"ments are contained all things necessary to
"salvation; and then only is our religion true,
"when that it doth hang upon this truth of
"God, and no other secondary means. Nearest
"thereunto cometh the Protestant religion, as
"I really and verily believe; teaching us that
"there is but one God, one Christ, one faith,
"one religion, which is the Gospel of Christ
"and the doctrine of His prophets and
"apostles. That other religion, therefore,
"which joineth with this doctrine of Church
"and His apostles the traditions and inven-
"tions of men, strange and superstitious wor-
"shipings, prayers to the Virgin Mary, to
"angels, and to saints, cringing and bowing
"and creeping to the altar, cannot, I say, be
"true, but is erroneous, nay devilish. All
"which being used and maintained in the
"Church of Rome to be as necessary as the
"Scripture to salvation, that Church is there-
"fore a false and erroneous Church, both in
"doctrine and discipline—a false worshiping
"of God, and not the true religion."

Where Hampden looked for true religion.

The two Testaments.

The Protestant Church true.

Bible alone needful to salvation.

Traditions and superstitions devilish.

The Romish Church false.

Very solemn and memorable words to have been spoken on such an occasion, containing in themselves, and promulgating for all, not merely a creed that men may live by, but a belief they will cheerfully die for. It is given to few among the sons of men to see the future in the instant, but Hampden was of the few. His manner at this eventful time, too, gave added weight to his words, which appear less to have impressed the lighter members and Royalists, indeed, this particular day, than the sudden and decisive change in the look and tone of him who uttered them. The mildness had for ever passed away. A fixed and stern resolution had replaced the old conciliatory bearing, and now truly might his enemies see, what Sir Philip Warwick tells us the scurf commonly on his face shewed plainly enough,* that beneath the quiet and seeming passionless self-control which he was able ordinarily to assume, lay a very sharp and acrimonious temper of the blood.

A creed to live by and die for.

Hampden's change of bearing.

Secrets of his character revealed.

They might have discovered or suspected it before. If Hampden had not until now assumed this uncompromising tone, if he had not earlier spoken thus, it was simply that before now the need had not shown itself, and the time for so speaking had not come. Clarendon charges him with begetting many notions the education of which he committed to

Waiting his time.

Charges by Hyde and D'Ewes.

---

* In speaking of his death at Chalgrove. The hurt, Sir Philip says, was not in itself mortal; but it was rendered so by the acrimonious condition of his blood, "as the scurfe " commonly on his face shewed."—*Memoirs*, 239.

§ XVII.   *Morning of the 4th of January.*   169

other men, and with leaving his own opinions with those from whom he pretended to learn and receive them.* D'Ewes attributes to him a "serpentine subtlety" which brought anything to pass that he desired, and "did still put others to move those businesses that himself contrived."† But these, as on a former occasion has been pointed out, are the imperfect and prejudiced judgments of a character whose very strength of self-reliance, self-containment, and silence, invited that kind of misconstruction. Upon no man of this great period, I would repeat, are so unmistakeably impressed the qualities which set apart the high-bred English gentleman, calm, courteous, reticent, self-possessed; yet with a persuasive force so irresistible, and a will and energy so indomitable, lying in those silent depths, that all who came within their reach came also under their control.

<small>"Serpentine subtlety."</small>

<small>Imperfect and prejudiced judgments.</small>

<small>What Hampden was.</small>

These are qualities which no craft however dexterous, and no subtlety the most serpentine, can in any manner or degree supply. When Clarendon, after taxing even his ingenuity to draw a bill of indictment against Hampden, ends by speaking of him as not only a very wise man and of great parts,‡ and who laid his designs deepest,§ but who had a great sagacity

<small>Admissions of Clarendon.</small>

---

* *Hist.* iv. 92—93.
† *Harl. MSS.* 163, f. 691 b.
‡ *Hist.* iv. 91.
§ *Hist.* i. 323.

in difcerning men's natures and manners, and was poffeffed with the moft abfolute fpirit of popularity, that is, the moft abfolute faculties to govern the people, of any man he ever knew; * he affigns to him the higheft form of power a ftatefman can poffefs. The richeft gifts are wafted in that direction, wanting this. To make the fpoils of differing intellects its own, to draw ftrength from the weakneffes of men, to affimilate the moft varied experiences, to render every mind it touches tributary, is to have that which the utmoft accomplifhment in eloquence, in learning, or in public affairs will fail to give, and which conftitutes pre-eminently a leader and governor of men.

Higheft power of ftatefman-fhip.

A leader and governor of men.

Nor was it that any lefs fupreme temper, or inferior felf-command, had appeared in Hampden as he repelled the King's charge of treafon, but fimply that what before was not called for had become neceffary now, and as the occafion rofe he rofe along with it. After the accufation of Treafon, fays the hiftorian of the Rebellion, Mr. Hampden was much altered; his nature and carriage† feeming

Change in Pym as well as

---

* *Hift.* iv. 91-92. Again (ii. 15) he fays of him: "He hath been mentioned before as a man of great underftanding and parts, and of great fagacity in difcerning men's natures and manners; and he muft upon all occafions ftill be mentioned as a perfon of great dexterity and abilities, and equal to any truft or employment, good or bad, which he was inclined to undertake."

Equal to anything.

† This is undoubtedly Clarendon's word, though Mr. Hallam ftrangely mifquotes it as "courage." *Conft. Hift.* ii. 127.

§ XVII. *Morning of the 4th of January.* 171

much fiercer than before. So also did he say Hampden after accusation of treason.
of Hampden's friend and fellow-labourer Pym.
From the time, too, of *his* being accused of
high treason by the King, he never entertained
thoughts of moderation, but always opposed All thoughts of moderation gone.
all overtures of peace and accommodation.*
They both saw, what men of such sagacity could
now hardly fail to see, that the armed struggle
was at hand, that it must be fought out to its
last issue, and that when, in defence of the Law
and Religion they so prized, the sword was No compromise possible.
once drawn, the scabbard must be flung away.

And so, to the close of what yet remained of
the lives they had given up freely to their country, these great men went in perfect harmony A memorable friendship.
together. They shared the same beliefs and
purposes, the same hopes and resolves, the
same enemies and friends, in common to the
end. Nor was it otherwise than well, remarked Remark to Hyde.
Hampden to Hyde when they next met in
the House after the incidents of this 4th of
January, that himself and Pym should hereafter Advantage of knowing one's friends.
know who *were* their friends. The trouble
which had befallen them had at least been
attended with that benefit; and he said also,
" very snappishly" adds Mr. Hyde (an expression that reveals himself if it fails to exhibit

---

* *Hist.* iv. 441. In another passage he says of Pym that Pym greatest in House of Commons.
" though in private designing he was much governed by Mr.
" Hampden, yet he seemed to all men to have the greatest
" influence upon the House of Commons of any man."
iv. 438.

Mr. Hampden), that he well knew Mr. Hyde had a mind they should both be in prison.*

Such, however, was not the mind of the House of Commons. Undaunted amid the perils that surrounded them, they at once resolved, upon the last of the accused members resuming his seat, to desire a conference with the Lords to acquaint them that a scandalous paper had been published, and to require their help in instituting inquiry who were the authors and publishers of the said scandalous paper, to the end that they might receive condign punishment, and the Commonwealth be secured against such persons. The *scandalous paper* was the Articles of Impeachment which the King had published by the hands of his Attorney-General.

Conference with the Lords demanded.

Impeachment denounced as a scandalous paper.

---

* This anecdote is in Hyde's *Life*, (i. 103), and his mode of telling it is still to mix up with it a purposed and deliberate misrepresentation of the real matter in issue. "Though "they," he says, referring to Hampden and Pym, "had a "better opinion of his discretion than to believe he had any "share in the advice of the late proceedings, yet they were "very willing that others should believe it; and made all the "infusions they could to that purpose amongst those who took "their opinions from them: towards which his known friend- "ship with the Lord Digby was an argument very prevalent: "and then his opposing the votes upon their privilege had "inflamed them beyond their temper; insomuch as Mr. "Hampden told him one day, that the trouble that had "lately befallen them had been attended with that benefit, "that they knew who were their friends: and the other "offering to speak upon the point of privilege, and how "monstrous a thing it was to make a vote so contrary to the "known law, he replied very snappishly, 'that he well knew "'he had a mind they should be all in prison;' and so "departed without staying for an answer." Hampden might well turn upon his heel and move silently away, for reasons far other than those imputed to him.

Hampden and Pym as to "discretion" of Mr. Hyde.

"Snappishness" of Mr. Hampden.

§ XVII. *Morning of the 4th of January.*

Another object of the Conference (of which Fiennes, Glyn, the younger Vane, and Hotham were named managers), D'Ewes adds, was to call immediate attention to the King's Guard at Whitehall, as not the lefs alfo " a breach of our privilege," and interruption to the freedom of debate. This is the firft hint he gives of any immediate alarm; and though there is little doubt, as will fhortly appear, that Pym had received notice the previous night of fome fpecific and violent defign in contemplation, he was not, as it would feem, made aware of the King's refolve to take part in it himfelf.* Clarendon fpeaks of a compofednefs appearing, during the events of this remarkable day, in the countenances of many who ufed to be difturbed at lefs furprifing occurrences; and this doubtlefs was an indication that the Houfe generally had been placed upon its guard. But its forced calmnefs was put to fevere tefts. " It was now generally " declared," fays D'Ewes, " that there was a " great confluence of armed men about White- " hall, and that between thirty and forty " canoneers went yefternight into the Tower " at ten of the clock. Alfo that the Hamlet " men, who were to be ordinary warders " there, had no arms given them: but that " the Bifhops' men were well armed.† Mr.

The Whitehall Guard an interruption to free debate.

Compofednefs of the leaders of the Commons.

Gatherings of armed men near the Houfe.

---

* *Hift.* ii. 128.
† *Harl. MSS.* 162, f. 304 b. Ten of my Lords the

Pym moves a deputation to City.

"Pym moved that we might send notice of these several informations and dangers into the city, to the Lord Mayor, Aldermen, and Common Council there assembled, and to let them know in what danger the Parliament was: all which was ordered accordingly."* And, for execution of the order, Alderman Sir Thomas Soame was joined to the two members, Pennington and Ven, who had so ably discharged themselves of the message of the House on the preceding day; "and they were,"

Deputation departs.

says D'Ewes, "sent instantly away into the City." In such haste, indeed, that a material point was forgotten. "After they were gone out, Mr. Peard" (the same who moved the printing of the Remonstrance) "was sent after them, to require them to let no man know

No man to know its errand.

their errand till they came into the City."†

Still there were members anxious that more should be done, as the rumour of what was preparing in Whitehall took more and more palpable shape. "Mr. Nathaniel Fiennes and

Alarm still increasing.

others," says D'Ewes, "moved that some members of this House might be sent to observe what numbers of armed men were about Whitehall, and to know by what authority they were assembled there: but this

Adjournment for an hour.

order was not fully agreed upon, when we adjourned the House, about 12 of the clock,

Bishops, it will be remembered, were at this time lodged, with of course all due attendance, in the Tower.
* *Harleian MSS.* 162, f. 305 b. † *Ib.*

" till one of the clock in the afternoon—for an
" hour's space."

§ XVIII. Betrayal of the Secret.

Momentous was the hour during which *A momentous interval.* the House thus adjourned its sitting, for within that brief space all the King's intention was betrayed. Up to the time of the adjournment, grave as were the causes of alarm, and the grounds for expecting some act of violence, the circumstance which gave its utmost gravity to the outrage contemplated does not appear to have been in any degree suspected even remotely. But now it was that Lady Carlisle *Lady Carlisle betrays all to Pym.* managed to convey to Pym that the King meant to put himself at the head of those Whitehall desperadoes, and in person to demand, and if necessary seize, the accused members as they sat in their places in the House of Commons. D'Ewes tells us that, " this day at
" dinner,"* the five members also received a secret communication of the King's intention *Private message from Lord Essex.* from the Lord Chamberlain of the household, Lord Essex, with advice that they should absent themselves.

Nevertheless that does not appear to have been their first intention. The Speaker re- *House reassembles: half-past one.* sumed his chair, says D'Ewes, between one and two o'clock, and the four selected members who,

* *Harl. MSS.* 162, f. 306 b.

by order of the Houfe in the morning, had been difpatched to the Inns of Court, rofe and made brief report of their miffion. Mr. Richard Brown, of Lincoln's Inn, the member for Romney, ftated " that he had done the mef-
" fage of the Houfe to the gentlemen of that
" fociety, whofe anfwer was, that they had at
" firft gone to the Court laft week only upon
" occafion of a report brought to them that
" the King's perfon was in danger: That
" yefternight they had received a meffage from
" his Majefty by Sir W^m· Killigrew and Sir
" W^m· Fleming, that they fhould keep within
" this day, and be ready at an hour's warning
" if his Majefty fhould have occafion to ufe
" them : That they brought likewife a paper
" of articles to them, by which the Lord
" Mandeville and five members of the Houfe
" of Commons were accufed of High Treafon :
" That they had only an intent to defend the
" King's perfon, and would likewife to their
" uttermoft alfo defend the Parliament, being
" not able to make any diftinction between
" King and Parliament: And that they would
" ever exprefs all true affection to the Houfe
" of Commons in particular." Mr. William Ellis, of Gray's Inn, the member for Bolton, next rofe, and " made the like relation " from that fociety. So, from the Inner Temple, did Mr. Roger Hill, member for Bridport, and who fat afterwards in judgment on the King. And

§ XVIII. *Betrayal of the Secret.*

so, finally, did Mr. Philip Smith, member for Marlborough, report from the Middle Temple; with the difference that this Society sent their reply in writing, and desired it should be added that their intention to defend the King's person was no more than they were thereunto bound by the oaths of allegiance and supremacy. "With which several answers from the Inns "of Court," D'Ewes adds, the House rested exceedingly well satisfied.

and from Middle Temple.

The House satisfied.

Then rose Nathaniel Fiennes, and, in proof that the royal messages to the learned societies just related were but part of a scheme which was under the same direction, and which depended for its execution on the armed assemblages in the vicinity of the House, "made relation "that he had been at Whitehall, and had asked "of one of the officers by what authority they "were there assembled, who answered that they "were commanded to obey Sir Wm Fleming "in all things that he should enjoin them." The member for Banbury was still speaking when Pym, Hampden, Hollis, Haselrig, and Strode entered and took their seats, whereupon the Speaker directed it to be entered in the Journals that they had done so.*

Armed crowds gathering nearer.

Re-entrance of the Five Members.

Communication was now made to the House of the secret intelligence received, and then followed a debate, brief and pressing, but

The Secret disclosed to the House.

---

* See *Commons' Journals*, ii. 368, where the entry still stands.

on which hung certain iſſues by which the future deſtinies of England were probably de-

Should the accuſed retire or remain? termined. Should the accuſed retire, or wait the King's arrival? Pym, Hollis, and Hampden, conſcious of all the danger, appear to have been for quitting the Houſe, Haſelrig and Strode for remaining; and the dſſentients were ſtill urging reaſons againſt retreat while yet, as they argued, no poſitive knowledge was before them of a neceſſity for abrupt departure, when

A new actor on the ſcene. a new actor came ſuddenly on the ſcene. Breathleſs with the exertion he had made to reach the Houſe rapidly, to which end he had even clambered over the roofs of neighbouring buildings,*there appeared at the door a friend of Nathaniel Fiennes, an officer of French birth ſettled in England, by name Captain Hercule Langres. Fiennes left his ſeat, exchanged ſome haſty words with the unexpected viſitor, and immediately paſſed up to Mr.

Lenthal announces King's approach. Speaker's chair: upon which Lenthal roſe and abruptly told the Houſe, now a ſcene of extraordinary excitement, that the King already had left Whitehall at the head of a large company of armed men, and was approaching Weſtminſter Hall.

Chronicler Heath. * *Harl. MSS.* 162, f. 310 b. Heath ſays (*Brief Chronicle*, p. 39) that Langres was a ſervant of the Queen. He declares alſo that the accuſed members were not able to get into the City on the night of the attempted arreſt, ſuch was the excitement prevailing; and that they lay hid all that night in the King's Bench Court, and did not find refuge in the City till next day. But nothing that Heath ſays is worthy of credit unleſs well corroborated by better teſtimony.

This closed debate. The motion before the House had been, that, considering there was an intention to remove five of their members by force, to avoid all tumult let them be commanded to absent themselves: but the motion now substituted, and at once affirmed, was that the House give their members leave to absent themselves, but enter no order for it. "It was "a question," Haselrig afterwards said, "if we "should be gone; but the debate was shortened, "and it was thought fit for us, in discretion, "to withdraw. Away we went. The King "immediately came in, and was in the House "*before we got to the water.**" Not, however, until violence had been used. For, even then, Strode, "crying out that he knew himself "to be innocent, and that he would stay in the "House though he sealed his innocency with "his blood at the door,"† had to be dragged bodily out by his friend Sir Walter Earle, and placed in the barge which had been hastily provided, and was in waiting at the Westminster stairs.

Leave to Five Members to absent themselves.

Away to the City by water.

Strode resists, and is dragged out.

§ XIX. THE KING'S APPROACH TO THE HOUSE.

MEANWHILE Charles and his companions had well-nigh reached the lobby of the House of Commons.

The King's attendants.

In the declaration of breach of privilege

---

* Burton's *Diary,* iii. 93.
† *Harl. MSS.* 162, f. 306 b.

As to their subsequently issued, it is stated that the number
number
and arms: of armed men who accompanied the King was
five hundred : nor does the King, in his reply,
dispute this, though he alleges that his own attendants were no otherwise armed than as gentlemen with swords. The remark pointed only
to his immediate Guard and Pensioners ; but
nothing was afterwards more distinctly proved
than that the bulk of the force who followed carried fire-arms as well. Here are the witnesses.

Testimony Sir Ralph Verney states, that, beside his
of Sir
Ralph usual Guard and all his Pensioners, his Majesty
Verney: was attended by two or three hundred soldiers
of Rush- and gentlemen.* Rushworth makes the same
worth: distinction between the royal guard of pensioners and halberdiers, and the miscellaneous
company who followed, and who constituted
the famous (or infamous) Whitehall Guard, of
commanders, Reformadoes,† and soldiers of
of Lud- fortune.‡ Ludlow, who might himself have
low: been (and probably was) an eye-witness, says
that Charles went attended not only with his
ordinary guard of pensioners, but also with
those desperadoes that for some time he had
entertained at Whitehall, to the number of
three or four hundred, armed with partizans,
of Thomas May: swords, and pistols.§ May, also a good au-

---

* *Notes*, p. 138.

Reformadoes. † A Reformado was an officer of a company disbanded, but whose own services had been retained as still belonging to the regiment of which his company had formed part.

‡ *Hist. Coll.* part III. i. 477. § *Memoirs*, i. 24.

§ XIX. *The King's Approach to the House.* 181

thority, puts down " the gentlemen soldiers
" and others armed with swords and pistols"
who were in immediate attendance on the
King, at the number of about three hundred.*
The wife of Colonel Hutchinson, implicitly to *of Mrs.*
be trusted as a witness, vouches likewise for the *Hutchinson:*
numbers that attended Charles as not less than
four hundred armed gentlemen and soldiers.†
D'Ewes, who shows the reverse of any wish *and of*
to exaggerate the circumstances, describes the *D'Ewes.*
attendant company as composed of "some offi-
" cers who served in his Majesty's late army and
" some other loose persons, to the number of
" about some four hundred."‡ Yet Clarendon, *Clarendon*
writing at a time when he had little need to *contradicts all:*
fear contradiction, has the inconceivable assurance to ask even his readers to believe, that it
was " *visible to all men* that the King had only *relating*
" with him his Guard of halberdiers, and fewer *what was " visible*
" of them than used to go with him upon *to all."*
" any ordinary motion ; and that fewer of his
" gentlemen servants were then with him, than
" usually attended him when he went but to
" walk in the park, and had only their little
" swords ! " §

But let us further hear Captain Slingsby on
this point, which goes indeed to the root of *Slingsby's*
the matter. Writing to Pennington on the *account to Penning-*

---

* *Hist.* lib ii. cap. ii. 21.
† Col. Hutchinson's *Memoirs*, 76.
‡ *Harl. MSS.* 162, f. 306 a.   § *Hist.* ii. 137-138.

6th of January,* the second day after the attempted arrest, he makes special mention of "the multitude of gentry and soldiers that had lately flocked to the Court." Never in his life, he remarks, had he seen it so thronged as it then was: and the effect had been to such an extent to terrify the Citizens, that they no longer appeared about Whitehall, from apprehension of the rough entertainment they were like to receive if they came again. But, he says, after thus describing the armed crowds in the King's palace, there had suddenly arisen something to breed expectation of troubles far transcending anything caused by the Westminster Hall tumults; and then, he continues, "all partes "of the Court being thronged with gentlemen

---

* MS. State Paper Office. The letter is dated, in manifest error, the 6th of December. It opens with the subjoined account of the articles of impeachment, as handed in the preceding day. "On Monday last the King's Attorney "did impeach the Lord Mandevill, and Mſſrs Pim, Hollis, "Strowd, Hamden, & Sr Arthur Haſlrigge, of High Treaſon, "in the Upper Houſe. The ſumme of the articles were sub- "verting the fundamentall lawes, placing ſubiects in arbitrary "& tirannicall government, calling in a forraigne army, "endeavouring to draw the King's army from his obedience, "depriving the King of his royall power, laying fals aſper- "ſions againſt the King to make him odious, countenancing "tumults againſt the King & Parliament, forcing the Parlia- "ment by terror to joyne with them, ſubverting the rights "& very being of Parliaments, practiſing to rayſe warre & "actually rayſing warr againſt the King: This charge was "ſent downe to the Comons houſe, who received it with the "tearme of a ſcandalous paper. A Serieant-at-Armes ſent "likewiſe to attach them, but was refuſed. Their cloſſetts "by the King's comaund ſealed up, but the ſame night, by "order from the Houſe, opened againe: the next day ſome of "them, notwithſtanding their impeachment, came and ſatt in "the Houſe."

§ XIX. *The King's Approach to the House.*

"and officers of the army, in the afternoone the King WENT WITH THEM ALL, his own Guard, and the Penfioners:" expreffly adding that by far the moft part, among whom he then and there had taken his own place, were " arm'd with fwords and piftolls." Such was Hyde's innocent party, and their harmlefs accoutrement, when they fet out on this famous expedition!

<small>Slingfby one of the King's company.</small>

<small>How innocently armed.</small>

Peaceful and innocent as they were, however, with their " little fwords," as Mr. Hyde ingenuoufly defcribes them, in their brief journey from Whitehall they had managed to carry difmay at every ftep; and, as they neared Weftminfter Hall, D'Ewes tell us, " it ftruck " fuch a fear and terrour into all thofe that " kept fhops in the faid Hall, or near the " gate thereof, as they inftantly fhut up their " fhops, looking for nothing but bloodfhed " and defolation."* Having reached the gate, the armed band formed fuddenly into a lane, ranging themfelves on either fide along the whole length of the Hall; and Charles, paffing through this lane, and entering the door at the fouth-eaft angle, afcended the ftairs into the Commons' Houfe. His armed company clofed up, and as many as could prefs in crowded after him. The King's command had been, according to Sir Ralph Verney and

<small>Difmay at their approach.</small>

<small>Shops fhut up.</small>

<small>The King paffes through Weftminfter Hall.</small>

---

* *Harl. MSS.* 162, f. 310 a.

Captain Slingſby, himſelf one of the company, that the great body ſhould ſtay in the Hall; but, ſays D'Ewes, "his Majeſty coming into the lobby, a little room juſt without the Houſe of Commons, divers officers of the late army in the North, and other deſperate ruffians, preſſed in after him to the number of about four ſcore, beſides ſome of his penſioners."* Captain Slingſby's account quite bears out D'Ewes. "When," he writes,† "we came into Weſtminſter Hall, wᶜʰ was thronged with the number, the King commanded us all to ſtay there; and himſelfe, with a ſmall trayne, went into the Houſe of Commons, where never King was (as they ſay), but once King Henry the Eight."

Lobby of Houſe of Commons ſuddenly filled.

Armed men ſtill preſs from without.

Charles enters the Houſe

where never king was but once.

§ XX. THE HOUSE ENTERED BY THE KING.

WITHIN the Houſe, meanwhile, but a few minutes had elapſed ſince the Five Members departed, and Mr. Speaker had received inſtruction to ſit ſtill with the mace lying before him, when a loud knock threw open the door, a ruſh of armed men was heard, and above it (as we learn from Sir Ralph Verney) the voice of the King commanding "upon their lives not to come in."‡ The moment after, followed only by his nephew Charles, the Prince

Voice of Charles heard as he enters.

---

* *Harl. MSS.* 162, f. 306 b.
† MS. State Paper Office. Slingſby to Pennington, 6 Jan. 1641-2.
‡ *Notes,* p. 139.

§ xx.   *The House entered by the King.*   185

Elector Palatine, Rupert's eldest brother, he entered; but the door was not permitted to be closed behind him. Visible now at the threshold, were the officers and desperadoes above named, of whom, D'Ewes proceeds, "some had " left their cloaks in the Hall, and most of them " were armed with pistols and swords, and " they forcibly kept the door of the House of " Commons open, one Captain Hide * stand- " ing next the door holding his sword upright " in the scabbard:" † a picture which Sir Ralph Verney, also present that day in his place, completes by adding that " so the " doors were kept open, and the Earl of " Roxborough stood within the door, leaning " upon it." ‡

Armed followers visible outside.

Door kept forcibly open.

Captain Hide and Lord Roxborough.

As the King entered, all the members rose

---

* This Captain Hide, who thus, holding his sword upright in its scabbard, signified his and its readiness that day for any desperate deed, was the same David Hide, "a Reformado in the " late army against the Scots and now appointed to go in some " command into Ireland" (*Rushworth*, part iii. vol. i. 463), who, upon that disastrous day of the Lunsford tumults which had its appropriate issue in the first blood shed in this Great Civil War (that of Sir Richard Wiseman, a London Citizen, mortally hurt on the 27th December), took a leading part in the conflict in Westminster Hall, " buffled " against the Citizen apprentices whom the hot Welsh wrath of Archbishop Williams had especially provoked, and, drawing his sword with an oath, said "he'd cut the throats of those Round-headed Dogs that " bawled against Bishops:" which passionate expressions of his, Rushworth remarks, " as far as I could ever learn, was the " first miniting " [minting, or coinage] " of that term or " compellation of Roundheads which afterwards grew so " general." (See ante, 63, 137). Hide was afterwards cashiered from his Irish command by the House, but he reappeared in Merrick's Regiment during the Civil War.— See *Rushworth*, iii. 1247.

Captain Hide:

Prominent in Westminster tumults:

Cashiered and reappointed.

† *Harl. MSS.* 162, f. 307 a.   ‡ *Notes,* p. 139.

and uncovered, and the King also removed his hat; and it would not have been easy, says Rushworth, to discern any of the five members, had they been there, among so many bare faces standing up together. But there was One face, among the Five, which Charles knew too well not to have singled out even there; and hardly had he appeared within the chamber, when it was observed that his glance and his step were turned in the direction of Pym's seat close by the Bar. His intention, baffled by the absence of the popular leader, can only now be guessed at: but, Rushworth adds, "his Majesty, not seeing Mr. Pym there, " knowing him well, went up to the chair."* We all, says D'Ewes, stood up and uncovered our heads, and the Speaker stood up just before his chair. " His Majesty, as he came " up along the House, came the most part of " the way uncovered, also bowing to either " side of the House, and we all bowed again " towards him, and so he went to the Speaker's " chair on the left hand of it, coming up " close by the place where I sat, between the " south end of the Clerk's table and me."†
As he approached the chair, Lenthal stepped out to meet him; upon which " he first spake," says D'Ewes, saying, " Mr. Speaker, I must " for a time make bold with your chair."

* *Hist. Coll.* III. i. 477.
† *Harl. MSS.* 162, f. 306 a.

§ xx. *The House entered by the King.*

And then the King stepped up to his place and stood upon the step, but sat not down in the chair. And after he had looked a great while, he spoke again.

Looks long before he speaks.

A break here occurs in the narrative of D'Ewes. His relation for a while is interrupted; and a note afterwards written, and substituted for it, refers us to what was "taken in characters by the Clerk's "assistant." Perhaps the only person wholly quiet and unmoved during the extraordinary scene, unless it were that most impassive of note-takers, Sir Simonds himself, was this lately appointed Clerk's assistant, young Mr. Rushworth, who was observed, as he sat at the Clerk's table, busily taking down the words of the King, as they broke upon the sullen and "awe- "full" silence. His report, drawn out in the evening by command of the King, who had noticed him writing at the table, was published in a broadside next morning, and D'Ewes, finding the King's words therein more exactly given than by himself, makes a reference in his Journal to those parts of it; but his Majesty had directed an omission which D'Ewes is careful to supply in his own record, and only a portion of which (the words spoken by Lenthal) we find Rushworth to have appended in after years to the account

Break in narrative of D'Ewes.

One unmoved spectator of the scene.

Young Mr. Rushworth.

His report and description sent for by King.

Important corrections made therein.

Copy so corrected in State Paper Office:

preserved in his *Collections.** But, in addition to what is so supplied by the manuscript Journal of D'Ewes, I have been fortunate enough to find, in the State Paper Office, what appears to be the original copy of Rushworth's report of what was said by the King, as taken during the evening to the palace and

a help to more vivid reproduction of the scene.

corrected by Charles; and, though the corrections, trivial in themselves, serve chiefly to show the accuracy with which Rushworth had taken his notes, the erasures yet enable us exactly to mark the characteristic breaks that occurred, and more vividly to reproduce the actual scene.†

The King's speech to the House.

" Gentlemen," said Charles, " I am sorry
" for this occasion of coming unto you. Yes-
" terday I sent a Serjeant-at-Arms upon a very
" important occasion to apprehend some that
" by my command were accused of High
" Treason; whereunto I did expect obedience,

* *Hist. Coll.* III. i. 477-8.

† I subjoin an accurate copy of the portions in which the material corrections or erasures occur, with the latter printed in facsimile:

Rushworth's report of the speech, corrected by Charles.

that albeit
I must declare unto you here, noe king that ever was in
to
England, shall bee more Carefull (of yor priviledges) ~~not~~
mentaine them to the uttermost of his power then I shall
be
~~be doer~~ Yet you must know y^t in Cases of Treason noe
person hath a priviledge. And therefore I am come to

§ xx. *The House entered by the King.* 189

" and not a meſſage. And I muſt declare Expects
" unto you here, that albeit no King that traitors to be de-
" ever was in England ſhall be more careful livered up to him.
" of your privileges, to maintain them to the
" uttermoſt of his power, than I ſhall be,
" yet you muſt know that in caſes of Treaſon

know, if any of thoſe perſons that were accuſed are here.
Then caſting his eyes uppon all the Members in the Houſe Eraſure by the King.
ſaid, I doe not ſee any of them; I thinke I ſhould know
them.

For I muſt tell you Gentⁿ· that ſoe long as thoſe perſons that
I have accuſed (for noe ſlight crime, but for Treaſon)
are here, I cannot expect that this Houſe can bee in the right
way, that I doe heartily wiſh it: Therefore I am come to
tell you, that I muſt have them, whereſoever I finde them.

Then His Maᵗⁱᵉ ſaid is Mr. Pym here? to wᶜʰ noe Body Enquiry for Pym
gave any weare. alſo eraſed.
                    the
Well, ſince I ſee all ~~my~~ Birds are flowen I doe expect from
you, that you ſhall ſend them unto mee as ſoone as they
                but aſſeure
returne hither: ~~I muſt tell~~ you in the word of a king I never
did intend any force, but ſhall proceed agᵗ them in a legall &
                    meant
faire way; for I never ~~intended~~ any other.

And now ſince I ſee I cannot doe what I came for. I
thinke this is noe unfitt occaſion to Repeat what I have ſaid
formerly that whatſoever I have done in favour, and to the
                                                   ~~moſt~~
good of my ſubjects I do meane to mentaine it.

Arrest of the Five Members.

Are the Five Members in the House? " no person hath a privilege. And therefore " I am come to know if any of these persons "' that were accused are here."

Then he paused; and casting his eyes upon all the members in the House, said " I do not see
No reply. " any of them. I think I should know them."

" For I must tell you, Gentlemen," he
Nothing will be well till accused are surrendered. resumed after another pause, " that so long " as those persons that I have accused (for no " slight crime, but for Treason) are here, I " cannot expect that this House will be in the " right way that I do heartily wish it. There- " fore I am come to tell you that I must
Must have them. " have them, wheresoever I find them."

Then again he hesitated, stopped: and called out, " Is Mr. Pym here?" To which nobody gave answer.

Painful hesitation and effort. The awkwardness and effort manifest in these pauses and interruptions, the words that again and again recur, the needless and bald repetitions, in which we seem to hear the flow and laboured utterance with which Charles covered his natural impediment of speech, impress the imagination painfully.

Addition supplied by D'Ewes: All the breaks and pauses, however, were omitted in the report directed to be published; and D'Ewes, surmising that not only such omissions had been made by the King's order, but also all mention of the reply given upon Charles's appeal to the Speaker, is careful to restore what was wanting. " But

§ xx. The House entered by the King.

"the King caused all that to be left out, namely, when he asked for Mr. Pym, whether he were present or not, and when there followed a general silence, that nobody would answer him. He then asked for Mr. Hollis whether he were present, and when nobody answered him, he pressed the Speaker to tell him, who, kneeling down, did very wisely desire his Majesty to pardon him, saying that he could neither see nor speak but by command of the House: to which the King answered, 'Well, well! 'tis no matter.' 'I think my eyes are as good as another's.' And then he looked round about the House a pretty while, to see if he could espie any of them."* Very welcome are all such additional touches to a picture so memorable.

<small>confirmation of report as corrected by the King.</small>

<small>Enquiries for Pym and Hollis.</small>

<small>Reply.</small>

<small>Looking for them himself.</small>

"May it please your Majesty," said Lenthal, to the appeal that he should say where Pym was (for, as Rushworth himself, when he published his *Collections*, inserted his own report of the discreet speech of Mr. Speaker, and as the good Sir Simonds, had he lived to see it, would certainly have copied it in his Journal, it will here be most properly appended to an account which first gives to it all its significance), "I have neither eyes to see nor tongue to speak in this place, but as the House is pleased to direct me, whose servant

<small>Speaker Lenthal's speech.</small>

<small>No eyes or tongue but as the House's servant.</small>

---

* *Harl. MSS.* 162, f. 306 a.

"I am here; and I humbly beg your Majesty's pardon that I cannot give any other answer than this to what your Majesty is pleased to demand of me." Words conceived indeed with a singular prudence. Impressed deeply by the attitude of the House, and inspired suddenly by the trust confided to him, a man little famous for magnanimity or courage displayed both for the moment in a remarkable degree, and rose to the occasion as greatly as the King sank beneath it. But sorrow and suffering are wiser teachers than anger and revenge. There was yet to come a day in Charles's life, when he too would rise to the demand of the time; when his natural infirmities would be visible no longer; and when men should wonder to behold, in one so infirm of purpose and difficult of speech, both unembarrassed accents and a resolute will.*

Extraordinary speech for an ordinary man.

Another greater but like example.

After that long pause described by D'Ewes, the dreadful silence, as one member called it, Charles spoke again to the crowd of mute and sullen faces. The complete failure of his scheme was now accomplished, and all its possible consequences, all the suspicions and retaliations to which it had laid him open,

"Dreadful" silence.

The King conscious of his failure.

* "He had," says William Lilly, "a natural imperfection
"in his speech: at some times could hardly get out a word:
"yet at other times he would speak freely and articulately,
"as at the first time of his coming before the High Court of
"Justice, where casually I heard him: there he stammered
"nothing at all, but spoke very distinctly, with much courage
"and magnanimity."—*Monarchy or no Monarchy.*

Charles the First's speech at his trial.

§ xx. The House entered by the King.

appear to have rushed upon his mind. "Well, *His birds* "since I see all my* birds are flown, I do *flown.* "expect from you that you will send them "unto me as soon as they return hither. "But, I assure you, on the word of a King, "I never did intend any force, but shall pro- *Protests he* "ceed against them in a legal and fair way, *never intended* "for I never meant any other. And now, *force.* "since I see I cannot do what I came for, I "think this no unfit occasion to repeat what "I have said formerly, that whatsoever I have *Means to* "done in favour, and to the good, of my *maintain the con-* "subjects, I do mean to maintain it. I will *cessions he has made.* "trouble you no more, but tell you I do "expect, as soon as they come to the House, *Expects* "you will send them to me; otherwise I must *the Five will be* "take my own course to find them." To *sent to him.* that closing sentence, the note left by Sir Ralph Verney makes a not unimportant addition, which, however, appears nowhere in Rushworth's report. "For their treason was foul, *Declares their* "and such an one as they would all thank *treason* "him to discover."† If uttered, it was an *foul.* escape of angry assertion from amid forced and laboured apologies, and so far would agree with what D'Ewes observed of his change of manner at the time: "After he had ended "his speech, he went out of the House in a *Leaves the* "more discontented and angry passion than he *House*

* " My " in Rushworth's original note : " the " substituted by Charles.
† Verney's *Notes,* p. 139.

Arrest of the Five Members.

in anger: "came in, going out again between myſelf and the ſouth end of the Clerk's table, and the Prince Elector after him."*

Captain Slingſby's narrative of the incident.

Harl. MSS. 162, f. 306 a. I will here add Capt. Slingſby's account, written the next day but one, but for which of courſe he muſt have been indebted to ſome Royaliſt members of the Houſe, as he had himſelf remained outſide the lobby. "He came very unexpectedly, and at "firſt coming in, commaunded the Speaker to come out "of his chayre, and ſatt downe in it himſelfe, aſking divers "times whether thoſe traytours were there, but had no

Silence of the Houſe explained.

"anſwere: but at laſt an excuſe, that by yᵉ orders of "the Houſe they might not ſpeake when there Speaker was "out of his chayre. The King then aſkt the Speaker, who "excuſed himſelfe, that he might not ſpeake but what the "Houſe gave order to him to ſay: whereupon the King "replied it was no matter, for he knew them, if he ſaw "them. And after he had viewed them all, he made a

Determined to have the accuſed.

"ſpeeche to them very maieſtically, declaring his reſolution "to HAVE THEM though they were then abſent: promiſing "not to infringe any of their libertyes of parlament, but "commaunding them to ſend the traytours to him if they came "there againe. And after his coming out he gave order to the "Sarieant att Armes to find them out; and attach them.

Houſe had ſent to City for 4000 men.

"Before the Kinge's coming, the Houſe were very high, and "as I was informed, ſent to the Cittie for ſower thouſand "men to be preſently ſent downe to them for their Guard. "But none came, all the Cittie being terribly amazed wᵗʰ "that unexpected charge of thoſe perſons: ſhoppes all ſhutt, "many of wᶜʰ doe ſtill continue ſoe. They lykewiſe ſent to "the trayned bandes, in the Court of Guard before White-

Shops all ſhut.

"hall, to commaund them to diſband but they ſtayed ſtill. "After the Kinge had beene in the Houſe, there was no more "ſpoke, but only to adjorne till the next day."—MS. State Paper Office. Captain Slingſby to Admiral Pennington, 6th January, 1641-2. To which may be added an extract from a letter, alſo in the National Collection, written on

Bere to Pennington: 6th Jan. 1641-2.

the ſame 6th of January by Under Secretary Bere, encloſing Ruſhworth's report of the King's ſpeech to the Admiral. "On Monday laſt, the King's Attorney accuſed 5 of the "Lower Houſe & one of the Upper of High Treaſon "as you will ſee by the Articles of accuſation herewᵗʰ. "In conſequence of wᶜʰ a Sergᵗ of Armes was ſent to demand "them, but yᵉ Houſe taking time to conſider of it, & having "ſent a meſſage inſtead of the delivery, His Matᶦᵉ went the "next day himſelfe in perſon to yᵉ Commons Houſe to demand "them, as you will ſee by the incloſed ſpeech. But it ſeemes

But he did not leave, as he had entered, in *but not amid silence.* filence. Low mutterings of fierce difcontent broke out as he paffed along, and "many "members cried out aloud, fo as he might "hear them, *Privilege! Privilege!*" With thofe words, ominous of ill, ringing in his ear, he repaffed to his palace through the lane, again formed, of his armed adherents, and amid audible fhouts of as evil augury from defperadoes difappointed of their prey. Eagerly in that lobby had the word been waited for, which muft have been the prelude to a terrible fcene. Lady Carlifle alone had prevented it.

Sidenotes: but not amid filence. " Privilege! Privilege!" fhouted after him. Paffes out through files of armed adherents.

§ XXI. IMPRESSION PRODUCED BY THE OUTRAGE.

WHAT briefly followed within the chamber whofe moft facred rights had thus been violated by Charles the Firft, is revealed to us only by D'Ewes. "As foon as "he was gone, and the doors were fhut, "the Speaker afked us if he fhould make "report of his Majefty's fpeech. But Sir "John Hotham faid we had all heard it, and "there needed no report of it to be made.

Sidenotes: Proceedings in Houfe after King's departure. Speech of Hotham.

" they had made themfelves out of the way, as they ftill alfoe
" remaine, wch fome conceive is but don till the Houfe fhall
" refolve what to doe wth them. *Others thinke that they are*
" *actually fled.* What will be of it, time muft tell. In the
" meane time this bufinefs filled every one wth feares whaf
" might enfue thereon, and the Cittie remained all that night
" in armes, and are not yett very well affured, every one
" being poffeft with ftrange feares and imaginations."

Sidenote: Uncertainty as to flight of members.

"And others cried to adjourn till to-morrow
at one of the clock in the afternoon; upon
which in the issue we agreed. And so, the
Speaker having adjourned the House to
that hour, we rose about half an hour after
three of the clock in the afternoon:* little
imagining for the present—at least a greater
part of us—the extreme danger we had
escaped through God's wonderful providence." †

"For the design was," pursues Sir Simonds,
writing at the close of his day's Journal, and
before the entry of the morrow, "to have
taken out of our House by force and violence
the said five members, if we had refused to
have delivered them up peaceably and willingly; which, for the preservation of the
privileges of our House, we must have refused. And in the taking of them away,
they were to have set upon us all, if we had
resisted, in an hostile manner. It is very
true that the plot was so contrived as that

---

* The day's entry, as it still stands in the Journals, well expresses, in its sudden and unfinished abruptness, the agitation and excitement in which the day must have closed.

"JAN. 4. P.M. The King came into the House of Commons and took Mr. Speaker's Chair.
"Gentlemen I am sorry to have this occasion to come unto you.
* * * *
"Resolved upon the question that the House shall adjourn itself till to-morrow one of the clock."

† Harl. MSS. 162, f. 306 b.

§ XXI.   *Impreſſion produced by the Outrage.*   197

"the King ſhould have withdrawn out of the
"Houſe, and paſſed thorough the lobby or
"little room next without it, before the maſ-
"ſacre ſhould have begun, upon a watchword
"by him to have been given upon his paſſing
"thorough them. But 'tis moſt likely that Armed
"thoſe Ruffians, being about eighty in number, deſpera-
does not
"who were gotten into the ſaid lobby, being to be
reſtrained.
"armed all of them with ſwords, and ſome of
"them with piſtols ready charged, were ſo
"thirſty after innocent blood as they would
"ſcarce have ſtayed the watchword, if thoſe
"members had been there; but would have
"begun their violence as ſoon as they had
"underſtood of our denial, to the hazard of The
"the perſons of the King and the Prince King's
perſon in
"Elector, as well as of us. For, one of them danger.
"underſtanding, a little before the King came
"out, that thoſe five gentlemen were abſent,
"'Zounds!' ſaid he, 'They are gone! and
"'we are never the better for our coming!'

"And the deliverance," adds D'Ewes, in Strange
this remarkable paſſage of his Journal, "will delive-
rance.
"appear to have been the more ſtrange, if we
"conſider how the plot being revealed to one
"M. Langres, dwelling in the Covent Garden,
"after the King had taken his coach at White-
"hall, and was coming toward us, he got
"through the multitude of thoſe ſouldiers and King's
"ruffians, and coming to the Houſe acquainted approach
told to
"Mr. Nathaniel Fiennes with the King's reſo- Fiennes.

Withdrawal of the members.
Oppofition of Strode.

"lution. Whereupon Mr. Denzil Hollis, Sir
"Arthur Hafelrig, Mr. Hampden, and Mr.
"Pym, who had notice alfo formerly given
"them that there was fuch a defign, did
"prefently withdraw: but Mr. William Strode,
"the laft of the Five, being a young man and
"unmarried,* could not be perfuaded by his

Identity of Strode with the earlier Strode difputed.

* I retain the opinion put forth in my Effay on the Grand Remonftrance (*Hift. and Biog. Effays*, i. 1-175) that this expreffion of D'Ewes, and the language ufed by Clarendon, are decifive againft the identity of the Strode of the parliaments of James and the early parliaments of Charles with the Strode of the Long Parliament. The grounds on which I formed and ftated that opinion have fince been contefted in a book of great ability, and full of valuable matter relative to the Commonwealth period (*Studies and Illuftrations of the Great Rebellion*, by J. Langton Sandford, Efq.); but I muft

Reply to objections made:

be permitted to think that Mr. Sandford's argument, though ingenious and elaborate, is not fatisfactory. The gift of it lies in this remark: " William Strode may very well have been " under forty in 1642; and this, in the eyes of 'an ancient " 'gentleman' fuch as D'Ewes, woulden title him to the name " of 'a young man'" (p. 399). Unfortunately for the fenfe

Original opinion ftrengthened, not weakened.

in which the argument is ufed, it tells with the greateft force in the oppofite direction. D'Ewes's own age was exactly thirty-nine (he was born in December 1602); and it entitled him to the name of 'an ancient gentleman.' No one acquainted with the focial ufages and characteriftics of that time would for a moment expect that a man of thirty-nine fhould be ftyled young. That is a modern ftyle altogether. But, even in our own polite days, a man of thirty-nine would not be likely to fingle out as a young man a perfon of his own

Ages of the principal men of the Commons.

mature age. Befides, Hollis himfelf was only forty-four, Hampden was not more than forty-fix, Hafelrig was fome years younger, and from fuch a company to felect and fet apart for his youth a man of years fo nearly equal, would have been fheer abfurdity. Since my attention was firft drawn to this " hiftoric

Miftakes of Thomas May.

" doubt," I have obferved that the hiftorian May afferts the identity, faying of Strode that he had "before fuffered many " years of fharp and harfh imprifonment for matters done in par- " liament" (lib. 2, cap. 2, p. 21), but when he publifhed his *Hiftory* in 1647 Strode had been fome years dead, and in perfonal queftions May is not always ftrictly accurate or careful. To give an inftance: his account (p. 27) of the Whitehall Guard is inaccurate both as to time and perfons. It is not much to

§ XXI. *Impression produced by the Outrage.*

" friends for a pretty while to go out; but
" said, that knowing himself to be innocent, he

add to the other proofs, but it may be worth remark that the same trivial and contemptuous mode of speaking of Strode, in comparison with the other members, is to be found in the lampoons of the day. In the verses subjoined, he and Haselrig stand in as marked contrast with the rest, even though all be set apart for abuse, as in the page of Clarendon: *Contempt of fame for Strode.*

> " My venom swells," quoth Hollis,
> " And that his Majesty knows."
> " And I," quoth Hampden, " fetch the Scots
> " Whence all this mischief grows."
>
> " I am an asse," quoth Haselrigge,
> " But yet I'm deep i' the plot;"
> " And I," quoth Strode, " can lye as fast
> " As Master Pym can trott."
>
> " But I," quoth Pym, " your hackney am,
> " And all your drudgery do,
> " I make good speeches for myself,
> " And privileges for you—"

So, in London's Farewell to the Parliament, the abuse of Hollis, Hampden, and Pym, is a good solid hate, and it is not till Strode's turn comes, that contempt seems to take the place of it: *Varieties of Royalist slander.*

> Farewell Denzil Hollis, with hey, with hey;
> Farewell Denzil Hollis, with hoe;
> 'Twas his ambition or his need,
> Not his religion did the deed,
> With hey trolly, lolly, loe.
>
> Farewell John Hampden, with hey, with hey;
> Farewell John Hampden, with hoe;
> He's a sly and subtle fox,
> Well read in Buchanan and Knox,
> With hey trolly, lolly, loe.
>
> Farewell John Pym, with hey, with hey;
> Farewell John Pym, with hoe;
> He would have had a place in Court,
> And he ventur'd all his partie for't,
> With hey trolly, lolly, loe.
>
> Farewell Billy Strode, with hey, with hey;
> Farewell Billy Strode, with hoe;

Arrest of the Five Members.

Will seal his innocency with his blood.

"would stay in the House though he sealed "his innocency with his blood at the door. "So as, being at last overcome" (D'Ewes gets a little confused in his sentences here) "by "the importunate advices and entreaties of his "friends, when the van, or fore-front, of those "ruffians marched into Westminster Hall: "nay, when no persuasion could prevail with

Sir Walter Earle pulls him out by the cloak.

"the said Mr. Strode, Sir Walter Earle, his "entire friend, was faine to take him by cloak, "and pull him out of his place; and so got "him out of the House. 'Tis very true, "indeed, that the Lord Mandeville" (Kimbolton continued to be more familiarly known by his old than by his new title) "and these "five gentlemen had notice not only yesternight "of this intended design, but were likewise

The accused warned at dinner hour by Essex.

"sent to, this day at dinner, by the Earl of "Essex, Lord Chamberlain of his Majesty's "household, that the King intended to come "to the House of Commons to seize upon "them there, and that they should absent "themselves: yet had they no direct assurance "that the said design should certainly be put "in execution, till the said M. Langres his "coming to the said House."*

Such was the view taken, such the opinion

He swore all Wharton's lyes were true;
And it concern'd him so to do,
For he was in the saw-pit too—
With hey trolly, lolly, loe.

* Harl. MSS. 162, ff. 306 b. 307 a.

§ XXI. *Impression produced by the Outrage.*

uttered, with no public object or design, but as a man communes with himself or his most intimate friend, of the proceedings of this eventful day, by a member of the House who with his own eyes had witnessed them, writing not many hours after the event; and who gave further decisive proof of *his* sense of the danger which from that day awaited all men who might discharge their duty fearlessly in the House of Commons, by at once arranging his affairs, setting his house in order, and executing his will. "Some," he remarked in a subsequent debate, "have said it were well "for the Parliament men to set their houses "in order, left they should shortly lose their "heads. For my part, I confess I have not "that work now to do; having ever since "the 4th day of January last past, left my "will with a third person in trust."* The

_{Unimpassioned character of D'Ewes's testimony.}

_{His sense of danger marked by execution of his will: and setting his house in order.}

---

* *Harl. MSS.* 163, f. 509 b. D'Ewes is speaking, on the 16th May, 1642, more than five months after the events to which I am referring, of the disputes in Yorkshire which immediately preceded the outbreak of civil war: "Mr. H. Bellasis, Sir R. Pye, and others, moved "that we might think of some way of accommodation. "Others moved that we might prepare to defend ourselves. "I said I was sorry to see things grown to such a height in "Yorkshire; and though his Majesty disavowed the injuries "offered the poor freeholders of Yorkshire, I did not hear "that he disavowed those offered his poor Parliament, although "their messages were hissed at when they were read, and "although some said it were well for the parliament men to "set their houses in order left they should shortly lose their "heads. For my part I confess I have not that work now to "do, having ever since the 4th day of January last past," the day of the attempted arrest, "left my will with a third "person in trust—(of which," D'Ewes adds with some com-

_{Question of accommodation with the King.}

_{Parliament-men in peril.}

Isolation of D'Ewes from mere party.

judgment so formed, too, and the course so taken on the instant, were those of a man not sharing vehemently in any of the popular passions; never admitted to the confidence of the leaders; having a strong personal dislike, as I shall shortly take an opportunity of showing, to some of them; and himself noted for a

His precision and sobriety.

particular precision and sobriety, as well in his habits of thought as in his ways of life. Nor is it in any degree reasonable to suppose that the King should *not* have resolved to give some sort of effect to his project, having once, however

Question of the King's conduct.

rashly, embarked in it. To have intended merely to go and ask for the members, and, having so invited the refusal which it was obvious would be given, to leave them unmolested in their seats and himself come discomfited away, would have been indeed to add to supreme rashness a supreme silliness. Armed

Could have had but one purpose.

men could have accompanied him for one purpose only, and this was baffled by the absence of the accused: nor was it possible that any one, writing of the occurrence in later times, should have found it reasonably open to any other construction, if upon this, as upon other great questions between the People and the King, Clarendon had not drawn off to a false issue successive generations of readers. Content to have profited by the act if it had succeeded,

placency, "the House took especial notice, as I was fain for a " while to stop from farther proceeding)".

§ XXI.   *Impreſſion produced by the Outrage.*   203

it was an act of which the failure was unpar- Not the act but the failure unpardonable.
donable : and every one in the confidence of
the King became eager to ſeparate himſelf
from it, to ſpeak of it as apart and iſolated
from other acts to which it was in truth no
way contraſted or oppoſed, to treat it as a
ſudden frenzy, and altogether to conceal the
real object which it aimed at, and, but for an
accident unforeſeen, and the failure of ſecret Succeſs narrowly miſſed.
meaſures here ſhown to have been daringly
attempted, it might have gone far to accompliſh.

Compare the tone ſo taken, after the
fact, with what men wrote upon the inſtant
who ſhared Hyde's opportunities of knowledge, who like him were behind the ſcenes, but
who wrote not to conceal, but to expreſs, the
truth.   " I pray God this very buſineſs," Under Secretary Bere's dread as to ultimate reſult.
wrote Under Secretary Bere to Admiral Pen-
nington on the 6th of January, " doe not
" render our condition in Court the worſe ; for
" things being now brought to a heighth, they
" cannot confiſt ſoe, but muſt change to the Change muſt be for the worſe.
" great prejudice of the one or other ſide : and
" I pray God wee find not that we have
" flattered ourſelves wth an imaginary ſtrength
" and party, in the Citty and elſewhere, w^ch
" will fall away, if need ſhould bee. A report Rumours as to whereabouts of accuſed.
" now goes that thoſe perſons accuſed are in
" London, and ſome will have itt they are
" ſitting wth the Comittee wch ſitts there. By

> "all this, you will fee the greate diftractions
> "that are here: foe that you may well fay
> "wee have no lefs ftormes here than you have
> "att fea—*I feare worfe and more full of
> "danger.*" *

<small>Worfe ftorms on land than at fea.</small>

That is not the language of a man who regarded the King's act as having fprung from a mere fudden unreafoning impulfe of anger, or who defired to underrate its gravity. The writer knew the circumftances too well. He had himfelf drawn up the warrant, which, but for a merciful accident interpofed, might have drenched London ftreets in the blood of the Citizens. He was perfectly aware of all the preparations made, of all the deliberation ufed; and his prayer to God is, that they who had taken part therein (of whom he was one) might not find they had flattered themfelves with an imaginary ftrength, in the City and elfewhere, which already was crumbling and falling away beneath them.

<small>Circumftances well known to Under Secretary:</small>

<small>His fears and forebodings.</small>

---

§ XXII. Lord Digby and Mr. Hyde.

NOT of the moderate or confcientious tem-

---

* MS. State Paper Office. The Under Secretary thus clofes his letter: "I humbly thank you for y^r kind invitation "abord this Xmas, where I would willingly be, but that I "may not well bee abfent: my bufineffe growing ftill more "and more: yett we have the addition of another fellow "Secret^y. by name Mr. Oudart, who was Secret^y to Sr John "Bofwell: fo y^t ye labour is very eafy, but difpenfes not "with abfence."

<small>An invitation for Chriftmas declined.</small>

per of the Under Secretary, however, were *Violent and reckless counsel.* those who had advised the King. It is a bare act of justice to say, of other and more active participators in the Royal Councils at this time, that they did not show fear, remorse, or apprehension of any kind. Lord Digby certainly does not seem to have shrunk from the proposal to carry the King's daring attempt, be- *Carrying attempt to its issue.* gun that day, to its natural issue. He was willing to take the utmost hazard upon himself, says Hyde; and would have redeemed his failure of promise in the matter of Lord Kimbolton by undertaking, with the congenial help of such gentlemen as Sir Thomas Lunsford, to seize the accused members in the very house *Digby's proposal:* in the City where they had taken refuge, and either bring them away alive, or " leave them " dead in the place."*

Elsewhere, too,† the same writer tells us, that, as soon as the failure of the enterprise at the House declared itself, Digby's great spirit was so far from failing, that when he saw the whole City upon the matter in arms to defend the Five Members, he, knowing in what house they were together, offered the King, with a select number of a dozen gentlemen, who he presumed would stick to him, to seize *To seize the Five Members dead or alive.* upon their persons dead or alive. And without doubt, adds Clarendon naively, he would

* *Hist.* ii. 130.
† Clarendon's *State Papers.* Supplement to third vol. lv-lvi.

have done it, "which muſt likewiſe have had "a wonderful effect."

Miſchief let looſe by King's act.

Such were the elements of diſcord and violence let rudely looſe by the act of the King; and to comprehend all that follows, to underſtand even the alarms we have ſeen expreſſed by D'Ewes after the King's departure, and what we ſhall obſerve hereafter of their ſudden, unexplained, and abrupt recurrence, the fact of ſuch miſchief being abroad, and ſuch rumours or threats of deſperate deſigns underlying men's ordinary diſcourſe, muſt ſtill be kept carefully in mind. "The publike voice "runs much," wrote Bere to Pennington,

Rumours againſt Briſtol and Digby.

"againſt Briſtol and his ſon, as great inſtruments of theſe miſunderſtandinges."* With more elaboration, and with alluſions that pointed to ſecret intrigues not leſs than to frank and open outrage, Mr. Smith of the Admiralty wrote to the King's favourite ſeaman. He began by telling his "honoured "compeer," what grief he feels that his rela-

Small comfort for the Admiral.

tion of affairs cannot be ſuch as might comfort the Admiral's languiſhing ſpirits, as in his lateſt letter he had deſcribed them, turmoiled and almoſt tired in thoſe tumultuous ſeas.

Suffering on waters, fear on land.

"You ſuffer on the waters, we feare on the "land." And he proceeded to explain the ſources of the fear. "The deſires and

---

* MS. State Paper Office, January, 1641-2.

"endeav^rs of men, especially of such as Rule, are so diverse, that wee seeme to bee now in this K.dom like to the pregnant wombe of Rebecca, which teemes of discourse and affections, some labouring to bringe forth the Honest Jacob of order, tranquillitie, and peace, others the Rough Esau of discord and ruine." Yet one advantage had already attended the attempt made on the House of Commons. It was expected that in future there would be less disagreement, and a more general co-operation for the public good, than before was noted therein. "Wee are not," continued Mr. Smith, "altogether out of hope of a Good Period in regarde those y^t rule in Parlem^t are both honest and able men. If distractions and confusions come, 'twill be from some factious firebrands that trouble the Court, abuse his Matie, and seeke to fish in troubled waters; and, through feare of being rewarded according to theire merit, do labor to bring all things to ruine with themselves. But the Good God will not suffer them long thus to divide betwixt O^r good King and his People, whom they traduce wth false report of Rebellion, whereas indeede they are the greatest and only Rebells I know in England, and go about ye K.dom raising tumullts and false reports to putt the land into an uproar if they can, and scandalize the hon^ble and just Proceed-

Side notes: Jacob and Esau. Two parties out of House: but the leaders honest: and only one party now in House. Sole rebels in England.

"ings of the Parlem^t wth lying and unjuft
"imputations."*

<small>Open and secret enemies.</small>

This difcreet and temperate man, writing thus a few days after the King's attempt, found not more mifery occafioned by firebrands fuch as Digby, than by thofe more fecret agents of confufion who went about creating jealoufies and diflikes againft the Parliament, of whom it will not be unjuft, upon his own account of his own proceedings at the time, to felect Hyde as by far the moft prominent example. And to underftand the pofition he had in that refpect taken up is neceffary, in his inftance not lefs than in that of Digby, to a proper comprehenfion of the fequel of thefe extraordinary fcenes.

<small>Caufe for this digreffion.</small>

Hyde acknowledges,† that, feveral weeks earlier than the attempted arreft, he had become fecretly the King's private counfellor, and had in confequence withdrawn from fo frequently or publickly as before taking part in the proceedings of the Houfe. So early as during the Remonftrance Debates, indeed, he was, as in a former work has been fhown,‡ fupplying the King with refolutions and papers of the Houfe in their firft rough draft ; and, in many paffages of the Memoir written by himfelf, his *modus operandi* is defcribed in

<small>Hyde the king's private advifer:</small>

<small>Supplies fecret papers and information.</small>

---

* MS. State Paper Office. Thos. Smith (from York Houfe) to Admiral Pennington: January, 1641-2.
† *Life*, i. 98-100.
‡ See my *Hift. and Biog. Effays*, i. 142, &c.

§ XXII.   *Lord Digby and Mr. Hyde.*

detail, entirely without difguife, and even with a chuckling felf-fatiffaction.* He feems to take an odd kind of pride, in avowing openly the double part he played in the Houfe and in the back fcenes of the Court; while he was unfcrupuloufly ufing his opportunities of obtaining knowledge of the fecrets of the popular leaders, for no other purpofe than to betray them to the King. Several curious unconfcious illuftrations of the fame double-dealing are recorded alfo in the Journal of D'Ewes. [*Playing double and falfe.*] [*Betrays the Commons to the King.*]

When, fhortly after thefe events, Lord

---

* For example (*Life,* i. 102-3): " And fo they (Vifcount "Falkland, Sir John Colepepper, and Mr. Hyde) met every "night late together, & communicated their obfervations & "intelligence of the day; & fo agreed what was to be done "or attempted the next; there being very many perfons of "condition & intereft in the Houfe who would follow their "advice, & affift in anything they defired . . . And after "their deliberation together, what was to be put in writing "was always committed to Mr. Hyde; and when the King "had left the town, he writ as freely to the King as either "of the others did . . . . and now when the governing "party had difcovered the place of the nightly meetings, "that a Secretary of State and a Chancellor of the Exchequer "every day went to the lodging of a private perfon, who "ought to attend them, they believed it a condefcenfion that "had fome other foundation than mere civility." And in another remarkable paffage he fays (i. 130-133): " They had "long detefted and fufpected Mr. Hyde, from the time of "their firft Remonftrance, for framing the King's meffages "and anfwers, which they now every day received, to their "intolerable vexation: yet knew not how to accufe him. "But now that the Earls of Effex and Holland had dif- "covered his being fhut up with the King at Greenwich, and "the Marquis of Hamilton had once before found him very "early in private with the King at Windfor, at a time when "the King thought all paffages had been ftopped; together "with his being of late more abfent from the Houfe than he "had ufed to be; and the refort of the other two every night "to his lodging, as is mentioned before; fatiffied them that "he was the perfon." [*Private meetings in Hyde's lodgings.*] [*Sufpicions againft him.*] [*Hyde fhut up with Charles.*]

P

Compton, the member for Warwickshire, and Sir Edward Baynton, who sat for Chippenham, had been sent with a message from the House *Complaint* to the King, replying to a complaint against *of the King* one of Pym's speeches, they reported on their *against* return that they had duly delivered the *Pym.* message, and that the King gave them for an answer that he was altogether unsatisfied that Mr. Pym had any ground for the bold assertion he had made. Whereupon Mr. Pym *Pym's* stood up and said he conceived there needed *rejoinder.* no further declaration to satisfy his Majesty; and Sir Edward Baynton called the attention of the House to the fact, that such reply from his Majesty was not given upon the sudden, for that, as they gathered from some expressions *Messages* of the King, "he had seen the said message *sent before voted.* "before they gave it him." * In like manner also, when, some week or two earlier, the famous struggle with the King upon the Newmarket Declaration had been in progress, D'Ewes relates†
The that "Mr. Pym delivered in a letter directed
House warned "to him, superscribed 'John Pym, Esq. at
against "'his Lodgings in Westminster,' which had
treachery. "been found by Simon Richardson and John
"Walker, two watchmen of Westminster, in
"the Palace Yard. It had no name to it:
Letter to "but the writer said in ye beginning of it that
Pym. "not knowing how to venture safely, he

* *Harl. MSS.* 163, f. 438 b. † *Ibid* 163, f. 246 a.

"had sent him this letter, and caused it to be
"dropped in the street, having done so with
"two formerly: notwithstanding his danger if
"he should be discovered, yet he had adven-
"tured out of love to his country to give him
"timely warning. *That nothing was done in* Able
"*the House, but some able members amongst us* members informed
"*sent it, as well as all messages intended for* against.
"*him, to his Majesty before they came from us,*
"*and sent him also heads ready framed for his*
"*answers.* That the King was resolved to King's
"use force, and that we should find the Navy preparations.
"of England turned against us. That he
"had heard the King say he had the nobility,
"gentry, and divers honest men of his side.
"That the Parliament had irritated the mili- Parlia-
"tary men and denied them employment in ment in danger.
"Ireland, and so prepared swords for their
"own throats."

The contents of the letter it is not necessary further to dwell upon, but circumstances gave to them afterwards much weight; and that Hyde was distinctly aimed at, every one ap- Charge pears to have taken for granted. Means were aimed at Hyde. adopted immediately after to put some check to his opportunities of treachery; but the fact of such secret enemies existing within the House, more dangerous than its open assailants, and suspected strongly while yet the truth was not perfectly established, should avail against any hasty or harsh judgment of the precaution-

Arrest of the Five Members.

Self-defence against treachery.

ary and repressive measures which it forced in sheer self-defence upon the leaders.

That suspicion should have lighted upon Hyde, moreover, as soon as the King's attempt was made, will hardly seem surprising after the secret history that D'Ewes discloses.

Hyde accused of advising arrest:

This suspicion he frankly confesses himself. He tells us* that some friends of his who loved him very well, had warned him that he was pointed at as one of the contrivers of the arrest, all the more certainly because of his known friendship with Digby; and they had

suggestion of his friends not to defend it.

advised him so to carry himself, in the debates which should arise upon it, that it might evidently appear that he did not approve of it, or was privy to it. Notwithstanding which good advice, he adds in another place, he did speak on a particular occasion in a sense adverse to the claim of parliamentary privilege in matters of treason, though amid noise and clamour, and with wonderful evidence of dislike.† He

Alleged speech upon impeachment.

even professes to give an abstract of what he said; and would appear to have said so ill, that, but for the purpose of showing how poor was the strongest case that such an advocate could put against the overwhelming argument on the other side, it would not be necessary to give an abstract of it here. It is only by a persistent

Gross misrepresen-

misrepresentation that he makes out any case at all; for it cannot be too often repeated that

* *Hist.* ii. 136. † *Hist.* ii. 138, 139.

§ XXII.   *Lord Digby and Mr. Hyde.*   213

never, from the firſt of theſe proceedings to the laſt, was it aſſumed on the ſide of the accuſed members that privilege of Parliament could or ought to run in a caſe of felony or treaſon. _{tation therein.}

On the occaſion now pretended (for no circumſtance of identification is connected with the ſpeech, and no clue given to when it was ſpoken, beyond the general ſtatement that it was upon certain votes being propoſed "at the "Committee" to be ſubmitted at the re-aſſembling at Weſtminſter), Hyde took upon himſelf to warn the Houſe to take heed that they did not, out of tenderneſs of their privilege, which was and muſt be very precious to every man, extend it further than the law would ſuffer it to be extended; that the Houſe had always been very ſevere upon the breach of any of their privileges, and in the vindicating thoſe members who were injured; but that the diſpoſing men to make themſelves judges, and to reſcue themſelves or others, might be of evil conſequence, and produce ill effects: at leaſt if it ſhould fall out to be, that the perſons were arreſted for treaſon, or felony, or breach of the peace; in either of which caſes, there would be no privilege of Parliament.* All which was as well known to Mr. Pym and Mr. Hampden as to Mr. Hyde, nor was the remoteſt pretence to aſſert or _{Pretended occaſion for ſpeech. Argument of ſpeech: no privilege for felony or treaſon: undiſputed by Pym and Hampden.}

* *Hiſt.* ii. 138-9.

juftify the contrary ever fet up by either. They muft have fcouted fuch arguments, if employed at all; and the real truth I believe to be, that fuch a fpeech was never fpoken.

Of courfe it tells extremely well in the Hiftory of the Rebellion, that Mr. Hyde, amid noife and clamour, and with wonderful evidence of diflike, fhould have taken a line of reafoning fo manifeftly juft, that if we believe him to have ufed it, and that fuch was the reception given to it, we muft attribute to the leaders on the other fide, to whom he profeffes to have been replying, a tone and argument as manifeftly *un*juft. It will hereafter be feen more plainly how falfe fuch an inference would be. Suffice it for the prefent to point out that no trace of any fuch remarks by Hyde, or of his participation in one of the debates arifing out of thefe tranfactions, is difcoverable in any fhape or form. From the expreffions ufed it might be affumed, that he was fpeaking on the Refolution of the Houfe that any one attempting to give effect to the confeffed illegality of the Impeachment, by arrefting the Members whom it accufed, and whom the King, in a fubfequent as illegal proclamation, had outlawed, would be guilty of a breach of privilege. But he was certainly not prefent when that refolution was moved. He feems to wifh us to infer, that the fpeech might have been delivered on one of the days when

Imputation againft leaders of the Commons.

No proof exifting that the fpeech was fpoken.

Hyde not in the Houfe:

§ XXII.   *Lord Digby and Mr. Hyde.*   215

the Grocers' Hall Committee were preparing resolutions to be passed on the House re-assembling.* But D'Ewes has carefully reported each day's proceeding of that Committee, without the remotest reference to Hyde.

It was easy, in short, with no record of the debates existing to confront him, to take the credit of having so spoken, and to fling upon the popular leaders the discredit of having forced him so to speak. D'Ewes now enables us to state, however, with an almost absolute certainty, that not even on one occasion did this active member of the House, this incessant and untiring orator against the Remonstrance, speak for or against the proceedings of the 3rd and 4th of January.† His name nowhere appears as having been even present. Culpeper and Falkland, Sir Ralph Hopton and Mr. Herbert Price, noted partizans of the King, are in the list of the Committee appointed to

nor at Guildhall or Grocers' Hall.

No evidence that Hyde took part in debates on arrest.

---

* It is a very significant circumstance, with reference to the Incondoubt thus suggested, that in his text as undoubtedly left by sistency himself (in a fair copy made by his secretary) for publication, in Hyde's the introduction to the mention of this speech is simply: MS. " And these votes the House confirmed, when they were " reported: though in the debate it was told them, &c." It is only from the notes and additions found by comparison with one of his additional illustrative papers (lettered B), that the words to be now quoted in Italics are supplied by the edition of 1826: "And these votes the House confirmed, when " they were reported: *which caused some debate, and Mr.* " *Hyde (notwithstanding the good advice that had been given* " *to him) told them,*" &c. &c. ii. 139.

† When upon a former occasion Hyde's absence was remarked, his friend Falkland had to suggest an excuse for it (Clarendon's *State Papers*, ii. 141, where the letter, manifestly belonging to March 1640-41 is placed under 1642): so constant and punctual were his ordinary attendances.

meet in the City; but not Hyde. Many not on the lift of the Committee, to which all who came had voices, are yet carefully recorded as taking part in the debates. But no where do we find Hyde's name. He feems to have been fo impreffed by that advice of the friends who loved him, to be careful not to fhow any approval of the King's attempt, as for the time to abfent himfelf from the Houfe altogether.

Reafons for abfenting himfelf.

Prudent advice it unqueftionably was, and given doubtlefs by men who not only knew the need for it in the particular cafe, but, friendly to the King as they were, faw the real iffue which his failure had made inevitable, and which Hyde could now better help by other methods than that of public fpeaking in parliament. It fhifted the ftruggle to other fcenes than thofe it had heretofore occupied. Mr. Hallam is no friendly critic of the popular leaders at this crifis, but he finds himfelf compelled to admit that the fingle falfe ftep which rendered the King's affairs irretrievable by anything fhort of civil war, and placed all reconciliation at an infuperable diftance, was the attempt to feize the five members within the walls of the Houfe.* Plainly, it was an

His help more ufeful elfewhere.

Appeal to force.

Hallam's view of impeachment.

* *Conft. Hift.* ii. 126 (ed. 1855). " An evident violation," Mr. Hallam adds, "not of common privilege, but of all " fecurity for the independent exiftence of parliament, in the " mode of its execution." The paffage of his *Monarchy or no Monarchy* (ed. 1651), in which William Lilly expreffly records his opinion that the act of the 4th January 1641-2 coft Charles the Firft his crown, is well worth fubjoining for

§ XXII. *Lord Digby and Mr. Hyde.* 217

appeal to force. Both parties felt it, and both
inſtinctively turned in the direction where alone,

the curious facts it contains, and for its incidental corroboration
of much that has been adverted to in my text. After remarking
that the reſult proved that the King had really no evidence
againſt the accuſed members but his own thoughts, as he himſelf confeſſed, he proceeds: "And ſurely, had it been in his
" power to have got their bodies, he would have ſerved theſe
" members as he did Sir John Eliot, whom without cauſe he
" had committed to the Tower, and never would either
" releaſe him, or ſhow cauſe of his commitment, till his death.
" This raſh action of the King's loſt him his crown. For, as
" he was the firſt of kings that ever, or ſo imprudently, brake
" the privileges by his entrance into the Houſe of Commons
" aſſembled in parliament, ſo, by that unparalleled demand of
" his, he utterly loſt himſelf, and left ſcarce any poſſibility of
" reconcilement; he not being willing to truſt them, nor they
" to truſt him, who had ſo often failed them. It was my
" fortune that day to dine in Whitehall, and in that room
" where the Halberts, newly brought from the Tower, were
" lodged for the uſe of ſuch as attended the King to the Houſe
" of Commons. Sir Peter Wich, ere we had fully dined,
" came into the room I was in, and brake open the cheſts
" wherein the arms were, which frighted us all that were
" there. However, one of our company got out of doors, and
" preſently informed ſome members that the King was pre-
" paring to come in to the Houſe: elſe I believe all thoſe
" members, or ſome of them, would have been taken in the
" Houſe. All that *I* could do farther was preſently to be
" gone. But it happened alſo the ſame day that ſome of
" my neighbours were at the Court of Guard at Whitehall,
" unto whom I related the King's preſent deſign, and con-
" jured them to defend the Parliament and members thereof,
" in whoſe well or ill doing conſiſted our happineſs or miſ-
" fortune. They promiſed aſſiſtance, if need were; and I
" believe, would have ſtoutly ſtood to it for defence of the
" Parliament or members thereof. The King loſt his reputa-
" tion exceedingly by this his improvident and unadviſed
" demand: yet, notwithſtanding his failure of ſucceſs in the
" attempt, ſo wilful and obſtinate was he, in purſuance of that
" prepoſterous courſe he intended, and ſo deſirous to compaſs
" the bodies of thoſe five members, that the next day he poſted
" and trotted into the City to demand the members there: he
" convened a meeting at the Guildhall, and the Common
" Council aſſembled: but *mum* could he get there; for the
" word, *London Derry,* was then freſh in every man's
" mouth." Some years before, againſt the advice even of
Strafford himſelf, the City of London had been dragged

William
Lilly as to
arreſt of
members.

Coſt the
King his
crown.

All confi-
dence at
an end.

A dinner
party on
day of
arreſt.

Belief as
to outrage
intended.

King's
obſtinacy.

Arreſt of the Five Members.

for either, now lay ſtrength and ſafety. Everything depended hereafter on the impreſſion to be
made upon the people, and on the reſponſe it
might be poſſible to obtain from the great maſs
of the inhabitants of London.

Impreſſion to be made on the people.

§ XXIII. SIR SIMONDS D'EWES AND
SPEAKER LENTHAL.

BUT before reſuming the courſe of my
narrative, already interrupted by the neceſſity
of interpoſing the foregoing ſection, it ſeems
deſirable to make further pauſe for introduction of other matter alſo of a perſonal kind,
from which not merely the general ſubject, but
the particular ſcenes in which its ſtriking intereſt
conſiſts, will receive eſſential illuſtration.
What is ſoon to paſs in debate within the
Houſe, or at Guildhall or Grocers' Hall in
the City, during thoſe days of excitement
following the attempted arreſt which wait to
be deſcribed, will have for its principal authority the Journal of D'Ewes; and while that
rich and curious manuſcript lies open before
me, I propoſe, before paſſing to thoſe later
ſcenes, to draw from it ſome inſtances and
examples in proof of its claim to be received
as an authentic record, by which the pecu-

Further pauſe in narrative required.

Manu-ſcript Diary of D'Ewes:

into the Star Chamber, and, on the falſe pretence of ſome
invalidity of a grant by James the Firſt, mulcted not only of
their plantation of Derry, but in a heavy fine as well.

§ XXIII.   *D'Ewes and Speaker Lenthal.*

liarities both of D'Ewes and Lenthal will be characteristically displayed, and amusing as well as valuable information afforded as to the forms, the usages, the discipline, and the management of the House of Commons,* in these memorable days of its history.   *illustrations to be drawn from it.*

Let me, then, first impress upon the reader (it cannot be done too often or too strongly) that Sir Simonds D'Ewes is really, in regard to all the matters under discussion in these pages, so far a most reliable witness, that his sympathies were never decidedly, or at all actively, with the members accused or any of their more intimate friends. Within certain limits, his strong Puritan opinions, and the deference really felt for, and paid to, his knowledge of precedents and constitutional forms, caused him to act steadily with them; but the more attention he received, the more he was disposed to claim, until, taking literally a half jesting remark made by Sir William Lytton † that really the House could not possibly spare him, he put himself forward so incessantly on every question, embarrassed so many by his pedantic exaggeration of trifling rules and   *D'Ewes a reliable witness.*   *Not a thorough-going party man.*

---

* For others I may be allowed to refer the reader (all repetitions here of matter formerly published being carefully avoided) to the notes to the Essay on the Debates of the Grand Remonstrance in *Hist. and Biog. Essays*, i. 1-175.

† He had been of material service to the member for Hertfordshire in exposing the forged signatures to a royalist petition from that county. See my *Hist. and Biog. Essays*, i. 89.

forms, and spared the House itself so little, that even his extraordinary learning lost its relish, and he fell into sad personal differences with the leaders, even while in hearty agreement with their general policy and aims. Hampden became too "serpentine" and "subtle" for him. Denzil Hollis was too "proud" and "ambitious." Strode was too much of a "firebrand" and "notable profaner of the Scriptures," and had "too hot a tongue." Glyn also was a "swearing profane fellow." Haselrig was too "violent." Harry Marten was a "fiery heathen," and had a too "scurrilous "and windy wit." With a sneer, in like manner, he qualifies an attack upon the impetuosity of Nathaniel Fiennes, "though he hath amongst "his other good parts an able voice." And if he does not use the same tone or apply similar epithets to Pym (all now quoted were applied within a very few weeks of the incidents in this narrative, for, at a later time, he used even less scrupulous speech), it is because that great popular leader, with a profound knowledge of the strength of his party, had also a wise deference for the weaknesses and vanity of individual members of it, and was always ready with the concession that substantially yielded nothing, while it softened anger, quieted fears, and was soothing to self-esteem.

To take one instance out of many, which will

[margin: Differences with the leaders. Epithets applied to the popular chiefs. Why more tolerant of Pym. Pym more tolerant of him.]

also show the personal position in which D'Ewes generally stood to the party with whom commonly he acted, I give his account of an incident, full of character, which arose out of the discussion of one of the answers to a message of the King in the course of the present differences. Pym had drawn up the answer, and some expressions in it were strongly objected to by Mr. John Vaughan, the Royalist member for Cardigan, when suddenly it occurred to D'Ewes that there might be something in the objection so taken.

Discussion upon answers to a royal message.

"Mr. Pym read the Answer, or Declara-
"tion, to his Majesty's message. Divers
"called to have it put to the question, but
"Mr. Vaughan stood up and desired us to
"consider well two things in it: 1. the King's
"raising of men to be to the terror of his
"people; 11. where we said we would not
"obey his Commissioners. Mr. Pym ans-
"wered him somewhat superficially" (D'Ewes
means, in the literal sense of the word, that
Pym spoke cursorily or slightingly), "and yet
"divers called to put the Declaration to the
"question: which made me, just as the
"Speaker was standing up to put the ques-
"tion, to say"—urging thereon more strongly
Mr. Vaughan's objection. "As I was pro-
"ceeding," he resumes, "some indiscreet
"and violent spirits interrupted me, and
"called — to the Question! Whom the

Objection taken by Royalist members.

D'Ewes supports objection.

Is assailed by violent spirits.

"Speaker having first reproved, I went on."
The worthy Baronet very decidedly expressed himself, in short, in favour of moderate and conciliatory speech. "It concerned us much to weigh all our expressions, and not leave the kingdom without all hope or possibility of an accomodation between his Majesty and us, lest so we precipitate things into speedy confusion. After I had done Mr. Peard stood up, and did with great vehemency reprove those indiscreet and foolish members who had interrupted me first: showing breach of privilege, &c. When I sat down, many discreet and sober members called on me still to speak and go on. And Mr. Pym also, who had made report of the said Declaration, did with much discretion and modesty approve what I had spoken, and coming himself to the Clerk's table, did amend the said Declaration according to the advice I had given." (It involved little beyond the change of a few letters.) "Which being read was approved of, and those indiscreet spirits that interrupted me had not a word to say against it."*

On the other hand observe the conduct of that "firebrand" Mr. Strode, on a precisely similar occasion, when what is called the Newmarket Declaration was under discussion. "Divers," says D'Ewes, "spake after me;

* *Harl. MSS.* 163, f. 467 b. Another similar instance

§ XXIII.   *D'Ewes and Speaker Lenthal.*

"and Mr. William Strode, having spoken *speaks thrice:*
"twice before, stood up and spake the third
"time, and related the same matter in sub-
"stance; which made me stand up and
"speak to the order of the house and inter-
"rupt him, &c.   He sat down, and divers *and gets*
"laughed, and some spake after him."* *laughed at.*

Generally it is to be remarked, upon all these
scenes, much to the credit of the House, that *Good humour of the House.*
the moderation and temper of D'Ewes, when
discreetly put forward, seems hardly ever to have
failed of its effect. When the Declaration was
under discussion, in which, upon intelligence
received of the schemes set on foot for raising
money abroad, some very plain truths were
addressed to the King, he interfered, almost *Moderation of D'Ewes.*
as zealously as Sir Ralph Hopton, and much
more successfully, to obtain abatement of some
of its terms. He had left the House between
four and five o'clock that afternoon,† while the
debate was in progress, and on his return
between five and six he found Sir Ralph withdrawn into the committee chamber, and the

---

will be found of a moderating expression moved by Pym and
seconded by D'Ewes, *Ibid* 163, f. 518 b.

* *Harl. MSS.* 163, f. 431 a.

† In a characteristic entry of earlier date, D'Ewes lets us
into the secret of these retreats from the House during the
afternoon hours of a long debate. "I returned into the
"House," he says, "between 5 and 6 o'clock at night, and
"it was my good fortune that I withdrew so seasonably *With-*
"between 2 and 3 as I did, having by that means freedom *drawing*
"for some hours, and convenience of supping in time, and on *for*
"my return I heard almost the whole matter debated over *supper.*
"again."   *Harl. MSS.* 162, f. 354 b.

Aˊrreſt of the Five Members.

<small>Propoſed cenſure of Sir Ralph Hopton.</small>
Houſe in ſharp debate what cenſure to lay upon him. "The words he had ſpoken were "occaſioned on the reading of that part of "the Declaration which ſhowed that the Pope's <small>Pope ſoliciting help againſt Engliſh Parliament.</small> "Nuncio had ſolicited the Kings of France "and Spain to ſend each of them 4000*l*. to "his Majeſty againſt the Parliament, and that "we did believe his Majeſty could not give "ear to ſuch counſels unleſs he meant to "change his religion. Upon which the ſaid "Sir Ralph Hopton ſtood up and ſpake "very vehemently againſt the ſaid article, "ſaying, amongſt other particulars, that we "did thereby charge the King with apoſtacy.*

<small>King accuſed of Popiſh deſigns.</small> * Clarendon refers to this incident, and ſays that Hopton charged the Houſe with accuſing the King of deſigns favourable to Popery on evidence that would not hang a conſtable. But, to ſay nothing of the letters found after Naſeby, all that has ſince been diſcovered of the ſecret purpoſes and deſperate expedients reſorted to by Charles the Firſt, tends directly to ſhow how thoroughly well informed, though unable always to give up their informants, the leaders of the Houſe of Commons <small>Too many grounds for ſuch imputation.</small> were. As to Charles's undoubted negotiations for the procuring foreign help againſt the Parliament on condition of ſpecial ceſſions to the Roman Catholic faith, ſee my *Eſſays*, i. 75-6. Let me add that there is a very curious letter in the Clarendon *State Papers* (ii. 141-2) which may be quoted, not only in aid of what has been ſaid (ante, 32 and 49) of the ſuſpicion of Secretary Windebank's illegal practices in favour of the Roman Catholic religion, but in proof of the <small>Engliſh politics at Rome.</small> intereſt with which Engliſh politics were now regarded in Rome, and of the prudent and ſomewhat ominous reſerve which, preciſely at the very date of the incident deſcribed in my text, had fallen ſuddenly on the Pope's nephew and one of the leading Cardinals, otherwiſe accuſtomed, as it would ſeem, largely to indulge in garrulity about England. Writing, to his <small>Letter to Hyde from brother-in-law</small> brother-in-law Hyde, from Rome at the cloſe of March 1642, Mr. Ayleſbury ſays: "The laſt week, we came from Naples; "where we met with an Engliſh Franciſcan Friar, called "Father Morton; who uſed us exceeding civilly, and has a

"After which, though he explained himſelf, and acknowledged his fault to proceed from his miſtake, yet the Houſe would not reſt ſatisfied, but cauſed him to withdraw."* When D'Ewes entered, Sir Henry Herbert, the member for Bewdley, was ſpeaking in mitigation of his offence (againſt a propoſition for diſabling him which the member for Bletchingly, Sir John Evelyn, had ſtarted), and in favour of the more moderate ſuggeſtion that he ſhould be permitted to purge his fault by a few days lodgment in the Tower. Such cen-

margin: Hopton's offence. His expulſion moved.

"great mind to go into England to accuſe Secr^y Windebank "of greater matters than the parliament ever laid to his "charge. I aſſure you the diſcourſe he makes of him is "very good ſport; and in theſe ſad times I could wiſh you "had him amongſt you to make you merry. At Rome there "are graver gentlemen; but I underſtand nothing of them "but their civility, which is as much as can be imagined. "Indeed, from the higheſt to the loweſt, they are all ſo. The "other day we were with the Cardinal Franceſco Barberino, "the Pope's nephew, and had a long audience of him, but "not a word of England, though I ſought all I could to put "him into that diſcourſe of which he is very well informed, "and at other times liberal enough. For, Sir Walter Pye "having been with him ſome days before, all his diſcourſe "was to perſuade *him* that the troubles of England and "Ireland have never been fomented by any of the Pope's "miniſters: and that they all wiſhed the flouriſhing eſtate of "our country. Beſides, he made particular mention to him "of Mr. Pym, Mr. Hampden, Mr. Hollis, and ſome others." What ſort of "particular mention" Pym and Hampden are likely to have attracted to themſelves in the halls and council chambers of the Vatican, it would not be difficult to imagine; and he muſt have been a very clever Cardinal indeed if he managed to impreſs any Engliſh traveller with the belief that he, one of the higheſt dignitaries of the Roman Catholic Church, took an impartial intereſt in the welfare of thoſe famous members of the Engliſh Commons. The reference, however, is at leaſt remarkable.

margin: The Pope's nephew: ſays he has not fomented Engliſh troubles. His "intereſt" in Pym and Hampden.

* *Harl. MSS.* 163, f. 410 a.-414 b.

sures being very much matter of precedent, Sir Simonds at once plunged into the debate, and claimed hearing from the Speaker. But Sir John Evelyn was so loudly called for, that D'Ewes was fain, after beginning his speech, to give way. "After Sir John sat down," he proceeds, "I stood up to continue my former
" speech where I left off; but some violent
" spirits, whom otherwise I esteemed very
" honest men, fearing that by my speaking I
" might prevent the putting of the question
" for disabling Sir Ralph, which I did, would
" fain have interrupted me, crying out He hath
" spoken! he hath spoken! But they, being
" soon ashamed of the breach of the order of
" the House and their own violence, became
" silent and I proceeded, showing that indeed
" my very worthy friend on the other side
" (and here I pointed to Sir John Evelyn)
" did break the order of the House in inter-
" rupting me after I had begun."

The result of Sir Simonds's interference was the more moderate course of sending Hopton to the Tower; and when Sir Walter Earle, upon this, moved that Sir Ralph should not be enlarged but in a full House, D'Ewes sensibly pointed out what injustice this vague expression might involve, and induced the majority to consent to receive the petition for release on any day when tendered, provided always it was between the hours of two and

[margin: D'Ewes's speech in mitigation. Interrupted by the hot spirits. Appeals to order. His suggestion adopted by House.]

§ XXIII. *D'Ewes and Speaker Lenthal.* 227

four o'clock. He then goes on to fay, that, the
original debate on the Declaration having Makes
been refumed, he objected himfelf to expref- ſimilar
                                              objection
ſions in it, " condemning them almoſt as to Hop-
" much as Sir R. Hopton had done, but with ton's:
" better fuccefs, for amendment enfued on my with
" motion." Still he was not fatiffied; and better
                                              fuccefs.
when, on the following day, it was finifhed and
paffed upon the queſtion, he adds: " many par-
" ticulars continuing in it, full of irritating and
" rigid expreffions to his Majeſty concerning
" his own words and actions, which I utterly
" mifliked: for we might have declared the D'Ewes's
" whole and naked truth as well in reverential love of
                                              moderate
" and humble words, as in fo high and afperous fpeech.
" terms."*

Upon another occafion, however, he found Another
himfelf lefs decidedly in fympathy with that cafe for
                                              cenfure.
ardent royaliſt, " Hopton of the Weſt," and

---

* *Harl. MSS.* 163, f. 414 b. On that fame day fo re- Remark-
markable an entry appears alfo in D'Ewes's Journal, carrying able entry
with it fuch marks of generous confideration on the part of in Journal.
the Houfe to the memory of a great opponent, that the reader
will thank me for fubjoining it. " Upon Mr. Denzil Hollis's
" motion it was ordered that the young Earl Strafford, being
" fome fifteen years old, being nephew to the faid Mr. Hollis,
" being his fifter's fon, and whom the King by letters patent
" created Earl Strafford fince the attainder of his father, fhould Generofity
" continue his troop in Ireland and receive his pay thereof, of Houfe
" though he were not there prefent: the faid Mr. Hollis under- to Straf-
" taking to fee his abfence properly fupplied." It is curious ford's fon.
that the order which rendered this fpecial application neceffary,
was one introduced under the government of the young man's
father, the great Earl; who refifted nothing more ſtrongly in
Ireland than the abufe of abfenteeifm and non-refidence in
every poffible form, whether it were in the captains of regiments
or the proprietors of eſtates.

by no means difpofed to mitigate punifhment to an offending member. This was when Sir Edward Dering, in lefs than a month after the arreft of the members, had printed his fpeeches againft the Grand Remonftrance, with a preface fo ill-judged and indifcreet, remarking upon members of the Houfe and otherwife fcandalizing its orders of debate, that opportunity was taken to vote his expulfion. The propofal found an ardent fupporter in D'Ewes. He had no mercy for any one who departed from precedent, violated old ufage, or committed breaches of parliamentary decorum; and, entering the Houfe juft as the debate began, and finding attempts made to evade the motion by no fharper cenfure than the Tower, he tells us that he loft all patience.

Sir Edward Dering's publifhed fpeeches.

D'Ewes's indignation thereat.

"After I had heard divers fpeak," he fays, "and faw a great part of the Houfe begin to "incline to inflict no other punifhment on "him than fending him to the Tower, I was "very much troubled at it; efpecially when "Sir R. Hopton faid that we might retain "him *becaufe of his great parts.*" At this, unable to contain himfelf any longer, he ftarted up; detailed the offences of the book; denounced the prefumption of the author; defcribed him fo overvaluing himfelf in his "moft fcandalous, feditious, and vain-glorious "performance," as if he had been able of himfelf to weigh down the balance of that Houfe

Would have Dering expelled.

Denounces his vain-glorious preface.

§ XXIII. *D'Ewes and Speaker Lenthal.*

on either side when he pleased; pointed out the evil consequence of printing such arguments, without allusion to the answers made thereto; dwelt upon the outrage to the freedom of debate as unpardonable, seeing that he had therein discovered the secrets of the House, had discredited the acts of the House, and had named members of the House (among them Mr. O. C. by which the member for Cambridge was plainly intended) to their disgrace; and he concluded by declaring that if he himself, member for Sudbury, should ever be so unfortunate as to offend that assembly in so high a nature, he would rather hide himself for ever in a cell than enter again within those walls! " As soon," he continues, " as I " had spoken, having delivered myself with " some vehemence, the Speaker said presently " to some about his Chair, 'You may see, now, " ' what Sir Edward Dering's friends have pro- " ' cured him, by endeavouring to have a small " ' censure passed upon him.'"* The tide had turned against Sir Edward. The determination became strong, not only to expel the writer, but to put a mark of opprobrium on the book; and though D'Ewes sensibly resisted Sir Walter Earle's motion for " calling it in," on the ground that such a proceeding would raise the price of it from fourteen pence to

Dering's attack upon the House.

Mr. O. C. libelled.

Mr. Speaker compliments D'Ewes.

Objection to suppression of a book:

---

* *Harl. MSS.* 162, f. 366 b.

Arrest of the Five Members.

<small>will raise value from fourteen pence to fourteen shillings.</small> fourteen shillings, and hasten a new impression,* he did not oppose Mr. Oliver Cromwell's suggestion for remitting it to the hands of the common hangman. It was, by a majority of 85 to 61, ordered to be burnt in Palace Yard, <small>Dering expelled and his book burnt.</small> Cheapside, and Smithfield, on the Friday following. Dering was expelled; and a warrant issued for a writ for Kent to choose a new knight.

Between that day and the next, however, a doubt seems to have occurred to the honorable member for Cambridge whether to burn a book were quite the best way of answering any dangerous matter contained in it; and D'Ewes relates accordingly what took place near the close of the sitting on the following day.†

<small>A suggestion from Mr. Oliver Cromwell.</small> "Mr. Oliver Cromwell," he says, "moved "that Sir E. Dering's book, lately set out by "him, had many dangerous and scandalous "passages in it, by which many must be de- "ceived and led into an ill opinion concerning "the proceedings of this House; and there- "fore desired that some able member of the "House might be appointed to make a short "confutation of the same. And then he "nominated Me. Which made me presently <small>Will D'Ewes answer Dering?</small> "stand up and answer, that I conceived that "the gentleman who last spoke did not dream

<small>* This passage of the debate was referred to in my *Hist. and Biog. Essays*, i. 89, but the details here given have not before been presented.   † *Harl. MSS.* 162, f. 368 a.</small>

§ XXIII. *D'Ewes and Speaker Lenthal.*

"that it was now near 7 of the clock at night,
"or elfe that he would not at this time have
"made fuch a motion as he did: for, if I
"could but gain fome fpare time from the
"public fervice of the Houfe, I have other
"things to print, of more public ufe and
"benefit than the confutation of Sir E.
"Dering's fpeech could be: and therefore I
"defired that the gentleman himfelf who
"made the motion, might be defired to under-
"take the tafk. The Speaker then defired
"that I would print that, that would be for the
"public good." And with this polite intimation from Mr. Speaker, unfeconded by any
eagernefs on Mr. Cromwell's part to affume
himfelf the literary labour he would have
impofed on D'Ewes, the fubject dropped.

D'Ewes declines: has better things to do.

Might not Mr. Cromwell do it?

It will not be out of place to connect with
it, and the illuftrations formerly given of the
general truftworthinefs, as well as temperate
and moderate fpirit, of a man to whofe manu-
fcript record of the events under notice this narrative has been, and will be, fo largely indebted,
further and very ftriking proof of his independent honefty and confcientioufnefs in regard
to his Journal. It is this in truth which gives
it a character of accuracy and original authority
that none of the many other exifting MS.
journals of this time, which on examination turn
out to be, for the moft part, mere tranfcripts
from the official records of the Houfe, can in

Other proofs of D'Ewes's accuracy.

Originality of his Journal.

the leaſt lay claim to. In the midſt of the events under notice, when a meſſage had been voted, late one evening, to the King, Denzil Hollis brought it again before the Houſe the following morning, with a view to an alteration in the wording which he deſired to ſuggeſt.

Hollis would alter a meſſage voted.

"But," D'Ewes continues, "Sir Guy
"Palmes ſaid he did not know how it could
"well be ordered, becauſe the votes were
"already printed. Thereupon ſome thought
"that the clerk or his men had given it out:
"others that it might be tranſcribed by ſome
"of the Houſe. So the clerk was aſked who
"did conſtantly write out of his Journal Book
"every night after the Houſe was riſen; and
"he ſaid the Lord Falkland only (who had
"lately been made principal Secretary). Then
"they aſked him who, alſo, did ſometimes
"write out of the ſaid Journal Book, or were
"preſent; and he ſaid, Mr. Moore and Mr.
"Bodvill did often write out of the ſame, and
"that myſelf was ſometimes preſent. But I,
"miſtaking him, and conceiving that he
"ranked me amongſt the tranſcribers (who
"ſcarcely wrote 3 words out of his Journal
"Book in 3 months), was very angry with
"him, and ſtood up and ſaid, that I was indeed
"often preſent when others tranſcribed out
"of the ſaid Journal, but did myſelf write *not
"out of that but out of my head:* and there-
"fore I deſired that the clerk might name the

The meſſage already printed.

Who copies nightly from Clerk's Journals?

Falkland and two others.

But not D'Ewes: he reports "out of his head."

" time when I tranfcribed anything out of his *never at*
" Journal. With which the houfe refting fatif- *fecond-hand.*
" fied, as I conceived, I troubled myfelf no
" further about it. But Mr. H. Elfyng, the
" clerk, came to me in Weftminfter Hall after
" we were rifen, and expreffed a great deal of *Clerk*
" forrow that I did miftake him; that he only *Elfyng's apologies.*
" named me as being prefent, and the rather
" that I could prove what he faid." *

An incident highly charaƈteriftic of D'Ewes, which occurred on the next following day, completes the piƈture of our learned and careful reporter, zealous for the originality of his notes, fenfible of the power derived from exercife of fuch an art, and refolved to abate no jot of the influence it gave him. A delicate matter coming under debate (being nothing *A delicate* lefs than information, fubmitted by Pym, of *matter difcuffed.* tamperings on the part of the Court with foreign powers, for the lending an army, if need fhould be, to put down the liberties of England) fome members arofe, in much excitement, to fuggeft that the debate be adjourned *Notetaking* for a day, and that no one meanwhile be per- *infeparable from* mitted to take notes. " Stop note-taking!" *ble from speechmaking.* cried D'Ewes.† " You cannot! Or, if you can, " make men hold their tongues, then, as well!"

Such being the recognized pofition of D'Ewes in the Houfe, and his admitted authority in everything conneƈted with its ufages *Relations of D'Ewes to Lenthal:*

* *Harl. MSS.* 163, f. 430 a. † *Ib.* 163, f. 432 b.

his authority in precedents: and the precedents of former times, he was naturally brought into frequent relations with the Speaker; and whether Lenthal found it more oppressive to submit to his critical objurgations, or to enjoy the advantage of his condescending patronage, it might be difficult to say. There is, however, hardly a week's *critic and patron of Mr. Speaker.* entry in his Journal that does not present him in one or other of these positions; and if nothing were known of Lenthal but the noble words we have seen him use on a sudden and great emergency, we might well be disposed to reject as incredible the impression which D'Ewes steadily conveys, that he was a timid, restless, indecisive, ill-informed, and ill- *Weaknesses of Lenthal.* conditioned man. Unhappily this impression is too well borne out by what otherwise is known of his life, and by what already this narrative has disclosed.* We know that this *Self-surrender of his only claim to respect.* was the man who, violating the principle laid down by himself on that memorable 4th of January, and flinging scorn and disrepute on the only act by which in history he is honorably remembered, actually had the baseness, at the *A witness against Scot the regicide.* Restoration, to give evidence against Scot the regicide of words which he had heard within the House when sitting in the Speaker's chair!† When Lenthal is credited, therefore,

---

* *Ante*, 22, 25.

Contract to Lenthal. † *State Trials*, v. 1063. As a contract let me mention, in justice to the Earl of Northumberland, whose conduct throughout these affairs seems to me to have been unworthy of his abilities

with qualities generally poor and commonplace, we may be only too well assured that the facts alleged will justify the charge. Such evidence abounds in every part of D'Ewes's Journal, and proves beyond all doubt, quite irrespective of the special proof given in a previous section of his eager desire at this time to offer servile homage to the King, that what he showed himself unmistakeably to be in later years, he now already was, and was known to be. And I gladly seize the opportunity of adding, to what was remarked upon the subject in a former work,* other traits and incidents relating to him from D'Ewes's curious manuscript, not merely characteristic and amusing in themselves, but such as, besides completing what was formerly said, will also help further to show D'Ewes's own position in reference to parties in the House.

A time-server always.

Traits and incidents from D'Ewes's diary.

A debate arose upon a question of privilege: a person having been arrested, after order had issued from the House that he should be

Question of privilege.

and his name, that when, upon the Restoration, he consented, like Lenthal, to receive favour from the Government, it was by no such base betrayal of acts and proceedings in which he had himself been a participator. Ludlow tells us in his *Memoirs* that Lord Northumberland (who had taken the oath of fidelity to the Commonwealth) was heard to say in the Convention Parliament at the Restoration, that though he had no part in the death of the King, *he was against questioning those who had been concerned in that affair, that the example might be more useful to posterity, and profitable to future Kings, by deterring them from the like exorbitancies.* iii. 10, ed. 1699.

Northumberland true to old friends.

An example profitable to future Kings.

* *Hist. and Biog. Essays* (Debates on the Grand Remonstrance), i. 82, 83, &c.

sent for as a witness. "When," says D'Ewes, "some spake to the case, and mistook it, and the Speaker would have informed them of the case how it stood, Sir A. Haselrig spake to the order of the House, and said that the Speaker ought not to stand up and interrupt any other member of the House when he was speaking. Whereupon the Speaker stood up and answered Sir Arthur Haselrig that he had not stood up to interrupt any member, but only to inform such as should speak of the truth of the case. But Sir A. H. not satisfied herewith, stood up again: saying he would speak to the order of the House, and under colour thereof endeavoured to reply to the Speaker, and to get said over again the same thing: which made me interrupt him, though I much respected him." He accordingly, with deference, but very decidedly, rebukes "that worthy gentleman in the Gallery," who, upon D'Ewes resuming his seat, "would have spoken again to the order of the House; but the House, it seems, being satisfied with what I said, would not hear him again."*

Marginalia: Haselrig and Lenthal. Attack on Mr. Speaker. D'Ewes rebukes Haselrig.

That was a great triumph for Sir Simonds, if not for Lenthal; but, upon a subsequent question of order and usage, Mr. Speaker himself seems to have been permitted to violate all precedent. Soon afterwards there occurred a

Marginalia: Lenthal out of order.

* *Harl. MSS.* 163 f. 405 b.

debate, very stiffly maintained on both sides, about the custom to be imposed on sugar. D'Ewes was the last speaker, and sat down with a solemn warning to the House that they should be wary of offending the Hollanders with such an impost. "Between which time "and the putting of the question itself," he continues, "some members came into the "House, and some called on them to with- "draw; and thereupon grew a debate, whether "by the order of the House they should with- "draw or not: and in the issue it was "observed that regularly no member of the "House could be commanded to withdraw, "but when he came in after the question "had been put the first time." But the extraordinary thing was, D'Ewes concludes, that upon going to the division, the Speaker not only claimed to vote, but actually voted, "the "like of which I never knew before or since."*

Sugar-duties' debate.

Members entering just before question put.

Not to withdraw.

Again, shortly after, occurred another instance of Mr. Speaker forgetting the dignity of his place. It arose out of Sir John Holland, the member for Castle Rising, objecting to the amount of the parliamentary levy on his county. "Sir John Holland," says D'Ewes, "a Norfolk man, seemingly anxious to show "his forwardness for the county, said he was "informed that Norfolk would not pay the

Extraordinary proceeding of Mr. Speaker.

Lenthal again at fault.

---

* *Harl. MSS.* 163, f. 429 b.

"sum laid on them by the £400,000 bill,
"except some abatement; and that if any dis-
"temper arose in Norfolk, it would be paid
"nowhere in England. Whereupon the
"Speaker stood up and interrupted him, and
"said such words were very dangerous and
"not fit to be spoken. But Sir J. H. stood
"up to justify himself, and averred that he
"only said he was informed so, and claimed
"the privilege of a member not to be inter-
"rupted, &c. Whereupon the Speaker, for-
"getting the dignity of his place, and deserting
"the just ground that was given him to
"interrupt him, gave some approbation to
"what he had said, and sat him down. So
"as Sir John Holland was proceeding on as
"if he had done very well before, which
"made me, with some indignation to see the
"Speaker's miscarriage, stand up and speak to
"the order of the House."* Here, beyond all doubt, was another decided success for D'Ewes; and the House loudly, and very properly, applauded him for thus vindicating Mr. Speaker, though against Mr. Speaker himself.

An hon. member interrupted.

Hon. member retorts.

Mr. Speaker succumbs.

D'Ewes's indignation.

But, even in the trivial duties and observances of his place, Lenthal was by no means expert. Some letters having been handed in to the Speaker, and among them one from the King, he gave it to the Clerk of the House, "who,"

Lenthal's deficiencies as Speaker.

* *Harl. MSS.* 163, f. 461 a.

says D'Ewes, "having read the superscription *A letter*
"*Charles Rex*, I stood up and reminded the *from the*
"Speaker that he was to read such letters *King.*
"himself: on which he acknowledged his
"error, and read it." It came at last, indeed, *D'Ewes*
to be very generally understood that the *the great authority*
member for Sudbury, and not the Speaker, was *as to order:*
the man to settle questions of order, and to
compose jarring discords in debate.* A curious
instance occurred when Sir Henry Mildmay,
the member for Malden, who sat afterwards *composer*
on the trial of the King, would have obtained *of discords in*
consent from the House to a bill for trade *debate.*
which threatened to interfere mightily with
the Coventry weavers; whereupon Mr. William
Jesson, an ancient alderman of that borough *Heat of*
who very worthily represented it, started up with *ancient burgess*
much heat and "spake very earnestly against *for Coventry.*
"such a bill, saying that by so doing we would
"destroy the whole trade of the kingdom.
"Whereupon Sir H. Mildmay took excep-
"tion, affirming that the said Mr. Jesson
"had looked very fiercely upon him when he

---

* Other duties appear at times to have been imposed which D'Ewes
he took upon himself with less relish. The following may serve *avoids*
as an example: "Between 4 and 5 the House resolved into *a chair of*
"Grand Committee on Tonnage: and when the Speaker *Com-*
"withdrew, and most of the House with him, some *to mittee.*
"Committees, and some clean away, so as we were scarce 40
"left, divers called on me to sit in the chair at the Committee.
"So as, fearing that I should not have excused myself, I with-
"drew out of the House, and after Mr. Ellis had taken the
"said chair, I returned again. The bill passed, and we rose
"between 5 and 6." *Harl. MSS.* 162, f. 357 a.

Fierce and unparliamentary looks:

"spoke, and that it was done in an unparliamentary way." Here was a novel case! and it must be confessed that D'Ewes, on appeal being made to him, treated it more sensibly than might have been expected. Desiring to

D'Ewes's opinion thereon.

qualify, as he says, such unnecessary heat, he declared that in all his knowledge of these matters he never knew exception taken at looks before; and, with some further goodnatured words, he perfectly reconciled the offended knight and too choleric ancient burgess.*

Ancient member again.

It fared not so well, however, with the good old member for Coventry some few months later, when, upon the unfurling of the Royal standard at Nottingham " about six of the " clock in the evening of a very stormy and " tempestuous day," † the House of Commons promptly met the King's proclamation against

Vote for allegiance to Parliamentary general.

Lord Essex as a traitor, by a vote calling upon every member to answer individually, upon the instant, whether he would venture and hazard his life and fortune with the Earl of Essex, Lord General. D'Ewes regarded this vote with little favour, and dwells upon the harsh way in which it was pressed by the "fiery

Disliked by D'Ewes.

" spirits" who had introduced it: wherein, he adds, they were seconded, in a manner un-

---

* Harl. MSS. 163, f. 502 a.
† "The standard," Clarendon subsequently tells us (Hist. iii. 190), "was blown down the same night it had been set up, " by a very strong and unruly wind."

§ XXIII.   *D'Ewes and Speaker Lenthal.*   241

worthy of himself and contrary to the duty of
his place, by Mr. Speaker. "And whereas _{Required}
" one Mr. Jesson, one of the burgesses for _{to say *Aye*.}
" Coventry, being an ancient man, did only
" desire a little time to consider of it before
" he gave his answer, they would not permit
" that, but compelled him to answer presently,
" whereupon he, not being satisfied in his con-
" science, gave his No.   At which those hot _{Says *No*.}
" spirits taking great distaste, the Speaker,
" unworthy of himself and contrary to the
" duty of his place, fell upon him with very _{Assailed}
" strange language for giving his No; and _{by Mr.
Speaker.}
" when the poor man, terrified with the dis-
" pleasure he saw was taken against him, would
" have given his Aye, they would not permit _{Wishes to}
" him to do that neither.   Sir Guy Palmes, _{say *Aye*:
but not}
" and Mr. Fettyplace" (the members for _{permitted.}
Rutlandshire and Berkshire, both of them
declared Royalists) " were so overawed by Mr. _{Other}
" Jesson's misfortune as they answered Aye _{members
fright-}
" without any further debate; and so did many _{ened.}
" others who came dropping in from dinner,
" not knowing what had been done and was
" doing in the House." *

Nor had the scene been less striking some
three months earlier (little more than six weeks
after the attempted arrest), when, amid the war
of declarations and replies that preceded the
unfurling of the standards, Sir Peter Wentworth

* *Harl. MSS.* 164, f. 1060 b.

Sir Peter Wentworth: (who fat for Tamworth, and afterwards on the High Court of Juftice) took the occafion of a particular meffage from Charles to fay " that *cannot truft the King.* " we could not confide in the King nor truft him: " which made Sir John Culpeper, Chancellor " of the Exchequer, who fat near him, rife up *Chancellor of Exchequer's horror.* " and fay that he wondered that any man " fhould dare to fpeak fuch language within " thefe walls—*That we could not confide in the* " *King!*" Confiderable excitement enfued, D'Ewes proceeds to tell us, but Sir Peter's plain fpeaking having found feveral backers, *Houfe overlooks this " folly."* he was permitted to explain himfelf. " And " fo the Houfe paffed by his folly."

But then followed an incident well worthy record in itfelf, and having a highly character-iftic fequel with D'Ewes for its hero. Old *Old Sir Harry Vane.* Vane, who fo long had ferved the higheft offices of ftate, had fignalifed himfelf, fince his lofs of Court favour and public employ-ment,* by difplaying in oppofition all the caution and prudence which accompany the expectation of being reftored to power. But, in *Startling fpeeches.* a fpeech he delivered on the prefent occafion, this referve was flung afide. He fhowed that things were come to a defperate condition. In a previous debate on the Cuftody of the young Prince of Wales, very ftartling allufions *Sir John Northcote's avowal.* had been made. Sir John Northcote, the member for Afhburton, had faid plainly he

* *Ante* 50, 51.

§ XXIII. *D'Ewes and Speaker Lenthal.*

would rather increase the jealousies between the King and the House than any way diminish them, and, amid continual excitement and interruptions, had persisted in naming an intention which they had all heard discussed elsewhere if not in that House, " to crown the prince and make him King."* But now, in a very full House, amid an unusual and sullen silence, Old Vane did not scruple to take something of a similar tone. He gave in his adhesion to the views expressed by Pym and Hampden upon the question of the Militia, declared his conviction that " the present flame would devour all " unless great care and wisdom were used for stopping it, " and wished that to that end we might lay " a new foundation." This called up Mr. Harry Killegrew of Cornwall, the member for West Looe,† who made a violent Royalist speech, and in the course of it propounded a constitutional doctrine of an extremely novel and disconcerting kind. He warned them that they were setting their feet on slippery places

marginalia: " Make the Prince our King." Old Vane declares for militia and " new foundation." Anecdote of Killegrew. Will " find " a good cause.

---

* Northcote's speech was delivered on the 14th January on the motion of Sir Henry Chomley, the member for Northallerton, for removal of jealousies between King and Parliament. *Harl. MSS.* 162, f. 328 a.

† The same " gallant gentleman and generally known," of whom Clarendon relates (*Life*, i. 140) that subsequently, on being invited with the other members to offer a contribution towards the formation of an army for the Parliament, stood up and answered, he would provide a good horse, and a good sword, and a good buff coat, and then he would find a good cause:" which for that time only raised laughter, though they " knew well what cause he thought good, which he had never " dissembled."

in what they called their new foundation, and that he could wish, before the gentlemen he saw around him concluded matters of so great moment then and there, as imposing the militia and all their new taxation on the people, they should send some members of that House into each county to have their consent; otherwise, they might come to feel the weight of the major part of the people; *for it was not the enacting of a law that made it in force, but the willing obedience to it.* "With some other words," D'Ewes adds, "to the like effect, at which " many of the House, laughing heartily when " he spoke them, it made him repeat them " once or twice." The laughers meanwhile desisted, for Young Vane arose with much gravity to take exception to words carrying such dangerous import. Others followed in the same tone; and some, says D'Ewes, did aggravate the words so far, that they were against allowing Mr. Killegrew to explain himself. With some difficulty Pym obtained hearing for him, "and so he made some little " justification, protesting in the presence of " God that he had no intention to do any dis- " service to the House." Upon this Pym opposed the motion for his expulsion, which was rejected by 131 to 97. He was however ordered to withdraw, and, the debate continuing, there came suddenly to his relief another Cornishman, Mr. Chadwell, the member for St.

§ XXIII.   *D'Ewes and Speaker Lenthal.*

Michaels, who professed to cite some ancient record supporting what the member for West Looe had said. D'Ewes no sooner heard it than he suspected an imposture. He withdrew very quietly, for it was against the order of the House; hastened over to his lodging, close at hand; looked through his papers and records; hurried back to the debate; and threw upon it a flood of antiquarian lore, underneath which poor Mr. Chadwell, and his misquoted, misdated, and wholly misrepresented record, were completely carried away. But it is a peculiarity of D'Ewes to be always magnanimous in his moments of triumph. He never tramples on the fallen. "No doubt, Mr. Speaker," he said, "I think this gentleman very faulty who "would presume to misquote Records for "Mr. Killegrew. But, not being well skilled "in Records, perhaps he did not know the "dangerous consequence." That was his tone. The House fell in with it; and both Killegrew and Chadwell, thanks to the moderation and good sense of Pym, escaped with but slight punishment.*

An indiscreet friend.

D'Ewes goes in search of records.

Exposes Cornish ignorance.

Is merciful in triumph.

These illustrations may now be fitly closed with some notice of the many efforts made to

---

* *Harl. MSS.* 163, f. 451 b. Being called to the Bar, the Speaker told them that the House conceived the offence to be of a very high nature, considering the circumstances of time and the opinions of some people abroad; and therefore they had commanded him to give them a sharp reprehension, and it was the mercy of the House that the censure was no severer.

A reprimand.

Attempts to force early attendance. compel early and full attendance at the Houſe, in which D'Ewes and Lenthal took prominent part. Under the form of fines for being late at prayers, theſe attempts were frequently renewed; and they had originated at a memorable time. As early as the previous May (1641), when the duties and reſponſibilities of memberſhip had become ſuch as to daunt and deter all but the moſt reſolute; amid the plots for Strafford's eſcape, and the tumultuous aſſemblages of the people demanding juſtice upon him; when the King ſtill pauſed on the verge of deſperate *Alarming time when firſt found neceſſary.* counſels; while each hour of every day came laden with its danger and its terror; only two days before Charles had gone to the Lords to warn them againſt paſſing the attainder, for that he never in his conſcience could conſent to it; on the very day when Pym aroſe in the Commons to explode the conſpiracy of Henry Percy and Goring for bringing up the army and ſeizing on the Tower,—D'Ewes makes the ſubjoined moſt ſtriking entry in his Journal. It adds another to many memorable inſtances of the *Tragi-comedy of the world.* cloſe intermixture of ſeriouſneſs and laughter in this tragi-comedy of the world, and is one more proof that men are never ſo prone to ſudden burſts of mirth as when heavy and overborne in ſpirit by a long ſtrain of anxiety, by nervous excitement or apprehenſion, by the over-wrought intenſity of either hope or fear.

"Prayers being done, after the Speaker had

§ XXIII. *D'Ewes and Speaker Lenthal.*   247

" fitten a good while, and all men filent, the The
" Clerk's affiftant began to read a bill touching Houfe in fadnefs.
" wire-drawers, which being prefently ftopped,
" did amidft our fad apprehenfions move
" laughter from divers that fuch a frivolous Suddenly
" bill fhould be pitched upon, when all matters moved to laughter.
" were in fuch apparent danger. After fome
" half-hour's filence more, or a quarter's, fome
" called to have the order read, which was
" made on Saturday, by which every member
" that came after eight of the clock was to pay
" one fhilling. And then, as men came in,
" divers cried, 'Pay! Pay!' When the Serjeant The fhil-
" demanded the faid fhilling, which bred a great ling fine.
" confufion."*

Such was the continued confufion, indeed, A failure.
that for this particular time it had to be
abandoned. But, ten months later, it was renewed; and Sir Simonds had again, upon the
fpecial fubject, though on this occafion with
inferior fuccefs to that we have feen formerly
attend him, to vindicate the dignity of Mr.
Speaker's place againft Lenthal's own forgetful-
nefs and non-affertion of it. On a Tuefday Shilling
the fine was propofed. "A motion made," fine again propofed.
fays D'Ewes, "as I came in, that fuch
" members as fhould not come up by 8 and
" be at prayers, fhould pay a fhilling. I faid, D'Ewes
" when that was tried twelve months ago oppofed to it.
" it was laid afide from its inconvenience,

* *Harl. MSS.* 163, f. 514 a.

"after one day's practice; and that the beft
"way would be to rife at 12, and not at 2 or
"3, to enfure members coming at 8. Divers
"others fpake againft it; but the greater
"number being for it, it paffed." *

Mr. Speaker late: Very little, however, as it would feem, to the immediate edification of Mr. Speaker, feeing that next morning, Wednefday, he did not himfelf make his appearance till a quarter to nine. "The Houfe by this time," D'Ewes remarks, "was very full at prayers, by reafon of the order "made yefterday. Sir H. Mildmay, after "prayers, ftood up and faid he was glad to fee

rebuked: "this good effect of yefterday's order ; and faid "to the Speaker that he did hope that hereafter "he would come in time; which made the

throws his fhilling on table: "Speaker throw down twelvepence upon the "table. Divers fpake after him, and others "as they came in did each pay his fhilling to "the Serjeant. I fpake to the Orders of the "Houfe: That the order made yefterday was "to fine 'after' prayers, and therefore you "(I fpake to the Speaker) cannot be fubject "to pay ; and for coming a little after 8, that "was no great difference. Although I fpake

will not take it up again. "truly, the Speaker having caft down his "fhilling, would not take it up again."†

One may perhaps infer, without difrefpect, that Lenthal had fulked a little ; and the ill effect of fo throwing down his twelvepence,

* *Harl. MSS.* 163, f. 474 a.   † *Ib.* 163, f. 475 b.

§ XXIII.   *D'Ewes and Speaker Lenthal.*   249

certainly difplayed itfelf next day, Thurfday, Ill refults of the fine when the action found an imitator well difpofed to exaggerate it. After obferving that on that morning only about forty were at prayers, D'Ewes proceeds to fay that it was ordered upon the motion of Mr. Rous, that the fines of yefterday and to-day be given to Dr. Leighton, being in fome diftrefs. Then came on a petition complaining of Dr. Fuller, parfon of St. Giles's, having chofen two churchwardens ill affected to religion, in oppofition to two chofen by the parifhioners.
" Some coming in and refufing to pay, whilft Refufals
" the aforefaid petition was reading, divers to pay.
" called out to them to pay, and fo inter-
" rupted the Clerk's affiftant, who was reading
" it.   Mr. John Hotham ftood up and faid
" that the time appointed for men to come
" yefterday by the order was 8, and that the
" chimes for that hour went juft as he came
" into the houfe.   But the Speaker telling Jack Hotham
" him that prayers being paft he muft pay, ordered to
" and he ftill refufing, it was put to the pay.
" queftion, ruled affirmatively, and ordered ac-
" cordingly.   Whereupon he took his fhilling,
" and threw it down upon the ground: Flings his fhilling on
" upon which fome called him to the bar, ground.
" others that he fhould withdraw : and the
" Speaker, ftanding up, did fharply reprove him
" for that action, as being a contempt to the
" Houfe.   Which caufed him, as I conceive, a

"little after, to withdraw out of the Houfe, though he returned again this forenoon."*

Beginning of the End.
Thefe various fcenes, and the attempts to check in honorable members a growing tendency to flacken and be remifs in their attendances, prefigure what was now rapidly approaching. The King's party had loft their laft venture, and filent defertions were reported daily.

Call of Houfe attempted.
A call of the Houfe had been attempted with ill fuccefs foon after Strafford's execution, and now another attempt was made. "Mr. D. Hollis," fays D'Ewes, "moved that the houfe might be called, and fuch as were abfent fined, for the relief of Ireland." But Sir Simonds ftoutly oppofed the motion, reminding Mr. Speaker that none of the members who were abfent at the firft calling had paid their £5 fine. In the end, the motion was overruled, and D'Ewes adds: "A number went to the conference with the Lords, and we had not *Not forty members prefent.* forty left, fo the Speaker left the chair, and we difcourfed feverally one with another for a pretty while."† Difcourfe which has all paffed away with the honourable members themfelves, but of which we might perhaps with flight effort, if it were worth the while, recal fo much as the fubjoined little incident of that day is likely to have called forth, as they fo talked feverally one with another. It had occurred while the Houfe yet fat, and bufinefs

* *Harl. MSS.* 163, f. 476 a. † *Ib.* 162, f. 401 b.

was proceeding. "One Mr. Shepherd, a *A strange in the House.* "stranger, came into the House and stood "behind the Serjeant. So divers espied him "out, and called him to the Bar. There, he "would not tell his name, but said he was a "Bedfordshire man. As divers knew him, *How dealt with* "he was dismissed."*

And now I resume the course of this narrative, which will not be held, I trust, to have been interrupted needlessly, by a series of incidents and illustrations intimately connected with it; all of them drawn from an unpublished manuscript record; ranging, in every instance, within a compass of not many weeks beyond the date of the Arrest of the Five Members; and not only supplying traits of history and personal character essential to any thorough comprehension of the circumstances and results comprised in that event, but testifying to the trustworthiness of one of the principal witnesses to be called in evidence for what yet remains to be described. *Resumption of narrative.* *Why interrupted.*

---

§ XXIV. APPEAL TO THE CITY.

CHARLES sent for Mr. Rushworth shortly after he reached Whitehall. James Maxwell, usher of the House of Lords, the same to whom Strafford yielded himself a prisoner, and in *Mr. Rushworth sent for by King.*

* *Harl. MSS.* 162, ff. 385 a. 389 a.

whose house at Charing Cross two right reverend prelates were now impounded, bore the message to the astonished Clerk's assistant. Arrived in the Royal presence, the King commanded him to give him a copy of his speech that day, which "his Majesty had observed "him to take in characters at the table in the "House." Somewhat alarmed at the order, and perhaps not without the ambition to show the King that Mr. Speaker's recent lesson of allegiance to the Commons had not been thrown away, Mr. Rushworth stammered out excuses; and proceeded humbly to remind his Majesty how a certain member had been committed to the Tower, for reporting what a certain other member had said in the House. Then said his Majesty smartly, "I do not ask you to tell me "what was said by any member of the House, "but what I said myself." Whereupon, Mr. Rushworth informs us, that, omitting what Lenthal had interposed, he "readily gave "obedience to his Majesty's command, and in "his Majesty's presence, in the room called "the Jewel-house, transcribed his Majesty's "speech out of his characters, his Majesty "staying in the room all the while, and then "and there presented the same to the King: "which his Majesty was pleased to command "to be sent speedily to the press, and the next "morning it came forth in print." But alas for the present chances of such an appeal!

Report of his majesty's speech demanded.

Mr. Rushworth's humble excuses.

King's sharp rejoinder.

Speech transcribed from notes, in King's presence.

Sent to press.

Every copy that could now be circulated had for its precursor, and illustrative comment, the printed and published Grand Remonstrance, already for nearly three weeks in the hands of every Citizen.

On the same night, after Rushworth quitted the King, there came forth a proclamation reiterating the charge of treason against the Five Members, and closing the ports against any attempt they might make to quit the kingdom. This proclamation is ordinarily confounded with that which forbade all persons under gravest penalties to receive or harbour them, and which was not issued until afterwards. Received and harboured, meanwhile, it was well known that they now were, in a house in Coleman Street in the City: whither already the King was resolved to proceed next day to demand them, and to try his final chances of authority and predominance in that stronghold of his kingdom. *Proclamation against Five Members. Ports closed against their escape. Their place of refuge.*

Of the influence and importance of the City of London at this time, it is needless to speak. It represented in itself the wealth, the strength, and the independence, which had made England feared and honoured throughout the world. Within its walls, and under the shadow and protection of its franchises, slept nightly between three and four hundred thousand Citizens. The place of business of the merchant, in those days, was also his residence *City of London. Merchants' home as well as place of business.*

and his home. The houses then recently built by nobles beyond its precincts, along the Strand of the magnificent river, scarcely transcended in extent or splendour those palaces of its merchant princes, which lurked everywhere behind its busy wharves and crowded counting-houses. But, beyond every such source of aggrandisements, its privileges were its power. From its guilds, charters, and immunities, wrested from the needs, or bestowed by the favour, of successive princes; from its own regulation of its military as well as civil affairs;* from its

Its palaces and privileges.

Sources of its power.

---

* Late in the night of the 4th of January, the day of the King's attempt, upon some suggestion which had reached him from Whitehall, Sir Richard Gourney sent round to the Aldermen of each ward in the City a letter of which the rough draft, brought back apparently to the Court, is now in the State Paper Office. It will be read with interest for the proof it affords of the military government and organization of the City at the time. Of course the object which the Lord Mayor had in view was frustrated by the very means thus proposed to give effect to it. He miscalculated, as the King did; and the organization and resistance they would have invoked to protect themselves, they found suddenly turned against them. The letter begins by stating, that, for the better suppressing and apprehending of all such insolent persons as shall be tumultuously assembled in and about the City and Liberties thereof, each Alderman do straightway appoint "substantial double watch and ward of able men, well "weaponed and furnished with Halberds and Musquetts, to "be from henceforth duly kept & continued every night and "day . . especially at every gate, posterne, & landing "place within the same, to beginne at eight of the clock in "the evening and continue until five in the morning. And "so from that tyme, by new supply, until eight at night "again," to go on until each Alderman have further order to the contrary from the Chief Magistrate. And further, each Alderman is adjured "that yourselfe take the service, the danger "of the tymes considered, personally to heart and care. And "that you, your deputy, & some of the Common Councilmen, "in person, do not only by turne watch every night, but that

Lord Mayor's letter to aldermen.

Military organization of City.

Instructions for watch and ward.

Personal service required from aldermen.

§ XXIV. *Appeal to the City.*

complete and thoroughly organized democracy, governed and governing by and within itself; was derived an influence which made it formidable far beyond its wealth and numbers. Clarendon, after speaking of its incredible accession of trade, of its marvellous increase in riches, people, and buildings, of its unvarying choice of the wealthiest and best-reputed men, of the wisest and most substantial citizens, to serve its offices and dignities, and of its several powerful companies " incorporated within the great " corporation," falls into a lament that wise men should not have foreseen, that such a fullness could not possibly continue there without an emptiness in other places; and that the government of the country should undergo neglect, while so many persons of honour and estates were so delighted with the City.* But this lament was not indulged until the City

Its complete and organised democracy.

Its incredible enrichment by trade.

Clarendon's lament.

" you provide the same watch and ward to be orderly sett " forth & continued in manner as aforesᵈ within your wards." Gates were everywhere to be shut and strongly guarded. Especial care to be taken that the said gates, and portcullises thereunto belonging, were speedily repaired and made sufficiently strong wheresoever required: and the portcullises made easy to let down and draw up when need should be. Also provision was to be made for setting right all chains and posts in any way defective, substantially and strongly. Also each parish in the ward was to be sufficiently furnished with hooks, ladders, buckets, spades, shovels, pickaxes, augurs, and chisels. Men were likewise to be provided in such numbers that the Trained Bands and watches might be kept constant to their stations, and always in full efficiency. And every householder was to be responsible for the good conduct of his apprentices. They were not to permit either them or their servants to go abroad without most severe penalties. It is signed "This 4th day of Janʸ. MICHELL."   * *Hist.* ii. 151.

Fortifications of the City walls.

The City disaffected to the Court.

had made itself, in the same writer's words, "eminent for its disaffection to the government of Church and State" (as then administered), and had in fact overthrown it. To its honour, be it said, that, from the hour the cause of public freedom was in peril, the City of London cast in its fortunes unreservedly with the opposition to the Court.*

Well affected to the Commons.

Its resolute refusal to join the league against the Scottish Covenant, had baffled the counsels and wasted the energies of Strafford; and its

Services in the war.

Trained Bands, under Skippon, were destined largely to contribute to the final defeat of the King.

Excitement on night of the arrest.

Throughout the night of Tuesday the 4th of January, a terrible excitement prevailed. Upon intelligence of the King's attempt, all the shops had been closed, and the City all night

---

Attack on City in Royalist satires.

* The City, it is almost unnecessary to say, is the constant object of unsparing and merciless attack in the Court Satires, but its power is freely admitted, and the sustaining force it imparted to the popular counsels is never for a moment questioned. The subjoined lines are from *An Address to the City*:

> Now do you daily contribute and pay
> Money your Truths and Honours to betray!
> Bigg with Fanatic thoughts and wilde desire,
> 'Tis you that blow up the increasing fire
> Of foul Rebellion! you that alone do bring
> Armies into the Field against your King!
> For wer't not from sustainment from your Baggs
> That "Great" and "Highest" Court that only braggs
> Of your vain folly, long 'ere this had been
> Punish'd for their bold sacrilegious sin . . .
> They would not then have so supreamly brought
> Their votes to bring the kingdome's peace to nought,
> Nor with so slight a value lookt on him
> King Charles, and only doted on king Pym!

§ XXIV. *Appeal to the City.*

was under arms.* From gate to gate paſſed the cries of alarmed Citizens that the Cavaliers were entering, that their deſign was to fire the City, and that the King himſelf was at the head of them. Threats of a contemplated ſeizure of the arms of the Citizens, by violent entry into their houſes under royal warrant, increaſed the prevailing dread and excitement.† Nor was the feeling likely to abate upon rumours

"Cavaliers coming."

Apprehended ſeizure of arms.

---

* "The ſhops of the City generally ſhut up, as if an enemy "were at their gates ready to enter, and to plunder them; "and the people in all places at a gaze, as if they looked "only for directions, and were then diſpoſed to any under- "taking."—Clarendon, *Hiſt.* ii. 160.

City ſhops all ſhut.

† That there exiſted too much ground for theſe ſuſpicions, I diſcover by the rough draft, in the State Paper Office, of the ſubjoined "Warrant to the Lord Mayor under the Signet," dated 4th of January 1641. "Whereas wee are informed "that ſix peeces of Ordnance, uſually belonging to the "Artillery Yard, have now lately been brought into that "Or City of London, and placed in Leaden Hall, but wᵗʰ "what intentions wee are not yett well ſatiſfied. [Conſidering "the diſtempers and troubles of theſe times,] Our will and "command therefore is, that you forthwith take an eſpeciall "care to ſee thoſe ſaid peeces ſoe ſafely diſpoſed of, that they ' onely ſerve for the guard and preſervation of the ſaid Citty, "if cauſe ſhould ſoe require. And whereas wee are farther "informed that ſeverall perſons of mean quality have of late "taken into their houſes an unuſuall number of muſquets, as "ſome 20, 30, 40, or thereabout, and amunition accordingly. "Our will and pleaſure is that you likewiſe cauſe a ſearch to "be made throughᵗ the ſaid Citty and the Liberties thereof, "and, when you ſhall find any ſuch quantities of armes, that "you examine thoſe perſons upon what grounds and reaſons "they have made ſuch proviſions, and, as you ſhall ſee cauſe, "that you take ſoe good aſſurance from them, that they may be "reſponſible for the ſaid armes and their intentions therewᵗʰ, "that through the ſame the peace and ſafety of that Our "Citty not any ways be endangered. And for ſoe doing this "ſhall be yʳ warrant. Given under our Signet, Whitehall, "4th Jan. 1641." The words within brackets are an interlineation in Nicholas's hand-writing.

Rough draft of royal warrant.

Ordnance ſafely diſpoſed.

Houſes to be ſearched for muſkets.

Poſſeſſors of fire-arms to be examined.

Arrest of the Five Members.

King's message to the Lord Mayor.

spread abroad with the dawn, of a message received by the Chief Magistrate from Whitehall, to the effect that his Majesty had matter of pressing occasion to address to the Lord Mayor and Common Council, and proposed to visit Guildhall before noon.

Warrants against accused.

Warrants of arrest, committed to the hands of the two Sheriffs of London, preceded him there; and no indication was wanting of a determined resolve that he would yet carry out his purpose of obtaining possession of the persons of the accused.

§ XXV. THE KING'S RECEPTION IN GUILDHALL.

An important day for Charles I.

SOON after nine o'clock on the morning of Wednesday the 5th January, or nearly four hours before the time to which the House of Commons had adjourned their meeting that day, Charles set out upon his enterprise of conferring with the City authorities; and the report in Rushworth, and half a page in Clarendon, are all that has hitherto come down to us of what passed at a meeting which may be said to have determined the King's fate.*

* *Hist. Col.* III. i. 479, 480; Clarendon, *Hist.* ii. 131. I subjoin Rushworth's account, which, brief and dry as it is, comprises all the detail known to us hitherto of what transpired. "His Majesty being arrived at Guild Hall, and " the Common Council assembled, he made this speech to

King's speech at Guildhall.

" them: ' Gentlemen, I am come to demand such persons as
" ' I have already accused of High Treason, and do believe
" ' are shrouded in the City. I hope no good man will keep
" ' them from me; their offences are Treason and Misde-

§ xxv. *The King's Reception in Guildhall.*

For, in this visit, he threw his last stake for the good-will of his citizen subjects. Declining to take any Guard with him, and counting to the last upon a greeting at Guildhall not less enthusiastic or loyal than had welcomed him on his return from Scotland, he left Whitehall with the confident belief that he should drive his enemies from their last refuge. Nor was he without so much ground for the delusion as, however scant and insufficient in reality, might perhaps have been expected to suffice to a mind so obstinate and narrow. He continued to have undoubtedly many adherents among those holding municipal places. One of the Sheriffs was his unflinching partizan. The Chief Magistrate wielded extraordinary powers in that day, long since fallen to disuse; and the devoted adherence of the present holder of the office, carried still an amount of support that in ordinary circumstances might have turned the scale. Royalty itself, moreover, had not lost even then all its old tradi-

His last stake for good-will of City.

His confidence still unabated.

Grounds for such false reliance.

Present supporters and old traditions.

"'meanour of an high nature. I desire your loving assistance
"'herein, that they may be brought to a legal trial. And
"'whereas there are divers suspicions raised that I am a
"'favourer of the Popish Religion, I do profess in the name
"'of a king that I did, and ever will, and that to the utmost
"'of my power, be a prosecutor of all such as shall any ways
"'oppose the laws and statutes of this kingdom, either papists
"'or separatists; and not only so, but I will maintain and
"'defend that true Protestant Religion which my Father did
"'profess, and I will continue in it during life.' His Majesty
"was nobly entertained that day in London at the house of
"one of the Sheriffs, and after dinner returned to Whitehall
"without interruption of tumults."

Assurances as to religion.

Dinner at Sheriff's.

tional and inherent authority; and the number of waverers, or men of no fixed opinion, whom all thefe circumftances would be likely to influence, could not have been inconfiderable. *Reception on his way.* Hardly had Charles paffed Temple Bar, however, when he muft have felt thefe fupports begin to crumble under him; and fuch warning had he *Caution to be wary of fpeech.* received to be wary of his fpeech by the time he reached Guildhall, that his declared and determined purpofe to have the five traitors delivered up to him, which he had come there exclufively to repeat and enforce, muft have founded ftrangely out of keeping with the *Forced mildnefs.* forced mildnefs of his tone. We are happily able to break through the referve of Rufhworth, and fully to defcribe the fcene.

Captain Slingfby an eye- and ear-witnefs. It was Captain Slingfby's fortune that day, as he writes to Admiral Pennington the day following,* " being in a coach," to meet the King with his fmall train going into the City. Whereupon, he fays, he followed him. His Majefty's reception in the ftreets was not favourable. Unfuppreffed cries of difcontent broke *" Privilege! privilege!"* forth. The multitude preffed around his coach with confufed fhouts of Privilege of Parliament! Privilege of Parliament! and one, lefs reftrained than the reft, made himfelf confpicuous by *" To your tents, O Ifrael."* flinging into the window a paper on which was written, "To your Tents, O Ifrael!"

* MS. State Paper Office: Slingfby to Pennington: 6th January 1641-2.

§ xxv. *The King's Reception in Guildhall.*   261

The offence was expiated at Sessions; but the
Ten Tribes had even now deserted the Reho-
boam, whom nevertheless the more gracious
company, the Mayor, the Sheriffs, the Alder-
men, and all the Common Council assembled in Arrival at Guildhall.
full order and ceremony at Guildhall, received
with every external mark of homage and
respect.

He at once addressed them. He had come, King's
he said, to demand such persons as he had speech.
already accused of high treason, and did
believe were shrouded in the City. He hoped
no good man would keep them from him, Resolved
their offences being treason and misdemeanor the Five
of a high nature; and he desired assistance to Members.
bring them to a legal trial. He was very
sorry to hear of the apprehensions the City had
entertained of danger, and he was come to Reliance
them to show how much he relied on their City's
affections for his security and guard, having good-will.
brought no other with him. Whereas there
had been suspicions raised that he was a favorer
of the Popish religion, he now declared to them
his wish and intention to join with the Parliament in extirpation not alone of Popery,
but of all schisms and sectaries. His resolve Will re-
was to redress all the grievances of the subject, grievances
and his care should be to preserve the privileges and respect
of the Parliament; but again and again, accord- privileges:
ing to Slingsby, he repeated, *he must question* but must
those Traitors. He justified the Military Guard Traitors.

Justifies Whitehall Guard. establifhed at Whitehall, and faid the reafon thereof was " for fecuring himfelf, the Parliament, and themfelves, from thofe late tumults." He added, fays Slingfby, " fomething of the Irifh; and at laft had fome familiar to the Aldermen" (fpoke them friendly words, that is), "and invited himfelf *Offers to dine with liberal Sheriff.* to dinner to the Sheriff's." He was careful to felect for that honour Mr. Sheriff Garrett, who was of the two, according to Clarendon, thought to be lefs inclined to his fervice.

Ominous filence: Oppofing cries. So far all had paffed very quietly; in an ominous filence, but without interruption. Then, fays Slingfby, after a little paufe, a cry was fet up among the Common Council, *" Privileges of Parliament," and "God blefs the King."* *Parliament! Privileges of Parliament!* And prefently another, *God blefs the King!* Thefe two, he writes, "continued both at once a good while, I know not which was loudeft." Sufficiently decifive evidence, it will be thought, out of fuch lips, that the refiftance to the loyal ejaculation muft indeed have been ftoutly and fturdily maintained.

Has any one anything to fay? Nothing can be more characteriftic than the fequel, as related by this eye-witnefs fo favorable to the King. " After fome knocking for " filence, the Kinge comaunded one to fpeake " if they had any thinge to fay. One fayd, *Yes—we vote you hear your Parliament.* " *It is the vote of this Court that your Matie* " *heare the advice of your Parlament.* But " prefentlie another anfwered, *It is not the*

§ xxv. *The King's Reception in Guildhall.*

"*vote of this Court : it is your ownn vote!* No—that is not our vote.
"The Kinge replyed, *Who is it that ſays I*
"*do not take the advyce of my Parlament : I*
"*do take their advyce and will : but I muſt*
"*diſtinguiſh between the Parlament and ſome*
"*Traytors in it :* and thoſe" (Slingſby tells
us that he again and again repeated this) "he
"would bring to tryall—tryall!" Then
there was ſilence again : but preſently, and
quite unexpectedly, another highly character-
iſtic interruption. "Another bold fellow, A bold fellow on a form.
"in the loweſt ranke, ſtood upp upon
"a forme, and cryed *The Priviledges of*
"*Parlament!* And another cryed out, *Ob-*
"*ſerve the man, apprehend him!* The King
"mildly replied, *I have and will obſerve* Rejoinder for him.
"*all priviledges of Parlament, but no pri-*
"*viledges can protect a traytor from a tryall—* "Trial—
"*tryall!* And ſoe departed. In the outer trial!"
"hall were a multitude of the ruder people,
"who, as the King went out, ſett up a greater
"cry *The Priviledge of Parlament!*"

Through theſe ruder people he paſſed to Dines with Sheriff.
Sheriff Garrett's houſe, was nobly entertained
therein until 3 o'clock, and, with the fatal and
determined ſhout of *Privilege! Privilege!*
again raiſed from the lips of thouſands, while
upon his own doubtleſs there trembled ſtill
the heſitating and painful, if not leſs obſtinate,
cry of *Trial—Trial!* he returned to White- "Trial— trial!"
hall. He had thrown and loſt the ſtake.

§ XXVI. HUMILIATION AND REVENGE.

<small>Incidents of the return to Whitehall.</small> Of the incidents of Charles the Firſt's return to his palace on this ill-omened day, when, as Clarendon mildly phraſes it, he failed of that applauſe and cheerfulneſs which he might have expected from the extraordinary grace he had vouchſafed, Captain Slingſby ſays nothing; but they are named by another correſpondent of Pennington, whoſe letter, contributing ſome heightening touches even to the relation juſt given, will find alſo here its appropriate place. "Noble Sir," writes Mr. <small>Wiſeman to Pennington: 6th January.</small> Thomas Wiſeman* to the Admiral of the Channel Fleet, "I am ſorry that the times are "ſuch they will afford little elſe to advize of, "than the daily diſtractions that increaſe upon <small>News of the week.</small> "us. The laſt weeke, 12 B^{ps} were impeached "of high treaſon by the Parlament; and this "weeke, 5 of the cheiffe memb^{rs} of the Houſe "of Comons, & the Lord Mandeville in the "Lords Houſe, by the King: as by the "charge given then, & theire names, you

---

<small>Bere to Pennington: 6th January.

Cries in City.</small> * MS. State Paper Office. 6th January. I append, from the ſame rich and unexplored materials of hiſtory, ſome ſentences of a letter, with ſame date, from Under Secretary Sidney Bere: "Yeſterday the King went to Guild Hall in perſon. . . . "They made a confuſed noiſe crying out for Privileges of "Parliament, to wch his Matie gave all the aſſurance poſſible "that his intention was not in the leaſte to infringe them. . . "But att this time he went not guarded as he did the day "before to Parliament. That afternoone the Lower Houſe "ſatt, & have adjourned until Tueſday next. . . wch cauſes "ſtill a greate diſtemper of apprehentions amongſt them."

§ XXVI. *Humiliation and Revenge.*

" may perceive by a particular herewth inclofed *Fears of*
" —wch hath bredd fuch a diftemper both in *infurrec-*
" ye Cittie & Houfes of Parlam^t that wee are *tion.*
" not free from the fears of an infurrection.
" The 6 perfons keepe out of the way; and *Accufed*
" although the Comons Houfe did promife for *keeping*
" theire forth coming, yet they are not *out of way.*
" coming forth. His Matie yefterday came
" into the Cittie, & made a gracious fpeech
" to the Lord Maio^r Aldⁿ & Comon Councill
" at the Guildhall, where they were affembled
" to take order for the faftie of the fame; and
" did, as much as in him laye, ftrive to give *Efforts to*
" them all fatiffacion. Many cryed out to *conciliate.*
" his Matie to mayntaine the priviledges of
" parlam^t, to whom he moft gently replyed it *Gentlenefs*
" was his defire foe to doe, & would not in *of King's*
" the leaft invade upon them; but they muft *voice.*
" give him leave to diftinguifhe betweene the *Firmnefs*
" Parlam^t and fome ill-affected members in it, *of his pur-*
" w^h have gon about by treafons to iniure *pofe.*
" his perfon, and to wthdrawe his people from
" their allegiance. And therefore, both for
" his owne faftie & theire goods, hee muft and *Muft*
" will finde them out, to bring them to Juftice *bring*
" —wch fhould be don in a legall and parlamen- *Traitors to trial.*
" tarye way, & no other wayes. And if they
" could cleare themfelves, he fhould bee glad of
" it; if otherwife, hee held them not memb^{rs}
" fitt to fitt in that affemblye, w^h were mett
" together to make good lawes, and to

"reforme the abuses of the kingdome, and
"not to betray their King. Afterwards, his
"Matie was pleased to bidd himselfe to dinner
"to Sheriff Garrett's, where hee stayed till 3 of
"the clock; and then, returning to Whitehalle,
"the rude multitude followed, crying againe
"*Priviledges of parlam^t, Priviledges of parlam^t*,
"whereat the good King was somewhat moved,
"and I believe was glad when hee was at
"home. The Comittee of the House of
"Comons—(being affrayed, as is conceived, of
"the King's Guards, wch hee hath lately taken
"to his own personne at Whitehaull, beinge
"there a Courte of Guard built, and the
"Trayne bands of Middlesex night and day
"attending, wth at least 6 score other officers,
"wch have theire dyett at Courte)—come into
"the Cittie at the Guildhaull to hould theire
"consultatōns, the Parlam^t being adjourned
"till Tuesday next. What these distempers
"will produce, the God of Heaven knowes;
"but it is feared they cannot otherwise end
"than in blood. The Puritan factionne, w^th
"the sectaryes & schismatickes, are foe preva-
"lent both in Cittie and Countrey, that no
"man can tell, if the King & Parlam^t should
"not agree, wch partie would bee strongest. On
"Tuesday his Matie went to the House of
"Comons to demand the persons of those
"that were accused for treason: but they were
"not there to be found. The House, it seemes,

Margin notes:
Dinner at Sheriff Garrett's.
Shouts of people against the King.
Glad to get home.
Why Commons left Westminster.
Expectation of bloodshed.
Doubts which party strongest.

§ XXVI. *Humiliation and Revenge.*

"taking it ill the King fhould come in that
"manner to breake their privilledges, for
"ought I can underftande refolve to protect
"theire memb^{rs}, & not to deliver them into the
"hands of the King. And to take them by
"force—they have fuch a partie in the Cittie
"that it will coft hott water! We have 3
"Privie Councill^{rs} more made: the Earl of
"Southa^{ton}, my Lord of ffaulkland, & Sr Jno
"Colpepper, whoe is likewife Chancell^r of the
"Exchequer; and my Lord of South^{ton} fworne
"Gentleman of the Bedchamber to the King.
"Thus you fee the changes of the times,
"whereon I pray God preferve our Gracious
"King, and fend us peace at home whatfoever
"wee have abroad: wh^{ch} is the hartye prayer of
"y^r moft affect^e & faithfull friende, THO.
"WISEMAN. My wife, and Doctor, wifh
"you a good new year, & fhee hath fent you
"a toaken of her refpects to you, & prays yor
"acceptance wherein I fhall acknowledge my
"thanks & reft once again yours, T. W."

Retrofpect.

More privycouncillors made.

God preferve His Majefty!

Meffage from Mrs. Wifeman.

Yet another, however, and perhaps worfe trial was referved for the King, when, within a couple of days after this vifit of evil omen, its refult declared itfelf in a formal anfwer from the magnates of the City to the demand he had made for fafe delivery into his cuftody of the bodies of Pym, Hampden, and the reft. He had to receive their furred and robed deputation in Whitehall; and to liften while Mr.

A worfe trial for Charles.

Vifit from Common Council:

Recorder read aloud their petition, representing the dangers which had arisen, and the greater that were impending, from the misunderstanding between his Majesty and his Parliament; and praying him again to resort to the advice of that great council, to abstain from further fortifying of Whitehall or the Tower, to place the latter fortress into the hands of persons of trust, to remove all unusual military companies and armament from the precincts of his palace, to appoint a known and approved Guard for the safety of himself and his Parliament, and not further to restrain of their liberty, or proceed against otherwise than according to parliamentary right and privilege, the members lately accused.

Marginalia: Their advice: consult with your Parliament: leave the Tower alone: disperse the Whitehall Guard: abandon impeachment.

Humiliating trials all these, no doubt; and it requires no effort to understand the emotion, and the eagerness to be home again,* which the good Mr. Wiseman attributes to his gracious sovereign while yet on the City side of Temple Bar. But it requires some effort, as well as a very intimate acquaintance with the character of this King, not to reject as almost incredible

---

Marginalia: Anecdote told by Slingsby.

* A curious incident followed upon his arrival at the palace, which is thus related by Slingsby. (MS. State Paper Office, 6th January.) "At the King's coming home, there "was a meane fellow came into the privy chamber, who had a "paper sealed up, wch he would needes deliver to the Kinge "himselfe. With his much importunitie he was urged to be "mad, or drunke, but he denyed both. The gentleman usher "tooke the paper from him, carried it to the King, and desiring "some gentlemen there to keepe the man. He was presently "sent for in, & is kepte a prisoner: but I know not "wherefore."

§ XXVI.   *Humiliation and Revenge.*

the suppofition, that his firft act, upon his return to his palace after receiving such a lesson, was with his own hand to pen a fresh instruction to Mr. Secretary Nicholas, for a new proclamation denouncing the accused members, specially directed against those who were harbouring them, and to be issued on the following day. The fact nevertheless is undeniable. Clarendon expressly mentions the publication of that particular proclamation on the "next day,"* and I have discovered in the State Paper Office the rough draft of it, with the date of the 5th of January, wholly in the handwriting of Charles himself. Kimbolton is not named in it. It is restricted to the five members of the Lower House, with probably a lingering hope that the Upper House, if the struggle with them were put aside, might yet be induced to act with the Court. It is endorsed by Nicholas, " His " Maties warr^{t} to me to draw upp a Proclama-" tion ag^{t} Mr. Pym, &c."; is addressed to " Our trusty and well-beloved Councell^{r} S^{r} " Edward Nicholas, Kn^{t}, our Principal Secre-" tary of State," and runs thus : " *Charles R.* " —Our will and pleasure is that you forthwith " prepare a draught of a Proclamation declar-" ing ye course of our proceedings upon the " accusation of High Treason and other high " misdemeanours lodged against Mr. Denzill " Hollis, Sr Arthur Haflerig, Mr. John Pym,

King's firft act on return from City.

New proclamation againft the members!

Rough draft in King's hand.

Kimbolton omitted.

Inftructions to Secretary Nicholas.

* *Hift.* ii. 131.

Arrest of the Five Members.

"Mr. John Hampden, and Mr. William
"Strode, members of Our House of Com-
"mons, who, being struck with the conscience
"of their own guilt of soe hainous crimes,
"have made their escape. And Our will &
"pleasure is, that you thereby commande all
"our officers ministers and loving subjects
"to use their diligence in ye apprehending &
"carrying of them, & every of them, to Our
"Tower of London, to bee kept in safe cus-
"tody, to bee brought to triall according to
"justice. And that, moreover, you prohibitt
"all ou^r loving subjects to harbor relieve
"& maintayne them, with any other fit
"clause. And for doing hereof this shall bee
"yor sufficient warrant. Given at our Court
"at Whitehall this fifth day of January in the
"17th yeare of our Reigne."

The guilty have escaped.

Injunction to seize them.

Prohibition against harbouring them.

The City threatened.

Any such prohibition against harbouring the accused was in effect a threat against the City, launched precisely at the moment when its author had discovered himself powerless to enforce it; and this circumstance, even if the warrant had not been entirely in the handwriting of the King, must have sufficed to declare it exclusively the King's act. Here no doubt can exist. It would have been sheer madness in any other man to assume, in such circumstances, the responsibility. It is not conceivable, for a moment, whatever part Nicholas or the rest may have taken before the declared

Solely the King's act.

and manifest failure, that they should now have encouraged a persistence so hopeless, so reckless, so impotently obstinate and vain. It will shortly appear indeed, in express terms, that by this time Nicholas very heartily had repented of having ever accepted his high office; and there is every reason to believe, that, from the day when the City thus declared against the King, Sir Edward required, for even the commonest ministerial act connected with the impeachment of the members, Charles's own sign manual. For the very printing of this proclamation the King has himself written the instruction, preserved also in the State Paper Office.*

Hopeless and reckless persistence.

Repentance of Nicholas.

Charles directs even printing of proclamation.

§ XXVII. REASSEMBLING OF THE COMMONS.

MEANWHILE, at some half hour after one o'clock on the same fifth of January, while the exciting scenes above described were in progress in the City, the House of Commons had reassembled at Westminster. The agitation of yesterday had not subsided. The first act was to order that the doors be locked,† and the outer lobbies cleared of all persons but ser-

Wednesday, 5th January, 1641-2.

Yesterday's agitation not subsided.

---

* "CHARLES R. Our will and Command is that you
" give orders to Our Printer to print Our Proclamation
" for Apprehending of Mr. John Pym, Mr. John Hampden,
" Mr. Denzil Hollis, Sir Arthur Haselrigge, and Mr.
" Wm. Strode. For which this shall bee yor warrant.
" Given at Our Court at Whitehall this 6 day of Jan^y.
" 1641.
 " To Sir Edwd Nicholas
 " Our Principall Secretary." † *Harl. MSS.* 162, f. 307 b.

King's instructions to printer.

vants to members; that no member should offer to go out without leave; and that some should send forth their servants, to see what numbers of people were repairing towards Westminster, and to bring notice to the House. So prepared and watchful for other than the conflicts of debate, and with hands nervously clutching at less peaceful weapons, there sat this day two hundred and sixty members, and among them nearly ninety of the party of the King. The Royalists had not assembled in such force since the debate and division of the 15th of December on the printing of the Remonstrance. When D'Ewes entered the House, he found Grimston, the member for Colchester, speaking of " the " great breach of their privileges by his Ma- " jesty's coming to the House yesterday with " so great a number of officers of the late " army, and men desperate of purpose and " in fortune, armed some of them with hal- " berds and swords, others with swords and " pistols, demanding to be delivered to him " Mr. Pym and other members of the House, " whom he accused of high treason."

Watches sent out.

260 members present;

90 of the King's party.

The member for Colchester leads debate.

Grimston's speech.

Its scope and value.

Mr. Grimston's speech was not only very able, striking skilfully several chords which elicited loud and vehement response, but it cleared the ground for all the subsequent discussions, and at once gave to the resentment which the King's act had aroused, its proper shape and right direction. Parliament,

§ XXVII.   *Reassembling of the Commons.*   273

he said, had always claimed and exercised power and jurisdiction above all other courts of judicature in the land; its wisdom and policy had been accounted of higher import than those of any other council; and all orders in the State had been brought frankly to admit its rights and privileges, its power and jurisdiction, its free continuance. Whence and wherefore had proceeded, then, the interruption of which they complained?   *Exposition of the power of Parliament.*

The answer to that question was to be found by inquiry into what circumstances they were which had given such "aweful predominancy" to the very name of a Parliament in this nation. It was because the ordinances and statutes of that high court struck with terror and despair all such evil-doers as were malefactors in the State. It was because, not alone the meanest of his Majesty's subjects, but the greatest personages of the kingdom, were in danger, if infringers of the law, to be called in question by this highest court, and to be by it punished. It was, on the other hand, because the drooping spirits of men, groaning under the burden of tyrannical oppression, had been from the same source enriched and comforted; while places and offices of power, both in Church and State, had been struck out of the hands of the wicked and the unmerciful.   He discovered the explanation to be, therefore, that the act of which they complained was the act of evil   *Why so awfully predominant? Because it punishes evil-doers; comforts the oppressed; and strips the wicked of place.*

T

The late outrage due to evil counsellors.

counsellors who desired, if possible, to break off and dissolve a Parliament which had declared its intention to bring all incendiaries and delinquents in the State to condign punishment for their crimes.

Offences charged.

Then Grimston pointed distinctly to specific offences given by members of that House, at which the articles of treason had been directed. He declared that no pretence existed for treasonable charge except such as conduct in the House itself might have provoked. In reply to which, amid stern expressions of sympathy from all around him, the member for Colchester claimed for himself, and for them all, the inalienable right, within the walls of Parliament, to speak freely, without interruption or contradiction, in all debates, disputes, or arguments, upon any business agitated therein. He claimed it as a privilege that they should not be questioned for this by any human power. Whether, he went on to say, with allusions he did not care to make less open and undisguised, it were freely to give vote, judgment, or sentence upon the reading of any bill to be made a law, or upon any bill *either of attainder* or other charge against delinquents and persons criminous to the State; or whether it were, by free vote, to issue Protestation, *Remonstrance*, or other Declaration; he claimed this for himself, and for all, as the solemn right and privilege of Parliament.

Conduct in Parliament.

Right to speak freely.

Title not to have votes questioned:

whether on bills of attainder or others:

or in drawing up Remonstrances.

Wherefore his conclusion was, that for

members of that House to be accused of any crime, or to be impeached for treason by any person whatever, during the continuance of Parliament, for things done in the same, without legal accusation and prosecution by the whole House—and further, that to be apprehended or arrested upon such impeachment, or to have studies broken open, and books or writings seized upon, without consent and warrant of the whole House—was a breach of the privilege and right belonging to the power, the jurisdiction, and the continuance of the High Court of Parliament. All which, he submitted, it was in the highest degree expedient explicitly and promptly to embody, in a declaratory resolution of the Commons of England.

[marginal notes: Conclusion: Members accused for conduct in House: lodgings entered and papers seized: a breach of privilege.]

Grimston resumed his seat amid cries of approval which his solid and masterly exposition had well deserved, and preparation was thereupon made to refer it to a Committee to draw up the necessary resolution. This, however, was stoutly opposed by several of the Royalists, headed by Hopton of the West. "Sir Ralph " Hopton and some five or six more," says D'Ewes, " excused his Majesty's coming with so " extraordinary a number." But the majority, led by Glyn the member for Westminster, steadily carried their point; and, proceeds D'Ewes, the House " nominated Mr. Glyn and " some few others to withdraw into the Com- " mittee Chamber, and to draw up a declaration

[marginal notes: Motion upon Grimston's speech. Opposed by Hopton. Excuses for the King. Committee to prepare resolution.]

"to that end and purpose." They withdrew accordingly; and then rose the member for Hertfordshire, Sir William Lytton, to suggest that no other business should be taken in hand until their return. He was warmly seconded in this: Sir John Clotworthy, on the other hand, pointing out the urgency of Irish affairs, and desiring that they might but append a short resolution to some propositions agreed upon by the Irish Committee. To the surprise of not a few, however, and of D'Ewes among them, it was found that this debate might have been spared; for, in the midst of it, Glyn and his friends returned. "During the "debate," says D'Ewes, "Mr. Glyn and the "rest who were commanded to withdraw into "the Committee Chamber, having stayed "there about a quarter of an hour, now "brought down a long Declaration ready "penned, which was doubtless prepared and "ready written by some members of the "House before we met this afternoon." D'Ewes here uneasily refers to consultations with Pym and the rest in Coleman Street, to which he had not been invited; but it is just to him to state, that, throughout the invaluable record he has preserved of these momentous scenes, from which details are here taken hitherto unknown, not even distantly referred to in the Journals of the House, and of which no mention is made in Sir Ralph

They retire:

do nothing till their return.

They return in a quarter of an hour:

with a resolution written before we met.

D'Ewes not in confidence of leaders:

§ XXVII. *Reassembling of the Commons.*

Verney's or any other memorial, his personal
jealousies and dislikes have small weight
against the gravity of the facts he reveals. *but his account trustworthy.*

He thus describes the Declaratory Resolution
brought back by Glyn: " It contained in
" substance that his Majesty had yesterday
" broken the privileges of this House, by
" coming hither with a great number of
" armed men, and striking terror into the
" members. And though we could not sit
" here in safety, nor properly fall upon the
" agitation or handling of any business till
" we had vindicated our privileges, yet our
" care to uphold this commonwealth, and the
" consideration of the miserable condition of
" Ireland, had induced us first to adjourn this
" House to (and so a blank was left for the
" day), and to appoint a Grand Committee
" to sit at the Guildhall in London at 3 of
" the clock this afternoon, to consider of the
" means of our safety, and of the assistance
" of Ireland, and to authorize the select
" committee of Irish affairs to sit when and
" where they pleased." *Glyn's Declaratory Resolution. Proposed adjournment: Grand Committee to sit in the City.*

This having been read by the Clerk, a warm
debate arose. The opposition was led by Sir
Ralph Hopton, who declared that there was
no precedent for what therein was proposed to
be done. For his own part, he thought that
many excuses might be urged for the King's
having come to the House with so great a *Warm debate thereon. Sir Ralph Hopton.*

number, and so unusually armed. And then he pleaded a necessity which the King himself had created (assuming this statement of it to be true), to justify the outrage he afterwards committed. "Had we not ourselves had divers of our "servants lately attending in the lobby without "the doors of this House, armed also in an un- "usual manner, with carabines and pistols?" He begged the House to remember, too, that the speech his Majesty made on the occasion had been full of grace and goodness. In conclusion, adds D'Ewes, "he did not think we could "appoint a Grand Committee to go into Lon- "don, nor would he have had us to have ad- "journed at all." Then followed some warm speaking on both sides; and the time originally named as the limit for the sitting of the House, as well as the hour for assembling elsewhere, had soon slipped away. In the end, D'Ewes tells us, "we resolved to alter it from a Grand "Committee to a Select Committee, and to "adjourn the sitting of this House to Tuesday "the 11th, and it being between three and "four of the clock we did alter our meeting "this afternoon till to-morrow morning at "nine of the clock." Not, however, without a division. Hopton and his friends objected equally to the Select Committee, and insisted upon dividing. "The Speaker," D'Ewes continues, "put the question as followeth: "As many as are of opinion that a Committee

Margin notes:
Did not we give first provocation?
And how gracious the King's speech!
Opposes Committee and adjournment.
"Grand" committee altered to "Select."
Adjourn till to-morrow at 9 o'clock.

§ XXVII. *Reassembling of the Commons.* 279

"shall be appointed by this House to sit at Division
"Guildhall in London, let them say Aye, to upon going into
"which there was a great affirmative: and to City.
"the negative, a less. Next, the Speaker
"appointed tellers for the Ayes, who went
"out (of which number I was), Mr. Arthur
"Goodwin and Mr. Carew. Their number
"was 170. And for the Noes, who sat still, 170
"he appointed tellers Mr. Kirton and Mr. against 86.
"Herbert Price, and the number was 86,
"and so it was carried accordingly."*

The naming of the Committee then took Selection of the Committee.
place. "And thereupon," continues the
precise Sir Simonds, "Sir John Culpeper,
"newly made Chancellor of the Exchequer,
"and divers others, were named to sit a com-
"mittee at the Guildhall in London to-morrow
"morning at 9 of the clock, and all that
"would come were to have voices: and they All who come to have voices.
"were to consider of the breach of the Privilege

* *Harl. MSS.* 162, f. 308 a. In little more than a fortnight
(see *ante* 36, 37), upon the impeachment of the Duke of Division as to Duke of Richmond.
Richmond (for his famous sally in the Lords upon the Militia
Bill being brought under consideration, when he broke in
upon sundry grave suggestions as to the day when discussion
should be taken thereon, by advising as a greatly preferable
course, "an adjournment for six months"), the King's party
mustered in larger force, but the popular leaders had made
corresponding exertion. The numbers then were 223 led 223 against 123.
into the lobby by Hollis and Stapleton, to 123 of whom the
counters were Culpeper and Herbert Price. From a speech
made on the occasion by D'Ewes, wherein he thought the only
excuse that could possibly be made for the Duke was his being
"a young man," some light may be thrown on the argument, *ante* 198, drawn from his applying a similar epithet to
Strode. The Duke of Richmond was now nine-and-twenty.
—*Harl. MSS.* 162, f. 356 b.

Its duties. "of Parliament by his Majefty's coming yefter-
"day, with other particulars mentioned in the
"before-recited declaration." The Committee
Comprifes included, befides Falkland and Culpeper, fome
feveral
Royalifts. ardent Royalifts, and feveral not unfriendly to
the King. Among thefe fat Herbert Price,
the member for Brecon ; Sir Richard Cave, who
Names fat for Lichfield ; Sir Ralph Hopton himfelf ;
on Com-
mittee. Sir John and Chriftopher Wray, the members
for Lincolnfhire and Great Grimfby; Sir
Benjamin Rudyard; the members for
Cockerworth and Chippenham, Sir John
Hippefley and Sir Edward Hungerford. It
comprifed, on the other hand, Glyn ; Sir
Philip Stapleton; William Pierrepoint (Earl
Kingfton's fecond fon, who fat for Great
Wenlock), and Nathaniel Fiennes ; Bulftrode
Whitelock, the member for Marlow ; Sir
Thomas Walfingham, who fat for Rochefter ;
the members for Weftbury and Ludgerfhall,
Mr. Wheeler and Mr. Walter Long; Sir
John Hotham; Sir Walter Earle ; Sir Robert
Cooke, who fat for Tewkefbury ; Mr. Grim-
fton and Sir Thomas Barrington, who fat for
Colchefter ; and the members for Devon-
fhire and Hertfordfhire, Sir Samuel Rolle and
Hyde, St. Sir William Lytton. Hyde's name nowhere
John, and
Cromwell, appears ; neither does that of Oliver St. John,
abfent
from it. the Solicitor-General ; and it is ftill more
remarkable that Cromwell's alfo fhould be
abfent. He may poffibly have had prefling

businefs to occupy him during thefe few days, on his coufin Hampden's affairs at Great Hampden.

Lord Lifle (Lord Leicefter's eldeft fon, who fat afterwards on the trial of the King), now moved that the Committee fo appointed fhould have power to iffue out fuch money as might be required for payment of the troops to be fent into Ireland. Another refolution connected with Irifh affairs was alfo adopted on the fuggeftion of Stapleton. And then followed a brief but fharp debate, raifed upon a motion by Nathaniel Fiennes, that a meffage fhould go up to the Lords to let them know, that, "by "reafon of his Majefty coming to our Houfe "yefterday in fuch a warlike manner, we had "adjourned the Houfe till Tuefday next, at one "of the clock, and that we had in the meantime "appointed a Select Committee to fit in the "Guildhall in London, to which all the mem- "bers of the Houfe who would come were to "have voices, to confider of the breach of the "Privilege of Parliament and the fafety of the "Kingdom." The debate ended in the naming of Mr. Fiennes and divers others to carry up this meffage accordingly. But the Houfe arofe, adds D'Ewes, before he returned, or was able to bring any anfwer.

Motion by Lord Lifle.

Irifh affairs.

Sharp debate led by Fiennes.

Meffage to Lords.

Abrupt rifing of Houfe.

§ XXVIII. A SUDDEN PANIC.

THE Houfe fuddenly arofe, in truth,

because there had broken out a sudden alarm. It was abruptly bruited at the doors that a body of armed men were in march upon them, and a panic of agitation ensued. Sir John Clotworthy was in the act of urging certain necessary resolutions for the service of Ireland, connected with the supply of men and arms, when shouts of " Move, move," and " Adjourn," interrupted him ; and though the imperturbable member for Malden would persist in having what he wanted, the votes were put without the usual forms. " All were " allowed," says D'Ewes, " and voted by the " House, but in such haste as they would not " permit the Clerk to read them." Then, in the like precipitate fashion, adjournment until the following Tuesday at one o'clock was resolved upon the question. Mr. Speaker ordered the adjournment accordingly ; and the House rose in extreme disorder " at about four of the " clock in the afternoon."

Armed men marching upon us.

Sir John Clotworthy persists with resolutions.

Voted without being read.

Disorderly adjournment, 4 p.m.

D'Ewes appends to the day's journal an explanation, from which it might seem that the sudden fright had not been wholly groundless. " For," he says, " we had new alarums given " us of the coming down of armed persons " upon us: and it was generally reported also, " that his Majesty had intended to have come " down to both the Houses this afternoon, " again attended with the desperate troop with " which he came yesterday, and to have

Reasons for the fright.

§ XXVIII. *A sudden Panic.* 283

"accused some other members, both of our Other members to be accused and seized.
"House and of the Lords House, of Treason,
"and to have seized upon their persons: but
"that, going into the City of London this
"morning, he was there so roundly and plainly City only had prevented it.
"dealt withal by people of all sorts, who
"called upon him to maintain the privilege of
"Parliament; to follow the advice of his
"Great Counsell in Parliament, without which
"they were all undone" (D'Ewes here appears
to be repeating the expressions of some excited
friend rather than quietly recording his own)
—" and that their blood would cry to Heaven
"for justice—and that they would with their
"lives and fortunes maintain the safety of his Alarm of the King.
"Majesty's person, and the safety and Privi-
"lege of Parliament; some also throwing the
"printed Protestation of the House of Com-
"mons into his coach as he went along; as
"that he both returned late out of the City, Change of purpose.
"and altered, it seems, his former resolution."*

It is now of course not difficult to make Results of 4th January.
light of these alarms, and to smile at their not
very coherent expression; but we may be sure
that they were then very real. It was of the
very essence of the King's attempt that it
should carry such consequences. Whatever
distrust or doubt had been in any direction en- Darkest rumours thought true.
tertained of the Sovereign, it confirmed. To
the rumours which had mixed him up with

* *Harl. MSS.* 162, f. 308 b.

Scottish "Incident." very recent and as desperate designs in Scotland against the leaders of the Covenant,[*] to

[*] *Offer of Montrose to kill Argyle and Hamilton.* In alluding to this transaction in my Essay on the Grand Remonstrance (*Hist. and Biog. Essays*), and to the statement by Clarendon (*Hist.* ii. 17), that Montrose had "frankly" suggested to the King the assassination of Argyle and Hamilton, I ought perhaps to have mentioned a highly elaborate argument in Mr. Napier's *Life of Montrose* (ii. 78-109), the drift of which *Mr. Napier's disproof quite untenable.* is not merely to defend Montrose from having made the offer, but to endeavour to establish that Clarendon's assertion that he had done so was not originally intended to stand as part of his text, and in fact only usurps the place of a suppressed passage restored in one of the Appendices of the edition of 1826. Upon the former part of this argument I offer here no opinion; but upon the latter I have simply to say that it breaks down altogether. It is not for a moment tenable. The *The text of Clarendon.* text of Clarendon must always now continue in the state wherein he left it himself after his last revision, clearly copied out by his secretary for publication or suppression, according to certain directions in his will; and the chief *Chief value of Edition of 1826.* value of the edition of 1826 will always be, that it enabled us for the first time to read it in that state. The confusion which exists as to the several MSS. left by him, and from which that important collation was made, arises from the fact that several years after he had planned his History and written the first four books, he resolved to recast the plan so as to admit therein of all the incidents of his own Life. He there- *Disclosed Author's plans and text.* upon began an Autobiography; but after pursuing it for some time, he threw it aside, and reverted to his design of a History, making great additions to that which already he had written, and completing it in 1673. His final task then was, to form, from the two MSS. thus drawn up (the Life having gone over, *History composed of two MSS.* in a more striking way, much of the ground of the first four books of the History), a third text, by taking the MS. of the History for the basis, and importing into it all the material portions and corrections of the MS. of the Life. The result was a fair transcript made by his Secretary under these in- *Secretary's transcript.* structions, which was found completed at his own death, in December 1674. Afterwards came the publication, mainly from a copy of this transcript, by his sons: with the modifications, alterations, and omissions, which, in exercise of the *Altered and corrupted by author's sons.* discretion left to them by their father, they had made to please their political friends, or out of delicacy to persons still living; and which so remained until 1826. The edition published that year was the result of an entirely new collation of the three MSS. above named: 1. The original MS. of History: 2. The original MS. of Life: 3. The Transcript constructed

§ XXVIII. *A sudden Panic.* 285

even thofe which had pointed to him as not unconnected with the awful outbreak in Ireland, out of both. The Editors, lettering the Tranfcript as A, the Life as B, and the Hiftory as C, collated the whole afrefh; reftored in Notes every word, fentence, and paffage omitted or in any manner altered in A; and, in a feries of Appendices, fupplied (reforting for the purpofe to B and C), in addition to all that the author's fons had rejected, ftill more which the author himfelf had already deliberately excluded from the Tranfcript made under his inftructions. We are thus enabled to compare particular ftatements made by Clarendon in his firft draft of the Hiftory, with accounts of the fame incidents manifeftly more authentic, and better confidered, which he had fubfequently inferted in the Life, and had finally directed to be fubftituted for the former in his Secretary's Tranfcript. The reader will at once perceive what I mean, if, to felect only one or two out of very numerous inftances, he makes comparifon of Appendix i. 536 (MS. C.) with i. 416 (MS. B.); or of ii. 61—2, note (MS. C.), with ii. 44—49 (MS. B.); or of Appendix ii. 575—9 (MS. C.), with ii. 13—19 (MS. B). The latter of thefe inftances is that under notice refpecting Montrofe; and it does not admit of the remoteft doubt that the account in the Appendix, taken from the firft four books of the Hiftory, written before 1648, and afterwards rejected, was meant by Clarendon to be entirely fuperfeded by the account in the Life, written many years later, and, by his own direction to his Secretary, placed in the final Tranfcript, where it has ftood ever fince, and muft continue to ftand. Even apart from the other irrefiftible evidence, the context fo conclufively fhows this, that but for Mr. Napier's extraordinary fuppofition to the contrary, fuggefted by zeal for his hero, and maintained with an air that impofes on readers fuperficially informed, the details I have entered into would fcarcely have been called for. It is fimply ridiculous to pretend that the paffage complained of, and (be it true or falfe) undoubtedly left by Clarendon, in the final difpofition of his papers, to ftand where it now does, could by poffibility have fallen into that place by accident. Lords Clarendon and Rochefter had no alternative but to print it; and with what reluctance they did fo is proved by what we now know of their fubftitution, for "to kill them both," of the words "to have them both made away." The point, however, was well worth clearing, becaufe all the illuftrative matter in the 1826 edition requires to be read with careful reference to the fact that the author had deliberately and defignedly excluded the greater part of it from his completed text (an inftance may be referred to, *ante,* p. 215, *note*); and it is exceedingly important, in reading Clarendon, to keep

Irifh rebellion:

Reftorations.

Scaffoldings of Hiftory.

Later and earlier verfions of fame events.

The Montrofe charge, the later verfion.

Intended fo to ftand.

Impoffible not to print it:

reluctance of firft Editors.

Additions in 1826

and Army plot:

it seemed to give deadly corroboration. It put undoubtedly beyond further queſtion what the popular leaders had all along maintained, that the deſign, clearly proved, of bringing up the army from the North, had had for its

King's ſuſpected ſhare in.

ſpecific object to overawe themſelves and ſuſpend the action of Parliament. Clarendon ſpeaks as if the failure of the Arreſt ſufficed to ſhow its futility, and there an end. But he

not to be confuſed with reſtorations.

the diſtinction always in view between that deſcription of new matter ſupplied in the 1826 edition, and the more eſſential reſtorations reconſtituting the original text, which had been corrupted and falſified in innumerable inſtances by his ſons, Lords Clarendon and Rocheſter, in preparing the firſt edition. The portions firſt printed in Notes and Appendices in 1826 are

Two kinds:

of two kinds: i. The reſtoration of the text to the condition in which Clarendon himſelf had left it, by reſtoring ſuppreſſed paſſages, and replacing modified or altered phraſes and ſentences: ii. The additional illuſtration of the text by ſupplying further notices or amplifications of ſpecial incidents treated therein, from the two manuſcripts, B and C, which I have

weight reſpectively due to each.

above deſcribed: and the degree of authority given to either ſhould be regulated according to the facts here ſupplied. I cloſe, as I began, by ſtating moſt expreſſly that, according to all the evidence we poſſeſs, it muſt have been, and was, the deliberate intention of Clarendon, upon reviewing all the materials he had collected, to convey to the readers of his Hiſtory, as his own final impreſſion, that Montroſe had

Charge deliberately intended.

"frankly" propoſed to the King the aſſaſſination of Argyle and Hamilton. Upon the probability or otherwiſe of ſuch an offer having been made, it is not neceſſary that I ſhould here give an opinion; but it is impoſſible to read the text in connection with the Appendix (of which, taken together, it is important to remark, as Mr. D'Iſraeli in his *Commentaries*, ii. 242-52, ed. 1851, has pointed out, that they are

The King its authority.

not in any reſpect irreconcileable), without an inference, amounting almoſt to certainty, that the King himſelf was Clarendon's informant. And the explanation of the two accounts may probably be, that, writing while Charles ſtill

Why firſt verſion of it changed.

lived, Clarendon preferred to expreſs the matter in paraphraſe; but that, writing of the incident at a later time, after the king's death, he had no heſitation in putting it, as he ſays Montroſe did the propoſal, "frankly."

§ XXVIII.   *A sudden Panic.*

well knew that this was not so; and that it
was less the first excitement attending so start- *Conse-*
ling an attempt wherein its troubles and danger *quences of*
consisted, than in its subsequent more enduring *outrage worse than*
effect upon men's modes and ways of regard- *itself.*
ing public affairs. He unconsciously admits as
much in another passage of his History, when he
remarks that everything formerly said of plots *Belief ob-*
and conspiracies against the Parliament, which *tained for grossest*
before had been laughed at, was now thought *charges.*
true and real ; and that all which before was
merely whispered of Ireland, was now talked
aloud and printed.

The various letters of the time are filled
with similar indications. "All things are now *Captain*
" in soe great distraction heare," wrote Cap- *Carterett's fears.*
tain Carterett on the day after this sitting of
the House, " that there is noe thinking of
" doeing anything ; but every-body are pro-
" viding after their owne safetie as if every-
" thing were inclainable to ruine."   " By
" the next post," writes Mr. Wiseman, " you *Mr. Wise-*
" may expect to heare of greate changes *man's.*
" either for the better or worse. The times
" are dangerous to discourse what I might.
" Only if God, in his greate mercie, doe not
" speedely looke upon us, wee are like to
" perish. The obedience of his Maties subjects *Obedience*
" hath been poisoned."   The incidents of *poisoned.*
the 3rd and 4th of January, in short, had
drawn up into hostile forces two powers in the

State whose agreement was essential to its welfare, but which never more could act in concert or unison till the struggle between them was over, and a victory won. This was a fact pregnant with general alarm for all men, and most for the thoughtful and reflecting.

Neither were reasons wanting for specific and well-grounded alarm as to the actual personal safety of the accused and other members of both Houses. From the very writer who laughs to scorn the notion that there was any sort of danger, we may learn what, and how great, the danger was. It is Clarendon, as we have seen, who relates the plan by which his friend Lord Digby, according to him the sole adviser of the attempt, proposed to redeem its failure by seizing himself upon the accused, backed by sufficient numbers to render it certain that they must either be taken or left dead in the place. It is Clarendon who says, that, if the King had not withheld his consent, without doubt Lord Digby would have done it. It is Clarendon who drily remarks upon that presumed success to a plan so atrocious, that it " must have had " a wonderful effect." Above all it is Clarendon who, by way of practical proof of his assertion that no personal danger could possibly have befallen the accused, actually puts forward a plan of his own by which, taking good care first to secure and lock up separately the persons of the five leaders, he fancies that such

Powers of the State in conflict.

Specific causes of alarm.

Digby's plan for securing members.

King withholds consent.

Clarendon's own plan.

To seize and throw them into separate prisons.

a blow might have been struck at what he calls "the high spirit of both Houses" that Charles might have reduced them to treat, and so have forced them to his own terms.*

§ XXIX. How History may be written.

THE assertion that the Five Members were at no time in any personal danger, admits but of one comment. It is not true. Conclusive proof has been given, in a former work,† of the faithlessness and untrustworthiness of Clarendon as any safe guide to a knowledge of the events for which Hume accepted him as the sole and implicit authority, and in which his lead has been more or less followed by every later historian. But if further similar evidence be desired, let me supply it by simple comparison of his account of the sitting of the House of Commons of Wednesday the 5th of January, with that which I have above derived from the manuscript of Sir Simonds D'Ewes, and from other contemporary sources. Until now, Clarendon's was the only account preserved to us of that sitting, except a memorandum of eight lines by Sir Ralph Verney, and another by Rushworth of exactly the same

Faithlessness of Clarendon.

Unsafe guide.

Comparison with D'Ewes:

Verney and Rushworth.

---

* See *ante*, pp. 143, 149, and 153, where the authorities are given for these various assertions.
† Essay on the Grand Remonstrance. See *Hist. and Biog. Essays*, i. 1-175.

Arreſt of the Five Members.

extent.* The record by D'Ewes was made on the day to which it refers; it is confirmed by Verney's and by Ruſhworth's notes; and its veracioufneſs is beyond queſtion.

Statement by Clarendon.
"When the Houſe of Commons next met," ſays Clarendon in his Hiſtory,† "none of the "accuſed members appearing, they had friends

Alleged tone of members' friends.
"enough, who were well inſtructed to aggravate "the late proceedings, and to put the Houſe "into a thouſand jealouſies and apprehenſions, "and every ſlight circumſtance carried weight

Verney's account of ſitting of 5th.
* Sir Ralph Verney ſays: "Wedneſday, 5th Janʳ. 1641. "The Houſe ordered a Comittee to ſit at Guildhall in London, "and all that would come had voyces. This was to conſider "and adviſe how to right the Houſe in point of privilege, "broken by the King's coming yeaſterday, with a force, to "take members out of our Houſe. They alowed the Iriſh "Comittees to ſit, but would meddle with noe other buſineſſe "till this were ended. They acquainted the Lords in a "meſſage with what they had donn, and then they adjorned "the Houſe till Tueſday next." (Verney's *Notes*, 139-40).

Ruſhworth's account.
Ruſhworth ſays (part III. vol. i. 478-9): "The Commons "ſent Mr. Fiennes with a meſſage to the Lords to give them "notice of the King's coming yeſterday, & that they "conceived it a high & great breach of privilege: & to "repeat their deſires that their Loᵖˢ would join them in a "petition to the King that the Parliament may have a Guard "to ſecure them as ſhall be approved of by his Majeſty, and "both Houſes; and alſo to let them know, that they have "appointed a Committee to ſit at Guildhall London, and "have alſo appointed the Committee for Iriſh affairs to meet "there." Then he quotes the order paſſed for adjournment

Adjournment to City.
to the City, on the ground "they cannot with the ſafety of "their own perſons, or indemnity of the rights & Privileges "of Parliament, ſit here any longer without a full vindication "of ſo high a breach, & ſufficient Guard wherein they may "confide:" to which, after appending the names of the Committee, and that all who will come are to have voices, he adds: "and then the Houſe adjourned till Tueſday the 11th "of January at one in yᵉ afternoon, according to the ſaid "Order."

† *Hiſt.* ii. 132, 133.

§ XXIX. *How History may be written.*

"enough in it to difturb their minds. . . .
"They who fpake moft paffionately, and
"probably meant as malicioufly, behaved
"themfelves with modefty, and feemed only
"concerned in what concerned them all: and
"concluded, after many lamentations, that they *Affected fears and griefs.*
"did not think themfelves fafe in that Houfe,
"till the minds of men were better compofed;
"that the City was full of apprehenfions, and
"was very zealous for their fecurity; and
"therefore wifhed that they might adjourn the *Propofal to adjourn Parliament.*
"Parliament to meet in fome place in the City.
"But that was found not practicable; fince
"it was not in their own power to do it, with-
"out the confent of the Peers and the concur-
"rence of the King; who were both like *King's wifh to get Parliament away from London.*
"rather to choofe a place more diftant from
"the City. And, with more reafon, in the end
"they concluded, that the Houfe fhould
"adjourn itfelf for two or three days, and
"name a committee who fhould fit both *Appointment of Committee.*
"morning and afternoon in the City; and
"all who came to have voices: and Mer-
"chant Tailors' Hall was appointed for the
"place of their meeting, they who ferved
"for London undertaking that it fhould be
"ready againft the next morning: no man
"oppofing or contradicting anything that was
"faid; they who formerly ufed to appear for *Royalifts filent.*
"all the rights and authority which belonged
"to the King, not knowing what to fay, .

"between grief and anger that the violent
"party had, by thefe late unfkilful actions
"of the Court, gotten great advantage, and
"recovered new fpirits: and the three perfons
"before named" (himfelf, Culpeper, and
Falkland), "without whofe privity the King
"had promifed that he would enter upon no
"new counfel, were fo much difpleafed and
"dejected, that they were inclined never more
"to take upon them the care of anything to
"be tranfacted in the Houfe."

Three King's advifers:

too dejected to fpeak.

Clarendon's account fummed up.

This account contains five alleged facts. 1. That the popular party went down to the Houfe with a propofal for the adjournment of Parliament. 2. That the propofal fubftituted was an adjournment of the Houfe itfelf for two or three days. 3. That Merchant Tailors' Hall was appointed as the place of meeting for a Committee named to fit in the interval, the members for London undertaking to have it ready the next morning. 4. That no man belonging to the King's party oppofed or contradicted anything that was faid. 5. That Hyde, Culpeper, and Falkland, were too much difpleafed and dejected to fhow any prefent inclination to take upon them the care of anything to be tranfacted in the Houfe.

Five fpecific ftatements, all untrue.

Confronted with D'Ewes, Verney, and Rufhworth.

On the other hand, the account preferved by D'Ewes, and confirmed in every refpect by the brief notes of Verney and Rufhworth, as

§ XXIX. *How History may be written.* 293

well as by the unpublished contemporary letters here adduced, furnishes a counterstatement to every one of these averments. 1. There never was mooted so absurd a proposition as to adjourn Parliament. The course had doubtless been concerted, as D'Ewes somewhat pettishly intimates, with the absent leaders; and the Declaratory Resolution was proposed and carried, as, prepared and ready written, it had been brought to the House. 2. The limit of adjournment was at once distinctly specified as Tuesday the 11th January, and it will be seen hereafter that the historian was not without a motive in substituting the loose and undetermined "two or three days." 3. Guildhall was from the first named and appointed, and not Merchant Tailors' Hall, as to which, therefore, the question of getting it ready could hardly have arisen. 4. So far from no man belonging to the King's party contradicting or opposing anything that was said, Sir Ralph Hopton (the King's servant, as Rushworth calls him) contradicted everything that was said without scruple; and the opposition was so determined that the Royalists divided 87 against the proposal of Glyn, which was four more than the division of the 15th of December against the printing of the Remonstrance. 5. Hyde undoubtedly took no part, and was probably not in the House; but Culpeper and Falkland were named for the

<small>Never proposed to adjourn Parliament.

Limit of stay in City specified.

Merchant Tailors' Hall not named.

Royalists not silent.

Culpeper and Falkland on Committee.</small>

Committee to sit during the recess, and served upon it.

§ XXX. Adjournment and Suspense.

Master-stroke of meeting in the City.

THE adjournment into the City was undoubtedly a master stroke of policy. The act of violence committed, the continued presence of the Court of Guard at Whitehall, the refusal of its officers to disband upon a

Necessity of suspending Westminster sittings.

message sent specially from the Commons on the morning of the 5th, the petition to the King for a Guard still uncomplied with, were all manifest and unanswerable grounds for suspending temporarily the sittings at Westminster. But the House could not afford that its visible action and influence should be withdrawn, even for an hour; and to sit by Committee in Guildhall, was not merely to make instant appeal, in the least resistible form, to

Policy of appealing to Citizens.

the sympathy and support of the Citizens, but at once to cast in the fortunes of the House with the fate of the five accused, who had taken refuge in a house in Coleman Street. Clarendon laughs at the notion of any member of the Commons conceiving for a moment

Alleged absence of danger.

that his accused colleagues were in the least danger. Not that the Five durst not, he avers, venture themselves at their old lodgings, for no man would have presumed to trouble them; but that the City might see that they relied upon that place for a sanctuary of their privi-

§ xxx.   *Adjournment and Suspense.*   295

leges against violence and oppression.* He says, as in a passage formerly quoted we have seen, that all cause for apprehension ceased upon the failure of the outrage of the 4th; and that nothing could equal the contempt the accused themselves felt for the power, of which they yet affected to put on a considerable show of dread. This last was merely " to " keep up the apprehension of danger and the " esteem of their darling the City."† But let us observe what tone, on the other hand, is taken by Admiral Pennington's well informed correspondents; men not alone intimately acquainted with all the movements of the Court, but the most important of them himself in office, and enjoying the confidence of the principal Secretary of State. It never once occurred to these men, at least until the shout of Privilege of Parliament was become universal, and the King had fled before it, that his impeachment of Pym and Hampden would be, or was meant to be, a mere dead and empty letter. For several days after the articles of accusation were published, the accused are spoken of everywhere, in each and all these letters, as men whose fate absolutely is hanging in the balance.

Fears pretended:

to get help from "darling" City.

But what say private letters in State Paper Office?

Serious alarm at impeachment.

Fate of members in balance.

Mr. Wiseman, four days after the outrage, fears it to be impossible but that the affair will have bloody issue, because the House is

Wiseman's view:

* *Hist.* ii. 130.   † *Ib.* ii. 178.

Arrest of the Five Members.

not more determined than the King still appears to be. The Under Secretary of State writes in doubt, on the third day after the failure of Charles's attempt at the House, whether the accused are not actually fled. And, on that same day, Captain Carterett describes his apprehension that there must be serious disturbance before all things could be rightly understood, for that many would have the accused members to be brought to their trial, and others not, saying it was against the privileges and liberties of the Parliament. "I " am not wise enough," continues the honest seaman, " to distinguish the Right of it, but " this I am certaine, that our good King is " much abused. On Tuesday hee went to the " House of Comons to demand those men w^{ch} " were acused, but noe answer was given him. " Yesterday hee went into the Citty, and after " he had spent some tyme in Guyldhall (to give " satisfaction of his good meaning towards his " people), he went to one of the Sheriffs to " dinner. The two Houses have adjorned " untill Tuesday nexte; and this day there was " a Comittee of both the Houses in Guyldhall, " where they have voted that those men accused " shall not be apprehended nor detained, soe " that I feare very much that this will increase " the disturbances of the tyme. This day, one " Serjant Dandie went into London to take " the accused men to aprehend them, where

the Under-Secretary's:

Captain Carterett's: 7th January. S.P.O.

Gives no opinion, but states the fact.

Vote of House for the accused.

Serjeant Dandie gone to seize them.

§ xxx. *Adjournment and Suspense.*

"hee was much abused by the worse sort of *Attacked by the people.* "people. My wife is y^r humble servant and "wishes you a mery new yeare, and soe doth
                "G. CARTERETT."

Strange, if what Clarendon says be true, that the King should have laboured so hard to bring upon himself the quite needless and gratuitous suspicion, and upon his agents and officers the abuse and hatred, of even the "worse sort" of his people! I have shown that with his *Obstinate resolve of* own hand, on the evening of his return from *King.* the City, Charles had drawn up the proclamation against such as should continue to harbour the traitors; and on the following morning, it is placed beyond doubt by Captain Carterett's statement, one of the Royal serjeants was dispatched into the City to endeavour again to complete the arrest. To what extent moreover, in the City itself, all this was thought to favour of an actual and present danger, I am further able to show on the testimony of a friend of the Earl of Northumberland's. "My noble *Thomas* "Compeer," writes on the 7th of January the *Smith to Pennington:* secretary of the Lord Admiral to the Admiral commanding in the Downs: "Though I writt *7th January.* "to you soe lately, yet I cannot choose but *S.P.O.* "give you ye occurrences of ye time. They "being of such importance. The six Delin- "quents continue in ye Citty, and are there pro- *Protection* "tected against ye King's mind. This breeds *of accused against* "displeasure in him, feare in all. Some have *King.*

> King will use force. "perſuaded yᵉ K. to raiſe force to fetch yᵐ
> "out. This made yᵉ Cittie laſt nighte to bee
> "/all in armes, and yᵉ gates and Portculliſes to
> "bee ſhutt; and for ought I heare, are ſo yet.
> "The Cittizⁿˢ delivered a Petition yeſterday,
> "humbly beſeeching his Maᵗⁱᵉ that thoſe men
> "might be proceeded agᵗ in a Parliamentary
> City reſolved to reſiſt. "way: no anſwer yet. 'Tis beleeved yᵉ Cittie
> "is reſolved to protect yᵐ. Some well affected
> "Nobles to both ſides do labor to pacifie the K.
> "Some ill affected labor as much to bring all
> "to confuſion with falſe tales. Wee knowe
> "God help us!" "both. God help us! Your true Friend and
> "humble ſervant, THOMAS SMITH."

This letter outruns by a day the point at which our narrative had arrived, but another remains to be cited which will take us back to that riſing of the Houſe at Weſtminſter on the 5th January, preparatory to the ſittings in Guildhall. "The Houſe yeſterday," wrote Captain Slingſby on the 6th, "were very high

> Slingſby to Pennington: 6th January. S.P.O. "againe, and, I perceive, not reſolved to
> "deliver the men in that are impeacht: they
> "adjorned the Houſe till Tueſday nexte, before
> "wᶜʰ time the King ſhall have no anſwere:
> M.P.s diſcourſing of adjournment to City. "but in the meantime a Comittee of the whole
> "houſe to meete at Guyldhall. This day, being
> "in the Privy Chamber, I heard ſome Parlia-
> "ment men diſcourſing of it. Some ſayd they
> Many refuſe to go. "would not go to Guyldhall, becauſe the men
> "impeacht wold be there: and, ſince the reſt

§ xxx. *Adjournment and Suspense.* 299

"would not deliver them, they might be all "acceſſories.* The Houſe is yett very thinne; "as I am tould, above 200 of them in the "country, who can not come up according to "the Proclamation, by reaſon of the greate "floodes; many in the towne forbearing to "come there. There is no other diſcourſe "but of open armes, if thoſe men be not "brought to tryall. The ill affected Partie "(wch are thoſe y^t follow the Courte) doe "now ſpeake very favourably of the Iriſh; "as thoſe whoſe grievances were greate, there "demaunds moderate, *and may ſtand the Kinge* "*in much ſtead*: many libells printed againſt "the King." *[side notes: Fear to be thought "acceſſories." Threats if accuſed not given up. Royaliſts begin to favour Iriſh.]*

No printed libel, however, it is much to be feared, could poſſibly have been worſe than this written one, of which Captain Slingſby is here unwittingly the author. It has been always one of the graveſt of the Royaliſt charges againſt Pym, that in his famous ſpeech before the Upper Houſe delivered in a week from this date (wherein he warned the Lords of the danger it might prove to themſelves if they left the great taſk of ſaving the liberties of the kingdom to the Houſe of Commons alone), he advanced a charge, unſupported by any kind *[side note: Pym's heavieſt charge proved true.]*

* Preciſely the argument uſed in the Houſe of Commons Hol-itſelf by Hyde's friend and fellow "rat," Holborne (*Hiſt. and* borne's *Biog. Eſſays*, i. 170), famous once for his ſplendid argument argument. againſt ſhip-money, delivered amid clapping of hands and ſhouts of popular delight which the judges found it impoſſible to reſtrain.

of proof, againſt the King and the King's friends, that ſo far from entertaining any laudable eagerneſs to bring to condign puniſhment the leaders of the cruel maſſacre and rebellion in Ireland, they had given the Houſes too much reaſon to ſuppoſe that they felt towards them ſympathy and favour. Can it be ſaid, after reading what is written by Captain Slingſby, that Pym had not good authority for the charge he made?

Sympathy with Iriſh rebellion.

§ XXXI. COMMONS' COMMITTEE AT GUILDHALL.

Thurſday morning, 6th January.
MEANWHILE the Committee at Guildhall, doubtleſs not greatly caring whether Captain Slingſby's friends may pleaſe to join them this day or not, have punctually aſſembled at the Guildhall on the morning of the 6th of January, and are now awaiting us.

No exiſting report of proceedings.
Of the proceedings of that Committee, beyond the fact that they took evidence as to the incidents of the 3rd and 4th which were ſubſequently reported, no account exiſts except in theſe valuable notes of D'Ewes. The Journals of the Houſe are entirely ſilent during the interval from the 5th, the day of adjournment, to the 11th, that of reaſſembling. Ruſh-

Slight notices in Ruſhworth and Verney.
worth devotes to thoſe days only a few lines, in which he makes brief alluſion to the evidence which was taken in the courſe of the ſittings. Sir Ralph Verney mentions but the

§ XXXI. *Commons' Committee at Guildhall.* 301

six resolutions * that were passed, on the days when the Committee sat at Grocers' Hall, in reference to the breach of privilege committed. Clarendon, not affecting to give particular account of anything, confuses everything. D'Ewes alone, who attended the Committee each day at Guildhall and at Grocers' Hall, has preserved anything like a regular record of its proceedings. And this is here given to the world as D'Ewes set it down each day. *Confusions of Clarendon. A regular record by D'Ewes.*

He begins his journal of Thursday the 6th of January, by stating that a great number of the House met at the Committee at the Guildhall, in London, that forenoon about ten of the clock. " I came thither about eleven of " the clock. We sate in the room within the " court into which the juries do ordinarily " withdraw." *Where the Committee sat.*

They had been greeted, on arrival at the committee room, by a deputation of the leading members of the Common Council, in their robes and chains; and a military guard composed of some of the wealthiest of the citizens, every man having his footman in suit and cassock with ribbons of the colours of his company, was in close attendance during all their sittings. Nor were the good old hospitalities of the City wanting; and D'Ewes has more than once to suspend his report that he *Welcome of the Citizens. Military guard in attendance.*

* See *Notes*, 140-141.

may inform us, that about one of the clock he withdrew out, intending to go away, but coming into the Hall he found a feaft prepared for the entertainment of the members, whereat he dined before he departed, and they had "great cheere."

The firft matter they fell upon at the Guildhall, D'Ewes proceeds to tell us, was the unjuft and illegal proceedings againft Pym and the other members, inftituted by the King's Attorney in the Lords' Houfe on the previous Monday. What Grimfton had treated generally in his very able addrefs, was now to be handled in detail. "It was firft debated and refolved "that the faid impeachment there was illegal "and a breach of the privilege of Parliament. "Then they fell in debate, which continued "when I came in, that the fealing up of the "doors of the chambers and ftudies of the "faid Mr. Pym and Mr. Hollis, on Monday "morning laft, was a breach of the liberty of "the fubject and of the privilege of Parlia"ment; and this was alfo voted upon the "queftion. Then we fell in debate concern"ing the King's iffuing out warrants, figned "with his own hand, to Mr. Francis and others "his Serjeants-at-Arms, to attach their "bodies: that they were illegal, and againft "the liberty of the fubject and the privilege "of Parliament."*

* *Harl. MSS.* 162, f. 309 a.

§ XXXI.   *Commons' Committee at Guildhall.*   303

The Committee thus wifely began at the beginning, queftioning the Attorney-General's proceeding by impeachment before difcuffing the outrage that followed. The folitary argument of any weight that is ufed by Clarendon in palliation of the conduct of the King, affumes that the popular leaders claimed their privilege of Parliament as an immunity even from the charge of treafon: we fhall now fee on what foundation this refts, and with how much truth any argument bafed thereon could be urged. Upon the laft propofition as to the warrants of arreft, a debate arofe, in which Nathaniel Fiennes and one or two more took part; and in the courfe of it a fuggeftion was made that the Committee fhould fend to Mr. Brown, the Clerk of the Houfe of Lords, for a copy of the proceedings in that Houfe againft the five members of the Lower Houfe. Upon this D'Ewes arofe, and made certainly the moft able fpeech, moft ferviceable in knowledge and illuftration, and going moft directly to the points in iffue, of any from himfelf that he has recorded in his Journal. Its reception by the Committee generally, is honourable evidence of their temper and fpirit.

Attorney-General's proceedings firft queftioned.

Motion to fend for warrants.

Refifted by D'Ewes.

"I did defire," he fays, "that we might
" not fend for the copies of any proceedings
" which had been there printed againft the faid
" members of our Houfe. We were not
" truly to take notice of fuch, becaufe thefe

Speech by D'Ewes.

Explains privileges against arrest.

"proceedings against our own members are first to begin in our own House. For there is a double privilege we have in Parliament: the one final, the other temporary. Our final privilege extends to all civil causes, and suits in law: and this continues during the

Final, and temporary.

Parliament. The other privilege, which is temporary, extends to all capital causes, as Treason or the like, in which the persons and goods of the members of both Houses are only freed from seizure till the Houses be first satiffied of their crimes, and so do deliver their bodies up to be committed to

Why such distinction.

safe custody. And the reason of this is evident, because their crime must either be committed within the same Houses, or without them. As for example. If any member of the House of Commons be accused for treasonable actions or words, committed or spoken within the walls of the same House, then there is a necessity that not only the matter of fact, but the matter of crime also, must be adjudged by that House; for

When the House to judge as to fact and penalty:

it can appear to no other court what was there done, in respect that it were the highest treachery and breach of privilege for any member of that House to witness or reveal what was done or spoken therein, without the leave and direction of the same House. And if it be for treason committed out of the House, yet still the House must be

§ XXXI. *Commons' Committee at Guildhall.* 305

"firſt ſatiſfied with the matter of fact, before
"they part with their members; for, elſe, all
"privilege of Parliament muſt, of neceſſity,
"be deſtroyed. For, by the ſame reaſon that
"they accuſe one of the ſaid members, they
"may accuſe forty or fifty upon imaginary and
"falſe treaſons, and ſo commit them to cuſtody
"and deprive the Houſe of their members.
"Whereas, on the contrary ſide, the Houſe
"of Commons hath ever been ſo juſt as to
"part with ſuch members when they have
"been diſcovered. As in the Parliament de
"A° 27° of Queen Elizabeth, Doctor Parry,
"being a member of the Houſe, was firſt
"delivered up by them to ſafe cuſtody, and
"afterwards arraigned and condemned of high
"treaſon, and executed for it. And ſo like-
"wiſe in Mr. Coppley's caſe. In the Parlia-
"ment in the laſt year of Queen Mary, he
"ſpake very dangerous words againſt the ſaid
"Queen; yet it was tried in the Houſe of
"Commons, as appears in the original journal-
"book of the ſame Houſe, and the ſaid
"Queen, at their intreaty, did afterwards
"remit it."

When as to fact only.

Otherwiſe Houſe might be thinned at pleaſure.

Yet members guilty to be ſurrendered.

Examples given.

Cries of "well moved," now rewarded *"Well moved."*
the firm yet moderate reaſoning,* and the apt

---

* Subſtantially this argument does not differ from that
which Clarendon ſays he took occaſion to urge upon the
Houſe in pointing out to them (*Hiſt.* ii. 139) that privilege *Why ap-*
of parliament did not run in caſes of treaſon, felony, or *plaud*
breach of the peace: but how is it that what was heard from *D'Ewes?*

x

constitutional learning, of the logical and well-read member for Sudbury: but these cries, grateful as he tells us they were to him, are to us the still more valuable testimony of a fair and just temper in the Committee itself, upon a question where Clarendon would have us believe the repeated asseverations he makes, that no man was for a moment listened to who attempted to explain what the law really was, or who asserted that a member of Parliament might have his responsibilities like any other citizen.

<small>Fair and just temper of Committee.</small>

<small>No desire to be irresponsible.</small>

D'Ewes with such approving cries, should have been received from the lips of Hyde with, as he is anxious to have us believe, noise and clamour, with wonderful evidence of dislike, and with some faint contradictions that no such thing ought to be done whilst a parliament was sitting? (See ante, 212-16.) The solution of this, as already I have ventured to suggest, appears to be that Hyde made no such speech; and that the assertion is a mere confusion of his memory between what he did or did not say, and what he had afterwards felt that he might have said. The charge he brings both in his History and his Memoir, as though the House claimed in these transactions to override both the judges and the law itself, is but another form of the doggrel Five Members' March, of which two or three out of the score of stanzas may amuse the reader.

<small>and object to Hyde?</small>

<small>Answer suggested.</small>

<small>Doggrel "Five Members' March."</small>

" And let no wights henceforth presume
To hold it rime or reason,
That judges shall determine what
Is Felony or Treason.

But what the Worthies say is so
Is Treason to award,
Albeit in Council only spoke
And at the Council-Board.
* * *
And for this Sea of Liberty,
Wherein we yet do swim,
Gramercy Kimbolton and Strode say I,
Haselrig, Hollis, Hampden, Pym."

§ XXXI.   *Commons' Committee at Guildhall.*   307

"But," proceeded D'Ewes, "for the cafe of D'Ewes
"thefe gentlemen that are now in queftion, it refumes.
"doth not yet appear to us whether it be for
"a crime done within the walls of the Houfe
"of Commons or without : fo that, for aught
"we know, the whole judicature thereof muft
"firft pafs with us. For the Lords did make an
"Act Declaratory, in the Parliament Roll de
"A° 4° Ed. III. N° 6°, that the judgment of As to cafes
"Peers only did properly belong to them ; fo Lords
"as I hold it fomewhat clear that thefe gentle- join.
"men cannot be condemned, but by fuch a
"judgment only as wherein the Lords may
"join with the Commons, and that muft be
"by Bill. And the fame privilege is to the Privileges
"members of the Lords' Houfe.   For we both
"muft not think that if a private perfon Houfes.
"fhould come there and accufe any of them
"of treafon, that they will at all part with
"that member, or commit him to fafe cuftody,
"till the matter of fact be firft proved before
"them. 'Tis true indeed, that, upon the Impeach-
"impeachment of the Houfe of Commons Lower
"for Treafon or any other Capital Crimes, Houfe :
"they do immediately commit their members
"to fafe cuftody : becaufe it is, firft, admitted compels
"that we accufe not till we are fatiffied in the furrender
"matter of fact ; and, fecondly, it is alfo perfon.
"fuppofed in law that fuch an aggregate body
"as the Houfe of Commons is, will do Malice not
"nothing *ex livore vel ex odio,* feeing they are prefumable.

x 2

Arrest of the Five Members.

Conclusion by D'Ewes.

" entrusted by the whole Commons of Eng-
" land with their estates and fortunes."
Sir Simonds closed his calm and temperate
exposition with a decisive assertion of opinion.
" So as upon the whole matter," he said, " I
" conclude that the proceedings against these
" five gentlemen have been hitherto illegal ;
" and that we ought to demand safety for
" their persons to come and sit amongst us,
" till their crime shall be proved before us."

Loud acclamation.

Then, as he resumed his seat, he proceeds to
tell us with pardonable complacency, " there
" followed a loud acclamation of *Well moved*,
" and Mr. Glyn spake after me, and said that
" I had abundantly and very well cleared this
" point both with authority and reason."

Glyn's speech:

But Glyn's speech was remarkable for more
than this. Some passages of it were hardly
less solid and weighty than Grimston's. Speak-

aimed at such counsels as Hyde's.

ing from the question of the Warrants to the
general consideration of breach of their privileges, he struck more nearly and directly
than Grimston had done at the evil councillors,
by whom misunderstandings had been for a
long period assiduously raised and encouraged
between his Majesty and that House. These

Private informers of the King.

men, he said, and such as these, had been,
and were still, casting aspersions, and spread-
ing abroad evil reports, not only of the members, but of the proceedings of the House of
Commons against them and others of their

§ XXXI. *Commons' Committee at Guildhall.* 309

favorites. For himself he would say that, of all
breaches of the privileges of Parliament, none
more grave could be committed than to in-
form his Majesty of any proceedings in the Spies in
the House.
House of Commons, upon any business what-
soever, before they had concluded, finished,
and made ready the same, to present to his
Majesty for his royal assent thereunto. Further,
he said, it was in his view a breach of Parliamentary privilege to misinform his Majesty
contrary to the proceedings in Parliament,
thereby to incense and provoke him against
the same. And to all men it was visibly a Manifest
most manifest breach of privilege, to come breach of
privilege.
to the Commons House sitting in free consul-
tation, and there, assisted and guarded with
armed men, to demand as it were *vi et armis*
any members singled out and accused, without
the knowledge or consent of that House.

Mr. Glyn had evidently, in the absence of the Glyn has
taken
leadership.
member for Tavistock, assumed in the Com-
mittee the place of leader to the popular party;
and, quietly taking their places by his side,
as of right entitled to claim the next rank to
that which all seem at once to have conceded
to Glyn's distinction as a lawyer and his position as member for Westminster, we find,
among the most active and influential, young Chiefs
under
him.
Sir Harry Vane, Nathaniel Fiennes, Grimston,
Maynard, Alderman Pennington, Stapleton
the member for Boroughbridge, and Wilde

the member for Worcefterfhire, who occupied the chair of the Committee more frequently than any other member.

<small>D'Ewes's argument on privilege.</small>

Glyn had fpoken truly in the compliment he offered to the learning and difcrimination of the member for Sudbury. D'Ewes had argued the matter of privilege, taking the King's proceeding as the bafis or ftarting point, upon incontrovertible grounds. He had anticipated and repelled the falfe infinuations of Clarendon, and now, covered by Glyn's authority againft fuch further objections as were made, he carried the committee with him to a pofition from which their right to refift was un-

<small>A firm pofition.</small>

affailable. Without minutely difcuffing a queftion which can no longer, with our fettled and afcertained rules of procedure, be viewed exactly as it prefented itfelf in thofe days, it is clear that the mere breach of privilege, grofs as it was, was not the King's worft

<small>More than one queftion at iffue.</small>

offence on that miferable day. Whatever, affuming that a cafe exifted on which to take proceedings at all, the form of thofe proceedings fhould ftrictly have been, whether by impeachment of the Commons themfelves, or by indictment preferred to a grand jury, the method taken by the King leaves quite imma-

<small>Clarendon's evafion.</small>

terial. When Clarendon afferts that "if the "judges had been compelled to deliver their "opinions in point of law, which they ought "to have been, they could not have avoided

§ XXXI. *Commons' Committee at Guildhall.* 311

"the declaring, that by the known law, which
"had been confessed in all times and ages, no
"privilege of Parliament could extend in the
"case of treason,"* he knows perfectly well
that he is not raising the real issue.† There **Not one but many breaches of law.**
were a dozen violations of the known and
settled law to be dealt with, before that could
even come to be considered. Each step had
been an outrage. Hyde was too good a lawyer
not to be perfectly aware, that, so far from the
King's having anything like the power he had **King powerless to arrest.**
assumed to exercise in this case, even an ordinary magistrate or justice of peace had a power
superior to the sovereign's. The King was in

* *Hist.* ii. 193.
† I find remarkable evidence, in a letter written the morning **Just opinions as to arrest.**
after the King's attempt, of how clearly, in opposition to all
these false statements and reasonings of Clarendon, the nature
of the outrage which had been committed was discriminated
by impartial bystanders, and how accurate and unexaggerated
was the measure taken of the breach of privilege involved.
Mr. Thomas Smith writes from York House (built for
Buckingham when Lord-Admiral, and since occupied by
holders of that high office), on the 5th January, to his
"true friend" Admiral Pennington. "Since the im- **Smith to Pennington: 5th January.**
"peachm^t and sending of the Bpps. to the Tower, His
"Matie hath sent ye Attourney Gen^{le} to ye Upper House to
"accuse my Lo. Mandeville, Mr. Pym, Mr. Hollis, Mr.
"Strode, Mr. Hampden, and Sir Arthur Haslerig, to bee
"guilty of High Treason. This was don on the 3^d of
"January. The Houses are much displeased at this manner of
"proceeding because, say they, Kings ought not to be the
"accusers of their subjects; and they complain that in y^e **King not to accuse Subjects.**
"manner of managing this businesse ye King hath done
"many things tending to breach of Priviledge. As Sealing
"up their studies, wch ye Parliam^t hath opened againe, and
"imprisoned those y^t sealed them. [And sending] his Sergeants
"into the House of Commons to attack ye persons of some
"who are supposed to be delinquents, &c. The Lords gave
"answer that if a Parliamentary Charge were given in against
"those Delinquents, they would be Comitted to custody, but
"till y^n they would not. The Kynge, offended that they were

Each step reality powerless. He could not draw up the
an out-
rage. impeachment. He could not carry it to the
Lords by his Attorney. He could not serve
it in the Commons by his Serjeant-at-arms.
He could not in person arrest under it. And
for the manifest reason that, presuming a wrong
to be done by such means, the subject would
Subject be left without a remedy. "A subject," said
may do
what King Chief Justice Markham to Edward IV,* "may
cannot. "arrest for treason; the King cannot; for,
"if the arrest be illegal, the party has no
"remedy against the King."
Shame of So strongly did the Attorney General,
Attorney- indeed, afterwards feel the humiliation in
General.
which considerations of this kind involved
him, that upon the proceedings subsequently
taken against him, he requested the Lord
Keeper to interest himself with one of his
Makes friends who sat in the lower House for Notting-
apology
through a ham, Mr. Francis Pierpoint, third son of Lord
friend. Kingston, to offer an apology for his breach of
the law. This curious passage, also revealed to
us by D'Ewes, has already been quoted in a
note†; but it seems impossible to understand, if

" not restrayned, came the next day himself in person well
" guarded into ye Commons' House (a thing never heard of
" before) to demand y^r p̃sons; but they were at that tyme
" absent, and do still absent themselves. The King much
" displeased departed, and is this day gone himselfe into
" London to have y^m p̃claimed Traytors. These violent
" proceedings of the King's give much discontent everywhere,
Discon-
tent with " and we are daily in feare of uproares; yet all care is taken
the King. " to prevent mischiefe."
* Quoted by Lord Macaulay in his *Essays*, i. 67.
† *Ante*, 128. My late extracts from the D'Ewes Journal will
be found in *Harl. MSS.* 162, ff. 308 a and b, and 309 a and b.

§ XXXI.   *Commons' Committee at Guildhall.*

Herbert really felt the "trouble" of mind al- *Apology*
leged, and saw before him so clearly the conse- *not be-*
quences of his act, how an officer of so much ex- *lieved.*
perience should have suffered himself to be
overborne in a matter where he was certain himself to be the first victim. One is rather disposed
to conclude with Mr. Strode, in the pregnant *Mr.*
remark he threw out on the occasion of Pier- *Strode's remark*
point's intercession, that he believed Mr. Attor- *thereon.*
ney did not only contrive the same, but knew
of the design itself also; for he was a man of
great parts, and well skilled in state matters.
The incredulity was at least pardonable.

But we left the debate of the 6th of January *Debate as*
before it closed, amid the cries of approval *to war-*
which followed the speeches of D'Ewes and *rants continued.*
Glyn. Divers, D'Ewes proceeds to tell us,
afterwards spoke respecting the warrants which
purported to have been issued out under the
King's hand, and no one ventured to af-
sert their legality. The speeches all went to *Sound*
one result. That such warrants could not be *principles stated.*
good: that the sovereign was himself a party
against all capital offenders: that, being entitled
on conviction to have their lands and goods,
he could therefore be neither judge nor accuser
in their trial: that his warrants were to be *No diffe-*
issued forth by his ministers, who were by *rence of opinion.*
the law appointed thereunto: "with much
" other matter to that effect."

A characteristic incident then occurred, which

further shows how clearly D'Ewes kept before himself, and how steadily before the Committee, the point it most behoved them to rest their case upon. Mr. Serjeant Wilde, speaking from the Chair, and taking advantage of exciting expressions thrown out in discussing these warrants of the King, would have had the Committee affirm that the mere charge of treason in the abstract, no matter how instituted, was, as against a member of the House of Commons, a breach of privilege; but the member for Sudbury wisely substituted a resolution against the mode of instituting such a charge which lately had been taken, and denouncing the issue of any additional warrants, as not only a violation of the privilege of parliament, but a breach of the liberty of the subject: and this the Committee adopted. The wisdom of such a course was manifest. Even supposing that the view could be supported, of a right in the Lords to entertain the accusation of treason at the instance of the Attorney-General, it was the Lords, and not the King, who should have issued the warrants: and D'Ewes was right to continue to fix the attention of the Committee upon the *mode* of procedure. Had the very right itself existed, the method would have turned it into wrong. "At length," he says, "Mr. " Serjeant Wilde propounded a question to be " put concerning the arresting of Mr. Denzil " Hollis, or any of the other four members

Dispute of D'Ewes with Wilde.

Wrong issue suggested.

Corrected by D'Ewes.

Lords to issue warrants.

How to make a right thing wrong.

§ XXXI.   *Commons' Committee at Guildhall.*   315

"accused of high treason, that it was a breach <small>D'Ewes's victory over Wilde.</small>
"of privilege: but I moved that the first
"question might be put touching the issuing
"forth of any fresh warrants; that the same
"was a breach of the liberty of the subject,
"and a violation of the privilege of Parlia-
"ment: which motion of mine was approved <small>Good sense of Committee.</small>
"by the Committee, and the same was resolved
"upon the question, and ordered by the Com-
"mittee accordingly."

There was no further objection to the reso- <small>Resolutions voted.</small>
lutions submitted. "We proceeded," says
D'Ewes, "to vote it a breach of privilege of
"Parliament, and of the liberty of the subject,
"for any person to arrest any of the said
"members by colour of such warrants; and <small>Against warrants.</small>
"we declared them public enemies of the
"Commonwealth. It was also further resolved
"upon the question, and ordered by the Com-
"mittee, that to arrest any member of either <small>Against persons arresting under them.</small>
"House without consent of that House whereof
"such person was a member, was against the
"liberty of the subject, and a breach of the
"privilege of Parliament, and that any person
"who should-so arrest such member should be
"declared a public enemy of the Common-
"wealth. Which votes being put and ordered,
"it was moved that a sub-Committee might
"be appointed to go out, and to draw out a
"Declaration to this purpose."

Then rose the younger Sir Henry Vane <small>Young Vane rises:</small>

Offers wife with a propofition, as the fequel to what the
fuggef- learned member fkilled in precedents had fo
tion. well moved, which he offered to the Committee as very neceffary to be included in the Declaration, and which was eminently characteriftic of his own fenfe of juftice. "He did
"move," fays D'Ewes, "that we might make
"fome fhort declaration that we did not intend
Guard "to protect thefe five gentlemen, or any other
againft
claiming "member of our Houfe, in any crime; but
privilege "fhould be moft ready to bring them to con-
for crime.
"dign punifhment, if they fhould be proceeded
"againft in a legal way." The Committee
affented; and young Vane, Glyn, Grimfton,
Sub-Com- Nathaniel Fiennes, and Sir Philip Stapleton, hav-
mittee to
draw ing been named as the fub-Committee to draw
provifo. the declaration, left the chamber for that purpofe. While they were abfent, "I departed,"
fays D'Ewes, "from the Committee, between
"two and three of the clock in the afternoon;
"but the Declaration was afterwards brought
Vane's "in by the faid Committee, and allowed and
claufe
voted and "voted by the Committee, and printed." He
printed. adds, that as the Common Council required
the Guildhall Chamber for City ufes, and it
Adjourn was moreover in itfelf fomewhat inconvenient,
to Gro-
cers' Hall. the Committee adjourned itfelf to meet next
morning in Grocers' Hall.

§ XXXII. FACTS AND FICTIONS.

THE elaborate particularity with which the

good Sir Simonds D'Ewes thus records in detail the proceedings of the Select Committee of the Commons, seems as though specially provided for refutation of the studied misrepresentations and disingenuous artifices of Clarendon. Speaking generally of the proceedings of the Committee described in the foregoing section, that writer deliberately states: 1. That all the resolutions voted were in support of, and simple corollaries from, the broad and unrestricted assertion, "that " the arresting, or endeavouring to arrest, any " member of Parliament, was a high breach " of their privilege." 2. That the House itself held short sittings, concurrently with the sittings of the Committee, for the mere purpose of confirming the votes so passed. 3. That when the votes in question were proposed for confirmation, he (Mr. Hyde) took part in the debate, and was received with noise and clamour, and with wonderful evidence of dislike, merely for stating what was a known truth to any one who knew anything of the law, namely, that where persons were arrested for treason, or felony, or breach of the peace, there could be no privilege of Parliament. And, 4. That after this debate "the House " confirmed all that the Committee had voted, " and then adjourned again for some days, and " ordered the Committee to meet again in the " City. . . . the House itself meeting and

[marginal notes: Clarendon fictions. Alleged restriction of votes. Concurrent sittings of House. Hyde's asserted speech. Pretended references to House itself.]

Arrest of the Five Members.

House confirming votes of Committee.
"fitting only to confirm the votes which were
"passed by the Committee, and to prosecute
"such matters as were by concert brought to
"them, by petition from the City, which was
"ready to advance anything they were directed:

All done during Five Members' absence.
"and so, while the members yet kept them-
"selves concealed, many particulars of great
"importance were transacted in those short
"sittings of the House.*"

Reply.
To which elaborate misstatement, the reply which D'Ewes enables us to make is very simple. It is: 1. That the votes of the

Votes not so restricted.
Committee distinctly limited and defined the breach of privilege as consisting, not in the accusation or the arrest, but in the means and process employed therein, whereby the law of the land and the liberty of the subject, not less than the privileges of Parliament,

House itself not fitting.
were violated. 2. That the House held no such fittings, the Committee having in the first instance received full powers, and exercising an entire jurisdiction over the matters

Hyde not speaking.
referred to them. 3. That it is therefore impossible that Mr. Hyde can have addressed the House; that there is no evidence of his having ever attended the Committee;† and that, assuming him nevertheless to have spoken at the Committee as alleged, what we have seen of their reception of D'Ewes's temperate speech renders it extremely improbable

* *Hist.* ii. 138-140. † See *ante*, 212-216.

§ xxxii. *Facts and Fictions.* 319

that Mr. Hyde's very innocent remark should have been hooted down. And 4. That there was only one adjournment of the House between the 5th and the 11th January, 1641-2; and that there were no short sittings whatever while the Five Members yet kept themselves concealed. Even if D'Ewes had not revealed this, the evidence of the Commons' Journals would have been decisive. They are a total blank between the two days named. No short sittings. Journals support D'Ewes.

Happily, too, the Declaration remains, which embodied the constitutional suggestions of D'Ewes and the manly proposition of Vane; and it needs but to quote a few of its noble sentences to dissipate these fictions of Clarendon. After stating the high breach committed against the rights and privileges of Parliament, and the liberties and freedom thereof, by the King's attempt to arrest the members, it proceeded: Evidence of published Declaration.

" And whereas his Majesty did issue forth
" several warrants, under his own hand, for the
" apprehension of the persons of the said mem-
" bers, which by law he cannot do; there being
" not all this time any legal charge or accusa-
" tion, or due process of law, issued against
" them, nor any pretence of charge made
" known to the House; all which are against
" the fundamental liberties of the subject, and
" the rights of Parliament: whereupon, we
" are necessitated according to our duty to
" declare, and we do hereby declare, that any As to warrants: King powerless to issue them. As to arrest:

Arrest of the Five Members.

King disabled from effecting it.

As to claim of privilege:

not defired to bar a juft charge.

Readinefs to bring guilty to trial.

"perfon that fhall arreft Mr. Hollis, Sir
"Arthur Hafelrig, Mr. Pym, Mr. Hampden,
"and Mr. Strode, or any of them, by pre-
"tence or colour of any warrant iffuing out
"from the King only, is guilty of a breach of
"the liberties of the fubject, and of the
"privileges of Parliament, and a public enemy
"to the Commonwealth.... Notwithftanding
"all which, we think fit further to declare, that
"we are fo far from any endeavour to protect
"any of our members that fhall be in due
"manner profecuted (according to the laws of
"the kingdom, and the rights and privileges
"of Parliament) for treafon, or any other mif-
"demeanor, that none fhall be more ready
"and willing than we ourfelves to bring them
"to a fpeedy and due trial: being fenfible
"that it equally imports us, as well to fee
"juftice done againft them that are criminal,
"as to defend the juft rights and liberties of
"the fubjects and Parliament of England."

§ XXXIII. AGITATION IN THE CITY.

Thurfday night, 6th January.

THE Declaration of the Commons on the Breach of their Privilege was printed and in circulation in the City, on the night of that firft meeting at Guildhall. Agitation and excitement had continued to increafe out of doors. Clarendon is no mean or incredible witnefs where his paffions or intereft do not deceive or miflead him to perverfion of the truth,

§ XXXIII. *Agitation in the City.*

and he fays that it cannot be expreffed how great a change there appeared to be in the countenance and minds of all forts of people, upon thofe late proceedings of the King.* The fhops of the City, while the members remained therein, were generally fhut up, as if an enemy were at their gates ready to enter and to plunder them; the people in all places, he adds, were at a gaze, as if, difpofed to any undertaking, they looked only for directions; and the wildeft reports were fpeedily accepted and believed. D'Ewes for once confirms Clarendon. On this Thurfday night, he tells us in a note appended to his Journal of the 6th January, the watch at

A change in the people.

Difpofed to any undertaking.

---

* The paffage is curious and valuable, though in its aim and object the reverfe of candid. "It cannot be expreffed," he fays (*Hift.* ii. 159), "how great a change there appeared " to be in the countenance and minds of all forts of people, " in town and country, upon thefe late proceedings of the " King." He afferts (with what likelihood I have attempted to fhow in my Effay on the Great Remonftrance) that the popular leaders had of late been lofing their fpirits, fo that fome of them were even refuming their old refolutions of leaving the kingdom; but that "now again they recovered greater " courage than ever, and quickly found that their credit and " reputation was as great as ever it had been: the Court being " reduced to a lower condition, and to more difefteem and " neglect, than ever it had undergone. All that they had " formerly faid of plots and confpiracies againft the Parlia- " ment, which had before been laughed at, were now thought " true and real; and all their fears and jealoufies looked upon " as the effects of their great wifdom and forethought. All " that had been whifpered of Ireland was now talked aloud " and printed; as all other feditious pamphlets and libels " were." Thefe remarks are fo coloured as to give a falfe expreffion to the facts they embody, but the facts themfelves are confirmed by what already has been quoted from private letters.

Evidence of Clarendon.

Tribunes exalted.

Court reduced.

All flanders believed.

Y

Sudden alarm at Ludgate. Ludgate was alarmed suddenly, between 9 and 10 o'clock, by information that the same band of desperadoes who had accompanied the King to the House on Tuesday, had a similar design to be executed in the City that night. The news spread simultaneously from several quarters, *Threatened attack on Coleman Street.* and the reported plan was that of an attack upon the house in Coleman Street, where the accused members were. The rumour had in all probability arisen from some oozing out of the project of Digby, as to which Clarendon, in the character he has left of that reckless personage* in the supplement to the third volume of his State Papers, gives us the particular *The Digby plot.* information, that it was conceived immediately upon the Citizens declaring absolutely for the members, and rejecting, as they had done the day before this to which D'Ewes refers, the King's personal overtures for assistance. Further he tells us, as we have seen, that Digby counted upon a select number of a dozen Gentlemen, who he presumed would stick to *Lunsford in it.* him (his friend Lunsford was one †), to help him out with this project, by seizing on the Five Members dead or alive; and he pro-

---

* *State Papers*, iii. lv. lvi. See *ante*, 205.

Speech of Stapleton. † Stapleton made rather a good speech when the Digby plot, and Lunsford's connection with it, became notorious the week after the present; describing Lunsford, "this "Colonel" as he calls him, not content, under the influence of *Lunsford's bragging.* the King's unmerited favour, " but imitating the water-toad, " and, seeing the shadow of a horse seem bigger than itself, " swelling itself straightway to rival the same, and so bursting."

§ XXXIII. *Agitation in the City.*

tefts that without doubt he would have done it, and that it muft have had a wonderful effect. A wonderful effect, even the rumour of it appears to have had.

The City and the fuburbs, fays D'Ewes, were almoft wholly raifed, fo that within little more than an hour's fpace there were forty thoufand men in complete arms, and near a hundred thoufand more that had halberds, fwords, clubs, and the like. Such was the military organifation of the City Train Bands in thofe days. Notwithftanding this, however, the panic ran its courfe, as it is in the nature of all panics to do. "Yet," D'Ewes tells us, in a fentence which exhibits not a little of the nervous derangement it commemorates, "the "general cry of the City, *Arm! Arm!* was "with fo much vehemency, and knocking at "men's doors was with fo much violence, "that fome women being with child were "fo much affrighted therewith that they "mifcarried." However, the Lord Mayor played his part of *pater patriæ* within the City walls with all neceffary promptitude and vigour, and put a timely check to thefe domeftic inconveniences. He had tried, but vainly, to prevent the Trained Bands from getting under arms; but he afterwards fent to Whitehall, and, in every direction where authentic intelligence was procurable, he difperfed it on all fides in place of the exaggerated rumours

The City in arms.

140,000 men with weapons.

Panic continues.

Women in terror.

Exertions of Lord Mayor.

flying about; and he took finally such skilful measures for clearance of the streets, that in little more than an hour from his first interference, the City was again quiet, and " every " man retired to his house." Two days later, he was specially thanked by an order of the Council Board, at which the King was present and the new Ministers of State; and at which demand was made, under their hands, for delivery up of the names of the persons who had " importuned " him to put the Trained Bands in arms."* Yet

Streets cleared.
City again quiet.
Thanks of Council to Lord Mayor.

---

* A copy of this Order from the Council-Board addressed to the " Lord Mayor &c. of London," and dated Saturday the 8th, exists in the State Paper Office, and furnishes remarkable evidence of the tone and spirit which must have animated the Council in discussing the incidents of the preceding Thursday, the 6th of January. It is to be borne in mind, in reading it, that the members for the City were notoriously those who had overruled the Lord Mayor as to the assembling of the Trained Bands, and that the Committee of the Commons, sitting in the City, held the step to have been essential to the safety of the citizens. The insertions within brackets are in the handwriting of Nicholas; and the intimations with which the Order concludes as to the swearing in of Lord Falkland at the Board that day, may perhaps be taken as an evidence of Nicholas's anxiety that the fact should be known in the City, and his own responsibility so far lightened by participation with one so recently engaged and trusted on the popular side in the House of Commons. " Hearty commendations to your L^p and " the rest. Whereas the King's Ma^y hath taken notice of a " great disorder & tumult within the Cittie of London & " Liberties thereof where many thousands of men as well of " the Trayned Bands as others were in armes on Thursday " night last [without any lawfull authority, as his Ma^y is " informed] to the great disturbance & affrightm^t of all the " inhabitants: for which neither his Matie, nor this Board, doth " [find] believe any cause given at all, nor the least danger to " have been intended to the said Citty, or inhabitants thereof, " by any person whatever. W^{ch} being of so dangerous conse- " quence, as the same may no way be connived at : but is " most requisite that the authors of the alarme be enquired " after, exam^d, and punished according to Law : that others

Order from Council, Saturday 8th Jan.
Members for City odious to Court.
Swearing in of Falkland.
Notices tumult of Thursday.
The authors must be punished.

§ XXXIII.   *Agitation in the City.*

the right fo challenged had never until now been Ill-timed defiance.
queftioned; and the time appropriately felected
for this note of defiance, was when bands of
armed men were being organifed, as well by the
King as by his followers, without any warrant
from the law.   D'Ewes concludes the very note
I have quoted, by faying that the alarm in the
City had been greatly increafed by the circum-
ftance of a troop of horfe, raifed by a Royalift Troop raifed by Royalift Squire.
Squire of Effex, having been billeted at Bar-
net, and reported, "upon what mifinformation

" may both hereafter be deterred from the like feditious
" attempts, & his Matie good fubjects better fecured in the
" peaceable quiet & enjoying of what is theirs.   And whereas Certain perfons (M.P.s) over earneft.
" his Matie hath been informed that before the alarme, certaine
" perfons were earneft wth yor Lo^p to put the Trayned Bands
" of the Cittie in armes; wch you refufing to doe becaufe [you
" faid] you knew no caufe of feare, yet the fame was after-
" wards done without yor commands & ag^t yor will [and
" without any authority].   His Maje^y, having duly confidered
" of the premiffes, hath thought fitt by advice of this Board
" hereby to pray and require you, together with y^r Brethren
" the Aldermen and the Recorder of the faid Cittie, forthwith
" to meete & to ufe all diligence for the enquiring and finding Find out authors of alarm.
" out, by what meanes and by whofe endeav^r foe great a
" diforder did happen; who were the authors of the alarme
" [by what & whofe order the trayned bands were raifed]
" and upon what pretexte; and fuch as you fhall difcover to
" be guilty of this fo great offence, that you take a fitting
" courfe that they may be forthcoming: and further that you
" certifie this Board with fpeed of yor proceedings therein,
" and what you finde [as alfo the names of thofe who at firft Give up their names. Muft be punifhed.
" importuned you to put the Trayned Bands in armes].   To
" the end fome further courfe may thereupon be directed for
" fettling the peace & quietneffe of the City, & for
" punifhm^t of the offenders according to the Laws & Statutes
" of the Realme.   Wherein not doubting of y^r care, we bid
" you very heartily farewell.   From Whytehall the 8 of
" January 1641.   Y^r very loving friends.—This day, his
" Ma^{ty} prefent in Counfell, and by his royall comand, the
" Vifc^t Faulkland was fworne one. of H. M. principal
" Secretaries of State."

"I know not, to be but the fore-runners of five hundred horse that were laſt night to come into the City of London."

Tendency to undue fears.

The univerſal tendency of communities and bodies of men to undue and exaggerated fears is well underſtood, and the preſent naturalneſs of ſuch ſudden fears and panics has been ſhown; nor was the character of the diſcloſures made at the reaſſembling of the Committee at Grocers' Hall the next morning, of a kind to diſcontinue or abate them.

§ XXXIV. First Sitting at Grocers' Hall.

Friday, 7th Jan.

On the day of the firſt ſitting at Grocers' Hall, Friday the 7th, it had been appointed to take evidence as to the circumſtances of the King's attempt of the previous Tueſday, and the character and conduct of the armed men who accompanied him. "The buſineſs was entered into," ſays D'Ewes,

Witneſſes as to outrage of the 4th.

"before I came in, and divers witneſſes were examined in my hearing." Of the ſtatements made by thoſe witneſſes he proceeds to

Abſtract of their evidence.

give an abſtract, confirming in all material points the account already given, and ſupplying ſome additional particulars not without intereſt.

It ſeems certain, from the great maſs of the evidence adduced, and ſupported even by witneſſes oppoſed to the majority in the Com-

§ XXXIV. *First Sitting at Grocers' Hall.*

mons, that, while the King was in the House, a *Concerted plan.* word or signal was expected to be given. It was distinctly deposed by several, that, when his Majesty was coming out of the House, divers officers of the late army in the North "and other desperate ruffians" called out *Signal to be given.* for the word, but, when they saw no word given, they "bade make a lane and so de- *Disappointment.* " parted." One of the witnesses, a Captain Ogle, deposed that while speaking, on the morning after the attempt, with one of the officers who came with the King, this person did not scruple to avow that he and others accompanied his Majesty to be his guard in consequence of having heard that the House of Com- *Necessity of forcing Commons to obey King.* mons would not obey the King, and that therefore it was necessary to force them to it. "And " he believed that if, in the posture that they " were set, the word had been given, they *Only the signal wanting.* " should certainly have fallen upon the House " of Commons." Another witness swore to having heard "one of the desperadoes" cry out, as he held up his pistol ready cocked, "I will " warrant you I am a good marksman, I will " hit sure." Another, Mr. John Chambers, deposed to the forcible keeping open of the *Forcibly keeping open door of House.* Commons' door; to the violence used against the servants of members of the House; to the firearms with which the King's party had come prepared; and to the interchange of questions he had overheard among them, as to what might

Counting numbers. be the exact number of members muftered in the Houfe that day. A fimilar piece of evidence muft be given in the words of D'Ewes: " That when the King entered the Houfe, and " it appeared that neither Mr. Pym, nor any " of the other four were there, one of thefe *Ingenuous confeffion.* " bloody ruffians faid ' Zounds! there are " ' none of them here, and we are never the " ' better for our coming!'"

An important witnefs. The moft notable piece of evidence, however, was given by Captain Hercule Langres, who played fo important a part on the memorable day; and D'Ewes enables us firft to publifh it. Dwelling in Covent Garden, he faid, he *At Whitehall the previous Friday.* had occafion to be in Whitehall on the laft day of December, the Friday preceding the King's endeavour to arreft the members. That he *What Lieut. Jenkin faid.* there underftood from Lieutenant Jenkin, who had command of a company of the Trained Bands at Whitehall, that he was then under orders to obey one Sir William Fleming. That he was with that officer again on the following *Again at Whitehall on the 4th.* Tuefday, having heard from a noble gentleman who wifhed well to this nation (doubtlefs the French ambaffador, Montreuil) of the defign *Previous intelligence of King's defign.* of the King's going to the Houfe to be, to take out thofe five members by violence which were accufed of treafon, if he found them there. That, feeing his Majefty was to be accompanied to that end with divers officers and foldiers armed with halberds, fwords, and pistols, among whom were divers Frenchmen, namely Monsieur Fleury and others, he passed through the roof, got to the House of Commons before his Majesty could come, and acquainted Mr. Nathaniel Fiennes therewith. Further, that the said Monsieur Fleury had told him, as long ago as some three weeks, that there would be troubles shortly here in England, that he had guessed so before, but that now he was sure of it. *Passes over roof to escape crowds.* *Knew of coming trouble three weeks ago.*

After this evidence had been taken, D'Ewes himself rose to state to the Committee the impression it had produced upon him, and to suggest a resolution in accordance therewith. "I moved," he says, "that seeing we had all "the material passages of this design proved "unto us by several witnesses, I was in mine "own conscience fully satisfied, that if God had "not in a wonderful manner prevented it by "the absence of those our five members, we "had been all in very great danger of having "been destroyed. And therefore I did desire "that we might resolve the same upon the "question. Others seconded me; and after "a pretty while, the question ensuing was "agreed upon. That the coming of the "soldiers to the House of Commons with his "Majesty, on Tuesday last, was a design to "take some members out of the said House, "and, in case they should find any opposition "or denial, then to fall in an hostile manner *Impression made on D'Ewes.* *Satisfied as to purpose aimed at.* *To find excuse for armed conflict with House.* *Moves and carries vote to that effect.*

"upon the Houſe of Commons; which was a traitorous deſign againſt the King and Parliament."

Sheriffs of London in attendance. Meanwhile Serjeant Wilde, reviving the queſtion on which D'Ewes had outvoted him on the previous day, had ſucceeded in obtaining orders from the Committee for the attendance of the two Sheriffs of London, with the warrants they had received under the hand of the King for the apprehenſion of the five members; and now their arrival was announced. They *Aſked as to warrants.* were called in, and aſked by Mr. Serjeant Wilde whether they had brought with them the warrants. Sheriff Garrett, who had entertained the King two days before, and whoſe ſympathies were with the popular party, *One replies, the other refuſes.* anſwered that he had; the other declined to anſwer, on the ground that the duty of his place enjoined ſecrecy.

At this point D'Ewes interpoſed, and upon his motion the Sheriffs withdrew. Serjeant Wilde then ſtarted up, from the Chair, to aſk whether *Difference between Wilde and D'Ewes.* the Committee did not mean to require them to deliver in the warrants: to which ſome having cried Aye, and more No, D'Ewes took upon himſelf bluntly to inform the Committee that *Don't ſhout "aye" or "no," but reflect and conſider.* the queſtion would not be determined by their confuſed crying Aye and No, but by their conſideration and debate what courſe was beſt to be taken. Suppoſe the Sheriffs *did* deliver up the warrants upon demand, what did they

§ XXXIV. *First Sitting at Grocers' Hall.* 331

propose to do with them? Unless they in- Against
tended to keep them, they were better not to calling in
demand them; and, as the case then stood, it warrants.
was his clear opinion that they should not
keep them, and therefore not demand them.
Because, he proceeded to argue (with that
guarded moderation of tone in reference to Discreet
the King, and that desire to avoid any personal tone as to
questioning of his prerogatives, by which the the King.
testimony he has just borne to the character of
the attempt of the 4th of January is rendered
greatly more valuable), though his Majesty,
being misled by evil counsel, had in many particulars violated their privileges, yet they still
owed him so much respect as not to assume Respect
authority to take from his ministers, to whom still due.
he had sent them, even these manifestly
illegal warrants. "Neither do I doubt,"
he continued, with a touch of the humour Touch of
wherewith he occasionally relieved the grave humour.
precision of his oratory, "but they shall sleep
" as quietly in the Sheriffs' hands as in our
" custody, *who, I believe intend to make but*
" *little use of them.* And indeed the City of
" London in general, and those gentlemen in
" particular have deserved so well of us, as I
" desire not that we should put them upon
" that strait as either to offend his Majesty, or An ill
" disobey us. One of them, you see, pretends choice.
" secrecy, and the other would gladly be ex-
" cused; and therefore I desire that they may

"be called in, and be informed of the good opinion we have of them, and so be dismissed. Some," D'Ewes adds, "seconded me, and others spake contrary; but it was overruled that they should be called in and dismissed, as I had moved: which was done accordingly."

Call in the Sheriffs and dismiss them.
Suggestion adopted.

The next resolution, however, moved in discharge of a duty which the circumstances unavoidably forced upon them, was in effect a direct challenge to the sovereign. It was that the five members accused might and ought to come to attend that Committee, notwithstanding any warrant issued out, or other matter or accusation, against them. It was opposed by some very strongly, and the discussion was still proceeding, when, at 4 o'clock, D'Ewes quitted Grocers' Hall. His opinion was, that this open defiance should not have been resorted to, until a direct demand for safety to the persons of the accused should have been refused by the King; and apparently he wished to avoid supporting a resolution which yet he could not conscientiously have opposed. It was carried, and the members invited to attend Grocers' Hall publicly on the following Monday.

Motion that Five Members attend Committee.
Disliked by D'Ewes.
Carried.

The King meanwhile had met, more than half way, the challenge of the Commons, and early on the morning following this vote, the very day when Falkland received the seals,

King meets the challenge.

there came forth a freſh Proclamation, reiterat- Freſh pro-
ing againſt the Five Members the accuſation of clamation againſt
High Treaſon, and commanding all magiſtrates accuſed.
and officers to ſeize and convey them to the
Tower. A letter from the Council Board
alſo reached the Chief Magiſtrate, of which the
object was to make the City members reſponſible for meaſures taken by them on the night
of the alarm to protect the Citizens. It was
impoſſible but that the courſe thus adopted
ſhould precipitate every danger, weaken what Unwiſe
chances were left to Charles the Firſt, and courſe.
give unexpected opportunities and power to
his antagoniſts.

§ XXXV. SECOND SITTING AT GROCERS' HALL.

WITHIN one hour after appearance of the Saturday,
King's proclamation on Saturday the 8th of 8th January.
January, commanding all loyal men throughout
the kingdom to apprehend the Five Members of
the Commons whom he had accuſed of treaſon,
the Committee of the Commons had aſſembled
in Grocers' Hall; and, after renewing the Reply of
order for the public appearance of the accuſed the Houſe to King's
members on Monday, preparatory to the return proclama-
to Weſtminſter on the following day, they tion.
paſſed two reſolutions. The firſt : that a
printed paper in the form of a proclamation
iſſued out for the apprehending five gentlemen, members of the Houſe of Commons,

was falſe, ſcandalous, and illegal. The ſecond: that all acts of the Citizens of London, or of any other perſon whatſoever, for the defence of the Parliament and the privileges thereof, or the preſervation of the ſame, were according to their duty, and the late proteſtation, and the laws of the kingdom, and that if any perſon ſhould arreſt or trouble them for ſo doing, he was declared an enemy of the Commonwealth. Then were tidings brought, while theſe votes were in progreſs, of a ſhip from Berwick laden with arms having neared the Tower; and this led to the moſt important ſtep yet taken by the Committee. Sir John Byron, Lieutenant of the Tower, and Captain Coningſley, Lieutenant of the Ordnance, having been ſummoned and examined, it was reſolved that meaſures ſhould be adopted with all diſpatch for the ſetting of a Guard upon that great fortreſs (the only ſecurity in thoſe days for even the ſanctity of commercial dealings),*

---

* Clarendon admits how vitally important it was to obtain ſecurity for the ſafe keeping of the Tower, even in the very language of cavil with which he complains of " the petition " brought and delivered in the names of ſeveral merchants " who uſed to trade to the Mint; in which they deſired that " there might be ſuch a perſon made lieutenant of the Tower " *as they could confide in* (an expreſſion that grew from " that time to be much uſed), without which no man would " venture bullion into the Mint, and by conſequence no " merchant would bring it into the kingdom."—*Hiſt.* ii. 154.

In that noble ſpeech (one of the greateſt monuments of eloquence, at once maſſive and perſuaſive, that exiſts in the Engliſh language) delivered by Pym before the Upper Houſe at the Great Conference of the 24th of January, but a few days ſubſequent to the preſent date, when the leader of the

under command of an officer having equally the
confidence of the City and the Parliament, and *Selection
of commanding
officer :*
irremovable "without the King's command sig-
" nified by both Houses." The officer selected
was the Captain of the Artillery Garden, Skippon; "a faithful and able soldier," says Whitelock; a man, says Clarendon, who had served
very long in Holland, and from a common
soldier had raised himself to the degree of a *Major-
General
Skippon.*
Captain, and to the reputation of a good
officer; "a man of order and sobriety, and
" untainted with any of those vices which the
" officers of that army were exercised in :" a *Character
and services.*
man, let me add, very notable in the coming
years, and whose part in our English history
dates from this day.*

Lower House invited the concurrence and help of the Lords
in saving the kingdom, but told them that their refusal would
not discourage the Commons in saving it without such aid, he *Effect of
political
troubles
on trade.*
also adverts to the evil influences upon trade arising from the
insecurity of the Tower. "But I must protest," he said,
" the House of Commons hath given no cause to these
" obstructions. We have eas'd Trade of many burdens and
" heavy taxes; we have freed it from many hard restraints by
" patents and monopolies; we have been willing to part with
" our own privileges, to give it encouragement; and we have
" sought to put the merchants into security and confidence in
" respect of the Tower of London, that so they might be
" invited to bring in their Bullion to the Mint as heretofore
" they have done. We are no way guilty of the troubles, *Defence
of the
Commons.*
" the fears, the public dangers, which make men withdraw
" their stocks, and keep their money by them, to be ready for
" such sudden exigents as in these great distractions we have
" too much cause to expect. I must clear the Commons.
" We are in no part guilty of this. Whatsoever mischief
" these obstructions in trade shall produce, we are free from it.
" We may have our part in the misery, we can have no part
" in the guilt or dishonour."
 * Whitelock (i. 191), has preserved for us a specimen of

Arreſt of the Five Members.

<small>Named Chief of the City Militia.</small> Captain Skippon was named, before the Committee aroſe, Major-General of the Militia of the City of London. It was an office never before heard of, Clarendon ſays afterwards in his Hiſtory, nor imagined that they had <small>How authority comes into being:</small> authority to conſtitute. Their authority, it might have been replied, ſprang into life with the proclamation iſſued on this 8th of January 1641-2, and the letter of that morning's date from the Council Board. It had become neceſſary that the Trained Bands of London <small>Attends upon neceſſity.</small> ſhould be under the command of a perſon fit to lead them, and authority waits upon neceſſity. A Sub-Committee was alſo appointed to confer and arrange, as to the Military arrange- <small>Order for poſſe comitatus.</small> ments for Tueſday, with the Common Council of London: order having been at the ſame time iſſued, to the Sheriffs of London and Middleſex, for the raiſing of the *poſſe comitatus* "for the "Guard of the King and Parliament" on the occaſion of the return to Weſtminſter. Little <small>No ſuch guard needed.</small> was that precaution needed. But even the men

<small>Skippon and his ſoldiers.</small> what he calls thoſe ſhort and encouraging ſpeeches to his ſoldiers which induced the City Bands, all through the Civil War, to march forth under his command with the utmoſt cheerfulneſs. " Come, my boys, my brave boys, let us pray " heartily and fight heartily. I will ſhare the ſame fortunes " and hazards with you. Remember the cauſe is for God, " and for the defence of yourſelves, your wives, and children. " Come, my honeſt brave boys, pray heartily and fight heartily. " and God will bleſs us!" Thus would he go all along with the ſoldiers, adds the grave Mr. Whitelock; talking to <small>Liking for ſhort ſpeeches.</small> them, ſometimes to one company, and ſometimes to another; and the ſoldiers ſeemed to be more taken with it than with a ſet formal oration.

§ xxxv.   *Second Sitting at Grocers' Hall.*   337

who fat at Grocers' Hall at the clofe of this eventful week of January, could not gauge the depth or force of the feeling, which, fince its commencement, had ftirred London and its adjacent counties to their depths, and already had determined finally the queftion of the fafety of Parliament againft the King. Though the Committee made arrangements and iffued orders as having no longer any fear, they could have formed but little notion as yet of the character and kind of triumph wherewith the great mafs of the people were preparing, againft the day of the propofed return to Weftminfter, to celebrate and glorify the men whom the King fo recently had denounced as traitors, and on that very day had again publicly outlawed and profcribed.

Committee ignorant of their power.

Triumph preparing.

Members to be borne back by the people.

A very ftriking incident occurred before the Committee, on this 8th of January, adjourned. Word was brought to them that the King, attended by certain members of the Houfe of Lords, propofed to come in perfon on Monday next to the Committee. It was probably a mere threat, thrown out in the hope that it might compel abandonment of the propofed public appearance of the accufed members on that day. But, whether really or only colourably entertained, the Committee, with confummate calmnefs and good tafte, intimated their readinefs to give dutiful welcome to fuch a vifit, by the degree of preparation they would make

Propofal of King to attend Committee.

Its reception.

z

Arrest of the Five Members.

Due respect to be paid.
Way to be made for King and Nobles.

for it. " Thereupon they ordered *the Captains*
" *of the Trained Bands that attended them as a*
" *Guard* should take especial care that his
" Majesty and the English nobility have way
" made for them to come in; and Sir Ralph
" Hopton and Mr. Charles Price, who were
" the King's servants, were desired *to stand by*
" *the Officers of the Guard to see the same*
" *performed*, and to shew them such persons
" as are of the English nobility." Of course
nothing more was heard of a visit from the King.

§ XXXVI. SUNDAY THE NINTH OF JANUARY.

Visitors in City streets and chapels.

SUNDAY, the 9th of January, saw groups of strange visitors in the London streets, churches, and chapels. The City had become suddenly and silently filled with other than the familiar faces of her Citizens. Men not known to each other but by the purpose that lighted up each countenance as they met, men who were com-

Strangers meeting as friends.

plete strangers, says Lilly, grasped hands firmly, and passed on without uttering a word. A settled and quiet determination everywhere shewed itself. Large numbers had poured

Petitioners for Pym.

into London that morning with a petition, signed by several thousands for protection of Mr. Pym. They were chiefly of the citizen and merchant class, but in attendance upon them were thickly gathering crowds of apprentices and artizans. Four thousand squires and

§ XXXVI. *Sunday the Ninth of January.* 339

freeholders had ridden up yesterday from Buckinghamshire to protect their beloved representative: substantial farmers and sturdy yeomen, born and bred within the shadow of Hampden's beeches; gentlemen of landed estate, who had selected him to obtain redress for their wrongs: the same, who, but a few weeks before the assembling of this parliament, had in great numbers preferred imprisonment to a timorous compliance with unjust levies of coat and conduct money in their several shires. They are here now to live or die with Mr. Hampden; to offer service to the Commons; respectfully to petition the King. And from many a pulpit issued forth, on this memorable Sunday, the solemn greeting of the great city to her welcome visitors. "We did "hear several most savoury discourses out of "the hundred and twenty-second Psalm." The noble old words bring back the fervour of the true faith, the belief in God and His word, the stern and indomitable resolution, which characterised this grand time. "Our "feet shall stand within thy gates, O Jerusalem! " Jerusalem is builded as a city that is compact "together: whither the tribes go up, the tribes "of the Lord unto the testimony of Israel, to "give thanks unto the name of the Lord. . . . "Pray for the peace of Jerusalem: they shall "prosper that love thee! Peace be within thy "walls, and prosperity within thy palaces!"

Petitioners for Hampden.

Savoury discourses.

122nd Psalm.

Text preached from.

§ XXXVII. Preparations for the Triumph.

<small>Monday 10th Jan^y:</small>
It was nearly ten on the following morning when the proceedings of the Committee were resumed. The Committee men had found it <small>Laſt ſitting in Grocers' Hall.</small> no eaſy matter to get to their places; ſo thronged were the narrow ways of the Poultry, and ſo difficult the approach to the magnificent old Hall which the wealthy Company of Grocers had placed at their diſpoſal. For, this was the day when the accuſed members were publicly to reſume their ſeats by the ſide of <small>Crowds aſſembled.</small> their colleagues, and denſe crowds of the people had aſſembled to give them welcome as they paſſed in from Coleman Street. When D'Ewes entered, Glyn had been explaining the conduct of the Roman Catholic Lord Herbert, in a matter which ſhowed his loyalty to the Houſe; and this elicited from all ſides <small>Speeches of Glyn and Pennington.</small> (the Puritan Sir Simonds himſelf chiming heartily in with it) an expreſſion of gratitude and reſpect. Alderman Pennington then roſe to make a communication reſpecting the Tower; and what he had to relate confirmed the alarms of the week preceding, <small>Suſpected tamperings at the Tower.</small> and eſtabliſhed the fact of interferences with the guard and defence of that all-important fortreſs, in direct oppoſition to the orders of the two Houſes. The hamleteers, who acted ordinarily as warders, had been diſcharged, and

§ XXXVII. *Preparations for the Triumph.* 341

were not suffered to re-enter; while others had
been introduced in their place. The body of
canoneers, upwards of forty in number, whose
residence was outside the walls, had been ordered to take up residence within; a company
of carbineers had joined them; and, acting with Evidence of danger.
these, there were now some forty or fifty re-
tainers of the accused Bishops: all disaffected
to the House. Several of the old hamleteers,
being called in, deposed also to acts of the new
Governor having a drift entirely opposed to
the resolutions of Parliament. The carbineers
had been introduced secretly; within the past
two days, considerable numbers of "cavaliers" "Cavaliers."
had been permitted to pass in and out; unusual
quantities of ammunition were in store; and
the flood was kept in the moat. A sub-com- Sub-committee appointed, and Byron summoned.
mittee was appointed, therefore, to examine
further; and direction was issued for the attendance of Sir John Byron.

Then rose Sir Henry Ludlow, the member
for Wiltshire, father of the more famous
Edmund (who upon Sir Henry's death in 1644
succeeded him in the representation of his
county), and submitted a vote to be passed by
the Committee, and reported to the House,
declaring it to have been a traitorous con-
spiracy in Sir William Killegrew and Sir Motion against Killegrew and Fleming.
William Fleming to publish to the Four
Inns of Court a scandalous paper against
Five Members of the Commons. But this

Moderation of Committee.

Violent language disliked.

resolution, says D'Ewes, in a passage that exhibits characteristically the prevailing desire to avoid all intemperance of expression, had to be "referred to Mr. Glyn and some others to "put into form, because it was very long, and "[contained] too high expressions of some "cruel and bloody intentions in the said Sir "William Killegrew and Sir William Fleming." Soon the sub-committee returned, and the subjoined resolutions were put. The wish seems to have been that all the votes having direct personal reference to the outrage committed on the Five Members, should be taken before their appearance among the Committee; and that what was reserved for settlement on their arrival should be simply the order of procedure for the Return to Westminster next day.

Resolutions modified and passed.

The Chairman rose, and read from the paper handed to him : That the publishing of several articles purporting to form a charge of High Treason against certain Gentlemen, members of this House, by Sir William Killegrew, Sir William Fleming, and others (in the Inns of Court and elsewhere, were afterwards inserted),

Against agents on the 3rd and 4th.

was a high breach of the privilege of Parliament, a seditious act maliciously (so written in mistake for manifestly) tending to the subversion of the peace of the kingdom, and an injury and dishonour to the said members, there being no legal charge or accusation against them.

Further, the Chairman read: That the privileges of Parliament, and liberties of the subject, so broken, could not be fully vindicated unless the King would discover who advised him to the sealing up of chambers, studies, and trunks of said members, the sending a serjeant to the House to demand them, and coming in his own person to Parliament to apprehend them, to the end that such evil counsellors might receive exemplary punishment.—But as these words were read, several members suggested the necessity of allusion to the warrants under the King's hand; and the fact of the appearance of Serjeant Dandie and his company in the City, for the declared purpose of seizing the accused, together with the simultaneous appearance of the Proclamation threatening penalties of the law against all who should be discovered entertaining, lodging, harbouring, or conversing with them, became the subject of excited conversation and dispute. In the end, the words "and to issue several "warrants under his Majesty's own hand to "apprehend the said members"* were inserted in the first resolution, and the vote was made to comprise this addition: And that it was lawful for all persons whatever to entertain, lodge, harbour, or converse with, those five gentlemen, and that whosoever should be

Against evil counsellors.

Against Proclamations issued.

Against warrants under King's hand.

---

* Interlineations of the votes as originally put, appear in Sir Ralph Verney's *Notes*, 141, 142.

questioned for the same was, and should be, under the protection and privilege of Parliament.

Speech by Maynard. Before the votes finally passed, a somewhat remarkable speech was made by Maynard, who sat for Totnefs. This was the same able and unscrupulous lawyer who, acting closely by the *His fellow-* side of Glyn throughout this great business, *ship with Glyn.* as a stickler for the rights of Parliament and the people, consented afterwards, with Glyn, to do the dirty work of the Restoration; had the inexpressible baseness to join with him in conducting the prosecution against Vane; and most justly drew down upon himself and his associate, even during the orgies of the opening *Remembered at the Restoration.* of Charles the Second's reign, contempt and hatred from the common people and citizens, who had not, through all that interval of nearly twenty years, forgotten these their old highflying efforts in behalf of popular rights against Court and King.*

For the present, however, it is to be admitted, in justice to the member for Totnefs,

Mr. Pepys' political rogues.

Popular view of them.

* "Blessed be God," says Pepys, devoutly, at the close of the long entry in his *Diary* (i. 179, 180, ed. 1854) of the 23rd April, 1661, in which he has been describing Charles the Second's Coronation, "I have not heard of any mischance "to anybody thro' it all, but only to Serjeant Glyn, whose "horse fell upon him yesterday, and is like to kill him, which "people do please themselves to see how just God is to "punish the rogue at such a time as this: he being now one "of the King's Serjeants, and rode in the Cavalcade with "Maynard, to whom people wish the same fortune." And who will not remember Butler's immortal couplet?

"Did not the learned Glyn and Maynard
To make good subjects traitors, strain hard?"

§ XXXVII. *Preparations for the Triumph.* 345

that he spoke forcibly, and drove the particular questions home. After enlarging, in the manner of the time, upon the nature of a Parliament, and its sovereignty in discovering and curing all diseases in a Commonwealth; after avowing his confident belief that the long intermission of those assemblies had been the sole cause of all the evils and troubles that had happened to his Majesty's kingdoms; he said that the worthy gentleman below him, indicating the member for Colchester, had, on a previous day, expressed in very pregnant terms the one great privilege of Parliament to which every other subserved. This was, Not to be questioned or accused, for or concerning any vote, argument, or dispute, during free sitting as the people's representatives, either in the continuance of a Parliament, or after the same might be dissolved or broken off, either legally or illegally. Applying which to the transactions of the 3rd and 4th, he would say that no greater breach could be committed than to accuse of High Treason five members of that House during the continuance of its sittings, for and on account of matters debated on and done in the House, in their character of members thereof; and then, upon such accusation, to proceed to break open their chambers, trunks, and studies, and seize upon their books and writings.

For if, said this skilful and popular speaker,

His present view of parliaments:

their privileges:

the attempted arrest:

and the unlawful seizures.

Arreſt of the Five Members.

<small>All public buſineſs in peril.</small> if to be queſtioned for free debating or arguing in Parliament were no breach of privilege, then could they not ſafely intermeddle with or agitate any buſineſs whatſoever, concerning either Church or State, but what ſhould be appointed and nominated by his Majeſty and his Privy Council. And further, if, for things done in the Houſe, if, repeated Maynard, amid <small>"Well moved."</small> cries of "very well moved," for things expreſsly done therein, freely choſen members of that Houſe might be accuſed of treaſon, then would it be dangerous longer to ſit in Parliament upon any buſineſs of diſorders in the State and grievances to the ſubject, committed or done by great perſonages, ſuch as Lords and Biſhops; ſeeing that theſe might at any <small>Lords and Biſhops. uncontrolled.</small> time, by their ſubtle inventions, induce his Majeſty to favour their actions, by merely pretending to uphold his honour, maintain his prerogative, ſupport his royal power, and the like.

And finally he had to ſay that if upon any ſuch accuſation, the chambers, trunks, and ſtudies of ſuch accuſed members might be broken open, and their writings ſeized upon, then would it altogether diſcourage any man to undertake any ſervice for the good of his country, who ſhould ſo perceive that he might at pleaſure be bereaved of ſuch means <small>Men of ſpirit diſabled.</small> and helps as alone enabled and rendered him fit for duties to the Commonwealth. He was for thoſe reaſons, therefore, favorable to the

§ XXXVII.   *Preparations for the Triumph.*   347

votes then submitted, and to a declaration to
be drawn up from the same for the information and encouragement of all loyal subjects.

The resolutions had scarcely been voted,
when a commotion outside the Hall gave notice Agitation outside.
of some fresh excitement, and it was announced
that a very numerous deputation of sailors and
mariners, masters and officers of ships, bring-
ing with them a petition signed on the sudden Petition of sailors.
by more than a thousand hands, had come to
proffer their services, in D'Ewes's phrase, " to
" be with us tomorrow, to defend the Parlia-
" ment by water with muskets and other
" amunition in several vessels; which was
" accepted by us," and all needful orders made Services of mariners accepted.
in relation thereto.* Permission was given, for
example, that all the vessels should be fitted
with artillery, proviso being made that no command for firing, save in the way of salute,
should be given that day, unless " the King
" and Parliament " should be first assailed.
Order was also drawn up for the place of ren- To meet at 3 next morning:
dezvous.   To take advantage of the tide, and
that the whole fleet might come through bridge
together, they were " to meet at the Hermi- at the Hermit-age.
" tage at 3 next morning."   All which being

* *Harl. MSS.* 162, f. 309 b. Rushworth, in his brief D'Ewes more cor-rect than Rush-worth.
allusion to these occurrences (*Coll.* III. i. 433), says that it
was on Saturday both the seamen and the apprentices attended
to proffer their service: but D'Ewes, who reports all the
details, is of course to be preferred as a witness, and he is
entirely supported by Sir Ralph Verney's brief record, *Notes,*
141-2.

fettled, away went the "water-rats," as the King bitterly called them, when, hearing this day of their proffer fo to guard the Commons back to their home at Weftminfter, he felt himfelf weaker by one defertion more, and faw that his mariners and feamen had gone over to his enemies.

The "water-rats."

But now came fhouts from without far exceeding any that had yet been heard, and the Five Members were known to be approaching. They entered amid what D'Ewes calls the "welcome of many," and took their places "in "among us." He remarks in what order they entered, Hollis and Hafelrig, Pym, Hampden, and Strode ; and the imagination fupplies all that his fimple expreffion includes, of the heartfelt fympathy that greeted them, and of the determination of the Committee to make common caufe with colleagues branded as traitors, whofe only title to that vengeance of the Court had been the extent of their fervice to the Houfe of Commons and the people. When they had taken their feats, it was found that cries and preffure ftill fo increafed from without that it was expedient to call in a certain number as fpokefmen for the great mafs of the common people and apprentices, who were faid to be thronging round the doors. They entered accordingly, and, fays D'Ewes, "in "their own names and in the names of all the "reft defired to guard the Parliament to-

The Five Members approach.

Enter and take feats.

Greeting.

Offers from the common people.

§ XXXVII. Preparations for the Triumph.

"morrow. Whereto Serjeant Wilde, by order
"from and in the name of the Committee,
"gave them hearty thanks for their prefent offer
"and former care and readinefs to guard the
"Parliament, wherein many of them had been
"wounded. For this the Committee hoped
"to fee them have redrefs in due time: but
"defired them to keep at home to-morrow for
"the guard of the City, whilft their mafters
"did guard up at the Parliament: and that
"whenfoever we had occafion to ufe them,
"they fhould have notice from us. One of
"them anfwered for the reft that they would
"obey our command, and fo departed."

Thanked by Committee.

Still another group from thofe eager crowds without, however, had by this time forced its way into the outer paffages of the Hall, and a paufe had to be made for its reception in the committee room. " Divers," fays D'Ewes, "of the borough of Southwark then came "and offered the affiftance of their Trained "Bands to us to-morrow, to come and be our "guard at Weftminfter. We told them that "we hoped the City of London would take "care for our guard: but accepted their offer "with thanks, and defired them to be in the "fields about Lambeth and in Southwark in "their arms."*

Offers from Southwark Trained Bands.

Accepted, and told to be in arms.

Sir John Clotworthy now rofe, and per-

---

* *Harl. MSS.* 162, f. 313 b. I may take this opportunity of faying that the entire proceedings of this Monday the 10th January are comprifed within ff. 312 a, and 313 b.

Protection of Sub-Committee. formed the great service of the day. He reported the heads of the various resolutions which the Sub-Committee named at the preceding sitting had settled with the Committee of the Common Council of London appointed to confer with them, for provision of the *Arrangements for Tuesday's guard.* Military Guard to accompany the Five Members on their return to Westminster on the morrow. This was the true pledge of welcome which the House and the City had been all these days preparing, and by which they became bound, in penalties of treason they would hardly themselves have questioned, *Irrevocable step.* never to recede from the conflict now provoked until a victory was won. Each article of the resolutions was put separately, and a vote taken upon it: not without resistance from some who were present (among them Hopton and Price, and Sir Edward Dering; what tone was taken either by Falkland or Culpeper is not ascertainable), but with a quiet and stern determination on the part of the great majority, as fully conscious of the responsibilities incurred. " It was really trea- *Raising troops without commission.* " son," exclaimed Philip Warwick,* " for them " to march without the King's commission." If it were in strictness so, then so let it be: they believed indeed otherwise, and that, even by royalist theories of the constitution, to secure the safety of the Parliament and Kingdom was

* *Memoirs*, 226, ed. 1813.

§ XXXVII.   *Preparations for the Triumph.*   351

to provide for the safety of the King : but to
the course they were now taking, whatever it
might involve, they had been driven in sheer Resolu-
self-defence by their assailant. tions voted:

The first resolution* was, that it had become First.
necessary to have a sufficient guard provided
for the safety of the King, Kingdom, and
Parliament. The second, that such guard Second.
should be raised out of the City and the parts
adjacent. The third, that eight companies Third.
should be appointed for to-morrow's guard, to
assemble at eight o'clock, under the command
of Captain Skippon. The fourth, that Skippon Fourth.
should receive rank as Serjeant Major General
of the City Forces, until the City ordered it
otherwise; and that all the officers and men
who should be of the Guard serving under
him, were to take the Protestation † before they
marched. The fifth, that eight pieces of ord- Fifth.
nance, with all accoutrements belonging thereto,

---

* These all important votes are now for the first time set
down as they were passed. A copy of them is in Verney's Verney's
Notes (142-3), but less correct than that of D'Ewes; and so mistakes.
unfamiliar still was the name very famous afterwards, that
"Skipworth" is written in every instance by Verney, instead
of Skippon. D'Ewes gives the right name.

† For the terms of the Protestation, see *Rushworth*, III. i.
241. And for the names subscribed to it of the members of
the Commons (between 4 and 500) and the Lords (numbering
with the judges and lawyers 106), *Ibid.* 244-8. The oath The Pro-
taken included a solemn profession of determination to main- testation.
tain "the true Reformed Protestant Religion, expressed in the
" Doctrine of the Church of England, against all popery
" and popish innovation within this realm, and also the
" power and privilege of parliaments, and the lawful rights
" and liberties of the subjects."

Arreſt of the Five Members.

should accompany the Guard; and that all the Trained Bands were to be at their colours, under

Sixth. Skippon's command. The sixth, that Serjeant Major General Skippon should not fail to perform what was ordered that day; and that, until such services were ended, he was not to stir upon any command or countermand whatever, without consent and direction from

Seventh. parliament. The seventh, that Skippon and his force were declared to have power, should violence be offered, to offend and

Eighth. defend. The eighth, that all Captains were to receive order to beat drum, de die in diem, from Skippon himself; and that all soldiers should repair to their colours in arms. The

Ninth. ninth, that all citizens who might be disposed to mount themselves should likewise be commanded by Skippon, and that such would be

Tenth. held as a most acceptable service. The tenth, that all ammunition necessary should be provided out of the Chamber of London. The

Eleventh. eleventh, that the Common Council Committee were to be considered free from all commands and arrests, and that they should not, until further leave obtained from the House of

Twelfth. Commons, stir out of the City. The twelfth, and last Resolution, declared that all this service in general, as well as in every particular, should be held good and acceptable service, *and legal;* and that it should be accounted to be for the safety of the King, Kingdom, and Parliament.

§ XXXVII.   *Preparations for the Triumph.*   353

These votes having been taken separately, Hampden was the first to break the silence which the Five Members had observed since they resumed their seats. He thanked the Committee for his friends and himself, craving their good counsel as to a matter it behoved him to lay before them. "Divers thousands "were coming out of Buckinghamshire with "a petition. The petition was to declare "their readiness to live and die with the Par- "liament, and in defence of the rights of the "House of Commons. He had to state that "they came in a peaceable manner, and that "he thought it his duty to acquaint the Com- "mittee therewith."* Upon this, however, the Royalist members present appear to have offered a resistance hardier than any by which the Resolutions were met. Very many, D'Ewes informs us, spoke to what Mr. Hampden had said; and several would have had the men coming out of Buckinghamshire sent unto to have returned thither. But this of course was

Hampden speaks.

Will you receive my constituents?

4000 from Bucks.

Better go back?

---

* The numbers of Hampden's petitioners are very variously stated. "As soon," says Clarendon, speaking of the day following the present, "as the citizens and mariners were "discharged, some Buckinghamshire men, who were said to "be at door with a petition, and had indeed waited upon "the triumph with a train of four thousand men, were called "in : who delivered their petition in the name of the inhabi- "tants of the County of Buckingham, and said it was "brought to the town by about six thousand men." ii. 166. Dering, in the same letter to his wife in which he states the number at five thousand, puts in a parenthesis his belief that they were not more than two thousand. Rushworth (111. i. 486) reckons them at four thousand; D'Ewes, at five or six thousand.

What number from Bucks?

Hyde.

Dering.

Rushworth and D'Ewes.

A A

over-ruled. "The greater fenfe of the Com- "mittee," fays D'Ewes, "being to let them "alone, becaufe we did not know fully the "intent of their coming." It was afterwards faid by Clarendon that only Mr. Hampden fully knew that ; that the levying of war in England dated from the day when thofe thoufands out of Buckinghamfhire were invited to tender their petition ; and that whatfoever afterwards was done, was but the fuper-ftructure upon the foundations which that day were laid.* The remark is at leaft rendered more intelligible by the picture D'Ewes has given us of Hampden on the eventful day. In the very moment of the pafling of refolutions claiming rights of the executive for the Commons' Houfe alone, to rife and direct attention to "thoufands" of his conftituents who had ridden up from their county to fhow readinefs, if need were, to die for that Houfe, difplayed at leaft the collected and determined fpirit of the member for Buckinghamfhire.†

No: we will hear them.

War beginning.

Hampden's attitude and bearing.

Laft acts of Committee.

Only two more acts of the Committee are recorded by D'Ewes. The firft was a report made from the Irifh Committee by Sir Robert Harley, to the effect that the Lord-Lieutenant of Ireland would, at their fuggeftion, difable

* *Hift.* ii. 170.
† Whitelock, in mentioning the arrival of thefe troops of Buckinghamfhire yeomen (1-156), fays that they brought up a petition on behalf of their knight of the fhire, "whereof "probably he was not altogether ignorant beforehand."

§ XXXVII. *Preparations for the Triumph.*

from his command Captain Hide,* notorious Captain Hide disabled.
for his infolent demeanour on the day of the
attempted arreft. The fecond was their anfwer
to a meffage from the Lieutenant of the
Tower. "A meffage," fays D'Ewes, "came
" from Sir John Byron, declaring that he
" heard there were fome complaints here Refufal to receive Sir John Byron's meffenger.
" againft him: and that he defired to know
" them, that fo he might make anfwer to
" them. We refufed to give his meffenger any
" anfwer, becaufe he took notice of what had
" been acted here, and did not apply himfelf
" to anfwer by petition."† With which cha-

Why fhould he have been? The fame imputation is repeated Hampden's fhare in Bucks petition.
with addition, in a Royalift Satire (*fpeech againft Peace at the Clofe Committee*).

   Did I for this my county bring
  To help their knight againft their king,
   And raife the firft fedition?
  Though I the bufinefs did decline,
  Yet I contrived the whole defign,
   And fent them their Petition.

A paffage from the Petition will be quoted fhortly, and it certainly bears throughout the Hampden mark very vifibly ftamped upon it. But the charge implied is, that though he Falfe charge. appeared to "decline" the fervices of his friends, he had really in fecret "contrived" them. It is the old accufation: and I name it here that the reader may fee, by Hampden's open and frank avowal before the Committee itfelf, how groundlefs it is.

 * See *Ante* 185. *Harl. MSS.* 162, f. 313 b. D'Ewes's Captain Hide. exact expreffion is: "that the Lord Lieutenant would put "out Capt. Hide as we had defired, and that he would fend "fuch lifts of the officers as we had defired."

 † *Harl. MSS.* 162, f. 313 b. The refult finally was, that New lieutenant of the Tower. Sir John Byron was difplaced, and Sir John Coniers, the fame who was felected by Strafford for the defence of Berwick, and whom Clarendon (in a paffage of his Hiftory, ii. 172, fuppreffed by his fons) admits the King had no other exception to than

racteriftic affertion of having maintained unimpaired the full plenitude of power with which the Houfe had invefted them, this famous Committee brought its fittings to a clofe. D'Ewes fhut up his note book and quitted the Hall a little after 3 o'clock.

3 p.m. 10th January. Clofe of Committee.

§ XXXVIII. Flight of the King.

At almoft the fame hour when the member for Sudbury was leaving the Committee room in the afternoon of Monday the 10th of January, Charles the Firft had formed the determination to quit Whitehall.

3 p.m. 10th January. Propofed flight of King.

As the incidents of that laft fitting of the Committee were communicated to him, by meffengers who paffed to and fro between the City and the Palace, in vain he had attempted to fupprefs his agitation. To an obftinate incredulity had fucceeded a difmay and bewilderment the moft extreme, and long did his partifans remember the forrowful humiliations of this day. It was, fays Clarendon, the trouble and agony which ufually attend gene-

Acts of Committee told to Charles.

Confeffed ufurpations.

that he was recommended by *them*, was named Lieutenant in his ftead. The Houfe did not affect to difguife from themfelves the real drift and tendency of thefe interferences with the executive. Clarendon characterifes their orders as to the Tower as " an act of fovereignty even of as high a nature " as any they have fince ventured upon." ii. 173. And fubftantially they did not themfelves deny this: but, according to D'Ewes, it was rendered abfolutely neceffary " in regard of " the great jealoufies and diftractions of London, the citizens " everywhere fhutting up their fhops and giving over trade " in confequence of the infecurity of the Tower.

Why neceffary.

§ XXXVIII.   *Flight of the King.*

rous and magnanimous minds upon their having committed errors. It was, says a less partial critic, the despicable repentance which attends the man, who, having attempted to commit a crime, finds that he has only committed a folly. {His trouble and dismay.}

His resolve at last was taken suddenly. He might have listened, comparatively unmoved, to the intelligence that the streets of his city were crowded with freeholders and yeomen of Bucks, who had ridden up by "thousands" to defend their representative Mr. Hampden. He might have heard in sullen silence, if not indifference, that such a gathering of the common people as had not been witnessed since the day of Strafford's execution, were about to surround Whitehall with a petition to defend Mr. Pym.* It would have mattered little to {Takes sudden resolve. Crowds for Hampden. For Pym.}

---

* As the copies of this petition, afterwards presented to the King at Windsor, are extremely rare (it is not among the King's Pamphlets, and I have indeed never seen but the single copy in my own possession which was obtained for me by the late Mr. Rodd), a few lines may be here taken from it. It deals with each article of treason separately; and thus comments upon that which charged the endeavour to subvert the fundamental laws: "This seems contrary, in regard that " hee hath laboured rather to ratifie and confirm the funda-" mental lawes; in his diurnal speeches ever specifying his " reall intent, as the institution and not the diminution or " subversion of law." As to the alleged traitorous endeavour to subvert the rights and very being of parliaments, this is the remarkable and emphatic comment: "To this we may " answer with great facility, *Hee was the chiefe cause that* " *this parliament was assembled,* and it seems very incongruous " that he should subvert the same. Moreover he is the sole " man that stands for the antient rights and liberties of parla-" ment, and it seems a stupendous thing that he should assail " the same." While on this subject I am tempted to add, {Popular Petition. Pym's support of law. Author of the Long Parliament.}

Arrest of the Five Members.

Alarming him that contemptuous cries and hooting from
defections. the populace were audible at the very gates of
his palace. But when it was told him that
sections of every class of his subjects had
offered allegiance and service to the men whom
he had publicly branded as traitors; that his

Attacks on Pym.

before the D'Ewes Journal is finally closed, some evidence of the abuse, not less than the praise, of which the great leader had so truly portentous a share as well now as to the end of the struggle. While, from this period to the outbreak of the war, his vast influence within the House renders poor D'Ewes himself, as his dissatisfaction with public affairs increases, daily more and more peevish and unhappy, in the Journal we also find almost daily evidence of assaults to which he was subjected out of doors. Now (to take a few instances from amid the events we have been describing) it is the "Examination of Jno. Sampson a mean fellow who said the "kingdom would never be in quiet till Mr. Pym & such "others as he was were hanged. His excuse, that he was "in drink. Sent to House of Correction. Sir A. Brown "showed that Mr. Nelson, a scandalous Minister in Surrey, "had said Mr. Pym was neither a gentleman nor a "scholar." *Harl. MSS.* 163, 377 b, 385 a. On another

"Not a gentleman or scholar."

day it is an "Information given against two men who "had said the King was no King because he did not "take up arms against the Scots, & that Pym was King "Pym, and that that rogue would set all the kingdom together "by the ears."—*Ib.* 163, ff.'322 a, 331 a. On a third day it is a "Report from the Committee of information of one "Thomas Shawberie, a graduate of Emanuel College about to "proceed a Doctor of Physic this commencement, who had "yester night at the Cross Keys in Gratious Street called Mr.

"Rogue and Rascal."

"Pym, a Member of this House, 'King Pym' & 'Rascal' "& that he would cut him in pieces if he had him."—*Ib.* 163, f. 424 a. Let me add, that out of numberless similar testimonies to Pym's unexampled influence in the State, and to the royalist hatred it inspired in a measure almost equal to the popular idolatry, one of the most remarkable will be found in a long poem in Mr. Wright's *Political Ballads of the Commonwealth* (pp. 30—38, Percy Society), which bears for its

"Penitent Traitor."

title, "The Penitent Traytor; or the Humble Confession of "a Devonshire gentleman who was Condemned for High "Treason, and Executed at Tyborne for the same, in the raigne "of King Henry the Third, the nineteenth of July 1267." Pym was of Somersetshire, but he sat for Tavistock in Devon.

§ XXXVIII. *Flight of the King.*

mariners and seamen, " the water rats," had
deserted him; that the Trained Bands of
London and Southwark were in arms against
him; that, for the men whom he would have
sent to a public scaffold, such a public triumph
was preparing as only waits upon Conquerors
and Deliverers; and that, finally, to protect
and consolidate their triumph, and in *his*
despite to " guard the Parliament, the King-
" dom, and the King," a military force had
been created, and military rank bestowed—he
appears to have yielded all at once to what
is known to have been the counsel of the
Queen, and to have given sudden directions
for the flight.

"Waterrats."
Trained Bands.
Triumph for "Traitors."
A sudden sense of danger.

" The issue is," wrote Sir Edward to Lady
Dering,* " that the King went suddenly out
" of town with the Queen and Prince, *angered*
" *and feared with the preparation of armes to*
" *attend us the next day.* Nor can I wonder
" at his purpose therein; but approve it. . . .
" The Commons go high: and not only the
" House, but a Committee of the House,
" have armed and imbanded the King's subjects,
" not only without his leave asked, but have
" made a Serjeant Major General *to the*
" *King's terror. For thereupon he went out of*
" *towne, and not till then.* . . . Jealousies are
" high, and my heart pitys a King so fleeting
" and so friendless, yett without one noted

Sir Edward Dering to his wife.
Commons going high.
King's " terror."
Pity for the King.

* MS. Letter (13th Jan. 1641-2) already quoted: *ante* 48.

"vice." It is not the "noted" vices which are moſt dangerous in kings. There was doubtleſs much, in the "noted" reaſons for this flight of a king from the capital of his kingdom, to awaken ſympathy from ſuch minds as Dering's: but more ſecret reaſons and purpoſes betrayed themſelves too ſoon, to permit the moſt ardent of the gentlemen who remained loyal to the ſovereign to deceive themſelves as to the temper in which London had been abandoned. It was not the fear of being deſerted by friends, but the mortification of being diſabled from ſtriking further at enemies. For Charles the Firſt, the hope of ſo ſtriking effectively exiſted now only in the provinces of his kingdom. Away from London, he might purſue his ſecret levies; and, while the actual outbreak of war was delayed, his abſence could not but diſorganiſe the operations of Parliament. The Queen had now reſolved, moreover, if ſhe could but ſcrew her huſband's courage to the ſticking place, to carry herſelf and her children for the preſent out of England, taking with her the Jewels of the Crown: and to leave London was to accompliſh the firſt ſtage. The watchful vigilance of the Commons compelled the detention of the princes; but, in little more than three weeks from this day, ſhe had ſucceeded in that moſt material part of her deſign which ſecured freedom of action and ſafety to herſelf, until the war ſhould

Marginal notes: Noted vices leſs dangerous than ſecret. Reaſon for quitting London. Hope of ſupport elſewhere. A project of the Queen. Vigilance of Commons.

§ XXXVIII. *Flight of the King.*

really begin, and to her hufband the means of waging it when once his troops were in the field. "By yours of this week," wrote Sidney Bere to Admiral Pennington, "I "perceive you are ready to fett faile upon "fome fervice, wherein I pray God to bleffe "you wth good fucceffe." That was on the 13th of January; and the fervice for which the Admiral fo held himfelf thus early in readinefs, was undoubtedly that which on the 23rd of February he performed, of conveying to the coaft of Holland the Queen and her daughter, and the Crown jewels of England. In little more than two months fhe had raifed two millions fterling.

Secret fervice by Pennington.

Conveys Queen to Holland.

The fame letter of the under-fecretary tells us further what it well imports us to know of the circumftances of the King's departure. After mentioning the triumph of the Commons in their return to Weftminfter, he continues: "The King and Queene toke the day "before a refolution to leave this towne, "w^h was alfoe foe fuddaine that they could "not have that acomodation befitted their "Maties. They went to Hampton Court that "night, next day to Windfor, whence its "confidered they will alfoe departe as this day, "*but whither is uncertaine.* The Prince and "Pr. Elector is with them, but few Lords. "Effex and Holland being here, who offered "up both their places before his going, but

Under Secretary to the Admiral: 13th January.

Reports King's flight.

Effex and Holland.

Arreſt of the Five Members.

Secretary Nicholas.
" His Maj^{tie} would not accept y^r ſurrender.*
" Mr. Secretary Nicholas is likewiſe gone, and

Refuſals to accompany the King.
* Eſſex, it will be remembered, was Lord Chamberlain of the Houſehold, and Holland Groom of the Stole. The fact mentioned by Bere confirms a portion of the ſtatement of Clarendon (*Hiſt.* ii. 163) that theſe officers of the King's Houſe had been aſked, and had refuſed, to quit London with him. It was not, however, until the 15th they applied to the Lords, and received order that " to attend the high affairs of " the realme as required by their writs was truer ſervice to His " Majeſty than any they could do him at Hampton Court." Clarendon ſays it was Holland who perſuaded Eſſex not to go: but I can find no evidence in ſupport of what he adds, that, after leaving the King to his ſmall retinue in a moſt diſconſolate perplexed condition, and in more need of comfort and counſel than they had ever known him, "inſtead

Waiting on Committee.
" of attending their maſter in that exigent, *they went together* " *into the City where the Committee ſat*, and where they were " not the leſs welcome for being known to have been invited " to have waited upon their Majeſties." Holland was capable of the act, but of Eſſex it is not to be believed. I may add, as the point aſſumed afterwards ſome importance, that one of the moſt curious of many ſimilar entries in D'Ewes's Journal of this date is one which marks the period of the

Final deſertions.
final and complete deſertion of the King by Holland and Warwick, when, caring no longer to reſort to the excuſe for non-attendance out of town, which their parliamentary obligations fairly ſupplied them with, they ceaſed to keep even a fair face to the King. On the day when the Houſe voted judgment againſt the Attorney-General Herbert for having preferred the articles of impeachment, D'Ewes himſelf handed

A libel upon
in a ſlip of paper purporting to contain the declaration of Walter Lumley, clothier of Lavenham, Suffolk; ſubſcribed ſeemingly in Lumley's own hand. He ſtated that he was ſitting in the houſe of Mr. Ferdinando Poulton, with two others; and that, they converſing together, the ſaid Poulton ſaid there were ſome verſes made about the Parliament, namely—

" One cuckold, two baſtards, and a pack of knaves,
Strive now to make ſubjects Princes, and Princes ſlaves."

Eſſex, Holland, Warwick, and Pym.
Who are theſe three, aſked Lumley, the declarant, for he proteſted he knew not of what was meant. To which Poulton ſaid all the world knew Eſſex to be a cuckold, and Warwick and Holland to be baſtards, and that they would make Pym prince. Having duly informed the Houſe of theſe facts, and put it in poſſeſſion of the document eſtabliſhing

§ XXXVIII.   *Flight of the King.*   363

" hath lefte mee here to attend fuch fervices Small
" as fhall occurre, w^{ch}, if the Kinge fhall per- work left for Under-
" fift in his refolution to retire,* *will not be* Secretary.
" *much.* Howfoever I will expect the iffue,
" and if I bee not fent for, thinke myfelfe
" not unhappy in my ftay to be freed of an
" expencefull and troublefome journey. *My*
" *Lady Nicholas is much afflicted, and I believe,* Grief of a Secretary
" *as well as hee, would for a good round fumme* of State's
" *hee had never had the feales. My Lord* wife.
" *Keeper refufing to put the greate feale to the*
" *King's proclamation ag^t the perfons accufed,* Lord Keeper
" *did alfoe make tender of his charge,* but how- offers to
" foever remaines ftill wth it. And thus, Sir, refign.
" you fee to what heighth of diftempers thinges
" are come." † In this fad condition, exclaims

the fame, D'Ewes goes on to remark that he took an oppor- D'Ewes
tunity of telling the Earl of Holland what he had done: and Lord
" who very well approved the fame with very fair expreffions Holland.
" to me for it."—*Harl. MSS.* 163, f. 462 b. I need hardly
add that Lord Effex is by no means to be put in the fame
category with fuch men as Lord Holland. Effex had been
confiftent throughout, and never concealed his popular views
and wifhes.
   * This expreffion (by which the Under Secretary means
perfifting in the determination to retire from Windfor and
Hampton Court as well as Whitehall) fhows that the real
defign of the King, not fimply to efcape the fight or neigh- King's
bourhood of the Triumph of the Five Members on the 11th, flight not
but actually and wholly to quit London and its vicinity until temporary.
he could return its mafter, had been difcuffed at Court, and
was already known in the Secretary's offices. The certain effect
of fuch entire withdrawal, it is alfo obvious from the remark of
Bere, was well underftood as an abdication of the functions
of the fovereign. It will leave us little to do here, fays the
Under Secretary to his friend the Admiral.
   † MS. State Paper Office. Bere to Pennington: 13 Jany. Union in
1641-2. In the fame letter the Under Secretary adds: "In Houfes.
" the mean time they are united in the Houfes, and the

Royal re-verſes.

Clarendon, was the King fallen in ten days,* from a height and greatneſs that his enemies

Literary entertainment.

"accorde between the Upper Houſe and Commons grows
"dayly more eaſy.... I ſend you herewth divers printed
"bookes of ſeverall ſtiles, all wch I leave for yor entertaynm^t
"att ſpare howers. Sir John Byron, Lieut^t of the Tower,
"it's thought will yett be diſplaced: the Parliam^t not being
"ſatiſfied wth his carriage, and having, as I am told, voted
"him a delinquent.. The Parliam^t, it ſeemes, having [have]
"taken into conſideration the ſmall Gard is att preſent att ſea,
"and ſoe have voted 30 ſaile to be ſett out forthwth. This is

Letters not ſafe.

"all I ſhall trouble you wth att preſent, in a time ſoe diſtracted,
"and wherein is ſoe little aſſurance into what handes letters
"may fall. Yours I humbly kiſſe and reſt, &c. &c."

* *Hiſt.* ii. 182. On that "tenth" day the King had gone to Windſor, and D'Ewes's journal gives us a glimpſe of the interior of the palace, from the reported ſpeech of a member of the Houſe who had accompanied a deputation with a meſſage, which ſeems to bear out what is ſaid by Clarendon.

Deſolate court at Windſor.

"They found," ſaid Sir John Holland, "a deſolate Court, "and ſaw not any noblemen, and ſcarce thirty gentlemen." (*Harl. MSS.* 162, f. 359 b.) A few days later, when the abſence of Endymion Porter from his ſeat (he repreſented Droitwich) was matter of remark, the ſame Sir John Holland, D'Ewes tells us (*Ib.* 162, f. 386 b.) "ſhowed that when he was "at Windſor with his meſſage, the ſaid Mr. Porter informed "him that he was at that time the only man attending upon "his Majeſty in his Bed-chamber to dreſs and undreſs him: "which was the chief cauſe that he could not attend the "ſervice of the Houſe: and deſired him to move the Houſe "in his behalf if anything ſhould be ſaid againſt him." To which I am fortunately able to add, out of the rich unpub-

Endymion Porter to his wife: 14th January.

liſhed ſtores of the State Paper Office, a letter from Endymion Porter himſelf to his "deare wyfe Olive Porter," dated from Windſor on the 14th January, that very "tenth" day from the arreſt to which Clarendon refers. It preſents a picture of the ſtraits of a married courtier during inauſpicious times, which is pleaſing as well as highly characteriſtic; and very curious is the view that is given us at its cloſe, of the jealous care with which the King and Queen were now guarding their children.

Very old ſtory.

"MY DEAREST LOVE,—As for monnies I wonder you
"can imagin that I ſhould helpe you, but you allwayes looke
"for impoſſibilities from mee, and I wiſh it were a tyme of
"mirrackles, for then wee might hope for a Good Succeſs in
"everie thing. Whither wee goe, and what wee are to dooe,
"I knowe not, for I am none of the Councell: My dutie &

§ XXXVIII. *Flight of the King.*

feared, to fuch a lownefs that his own fervants durft hardly avow the waiting on him! *Gloomy picture.*

To the gloomy picture another touch is added by a letter of Captain Slingfby * to his

"loyaltie have tought mee to followe my King and Mafter,
" and by the Grace of God nothing fhall divert mee from
" it: I could wifh you and your Children in a fafe place, but
" why Woodhall fhould not bee foe I cannot yet tell. I could
" likewife wifh my cabinetts and all my other thinges were at
" Mr. Courteenes—but if a verrie difcreete man bee not there,
" and take the advife of the joyner to convaye them thither,
" theye will bee as much fpoilde in the carridge as wth the
" rabble. Deareft love, to ferue God well is the waye in
" eueriething that will leade us to a happie end, for then
" hee will blefs, and deliver us owt of all troubles : I praye
" you have a care of your felfe, and make much of your
" children, and I prefume wee fhall bee merrie and enioye
" one another long. I writt to you and fent the letters by
" Nick on tuefdaye, but that rogue is drunke, and I heare
" not of him. If you remember my fervice to Mrs Eures, and
" tell her that I am her faithefull Servant, I will give you
" leaue to kifs Mrs Marie for mee: *I wifh fweete Tom wth mee,*
" *for the King and Queene are forced to lie wth theire children*
" *nowe and I enuie their happines.* I praye you lett this
" berer cum to me againe, when you heare where wee reft :
" and foe Godnighte, fweete Noll.

Troubles of a courtier.

Fear of "rabble."

King and Queen lying with their children.

" Y^r true frend and moft loving hufband,
" ENDYMION PORTER."

" Windfor this 14th of Januarie 1641."

I may add a further very notable illuftration, from an unpublifhed letter of Dering's, of the difficulties and hardfhips now incident to the courtier's trade. "The times," he writes to his wife, "are defperate, and £100 in hand may quickly " be worth £100 per annum. Will. Gibbes wrote yefter- " night for my advice. He would faigne attend the King " with his perfon, as other Cavaliers do: but his purfe is " empty, and the King foe poore that he cannot feed them " that follow him. I was told that the prince one night " wanted wine, and another candles." By the Prince muft be intended the Prince Elector.

Defperate times.

King's poverty.

* As this is probably the laft time I fhall have to refer to Captain Slingfby, I may mention that on the Reftoration he was made a Baronet and Comptroller of the Navy; that he is frequently referred to in Pepys's Diary; and that, in recording his death at the clofe of October 1661, Pepys fpeaks of him as "a man that loved me, and had many qualitys that made me

Slingfby and Pepys.

Arrest of the Five Members.

Slingsby Admiral one day later, on the 14th of January,
to Pennington: which reveals somewhat more of the alarm and
14th January. danger of the time. He describes what had
happened since the famous day at Guildhall;
and how that he, and all who accompanied the
King on the 4th, were now set apart and
Unexpected change of position. "esteemed criminals," while the gentlemen accused of treason passed with greater honour and
applause than ever, having been brought back
magnificently guarded to their seats at Westminster. "The King the day before," he
continues (I omit his allusion to the Buckinghamshire horsemen who had ridden up to town
to offer their service to the Parliament), "wth
" the Queene and all their children, went
" away discontentedly, attended not with
" many lords or old courtiers, but with the
Officers following the King. " officers of the late army in good numbers.
" He went first to Hampton Court, then to
" Windsor: this day removed from thence,
" whither I knowe not: but some say to
" Portsmouth, others to Woodstocke, and
" from thence to Yorke. There was yester-
" day a great feare in the Cittie by reason it
Lunsford at Kingston. " was reported that Coll. Lunsford had made
" proclamation in Kingstone for all of the
" Kinge's party to come to him. If any such

Carterett. " to love him, above all the officers and commissioners in the
" Navy." *Diary* (ed. 1854) i. 229. Captain Carterett, though
an older man, survived Slingsby eighteen years. He did important Royalist service during the Civil War, and obtained
high rank as well as several lucrative employments at the
Restoration.

§ XXXVIII.   *Flight of the King.*   367

"thinges were, I believe it was but some "Drunken
"drunken flourish of some of those souldiers flourish."
"that followed the King: yett the House
"hath sent order to the Sheriffs to apprehend
"them, and have, as I heare, sent likewise to
"Portsmouth to forbid the admittance of any
"such into the towne, as may breed tumult
"there."*

Capt. Slingsby makes light of the Lunsford Suspicious
proclamation as a "drunken flourish," but he tions.
yet connects it with the soldiers who were following the court,† and we have seen with
what designs at this time, at least not unknown
to the King, Clarendon couples Lunsford's and
Digby's names.‡ Except for Charles the First's Digby and
express disapproval on the scheme being sub- Lunsford.
mitted to him, he tells us that the accused members would either have been seized and taken

*MS. State Paper Office. Slingsby to Pennington: 14 Jany.
1641-2. The close of the letter is very characteristic. "All Agree-
"thinges go now currantly on in the Parlament with out any ment in
"apparent opposition: the malignant partie having all left Houses.
"the towne: only the Tower doth yett breede some jealousies.
"The Left* refuseing to come to the house, being sent for:
"and refusing to take the Protestation wch was sent to him. One ex-
"Some Victuals going to the Tower were stopped, and this ception.
"day I heare it is absolutely blockt up: the seamen have
"offerd their service to batter it. A day or two since it was
"soe dangerous saying anything, y^t a man could not be
"assured of his life in speaking anything. Factions were so
"hott. But now the Language of the Par: is only currant. Factions
"I pray God send us better unitie, but I can hardly expect subsiding.
"it: though I thinke there are twice as many plotts dis-
"covered and printed than are really contrived."

† Clarendon also states (ii. 163) that besides his own
gentlemen, "thirty or forty" of the officers of the Whitehall
Guard also attended him.

‡ *Ante*, 205, 288, 322.

to prison, or left dead in Coleman Street; and it is certain that the King's rejection of either this, or some other plan, which he had been disposed to entertain on the first failure of the arrest, was made matter of warning to him in later years. "You see," wrote the Queen, urging him afterwards to as rash an enterprise, "what has happened *from not having followed* "*your first resolutions when you declared the Five* "*Members traitors.* Let that serve you for an "example, and dally no longer with consulta-"tions."*

Under such advice is the ill-fated King abandoning the metropolis of his Kingdom. He confidently believed that he should soon return to it as its master, but he never again saw Whitehall until he was led through it to the scaffold. Before 4 in the afternoon he stepped into his coach with the Queen and their children, called to the window the Captain of the Trained Bands who had been in attendance at the palace during the last two eventful months, thanked him for what he had done, and drove off to Hampton Court.†

---

* *Harl. MSS.* 7379. Quoted in the *Fairfax* Correspondence, ii. 335.

† Let me refer the reader who is not acquainted with the book to M. Guizot's lately revised and enlarged edition of his *Histoire de la Révolution d'Angleterre.* I know of no narrative of the incidents of Charles the First's reign, within the same compass, at all comparable to it for fulness, accuracy, and picturesqueness. The account of the incidents under notice is a delightful specimen of narration, close and spirited; the observations are always thoughtful, considerate, and tem-

And now, to adopt the expreffion of Cla- *The Five placed on their "thrones."* rendon, it only remained to place the Five Members "*on their thrones.*"

§ XXXIX. RETURN OF THE FIVE MEMBERS.

TUESDAY the eleventh of January, 1641-2, *Tuefday, 11th January.* was a clear bright winter day, and never had the great river, or either of its fhores, prefented fuch a fcene as had there been vifible fince day break, from London Bridge to Weft- *March of City by land.* minfter ftairs. By land, the City Trained Bands on the one fhore, and on the other the Trained Bands of Southwark, lined the road up to the very avenues of the Commons' Houfe; and by water, guarding that filent *Guard by water.* highway through which the members were to pafs, appeared on either fide, connecting both the bridges in two compact and glittering lines, a fleet of veffels and long boats, armed with ordnance, and "dreffed up with waift- " clothes and ftreamers as ready for fight."* On all fides the afpect of a feftival; eager *Great feftival.* animation, movement, light, and colour: but no mere holiday gaiety. Blending with whatever could give brilliancy to the fcene, were figns everywhere of the folemn and earneft work in *No mere holiday.* hand. The men who ferved the ordnance on board the veffels ftood with their matches

perately juft; and the ftyle throughout is charming. This enlarged edition has been fairly tranflated by Mr. Scoble (Ed. Bentley: 2 vols. 8vo. 1854).
 * Clarendon, *Hift.* ii. 164.

Soldiers' pikes and muskets:

carrying printed votes of Houses.

lighted; and, fixed upon the pikes of the soldiers, attached to their muskets, flapping round their enfigns and colours, looped in their hats, or fastened on their breasts, were printed copies of the solemn Proteftation, which bound all who took it to the rendering up life itself on behalf of the liberties of Parliament and the maintenance of the Proteftant religion.* Manned by officers and seamen of the navy who had volunteered this service, one of the largest and richeft of the City Companies' Barges had been provided and fitted for the

Embarkation at "Three Cranes."

Five Members; and in this, at midday, they embarked "from the Three Cranes,"† and so returned to the feats from which their sovereign had vainly hoped to banifh them for

Under-Secretary's account.

ever. "They returned," wrote the Under-Secretary to Pennington, "with such multitudes as had " far more of Triumph than " Guard; and the feamen made fleetes of boates " all armed with musquetts and murdering " pieces, wch gave vollees all the way they

What Clarendon faw.

* "There was one circumftance," fays Clarendon, "not " to be forgotten in the march of the City that day, when " the fhow by water was little inferior to the other by land, " that the pikemen had faftened to the tops of their pikes, and " the reft in their hats, or their bofoms, printed papers of the " Proteftation which had been taken and enjoined by the " Houfe of Commons, the year before, for the defence of the " privilege of Parliament; and many of them had the Printed " Votes of the King's breaking their privileges in his coming " to the Houfe and demanding their members." ii. 166. D'Ewes will be found to notice this alfo, *poft*, 364.
† *Rufhworth*, III. i. 484.

§ XXXIX. *Return of the Five Members.*

"went."* Arrived at Weftminfter, the enthufiaftic applaufes of the people who had crowded to give them welcome, outrang even the clattering difcharges of ordnance which faluted them as they landed. They paffed up the ftairs, and into the lobby of the Houfe.

Welcome at Weftminfter.

The Speaker and the members ftood up as the Five entered and took their accuftomed places. The inftant after, all the Five arofe, and while Hampden, Hollis, Hafelrig, and Strode ftood filent and uncovered, Pym tendered in the moft earneft language their hearty thanks to the citizens of London. He faid that he could not but refer to the unexampled fcene they had that day witneffed. Such had been the kindnefs, the affection, they had found in the City, that if the mode of expreffing it, on this extraordinary occafion, had been fomewhat unufual, the honour of the Houfe was neverthelefs engaged to protect and defend the citizens againft all poffible confequences thereof. The words (reported by Clarendon)† are extremely ftriking; and moft fignificant was the appeal they involved from one fupreme power

Entrance into Houfe.

Pym thanks the City.

Striking expreffions ufed.

---

* MS. State Paper Office. Sidney Bere to Pennington, 13th January, 1641-2. The title begins: "The laft weeke I "told you but the beginning of thofe bad enfuing newes wee "muft now dayly expect, unleffe it pleafe God to give a ftrange, "if not miraculous change, whereby to fettle the diftraction of "affaires. The Committee fitting all laft weeke in yᵉ Citty, "returned againe to Parliament on Tuefday, and the perfons "accufed wᵗʰ them, for whom both city and country have "fhown foe much affection!"

† *Hift.* ii. 165.

Bere to Pennington, 13th January.

Impreſſion made on Royaliſt member.
in the State, to another which was to aſſume from that day a more than equal ſovereignty. Some idea of the impreſſion made upon even a member of the Houſe who ſympathiſed with the King, appears in what Sir Edward Dering now wrote to his wife. *"If I could be Pym*

Would you be King Charles or King Pym?
*" with honeſty, I had rather be Pym than King Charles."**

In the ſame letter, written the next day but one after the great feſtival, the member for Kent, after telling his wife that "heere have been five

Letter of Sir Edward Dering.
" thouſand petitioners out of Buckingham- " ſhire to offer their lives to execute our com- " mands," proceeds to tell her further, that by the help of God ſhe was not to fear for his perſonal ſafety, for that many thouſands had guarded them on the Tueſday, and that each day now the Houſe itſelf was provided with a

Guard againſt no enemy.
ſufficient Guard "againſt no enemy." But ſome members of the Houſe had been in danger, and how could any ſingle member in future be reckoned ſafe? In vain did even this loyal knight of the ſhire for Kent, notorious for his reſiſtance to the Remonſtrance, aſſure and re- aſſure his friends down in his native county.

Members thought ſtill in danger.
" Mr. Bullock came and offered," he writes, " with his friends, to be my perſonall Guard. I " refuſed itt, *but could not perſuade him from my* " *ſide, from morning to night, unleſs in the* " *very Houſe.*" The incident better explains

* MS. Letter before referred to, 48, and 358.

§ XXXIX.   *Return of the Five Members.*   373

what the feeling was, which had brought thou- Why
sands out of Buckinghamshire to the side of Bucks men came.
Mr. Hampden.

When Pym had ceased speaking, and when Thanks
there had been called in, successively, the by Mr. Speaker.
Sheriffs of London, the Masters and Officers of
ships, and Serjeant Major-General Skippon, to
receive thanks from Mr. Speaker, Hampden's
colleague in the representation of Buckinghamshire (Mr. A. Goodwin) arose, and begged of Speech by
the House that such of the gentry of that Goodwin.
county as had been appointed to bear their
petition* might be called in to deliver it.

* The opening sentences of this petition, which, if not written Bucks
by Hampden, may be safely taken as the exact expression of his petition to
views, are characteristic and worth quoting: "That whereas, House.
" many years past, we have been under very great pressures, for
" *which are clearly set forth in the late Remonstrance of the*
" *House of Commons*; the Redress whereof hath for a long
" time been by you endeavoured with unwearied pains, tho'
" not with answerable success; having still your endeavours
" frustrated or retarded, and we deprived of the fruit thereof,
" by a malignant faction of Popish Lords, Bishops, & others; Views held
" and now, of late, to take from us all that little hope which by Hamp-
" was left of a future Reformation, the very Being of the den.
" Parliament shaken; and, by the mischievous practices of
" most wicked counsellors, the privileges thereof broken in
" an unexampled manner, and the members thereof unassured
" of their lives, in whose safety the safety of us and our
" Posterity is involved: We hold it our duty, according to
" our late protestation, to defend and maintain the same
" Persons and Privileges, to the uttermost expense of our lives
" and estates." The last sentence is also remarkable. After
stating such measures against evil counsellors as they believe
to be called for, they close thus: " Without all which, your
" Petitioners have not the least hope of the kingdom's peace,
" or to reap those glorious advantages, which the fourteen Petition to
" months Seed-time of your unparallelled endeavours have King.
" given to their unsatisfied expectations." A similar petition was taken to the King at Windsor two days after
this was delivered to the Commons. Nor was it the Bucks

Bucks petition brought in.

Whereupon, the same being assented to, the petition was brought in, and they who bore it informed the House that it had been accompanied to the town by above six thousand men, not one of whom but was ready with their lives and fortunes to defend them, the honorable members of the Commons, or, if need were, against whomsoever should in any sort illegally attempt upon them, *to die at their feet.*
"And then," says D'Ewes, "they withdrew out of the House: but they were so many, and the press was so great in the Lobby and room next without the door, that they were a good while before they could get out."*

Its guard of 6000.

Crowd and pressure in lobby.

D'Ewes followed them, and went to walk a while in Westminster Hall. There, clustered in various groups, stood citizens of the Trained Bands belonging to the eight companies who had guarded the Members that day. And D'Ewes noted upon the tops of their pikes, hanging like little square banners in the now still and quiet air, copies of the Protestation for defence of parliament and maintenance of religion.†

D'Ewes in Westminster Hall.

"Little square banners."

Other counties petition the King.

men alone who thus followed the King to his retirement. Others, according to Clarendon, promptly followed the example: "Though the King had removed himself out of "the noise of Westminster, yet the effects of it followed him "very close; for besides the Buckinghamshire petitioners, who "alarumed him the same or the next day after he came to "Hampton Court, *several of the same nature were every* "*day presented to him, in the name of other counties of the* "*kingdom.*"—*Hist.* ii. 176.

* *Harl. MSS.* 162, f. 317 b.   † *Ib.* 162, f. 318 a.

§ XXXIX.   *Return of the Five Members.*   375

Meanwhile, before the House rose, between 7 and 8 on that "ever to be remembered" day, the departure of the King from London had been remarked upon by honorable members, and the matter was reserved for debate until the following morning. Accordingly, on that Wednesday the 12th, the Chancellor of the Exchequer wished to know if he should move his Majesty to return to London, to come to a proper understanding? But Sir John Culpeper failed to elicit any satisfactory reply. Again, next morning, Thursday the 13th, the question was renewed; and, says D'Ewes,* "Sir Henry Cholmely moved that we should "send to his Majesty to express our grief "for his absenting himself from us, and to "desire him to return, and to conceive that "we are his best and surest guard. *But Mr.* "*Denzil Hollis stood up, and said, that till* "*himself and the other members of this House* "*accused of High Treason were cleared, and the* "*violation of the privileges of this House in their* "*persons were redressed——*" {Departure of King noted. Question by Culpeper. Question by Sir Henry Chomley. Answered by Denzil Hollis.}

My Narrative closes here. The blank left is D'Ewes's own; and what yet there might have remained to tell, is better expressed in that eloquent silence. Of one of the most memorable incidents in our English history, more than enough will perhaps be thought to have been said in these pages. But it had consequences which {Close of narrative.}

* *Harl. MSS.* 162, f. 329 b.

Question not settled in one generation. were not determined even when the struggle of that generation ceased, and its actors, noble and ignoble, were also passed into silence. Every popular privilege won by the Commons in the long subsequent struggle with the *Struggle of Commons against Crown.* Crown, owed something to this first grand conflict: and if their rights and powers are at last harmoniously adjusted, it is because, in the momentous scenes which have been here described, violence in the Chief of the State was at once met by prompt resistance; and allegiance to a sovereign who had broken the *Why successful.* laws, was held of less account than that higher allegiance which all good men owe to their country and to posterity.

§ XL. Conclusion.

Arrest of members a deliberate act. In my introductory remarks it was stated that the Arrest of the Five Members was no exceptional act on the part of Charles the First, extreme and violent as it was, but showed a strict agreement with what had gone before it; and, happily for those against whom it was *How baffled.* aimed, only baffled its own deliberate and well-planned design by betraying it prematurely. The justification of the leaders of the Commons for the course they immediately took, with all its daring responsibilities, consisted *Only to be met one way.* solely in this. Force was to be met by force; and when Charles and his armed attendants passed through the lobby of the House of

§ XL. *Conclusion.*

Commons on the 4th of January, the Civil War substantially had begun. Clarendon himself admits as much when he calls it "the most visible introduction to all the misery that afterwards befell the King and Kingdom."*

The arrest of the Five Members was the final stage of the struggle against the Grand Remonstrance. That Appeal to the nation was designed to express the danger which had arisen to the popular cause from defections of its former supporters, to exhibit the past as a warning for the future, plainly to set forth the present insecurity of every concession that had been wrung from the King, and to invoke the People to defend and keep what had been won for them so hardly. The Arrest was a violent effort to reverse the eleven votes by which the victory was achieved, and to constitute the leaders of the minority, to whom the highest offices in the State had meanwhile been given, masters of the House of Commons. The issue was a plain one, and admitted only of the harsh arbitrament to which finally it was brought.

The Civil War begun by it.

Its connection with Remonstrance.

Design of Remonstrance:

object of Arrest:

to make the minority masters of the House.

If, indeed, it had been possible to believe that it was in the nature of Charles the First to have left it honestly to such men as Falkland, Culpeper, and Hyde to administer the Government subject to such concessions and safeguards as had been wrested from the prerogative during

Improbable case.

---

* *State Papers:* Supplement to vol. iii. p. lv.

the paſt year, there might have been a caſe against the adoption of meaſures which forbade the poſſibility of compromiſe. But a peculiar neceſſity was created by the character and opinions of the King. It was not merely that his bad faith was ineradicable; it was not even that he was underſtood to hold the high monarchical theory of the nullity of ſtatutes in direct reſtraint of the prerogative; but that he was known to entertain the belief, that, in reluctantly giving aſſent to the moſt important of the meaſures paſſed by the Long Parliament, he was giving it under compulſion, and that ſuch aſſent was therefore *ipſo facto* invalid. With theſe views, let him once be relieved from preſſure and everything gained for public liberty was loſt. Clarendon himſelf informs us that his Attorney-General, Herbert, had encouraged him in the notion that the act againſt the diſſolution of the Parliament without its own conſent was for ſuch reaſons void;* and in mentioning his aſſent to the Bill excluding the Biſhops from Parliament, he makes uſe of theſe remarkable expreſſions:† " An opinion that the violence " and force uſed in procuring it rendered it " abſolutely invalid and void, made the con- " firmation of it leſs conſidered, as not being " of ſtrength to make that act good, which " was in itſelf null. *And I doubt this logic had*

<small>Peculiar opinions of King.</small>

<small>Nullity of ſtatutes in bar of prerogative.</small>

<small>All recent acts in peril.</small>

<small>Aſſent under compulſion void.</small>

<small>Dangerous logic.</small>

---

* *Life and Continuation,* i. 206-211.
† *Hist.* ii. 252.

§ XL. *Conclusion.* 379

" *an influence upon other acts of no less moment*
" *than these.*" How was it possible to deal
on equal terms with such an antagonist?

Let the position be considered, too, in which *Position of accuser to accused.*
a charge of treason specifically made, and which
yet the accuser would neither prosecute nor
retract, left those who were so accused. That
startling remark of Hollis with which my narrative closes, throws considerable light upon
this point; and Whitelock has an observation
to the effect that the most powerful of the *Refusal to prosecute or withdraw charge.*
members accused (he alludes to Pym and
Hampden) peculiarly resented the King's refusal specifically to withdraw the charge.* So
much indeed has been frankly avowed by
Pym himself. In the Vindication which he
published when the war broke out, he does not
hesitate to avow that from the hour of that *"Vindication" of Pym.*
unjust impeachment his own conduct was
changed. "When," he says, "I perceived
" my life aimed at, and heard myself pro-
" scribed as a traitor, merely for my intireness
" of heart to the service of my country; when
" I was informed that I, with some other
" honorable and worthy members of the par-
" liament, were, against the privileges thereof, *Why he changed his conduct after arrest.*
" demanded even in the parliament house by
" his Majesty, attended by a multitude of
" men-at-arms and malignants, — while for
" my own part I never harboured a thought

* And see *Memorials*, i. 158 (Ed. 1853).

"which tended to any diſſervice to his Ma-
"jeſty, nor ever had any intention prejudicial
"to the State,—no man will think me blame-
"worthy in that I took a care of my own
"ſafety, and fled for refuge to the protection
"of the Parliament." But how much more
intolerable ſuch conduct to a man who had
refuſed, only a few days earlier, one of the
higheſt employments in the State, proffered
to him by his accuſer!

The dogged obſtinacy which was alſo a moſt
material feature in the character of the King,
had been here indeed ſtartlingly diſplayed.
The day after the return of the Five Members, he ſent a meſſage to ſay that he waived
the impeachment begun on the 3d, and intended to proceed thereupon in an unqueſtion-
able way. The next morning, replying at
Windſor to the petition of the Freeholders of
Bucks, he told Mr. Hampden's conſtituents,
not that the charge was withdrawn, but that
he would much rather that worthy gentleman
ſhould prove innocent than be found guilty,
and that meanwhile he ſhould not conſider his
crimes as in any ſort reflecting upon thoſe
good ſubjects who had elected him as their
knight of the ſhire! Eight days later, the
Houſe aſked for proofs of the charge: to
which after three days he replied, that he could
not diſcloſe his proofs, but that no time ſhould
be loſt in preferring an indictment at common

§ XL.   *Conclusion.*   381

law in the usual way. Nine days later, the House demanded once more to be informed, before a special day named, as to the nature and proofs of the alleged treason with a view to early and legal trial thereof: to which the King replied by deserting the intended prosecution altogether, and by offering a general pardon. The House then specifically claimed as their right, under certain statutes which they cited, that the King should not only, in addition, clear the members personally, but give up the names of the counsellors under whose advice they had unjustly suffered. Still he was immovable. A Bill for the acquittal of the Members was thereupon passed, and an impeachment of the Attorney-General voted. To save Herbert from punishment, he would at once have taken all responsibility to himself; and he offered the House any kind of satisfaction, excepting always that which they claimed. Immediately before the civil war broke out, the Attorney-General was disabled from being a member assistant, or pleader, in either House of Parliament, and committed to the Fleet: but still the King remained obdurate and unimpressible as ever. Nay, after the civil war had begun, and when the first attempt was made to mediate at Oxford after the battle of Edgehill, "a bill to " vindicate the 5 members" was among the propositions submitted; when again he refused it, and angrily interrupted the Commissioners.

will abandon all proceedings:

will give general pardon:

but nothing else.

Attorney-General impeached:

and punished.

King still immovable.

One of the Oxford propositions.

So angrily, adds Whitelock,* that the Earl of
Northumberland, who led upon the Parliament
fide, fhowed a fober and ftout carriage, and
on being once more interrupted, faid fmartly,
"*Your Majefty will give me leave to proceed?*"
"*Aye, aye!*" replied the King.†
  It need hardly furprife us, after this recital,
to be told by the memorialift that the moft
moderate members of parliament held it
matter of great difcontent, that, except by
general waiver and withdrawal of further
proceedings, the imputation of treafon was
never removed from men in whom the Houfe

The Earl and the King.

Strong ground for difcontent:

ftated by Whitelock.

  * *Memorials,* i. 196.
  † The greater portion of this paper war of petitions and replies which had enfued will be found in Rufhworth (*Coll.* III. i. 434-494). Clarendon (*Hift.* ii. 173-178) has alfo largely quoted them, and it is manifeft that fome of them bear the marks of his hand. Nor do I ever read one of Hyde's ftate papers of this kind without feeling the truth of that old courtier's comment on their new ally which is mentioned by Sir Philip Warwick (*Memoirs,* 217): "Our good pen will "harm us:" or, as Sir Philip himfelf puts it, "A blunt "would have ferved us better than fo keen a nib." An ivory knife cuts paper better than a fteel blade (as Swift had occafion to remind a high-flying Secretary in later time), and it is quite poffible, both in the higher and lower departments, to have the work of the State too fharply done. There is a ftory told, fomething to the purpofe, of Lord Burleigh and his fon Cecil. Being at Council, and reading an order penned by a new clerk who was reputed a wit and fcholar, he flung it downward to the lower end of the table to his fon, the Secretary, faying, "Mr. Secretary, you bring in "clerks of the council who will corrupt the gravity and "dignity of the ftyle of the Board:" to which the Secretary replied: "I pray, my Lord, pardon this. The gentleman "is not warm in his place, and hath had fo little to do, that "he is wanton with his pen; but I will put fo much bufinefs "upon him, that he fhall be willing to obferve your worfhip's "directions."

Paper war.

Blunt better than keen nib.

Burleigh and Cecil.

Too clever Clerk of Council.

repofed its higheft confidence. But, in the face of fuch facts, what becomes of Clarendon's affertion that the Arreft was a fudden act as fuddenly repented of; that no circumftance of deliberation attended it; and that it was followed, not by hardy and obftinate per- fiftence, but by the inftant trouble and agony which attends ufually the generous mind, upon its having unreflectingly com- mitted what it promptly perceives to be an error.

<small>Claren-don's de-fence of Charles.</small>

It feems to me very neceffary, in clofing this work, to fix attention upon fuch deliberate perverfions of the truth, becaufe they con- ftitute for the moft part, with all writers of a particular clafs, the fole ground of attack againft the Commons for having treated the outrage of the 4th of January as a challenge to civil war. Nothing is more certain than that, even while the outrage itfelf was ftill in progrefs, there was time for reflection pre- fented to its author; and that if this had been properly employed, at leaft fome of the difaftrous confequences might have been in- tercepted. Let me here, therefore, briefly recall in what way it *was* employed.

<small>The truth mif-ftated: as a ground for affailing Commons.</small>

Without adopting Whitelock's view that if Charles had promptly withdrawn the im- peachment little more trouble might have attended it (a view which makes too fmall allowance for the fettled diftruft which his

<small>Doubtful affertion of White- lock.</small>

previous conduct had inspired), it is yet very far from impossible but that, frankly done at the first, it might certainly have recovered so much ground for the King as not wholly yet to have broken and dispersed his party in the City. Not only, however, did he sullenly leave the charge rankling in the breasts of such men all powerful in debate as Hampden and Pym, whom it ever afterwards indisposed to any mediation or compromise; not only did he refuse to withdraw it, as we have seen, when finally compelled to withdraw all proceedings; but, up to the day when the storm broke over him under which he had to yield, and which with an obstinate impassiveness he had watched as from day to day it made darker the skies above him, not a word was uttered by him, or an act done, of which the manifest and unmistakeable tendency was not to exaggerate every danger, and to confirm and extend all the fears, generated by his first rash attempt.

There was but an interval of six days between his entering the House of Commons and his flight from Whitehall; and in that interval, Clarendon tells us, he had renewed his commands to himself, Falkland, and Culpeper, to give him constant advice what he was to do.* What, then, having the inestimable benefit and advantage of such confessed advisers, *did* he do? In

---

* *Life and Continuation,* i. 101-2.

full view of the danger escaped by failure of his instructions on the evening of the 3rd of January for firing on the Citizens, and of the mistake committed by failure of his attempt on the morning of the 4th for seizing on the Members, what were the steps taken, under such advice as Hyde admits him now to have had the full opportunity to profit by—to express regret or make reparation? What, in a word, was the course he took at that point of time which Clarendon fixes beyond question as "before he left Whitehall?" *Result upon the King.*

Events between 4th and 9th January.

On the night of the 4th, with those ominous sounds of Privilege! Privilege! still ringing in his ears which had followed him as he left the House that day, he caused a Proclamation to be issued, declaring that certain members of the House of Commons were under accusation of High Treason, and ordering the ports of the kingdom to be closed against any attempt they should make to evade justice. On the morning of the 5th, he issued under his own hand Warrants for their arrest addressed to the Sheriffs of London. On that day, also, he went himself to the City, and in person demanded that the accused, whom he knew to be concealed therein, should be delivered up to him. On that evening, he drew up with his own hand a second Proclamation against harbouring the men whom he designated as traitors. On the morning of the 6th, he dispatched a

4th: P.M. Proclamation against Members.

5th: A.M. King's Warrants and Visit to Guildhall.

5th: P.M. Second Proclamation.

o c

386   *Arreft of the Five Members.*

6th: A.M. Royal Serjeant into the City with orders to
Serjeant effect the arreft. On the 7th, the Common
fent to
arreft. Council voted their petition in behalf of
popular rights; and on the fame day, fuch
evidence was taken by the Committee at
7th: A.M. Grocers' Hall ("upon queftions," fays Claren-
Common
Council don, " whereof many were very imperti-
Petition. "nent and of little refpect to the King")
as conclufively eftablifhed the danger to which
the Commons had been expofed. On the
8th: A.M. 8th, the day when Lord Falkland was formally
New
Minifters fworn in before the Council as one of His
at Council- Majefty's principal Secretaries of State, and
Board.
the morning after that vote of the Committee
which invited the accufed publicly to refume
on the following Monday their places and duties
as reprefentatives of the people, there came
Same day: forth a third Proclamation from the King
Third
Proclama- reiterating againft the members the accufation
tion
againft of high treafon, and commanding all magif-
Members: trates and officers throughout the kingdom
to apprehend them and convey them to the
Tower. Moreover, on that fame day of the
and 8th, a private order was fent from the Council
private
order from Board, at which Falkland had taken the oaths
Council
Board. and his feat but an hour or two earlier,
giving inftructions for proceedings againft
thofe (notorioufly the members for the City)
who, upon the fudden alarm of two nights before,
had called out the Train Bands for protection
of the Citizens. Was it poffible that the

§ XL.   *Conclusion.*

Houfe of Commons, how reluctant foever to enter on the ftruggle, could in fuch circumftances as thefe have declined or evaded it?

There was manifeftly no alternative left. Such middle courfe as D'Ewes would have propofed before reforting to an open defiance, was fimply hopelefs.   It had become clear that the attempt upon the Members could not be defeated without a complete overthrow of the power of the King.   He could not remain at Whitehall if they returned to Weftminfter.   Charles raifed the iffue, the Commons accepted it, and fo began our Great Civil War.   The King drew the fword upon the day when he went with his armed followers to arreft the Five Members in their places in the Houfe.   The Houfe of Commons unfurled their ftandard on the day when, declining to furrender their members, they branded with the epithet of a Scandalous Paper the articles of impeachment iffued by the King.

<small>No middle courfe poffible.</small>

<small>Acceptance of iffue raifed.</small>

<small>Civil War.</small>

INDEX.

Alison.

ALISON, Sir William (York,) speaks againſt Lunſford, 36.
Argyle, Archibald Marquis of, made Scottiſh Chancellor, 17. (See *Montroſe*.)
Arreſt, privileges of Commons againſt, explained and aſſerted, 213-14, 304-5, 307-8. 315.
Arreſt of the Five Members. See *Five Members*.
Attorney-Gen. See *Herbert, Sir E.*
Authorities cited or referred to: MS. See *Bere. Carterett. Dering. Dowſe. Latche. Marſton. Nicholas. Porter. Slingſby. Smith, (Thomas). Windebank. Wiſeman, (Thomas).*
PRINTED. See *Bramſton. Bruce. Butler. Clarendon. Echard. Eikon Baſilike. Filmer. Forſter. Guizot. Hacket. Hall. Hallam. Heath. Heylyn. Hobbes. Howell. Hume. Hutchinſon. Lewis. Lilly. Macaulay. Nalſon. Napier. Pepys. Ruſhworth. Ruſſell, (Lord John). Sandford. Verney. Warwick, (Sir P.). Whitelock. Wright.*
Ayleſbury, Mr. writes from Rome to Hyde, 224, 225 *note*.

BAAL, or Ball, Peter, Queen's Attorney, 129 *note*.
Balfour, Sir William, removed from governorſhip of the Tower, 34. Clarendon's Note thereon, and on his Succeſſor, 35 *note*.
Balgony, Leſlie, Field Marſhal of, made an Engliſh Earl, 17.

Bere.

Banks, Sir John, to be Lord Treaſurer, 30 *note*.
Barberino, Cardinal Franceſco, makes "particular mention" of Pym and his friends, 225 *note*.
Barrington, Sir Thomas (Colcheſter), 37. Named on Committee of Safety, 280.
Bates, Dr. on Lady Carliſle's connexion with Pym and his friends, 137. On Adviſers of the King's Viſit to the Houſe, 137. 140. 141.
Bath, Earl of, to be a Privy Counſellor, 58.
Baxter, Richard, on the term "Roundhead", 136—7 *notes*.
Baynton, Sir Edward (Chippenham), on ſecret communications to the King, 210.
Bedford, Earl of, joins in Proteſt relative to Lunſford's removal, 36 *note*. 65.
Beedham, Mr. 87 *note*.
Bellaſis, H. (Yorkſhire), motion of, relative to the Biſhops, 102 *note*. Suggeſts attempt at accommodation with the King, 201 *note*.
Bere, Sidney (Correſpondent of Admiral Pennington), appointed Under Secretary, 5. Deſcribes Oppoſition to printing the Remonſtrance, 5, 6. On Charles's Viſit to City, 22. Fears and diſtractions daily increaſing, 26. On Secretary Nicholas's worth, 26, 27. *notes*. Court diſmiſſals and appointments, 30 *note*. Diſmiſſal of

D D

Biron.

Young Vane, 53. Further on Official changes, King's movements, and his own probable dismissal, 56 and *note*. On Commotion arising out of the Lunsford affair, 69, 70. On the Bishops and their Protestation, 96 *note*. Reports their Committal to the Tower, 98. His fears and hopes on the occasion, 99 and *note*. On King's Visit to the House to seize the Five Members, 194, 195, *notes*. His dread as to ultimate result: flying rumours, 203, 204. Why he declines a Christmas Invitation, 204 *note*. Rumours against Lords Bristol and Digby, 206. On Secret Service assigned to the Admiral, 361. King's flight and disquietude of his Counsellors, 361—363. Union between the two Houses, 363, 364 *notes*. Describes Return of Members, 370. 371 *note*.

Biron, Sir John, appointed Tower Governor, *vice* Lunsford, 70. " Little better accepted than the other", 77. Called before Commons' Committee, 334. 341. His Message to them, 355. Superseded, 355 *note*. 364 *note*.

Bishops, Petition against enforcement of Liturgy by the, 32 *note*. Course taken by them on account of the Tumults, 89. Purport of their Protestation thereon, 89—91. Real Author of Protestation: object contemplated by him, 91. What might have followed had Protest been admitted, 92. Provocation given, 92, 93. Bishop Hall's account of what led to the Protestation, 93, 94. Clarendon's Account: Course taken by King, 94, 95. Prompt action of Commons, 95. Cromwell as to Episcopal Spirit, 96. Sidney Bere's strictures on the protesting Prelates,

Buckingham.

ibid. note. Their conduct condemned by Clarendon, 96, 97. His opinion of their Impeachment, 97. View taken by Pennington's Correspondents, 97—100. Real drift of Protest, 100. Glyn sent up to impeach them, 101. Hacket's Lament for them: feelings of the Lords, *ibid. note*. Tower Gates closed upon them, 102. Civilities exchanged while in durance, 103 *note*. D'Ewes's comments, 104, 105. Tower preferable to Black Rod's Custody, 105 and *note*. Delight of Commons at their folly, 105, 106. See also 173. 174 and *notes*. 341.

Bodvill, Mr. John (Anglesey), and the Clerk's Journals, 232.

Bolingbroke, Earl of, 36 *note*.

Boswell, Sir John, 204 *note*.

Bramston on Attack on Archbishop Williams, 71, 92. His account compared with Clarendon's and Hacket's, 89 *note*.

" Bridle " the, for too restless Citizens, 33.

Bristol, John Earl of: to be Chamberlain, 30 *note*. Commons' Charge against him, 78. 82, 83. Spanish Match expedition, 82. Best account of that mad freak, 82 *note* ‡. Cromwell denounces him, 83. Rumours against him and his son, 206. See *Digby*.

Brooke, Lord, 36 *note*. Honour designated for him, 58.

Brown, Mr. Clerk of House of Lords, 303.

Brown, Mr. R. (Romney), brings up Lincoln's Inn reply, 176.

Brown, Sir A. (Surrey), reports slander on Pym, 358 *note*.

Bruce, John, Esq. Note by, 20 *note* *.

Buckingham Freeholders come to London, 338, 339. 357, 373. Their numbers, 339 *note*. Hampden's share in their peti-

Buckle.

tion, 340, 341 *notes*. 373 *note*. Debate as to receiving them. 353, 354. 373. Called in, 374. King's reply to their Petition, 380. See *Goodwin. Hampden.*

Buckle, "One Mr."; Threat uttered by, 169.

Bullock, Mr. 372.

Burleigh, Lord, Anecdote of, 382 *note.*

Butler, Samuel, couplet quoted from, 344 *note.*

Byron. See *Biron.*

CAMDEN SOCIETY BOOKS rich in illuftrations of period comprifed in this work, 49 *note.* Quotations therefrom. See *Bramfton. Verney.*

Carew, Alexander (Cornwall) 279.

Carlifle, Earl of, 36 *note.* 37 *note.* See *Hay, Lord.*

Carlifle, Lucy Countefs of: has Intercourfe with both parties, 15. Communicates Court Secrets to popular Leaders, 16. Caufes of her betrayal of the King's party, 133—135. Sir P. Warwick's Scandal about her, 135, 136 and *notes.* Dr. Bates's more complimentary interpretation, 137. Refult of her clofetings with the Queen, 138, 139. Gratitude expreffed for her fervices, 140. Dangers averted by her warning, 144. 145 *note.* 195. Precife moment of her communication of King's intentions, 175.

Carterett, Captain, Correfpondent of Admiral Pennington, 51. Clarendon's teftimony to his eminence, 52. Reports difmiffal of the two Vanes, *ibid.* Parliamentary appreciation of his fervices, *ibid. note.* Announces the publication of the Remonftrance, 60. His reflections on affairs, 60, 61. Confirms fact of Lunfford's knighthood and penfion, 70 *note.* On caufes of popular

Charles I.

difquietude, 287. 296, 297. His later career, 366 *note.*

Cavalier, firft ufe of the epithet, 62. Senfe in which it was ufed: inftances cited, 62, 63 *notes.* William Lilly on the fame fubject, 64, 65 *notes. See* 341. See Roundhead.

Cave, Sir R. (Lichfield) named on Committee of Safety, 280.

Cecil's excufe for a Clerk's "wanton pen", 382 *note.*

Chadwell, William (St. Michaels), munimental trick attempted by, 244, 245. His narrow efcape, 245 and *note.*

Chambers, John, depofes to violence of King's Guard, 327.

Chandois, Lord, 37 *note.*

Charles, Elector Palatine, accompanies the King into the Houfe, 184, 185. Joins him in his flight, 361. A Prince's privations, 365 *note.*

Charles the Firft, fatal day in the life of, 1. His attempt on Five Members correctly ftated in *Eikon Bafilike*, 2. Services rendered to him by Admiral Pennington, 3. Was Lord Digby fole advifer of the arreft? 10. Charges intended againft Pym and Hampden, 12. His ways of dealing with opponents: always too late, 12, 13. Refults of his obftinacy, 14. Clarendon's verfion of his confultations with Lord Digby and their betrayal, 15 *note.* Nicholas's communication relative to Lord Kimbolton, 15, 16. His conduct towards avowed Rebels and popular Leaders contrafted, 17, 18. Enlarges fcope of his accufation againft the latter, 18. His "confident and fevere look", 20. His felf-deception on ftrength of Royalift party in City, 21. Contemporary accounts of his reception there,

Index.

Charles I.
21, 22. Confers honours on City Magnates, 22. Adulatory Reports, *ibid. note*. Probable effect of Lenthal's defire to refign, 22, 23. 25. Inftances of his foolhardinefs, 29. Affails privileges of Commons, 30, 31. His double provocation of the Puritans, 31. Confequences of his reprieve of condemned Jefuits 31, 32 *note*. His Warrant appointing Lunfford Tower Governor, 34 *note*. Refponfibility for that act, 35 *note*. Alleged reafon for difmiffal of Lord Newport, 37. Gives Lord Newport the lie and retracts, 38, 39. Endeavours to win Pym to his fide, 42, 43. Why his efforts failed, 42 *note*. Pym's fecret influence over him, 44—46. Renews offers of place to Pym, 47. Dering on his overture to Pym, 48. Effect on Commons of his difmiffal of young Vane, 53. Propofal of Regency during his fojourn in Scotland, 56-7 *note*. Negotiations in London with popular leaders, and fudden change in Scotland, 57—8. His ill-advifed act on the Faft day, 61. Its fatal confequences, 62. His indifcretion relative to Volunteer Guard, 72. 73—75. How he received Declaration of both Houfes, 75. Juftifies his acceptance of the Guard, 75, 76. Anticipated refult of his noncompliance with Commons' defires, 80. His conduct on receiving Bifhop's Proteftation, 95. Commons' Demand for Guard, 109, 110. His expedients pending his anfwer, 110, 111. His reply and its accompaniment, 112. Impeachment of Five Members laid folely at his door, 113. Anfwer, in his own hand, to Petition of both Houfes for Guard, 114 *note*. His choice of Commander a proof of

Charles I.
infincerity, *ibid*. His Interview with the Commons' Deputies, 126. Queftion of his refponfibility further difcuffed, 127—129. Pernicious fruits of the Queen's interference, 129—139. (See *Henrietta*). His abettors in renewed attempt on the Commons, 139—142. Alleged evidence in fupport of his charge, 142, 143. Clarendon's view of the matter, *ibid. notes*. Incapable of a wife Fear, 145. Iffue raifed by his attempt, 145. Its alleged "gentlenefs," 150 *note*. His ftyle of writing, 151. His advifers and their fhare of refponfibility, 153, 154. Attempts to induce the citizens to aid him, 155—157. His Warrant for that object, 157. 158. Whitehall clocks too late, 156. 159. Goes to the Houfe to demand the Five Members, 179. Number and equipment of his attendants, 180—184. Enters "where never King was but once", 184, 185. His reception by and bearing towards the members, 185—187. His Speech to the Houfe, with corrections by his own hand, 188—190. Lenthal's Reply to his appeal, 191, 192. William Lilly on his manner of Speaking, 192 *note*. His Speech on finding his "birds flown", 193. His bearing on leaving the Houfe, 193—195. Accounts of the fcene by Slingfby and Bere, 194 *note*. D'Ewes's account of what took place on his departure, 195—200. Mifchief let loofe by the act, 206. Hyde his private advifer, 208. Clofeted with him, 209 *note*. Lilly's verdict on his "rafh action", 217 *note*. Money folicited for him from Foreign Rulers, 224. How the Commons met his Proclamation againft Effex, 240.

Index. 393

Charles I.
Sir Peter Wentworth's plain speaking, 242. Sends for Rushworth, 251. Their interview, 252. Issues Proclamation against Five Members, 253. His Warrant for seizure of arms in City, 257 *note*. Announces intention of addressing City Authorities, 258. His reception in Guildhall, and how he fared by the way, 258—263. Wiseman's account of the affair, 264—267. Citizens' answer to his demand for Five Members, 267. Their advice to him, 268. His first act on return from City, 269. 297. Its responsibility entirely his own, 270, 271. Commons' Proceedings arising out of Arrest, 271—281. Apprehensions natural to the times, 283. Montrose's offer to assassinate Argyle and Hamilton, 284, 285, 286 *notes*. Pym's heaviest charge against him proved, 299, 300. Commons' Declaration against his conduct, 319, 320. His Order in Council on position taken up by the City, 324, 325 *notes*. Evidence as to intended violence by his followers, 316—329. Further proclamation against the Five Members, 333. Threatens a Visit to Commons' Committee, 337. 338. Determines to quit Whitehall, 356, 357. His terror and its causes, 359. His reasons for leaving London, 360. MS. references to his flight, 361—368. (See *Bere—Dering—Slingsby*.) Off to Hampton Court, 368, 369. Case between him and the Commons summed up, 376—387. (See *Clarendon. Commons. Five Members*.)

Charles II. Glyn's accident at Coronation of, 344 *note*.

Chaucer, Bishop Hacket's estimation of, 91 *note*.

Chomley, Sir Henry (Northal-

City.
lerton), object of Motion by, 243 *note*. Question put by him, 375. City; strength of Royalist party in the, 21. Hopes founded by King on his reception there, 21, 22. Honors conferred on City Dignitaries, 22. Reappearance of "factious Citizens" at the Houses of Parliament, 26. "One of the House" catechized by them, *ibid. note* *. Their anti-royalist feelings further manifested, 27. Lord Mayor's unpopular acts, 28. Agitation by reason of reprieve of Popish Offenders, 31, 32. Petition against enforcement of Liturgy and offensive proclamation thereon, 32. Result of Attack on Newgate, *ibid. note*. Indignation provoked by King's Acts, 32, 33. City 'Prentices attacked by the Soldiery, 68, 69. Citizens assailed by King's Guard, 73, 74. Attitude assumed by them: Slingsby's apprehensions, 80. Solicited by Commons for Military Aid, 124. 155. 157. Efforts of the King to forestal Commons in this matter, 155—159. Five Members' place of Refuge, 253. Character of the City and habits of its Merchants, 253—254. Its Military Organization: Duties imposed on Aldermen, 254 *note*. Its fortifications and other defensive appliances, 255 *note*. Its enrichment by trade : cause of Clarendon's lament, 255, 256. Its adherence and services to the popular cause, 256. Comes in for its share of Court Lampoons, 256 *note*. Scene presented on night of Arrest, 256, 257. Apprehended Seizure of Arms, 257 and *note*. King's self-invitation to Lord Mayor, 258. King's progress to and reception in Guildhall, 258 —263. (See *Rushworth. Slings-*

Civil War.

by, *Wifeman, T.*) Anfwer to King's demand for the Five Members, 267. Advice tendered to him therein, 268. Meeting of Commons Committee at Guildhall, 300, 301. How the Committee was welcomed and treated, 301, 302. Proceedings of Committee, 302—316. (See *Commons*.) State of City on Publication of Commons' Declaration, 320, 321. Caufes for alarms afloat, 322. Number of armed men within call for defence, 323. Judicious arrangements of Lord Mayor: Proceedings of King and Council, 323, 324. King's Order againft thofe who "put the Trained Band in arms", 324, 325, *notes*. One caufe for increafe of Civic alarm, 325, 326, 333. Appearance of City on 9*th January*, 338. Its march with the Members, 369. Pym's thanks to the Citizens, 371.

Civil War, Great, firft blood fhed in the, 64. Who were the firft aggreffors, 66. Afpect of the Elements on its eve, 67, 68. Captain Slingfby's apprehenfions 80. Refponfibilities incurred by its inftigators, 80, 81. Its real beginning, 377, 387.

Clare, Earl of, 36 *note*, 37 *note*.

Clarendon, Edward Hyde, Earl of; mifreprefentations of, relative to Charles's attempt on Five Members, 1. His character of Admiral Pennington, 3, *note*. Mifftates caufe of Palmer's Committal to the Tower, 8. Afferts Lord Digby was fole advifer of King's attempt, 10—12. His character of and friendfhip with Digby, 11 *note*. His Opinion of guilt of the Five Accufed, 14. Affects ignorance of Lord Kimbolton's complicity, 14, 15. His verfion of Charles's

Clarendon.

Confultations with Digby, 15 *note*. Effect on the King of tone adopted by him and his Colleagues, 18. His character of Lenthal, 23 and *note*. His comments on Windebank's flight a key to his views on the Popifh Reprievals, 32, 33 *notes*. Explains object of Lunfford's appointment, 34, 35. His difingenuous note on Balfour's difmiffal, 35 *note*. Throws refponfibility of Lunfford's appointment on Digby, *ibid*. His eftimate of Captain Carterett, 52. His opinions and admiffions relative to King's Guard, 72, 73. His verfion of their attacks on the Citizens, 73, 74. On the epithets "Roundhead" and "Cavalier", 74. His account of attack on Archbifhop Williams contrafted with others', 89 *note*. Way in which Bifhops' Proteft was concocted, 94, 95. His opinion thereon and on their fubfequent punifhment, 96, 97. His charge againft Digby *in re* Kimbolton's Impeachment, 116, 117. Abfent from Houfe during debates on arreft, 121. Queen's part in Impeachment of Five Members, 132, 133. His apology for Lady Carlifle's defection, 134. On the legality of the King's Proceedings, 150 and *note*. 151, 152. Imputation againft him and his friends, 153. Their way of getting out of the dilemma, 153, 154. His charges againft and eftimate of Hampden, 168—170. Hampden's fignificant remark to him, 171. Bearing of Pym and Hampden towards him, 172 *note*. On number and equipment of King's Guards, 181. Falfe iffue raifed by him on King's failure, 202, 203. Period at which he became King's private Advifer,

Index. 395

Clarendon.

208. A double dealer by his own confession, 209 and *note*. Suspected of Treachery towards the Commons, 210—212. Accused of advising the Arrest, 212. Reasons for disbelief as to alleged Speech by him, 212 —214. Why Falkland excused his absence from the House, 215 *note*. No evidence of his presence during debates on Arrest, 215, 216. 293. Letter to him from Rome, 224, 225 *notes*. Why he laments absorption of Wealth by City, 255. Not named on Committee of Safety, 280. Question raised on his statement of Montrose's murderous offer, 284, 285, 286 *notes*. Liberties taken by his Sons with his MSS : 1826 Edition, how made up, *ibid*. His inferences relative to fears excited by King's conduct contrasted with his own admissions, 286, 287. 294. 295. Plans of himself and Digby for seizing Five Members, 288, 289. His faithlessness as an Historian, 289. Comparison of his Statements of Proceedings of 5th January with those of D'Ewes, Verney, and Rushworth, 289—293. His sole Argument of any weight, 303. His insinuations repelled by D'Ewes, 310. Real points at issue evaded by him, 310, 311. Construction put thereon by impartial bystanders, 311 *note*. Value of D'Ewes's Notes as correctives of his misstatements, 317. Recapitulation of such misrepresentations, 317, 318. Answers thereto furnished by D'Ewes, 318, 319. Trustworthy when not misled by his feelings, 320. What he says of the "great change in all sorts of People", 321 and *note*. Alarms traceable to the threats of his friend Digby, 322. Too keen

Commons.

a pen, 382. Deliberate perversion of the Truth, 383. See also 369, 335, 353, 356, 362, 364, 367, 370, 371, 374.
Clarendon, Henry Hyde, Earl of, Liberties taken by him and his brother, Lord Rochester, with the MS. of their Father's History, 284, 285, 286 *notes*.
Clotworthy, Sir John (Malden), 38, calls attention to Irish Affairs, 276 ; Persists in his object, 282. Service performed by him, 349, 350.
Coke, Sir Edward, 39.
Coke, Sir William, Anecdote told by, 126. 137, 138. Credit given to it by Haselrig, 140, 141.
Commons, House of ; growing alarms amongst Members of, 20. Proceedings of the Lord Mayor resented by them, 28. Their dissatisfaction at Young Vane's dismissal from Office, 30 *note*. 53. Their privileges assailed by the King, 30, 31. House much distracted at "reprieve of the Priests," 32 *note*. Course taken on Lunsford's appointment, 36. Their supporters and opponents in the Lords, *ibid*. and *note*. Address voted for Lunsford's Removal, 37. Their request to Lord Newport to take command of Tower, 37, 38. Their reception of Old Vane on his dismissal, 52. Time supposed ripe for destruction of their Leaders, 67. Their proceedings on Lord Newport's Dismissal, 82. Course taken with reference to Lords Bristol and Digby, 82, 83, 84. Long silences in the House ; Officering of the Army debated, 84, 85. Members alarmed by a suggestion of Pym's, 106. D'Ewes's Proposition, and the Speaker's rider to it, 106, 107. Pym's remedy for apprehended dangers, 107, 108. D'Ewes's

Commons.

troubles and doubts on the occasion, 108, 109. Demand for Guard for the House, 109. How the King received and answered such demand, 110—112. Joined by the Lords in demand for Guard, 115. Result of Proceedings on seizure of Members' Papers, 120—126. Ald. Pennington and Captain Venn sent to City for Guard, 124. 155. 157. Course taken by King to defeat this step, 155—158. Resolution adopted in consequence of King's tampering with Inns of Court, 161. Result of Messages sent to the four Inns, 176, 177. Re-entrance of the Five Members: King's Secret disclosed to the House, 177. Further disclosures, 178. Five Members depart, 179. King's approach to the House *4th January:* his retinue, 179—184. Appearance of House on his entry, 184—187. Speaker Lenthal's memorable Speech, 191, 192. King's Speech and departure, 193—195. Slingsby and Bere's Account of the Transaction, 194 *note.* Copy Entry of this day's proceeding in Journals of House, 196 *note.* D'Ewes's minutes of what passed after the King's departure, 195—200. Discussion on answers to Royal message, 221—223. Why Sir R. Hopton incurred displeasure of House, 223—227. Proceedings in Sir Edward Dering's Case, 228—231. Conflicts between Speaker and Members, 236. 238. 241. Cause of House's laughter " amid sad apprehensions ", 247. Result of attempts to enforce Members' early attendance: The Shilling Fine, 247—249. Precautionary steps taken on reassembling of House on *5th January,* 271, 272. Mr. Grimston's telling

Commons.

speech, 272—275. Result of motion thereon, 275. Upshot of Discussion of Declaratory Resolution, 275—279. Numbers on two important Divisions, 279, and *note.* Constitution of Committee then named, 280. Motions by Lord Lisle, Sir P. Stapleton, and N. Fiennes, 281. Cause of House's abrupt rising, 281, 282. Reasons for alarm, 282, 283. Clarendon's report compared with contemporary accounts, 290—293. Point gained by adjourning Sittings to Guildhall, 294. What Slingsby "heard some Parliament men discoursing of", 298, 299. No hitherto known report of Proceedings at Guildhall, 300. Value of D'Ewes's Notes, *ibid.*
Committee at Guildhall, (*6th Jan.*). Rushworth's and Verney's notices: Clarendon's confusion, 300, 301. Subjects treated of at this Sitting, 302—313. Dispute between D'Ewes and Wilde, 314, 315. Resolutions ultimately adopted, 315, 316. Hyde's aspersions read by the light of D'Ewes's Journals, 317—319. Declaration of Breach of Privilege, and Publication of same, 319, 320. State of public feeling, 320—326.
First Sitting at Grocers' Hall (*7th Jan.*). Abstract of evidence as to outrage of the *4th,* 326—329. Proceedings thereon: another dispute between D'Ewes and Wilde, 330—332. Effect of Resolution to invite return of Five Members, 332. How the King met that resolution, 332, 333.
Second Sitting at Grocers' Hall, (*8th Jan.*) Measures on King's further Proclamation, 333—336. King's threat to attend Committee, 337. Orders issued thereon: its upshot, 338.

Compton.

Laſt Sitting at Grocers' Hall.
Glyn's communication, 340.
Alderman Pennington's ſuſpicions relative to the Tower, 340, 341. Reſolutions againſt Killigrew and Fleming, 341, 342. The like againſt Evil Counſellors, Proclamations, and Warrants, 343. Maynard's effective Speeches, 344—346. Sailor Volunteers and their offers, 347 and *note.* Directions given to the "Water Rats", 347, 348. Arrival of the Five Members, 348. Common People's offers at this juncture, 348, 349. Defenſive arrangements made for return to Weſtminſter, 350—352. Hampden's 4000 men from Bucks, 353, 354. Laſt acts of Committee, 354—356.
At Weſtminſter again. Reſumption of their ſeats by the Five Members, 371. Proceedings on the occaſion, 371—373. Bucks Petition and its Guard of 6000, 374. Queſtions about the King anſwered, 375. Fruits of Struggle between Commons and Crown, 376. Caſe between the two parties ſummed up, 383—387. See *Biſhops, Charles I. Clarendon, D'Ewes, Five Members, Lenthal.*
Compton, Lord (Warwickſhire) communicates King's anſwer to Houſe's Meſſage, 210.
Coniers, Sir John, made Lieutenant of the Tower, 355 *note.* Ground of King's exception to him, *ibid.*
Coningſley, Captain, Lieutenant of Ordnance, examined before Commons' Committee, 334.
Conway, Viſcount, 37 *note.*
Cooke, Sir Robert (Tewkeſbury), named on Committee of Safety, 280.
Coppley's Caſe, temp. Q. Mary, 305.
Corbet, Miles (Yarmouth, Nor-

Culpeper.

folk), purport of relation made to Houſe by, 79 *note.*
Cotton, Sir Robert, one of the earlieſt Martyrs of the Stuarts, 40. His Sufferings at the Seizure of his Books and MSS. *ibid. note.*
Cromwell, Oliver (Cambridge), addreſſes House on Lord Newport's diſmiſſal, 82. Grounds of his complaint againſt Lord Briſtol, 82, 83. His advice on the officering of the Army, 85. His complaint relative to Captain O'Connel, *ibid. note.* What he ſaid of the Biſhops and their Proteſtation, 95, 96. Reflected on in Dering's Book, 229. Suggeſts that D'Ewes write an anſwer to ſame, 230. D'Ewes's recommendation, *per contra,* 231. Not named on Committee of Safety, 280.
Crown Jewels carried acroſs the Channel, and why, 3, 4. 132. Pawned by the Queen, 361.
Culpeper, Sir John (Kent), appointed Chancellor of Exchequer, 11. 48. 49. 111. 267. His obligations to and intimacy with Lord Digby, 11 and *note.* Suſpicions againſt him and his coadjutors, 12. 111, 112. Influence on Charles of the courſe taken by him and his Parliamentary aſſociates, 18. Silent on an important occaſion, 121. Has audiences with the King, 126, 140. What he and his friends would have done with the Five Members, 149 *note.* His confidence to Dering, 152. How he and his aſſociates endeavoured to evade reſponſibility, 153, 154. Holds ſecret meetings with Hyde and Falkland, 209 *note.* His horror at Sir Peter Wentworth's plain ſpeaking, 242. Named on Committee of Safety, 215. 279, 280. "Diſpleaſed and dejected", 292, 293.

Cunningham.

His unanfwered queftion, 375.
See alfo 279 *note*. 377, 384.
Cunningham, Mr. Letter of Marfton found by, 87, *note*.

DANDIE, Serjeant, fent to apprehend the Five Members, 296. His reception by "the worfe fort of people", 297. See 343.
Dering, Sir Edward (Kent), in trouble "for fomething he hath fpoke in the Houfe", 26 *note**. His note on Charles's overture to Pym, 48. His MSS. to be publifhed by Camden Society, 48 *note*. Source of his Information, 152. Act whereby he incurred Houfe's difpleafure, 228. D'Ewes's reafons for voting his expulfion, 228, 229. Sentence paffed on him and his Book, 230. Cromwell's fuggeftion as to anfwering fame, 230, 231. On Bucks Petitioners, 353 *note*. King's flight and Commons' Proceedings, 359, 360. Cavaliers' diftreffes, 365 *note*. "Rather be Pym than Charles", 372. His friend Bullock, *ibid*.
Derry Plantation, 217 *note*.
D'Ewes, Sir Simonds (Sudbury), Signs of danger, 19. Notes the King's look, 20. His Character of Lunfford, 34. His mifgivings, 36, 37. Recounts Cotton's fufferings at feizure of his Library, 40 *note*. King's intentions, 79, *note*. Houfe's proceedings on firft day of tumults, 81, 82. Character and condition of his Journal in the Harleian Collection, 81 *note*. "Long Silences" in the Houfe, 84. French Papiftical Threats, 85. Makes merry over Bifhops' fall, 103—105. On fubfequent Proceedings of Commons, 105, 106. Much troubled by Pym's propofition, 108. His Remarks in oppofition, 109, 110. Com-

D'Ewes.

mons' Proceedings on King's refufal of a Guard, 118, 119. Seizure of impeached Members' Papers, 120. Ufages of the Houfe in his day, 129 *note*. 223 *note*. Proceedings on the 4th of January, 160. 161. 164. 169. 173. 174. 175. On number of, and terror excited by, the King's Guards, 181. 183. 184. Charles's Vifit to the Houfe, 185, 186. Expreffive break in his Narrative, 187, 188. On Charles's Corrections of his Speech, 190, 191. King's afpect as he left the Houfe, 193, 194. Proceedings after King's departure, 195—200. His ufe of the term "Young Man", 198 and *note*. 279 *note*. His fenfe of danger, how marked, 201 and *note*. Not a mere party man: his ways of life, 202. 219. Light thrown on Hyde's double dealing, 209. 210. 211. 212. 215. Claim of his Journal to be received as authentic, 218. Sir W. Lytton's compliment to him, 219. His Service to Sir William, *ibid. note*. Epithets beftowed by him on Popular Leaders, 220. Mutual tolerance between him and Pym, *ibid*. His Pofition in the Houfe, 221. Debates wherein he acted as moderator, 221 —227. 236. 238. 240. 303—6. Young Lord Strafford, 227 *note*. His Part in difcuffion on Dering's conduct, 228, 229. His reply to Cromwell's Suggeftion that he anfwer Dering's Book, 230, 231. Further proof of his accuracy: How he makes up his Journal, 231—233. Stands up for Note-taking, 233. His pofition towards and opinion of Lenthal, 233—235. Rebukes Sir Arthur Hafelrig, 236. Avoids Chair of Committee, 239 *note*. How vote of alle-

D'Ewes.

giance to Parliamentary General was carried, 240, 241. His note on Sir Peter Wentworth's "folly", 242. Detects Chadwell's attempt to impose upon the House, 244, 245. His share in efforts to enforce early attendance: how the divers expedients worked, 245—249. Opposes Motion for Call of House, 250. A Stranger in the House, 251. Proceedings on reassembling of House, 5th *January*, 272. 275 —281. Explains cause of Panic in the House, 282, 283. Sole Recorder of Guildhall Sittings of 6th *January*, 300, 301. City hospitalities, 302. What was first debated, *ibid*. His arguments against Motion to send for warrants, 303—305. 307, 308. Cases in point cited by him, 305. Why applaud him and object to Hyde? 305, 306 *notes*. His Speech commended by the House, 308. Position achieved by his Argument, 310. Issue raised by Serjeant Wilde, 314. 315. Reports House's conclusion and departs, 315, 316. Value of his Journals as Correctives of Clarendon's misstatements, 317. Proofs furnished by him towards that end, 318, 319. Civic Alarms and defensive preparations on 6th *January*, 321 —323. One cause for increase of Alarm: 325, 326. His abstract of evidence as to Outrage of 4th *January*, 326—329. Speech and Motion then made by him, 329, 330. Again discomfits Serjeant Wilde, 330— 332. Avoids Voting on Motion for return of Five Members, 332. On number and object of Bucks Petitioners, 353. 353 *note*. 354. 374. Proceedings of Committee, 354—356. Commons usurpations why necessary, 356 *note*.

Dowse.

On Pym's traducers, 358 *note*. Lumley's Story, 362 *note*. Earns Lord Holland's approval, 363 *note*. On forlorn aspect of Court, 364 *note*. Soldiers' Pikes, 374. Abrupt close of his narrative, 375. Hopelessness of middle course, 387. See also 88. 206. 289. 290. 291. 292. 293. 312. 313. 370 *note*.
Digby, George, Lord: conveyed out of England, 3. Asserted sole adviser of Charles's Attempt, 10, 11. His Friends and Colleagues: Clarendon's analysis of his Character, 11 *note*. His intimacy with Lunsford, 34, 35. Extent of his responsibility for Lunsford's appointment, 35 *note*. Consequence of his Speech on Strafford's Attainder, 54. Employment designed for him by the King, *ibid*. Singled out for Royal favour, 60. Hollis's complaint against him, 83. Extent of his complicity in King's obnoxious proceedings, 83. 84. His Impeachment resolved on, 84. How he conducted himself on Kimbolton's Impeachment, 116—118. Further note on the disloyal conduct of the Digbys, 119. Closeted with the King, 129. Not unwilling to push matters to extremities, 205. His offer to take Five Members, dead or alive, 205. 288. 322. Rumours against him and his father, 206. Not the only guilty one among the King's prompters, 208. One probable result of his intimacy with Hyde, 212. Civic alarm possibly due to his murderous project, 322. Charges against his father. See *Bristol, Earl of*.
Dorset, Earl of, on Col. Lunsford's antecedents, 34. 34 *note*.
Dowse, Capt. (Correspondent of Admiral Pennington), solicits

400   Index.

Dungarvon.
a place for the Admiral, 51 *note*.
Dungarvon, Lord, 38.
Dunsmore, Lord, 34 *note*.
Durham, Bishop of, at the door of the House, 102 *note*. Lodged in "close air," 104, 105.

EARLE, Sir Walter (Weymouth), Service rendered to Mr. Strode by, 179. 200. His motion relative to Sir Ralph Hopton, 226. Why D'Ewes resisted his motion for "calling in Dering's Book", 229. Named on Committee of Safety, 280.
Echard, the Historian, Source of anecdote published by, 126.
Eikon Basilike, Charles's Attempt on the Five Members correctly interpreted in the, 2.
Eliot, Sir John, 39, 40 *note*. 147 *note*. 217 *note*.
Elizabeth, Queen, 33 *note*. 305.
Ellis, Mr. William (Boston) brings Gray's Inn Reply, 176. Made Chairman of Committee, 239 *note*.
Elsyng, Henry, Clerk of Commons, who copies from Journals of? 232. His explanation to D'Ewes, 233.
Essex, Robert, Earl of, joins in the Lunsford Protest, 36 *note*. 65. Military appointment conferred on him, 57. Commons demand Guard under his command, 109. Refused, 112. See also 116 *note*. His advice to the Five Members and to Kimbolton, 175. 200. Discovers Hyde closeted with the King, 209 *note*. How Commons acted when he was proclaimed traitor, 240. Refuses to attend King out of London, 361, 362. What Clarendon says of him, 362 *note*. Libel upon him, *ibid*. Honester man than Lord Holland, 363 *note*.
Evelyn, Sir John (Bletchingley),

Fiennes.
84. Proposes Hopton's expulsion, 225. Comes into collision with D'Ewes, 226.

FALKLAND, Lucius Cary, Lord (Newport, Hants): his asserted ignorance of intended Arrest, 11. 12. His intimacy with Lord Digby, 11 *note*. Suspicions against him and his Colleagues, 12. 111. 112. Influence on Charles of tone adopted by them, 18. Appointed Secretary and Privy Counsellor, 27 *note*. 50. 111 and *notes*. 324, 325 *notes*. Silent on an important occasion, 121. Only Member of Commons Deputation spoken to by the King, 126. Closeted with the King, 140. What he and his Colleagues would have done with the Five Members, 149 *note*. Reports King's Reply to Commons' Message, 160. Attends private Meeting at Hyde's lodgings, 209 *note*. Excuses Hyde's absence, 215 *note*. Copies from the Clerk's Journals nightly, 232. Named on Committee of Safety, 215. 280. As to Clarendon's assertion of his being "displeased and dejected", 292. 293. See also 332. 377 384. 386.
Fane. *See* Vane.
Fettiplace, John (Berks), overawed, 241.
Fiennes, Nathaniel (Banbury), 38. Believed to be "for root and branch", 47 *note*. Cause of sudden close of his speech, 119. Appointed a manager in Conference with the Lords, 121. Object of another Conference on which he was named, 173. Resolution moved by him, 174. His relation about armed crowds near the House, 177. Communicates Intelligence brought by Langres, 178. 195. 329.

Filmer.

Qualifying epithet bestowed upon him by D'Ewes, 220. Named on Committee of Safety, 280. Purport of Message to Lords proposed by him, 281. Prominent in Guildhall Committee Debates, 303. 309. 316.

Filmer, Sir Robert, and his followers, 166.

Five Members, arrest of the, misrepresented by Clarendon, 1. Interpretation put on the act in the *Eikon Basilike*, 2. Summary of the Seven Articles of Treason against them and Kimbolton, 113. 114. Copy of the MS. Articles in State Paper Office, 114, 115 *notes*. Seizure of their papers by King's Warrant, 120. Their persons demanded by King's Serjeant, 122. Course taken by House on this demand, 123. Ordered to attend House daily, 124. Reason why they withdrew, 145. What Charles's new Ministers thought of their guilt, 149. How Falkland, Culpeper, and Hyde would have disposed of them, *ibid. note*. Views of the arrest held by King's party after its failure, 150—152. Members successively defend themselves, 161 — 168. Impeachment voted a "Scandalous Paper," 172. Lord Essex's Message and advice to them, 175. Proceedings on their re-entrance, 177, 178. Leave given to them to absent themselves, 179. Digby's offer to seize them dead or alive, 205. 288. 322. What William Lilly thought of their arrest and of the King's intentions, 217 *note*. Their place of Refuge in the City, 253. City's answer to demand for them, 267, 268. New Proclamation against them, 269—271. Credibility of assertion that they were in no danger, 289. "Five Members'

Fuller.

March", 306 *note*. Vane's motion with regard to them, 316. Commons' Declaration against their arrest, 319, 320. Exclamation of a King's Guard on not finding them in the House, 328. Purpose aimed at by way in which King came to demand them, 329. Their attendance at Committee resolved on, 332. How the King met this defiance of his threats, 332, 333. Order for their public appearance renewed, 333. Further Proclamation against them condemned by the Commons, 333, 334. London invaded by their Constituents, 338, 339. No greater breach of privilege than their accusation, 345. How greeted on their return, 348, 369—371. Thanked by the Committee, 349. Hampden the first to break silence, 353. See *Commons. Hampden. Haselrig. Hollis. Pym. Strode.*

Fleming, Sir Wm. ordered into Custody, 125. Court Guards put under his command, 147. 177. 328. Delivers Message from King to Inns of Court, 176. Charged with Conspiracy, 341, 342.

Fleury, a Frenchman, nature of warning given by, 86, 329.

Francis, Mr. King's Serjeant-at-Arms; how received by the Commons, 121, 122, 123. 124. 302.

French Interference threatened against English Liberties, 85. Insolence of a French priest, 86. Obligation of the popular Leaders to French Informants, *ibid.*

Forster's Historical and Biographical Essays: references to, 1. 8. 20. 23. 63. 88. 92. 198. 208. 219. 230, 235. 284. 289. 299. 321. *notes.*

Fuller, Dr. Subject of Petition against, 249.

Index.

Garrett.

GARRETT, Sheriff Charles's motive in offering to dine with, 262. Entertains the King, 263. 266.
Gerbier, Sir Balthazar, 56 *note*.
Gerrard, Sir Gilbert (Middlesex), speaks against Lunsford, 56.
Gibbes, Will and his empty purse, 355 *note*.
Glyn, John (Westminster), sent up to impeach Bishops, 101. Watch duty imposed on him, 110. A Manager in conferences with the Lords, 121. 173. Epithet bestowed upon him by D'Ewes, 220. Committees on which he was nominated, 275. 276. 277. 280. 316. His compliment to D'Ewes: 308. 310. Follows D'Ewes: purport of his Speech, 308, 309. Leader in Pym's absence, 309. Reports Lord Herbert's loyalty, 340. His baseness at the restoration, 344. Pepys's glee over his accident, 344, *note*. See 342.
Goring, George (Portsmouth), object of Conspiracy with Percy, 246.
Goodwin, Arthur (Bucks), appointed a Teller, 279. Moves admission of Bucks Petitioners, 373.
Gourney, Sir Richard, Lord Mayor, made a Baronet, 22. Solicited to send Military Aid to King, 156. How his Instructions were carried out, 254 *note*. His extraordinary Powers, 259. Suppresses alarms, 323.
Grays Inn, Copy of Royal Letter to Benchers of, 147. 148. *notes*. Their Reply to the Commons Message, 176. *See* Inns of Court.
Grey Anchetil, 126. 137, 138.
Grey de Werk, Lord, 36 *note*.
Grimston, Harbottle (Colchester) 309. 316. Leads debate on breach of Privilege, 272. Summary of his Speech, 272—275. Named

Hampden.

on Committee of Safety, 280. Subject of his Speech handled in detail, 302.
Grocers Hall Sittings. *See* Commons.
Guildhall. *See* City.
Guildhall Sittings. *See* Commons.
Guizot's *Revolution d'Angleterre*, merits of, and of Mr. Scoble's Translation, 368. 369 *notes*.

HACKET, Bishop, Story told of a Hampshire Vicar by, 63 *note*. His account of the Westminster Tumults, 89 *note*. His *Scrinia Reserata* worth reprinting as a Curiosity of Literature, 90 *note*. His whimsical vituperation of Milton, *ibid*. Extent of his acquaintance with English Poets, 91 *note*. His lament for the Impeached Bishops, 101 *note*.
Hall, Joseph, Bishop of Norwich, Account by, of what led to the Bishops' Protest, 93—95. Hour at which " we were voted to the Tower", 101 *note*. Thankful at not being . Black Rod's prisoner, 105 *note*.
Hallam, Henry, View taken of Charles's conduct by, not consonant with King's Character, 127 and *note*. Scope of His note on Queen's intended Journey to Spa, 132 *note*. Inadvertent misquotation by him, 170 *note*. His view of Impeachment of Five Members, 216 and *note*.
Hamilton, Marquis of, "to be displaced", 30 *note*. Finds Hyde closeted with the King, 209 *note*. See *Montrose*.
Hampden, John (Bucks, one of the Five Accused), Clarendon's insinuation regarding, 12. Charles's contemplated charge against him, 12. 14. 15. Clarendon as to result of offer of place to him, 13 *note*. Songs

Harley.

and libels on him 16, 17. 119 note, 335 note. State-Offices to which he was designated, 54, 55. 58. His papers seized by King's Warrant, 120. Justifies resistance to an unconstitutional King, 166. His Confession of Faith, 167, 168. "Acrimonious condition of his blood", 168 and note. His "Serpentine Subtlety": what he really was, 169—171. Clarendon's estimate of his character, 169, 170 and note. Unity of purpose between him and Pym, 171, 172. Their opinion of Clarendon: Hampden's "Snappishness", 172 note. Epithet bestowed upon him by D'Ewes, 220. Petitioners for him, 339. First of the Five to break silence after Arrest, 353. Determined spirit, 354. King's hope concerning him, 380. See *Buckinghamshire*. *Five Members*. See also 47 note. 177. 178. 182 note. 198. 213. 225 note. 245. 267. 270. 271 note. 281. 295. 311 note. 320. 348. 357. 371. 373.

Harley, Sir Robert (Herefordshire), reports as to Captain Hide, 354, 355. 355 note.

Haselrig, Sir Arthur (Leicestershire, one of the Five Accused), reports insolence of a French priest, 86. His account as to Lady Carlisle and the Queen, 140. 141. Clarendon's contemptuous allusion to him, 149 note. Defends himself against Impeachment, 165. His age at the period, 198 note. Allusions to him in Royalist Songs, 199 note. Epithet bestowed upon him by D'Ewes, 220. Rebuked by D'Ewes for taking the Speaker to task, 236. See *Five Members*. See also 177, 178, 179. 182 note. 198. 269. 271 note. 311 note. 320. 348. 371.

Herbert.

Hay, Lord, Lady Carlisle's husband, 136 note.

Heath, Chronicler, on movements of the Five Members, 178 note.

Henrietta Maria, Queen of Charles I., by whom conveyed across Channel, 3. Windebank's Secret Understanding with her, 49 note. 50 note. William Lilly on Secret Counsels of herself and Party, 65 note. Use made of their knowledge of Court Secrets by French people about her, 86. 88. 130, 131. 138, 139. King's unconstitutional acts, how far due to her influence and intermeddling, 129—131. Her designs truly suspected by the Commons, 131, 132. Five Members' impeachment traceable to her own fear of accusation, 132, 133. Lady Carlisle's possible motives for betraying her Secrets. (See *Carlisle*). Words wherewith she is said to have incited the King, 138. 140. Misleads herself and betrays her Secret, 139. Source of her self-reproach on the King's failure, 146. Accompanies King in his flight, 359. 361. 366. 368. Course resolved on by her, 360. Carries off and pawns Crown Jewels, 361. Lying with her Children, 365 note. Reproaches King for abandoning first resolve against Five Members, 368.

Herbert, Sir Edward (Old Sarum), Attorney-General, delivers Impeachment of Five Members to the Lords, 112. Disclaims having advised such Impeachment, 113. 128. 113. 128. 312. What credit Strode gave to his denial, 128 note. 313. See 348. 371. 379.

Herbert, Sir Henry (Bewdley), speaks in mitigation of Hopton's Offence, 225.

Herbert, Lord, a Catholic Peer,

Hertford.

why complimented by Commons, 340.
Hertford, William Seymour, Marquis of, gives note of alarm to the Bishops, 93. Inference deducible therefrom, 95.
Heylyn, Dr. Peter, characteristic extracts from Laud's Life by, 102, 103 and *note*.
Hide, Captain David, with his sword upright, 185. His character and career, *ibid. note.* Lord Lieutenant willing to disable him, 354, 355, 355 *note*.
Hill, Roger (Bridport), brings up Inner Temple Reply, 176.
Hippisley, Sir J. (Cockermouth), named on Committee of Safety, 280.
History, how it may be written, 289—294.
Hobbes, Thomas, on sharers in King's responsibility, 140, 141. On King's refusal to disclose his Advisers' names, 141 *note*.
Holborne's R. (St. Michael's), Argument for giving weight to a minority, 20. Another argument of his, 299 *note*.
Holland, Sir John (Castle Rising), in conflict with Speaker Lenthal, 237, 238. Finds desolate Court at Windsor, 364 *note*.
Holland, Lord, 36 *note*. 75. 209 *note*. In disgrace with the King, 29 *note*. How "the speech goes" with regard to him and others, 30 *note*. Offers up his place, 361. Refuses to attend King, 362 *note*. Libel upon him, *ibid*. Contrast between him and Essex, 363 *note*.
Hollis, Denzil (Dorchester, one of the Five Accused), Clarendon's Speculations on possible result of offer of place to, 13 *note*. Office proposed to be conferred on him, 54. 55, 58. Denounces Lord Digby, 83. Delivers to Charles the Commons' Demand

Howard.

for a Guard, 109. His Papers seized by King's Warrant, 119, 120. 302. Defends himself against the Impeachment, 165. Inquired for by the King, 191. His age at this period, 198 *note*. Allusions to him in Royalist Songs, 199 *note*. How D'Ewes characterized him, 220. His motion in favor of young Lord Strafford, 227 *note*. His motion for Call of House, 250. Answers Chomley's Question, 375. See *Five Members*. See also 47 *note*. 177. 178. 179. 182 *note*. 198. 225 *note*. 232. 269. 271 *note*. 279 *note*. 311 *note*. 348. 317. 379.
Hopton, Sir Ralph (Wells), 136 *note*. 215. Incurs censure of the House, 223, 224. Clarendon's version of his Charge against the House, 224 *note*. His expulsion moved, 225. D'Ewes speaks in mitigation, 226. Determination come to, 226, 227. His reason for opposing Dering's expulsion, 228. Attempts an Excuse for the King's conduct, 275. 277. 278. Nominated on Committee of Safety, 280. Epithet given to him by Rushworth, 293. Duty assigned him in anticipation of second Visit from King, 338.
Hotham, John (Scarborough), behaves disrespectfully to the House, 249.
Hotham, Sir John (Beverley), deputed to carry message to King, 123. 126. Named a manager of conference with the Lords, 173. His remark on King's Speech in House, 195. Named on Committee of Safety, 280. Charged with Conspiracy, 341, 342.
Houses of Commons and Lords. See *Commons. Lords. Parliament.*
Howard de Escricke, Lord, 36 *note*.

Howell's Letters, best account of the Spanish Match contained in, 82 *note*.
Hume, David, misled by Clarendon, 289.
Hunsdon, Lord, 37 *note*.
Hungerford, Sir Edward (Chippenham), named on Committee of Safety, 280.
Hutchinson, Mrs. on number of King's Guard, 181.
Hyde, Edward (Saltash). See *Clarendon, Edward, Earl of*.

IMPEACHMENT of the Bishops. See *Bishops*.
Impeachment of the Five Members. See *Five Members*.
Inns of Court, Armed Assistance sought from the, 147. King's Letter in 1628 for Volunteer Guard, 147. 148 *notes*. Proceedings in House before the arrest, 160. Message resolved on, 161. Anecdote related by Ludlow, 161 *note*. Answer of each Inn to Commons' Message, 176, 177.
Irish Affairs, references to and motions on, 276. 281. 282. 290 *note*. 299. 300. 354. 355.

JAMES THE FIRST'S welcome to the "twal Kynges", 40.
Jenkin, Lieutenant, what Captain Langres heard from, 328.
Jesson, Alderman W. (Coventry), called to account for his fierce looks, 239, 240. Incurs Mr. Speaker's anger, 241.
Jesuit Priests reprieved from execution, 31. Commotion excited thereby, 32 and *note*. Prison for offenders of this class, 88.
Jonson, Ben; Bishop Hacket's estimation of, 91 *note*.

KILLEGREW, Harry (West Looe), novel doctrine propounded by,

243, 244. Anecdote of him related by Clarendon, 243 *note*. Trouble into which his inconsiderateness brought him, 244. Trick attempted by his friend Chadwell, 244, 245. His obligations to D'Ewes, 245. Extent of his punishment, *ibid. note*.
Killigrew, Sir William, ordered into custody by Commons, 125. Master Longe's diamond hatband and ring, *ibid. note*. Sent round to Inns of Court by the King, 147. 148. 176. Charged with Conspiracy, 341, 342.
Kimbolton, Lord (*See* also Mandeville, Lord), 36 *note*. Why charged with Treason, 14, 15. Clarendon's objection to his being included, 15 *note*. 149 *note*. His doings watched: His consultations with Pym and others, 15, 16, 37. Warning sent to him by Marston the Dramatist, 87. 117. Copy of Marston's Letter, *ibid. note*. Source of Marston's information, 88. Articles of treason against him and the Five Members, 113, 114. How he met the charge, 116. Embarrassment and flight of his expected accuser, 116—118. Lady Carlisle's intercourse with him, 133. Lord Essex's warning to him, 200. Omitted from King's Proclamation, 269. See also pp. 205. 269.
Kirton, Mr. (Milborne Port), 279.

LANGRES, Captain, source of warnings received by, 86. Nature and scope of his evidence, 147. His communication to Fiennes, 178 and *note*. 197. 200. Fuller report of his Evidence, 328. 329.
Larking, Rev. Lambert; Surrenden Papers to be edited for

Latche.

the Camden Society by, 48, 49 notes.

Latche, John, recounts his failure to enforce obedience to the King's Warrant, 159.

Laud, William, Archbishop of Canterbury, tyranny of, broken down by Pym, 41. His rule, not the Church itself, obnoxious to Pym, 47. He and his old rival in prison together, 102. Makes merry over a caricature of his rival, 103. Civilities between him and his fellow-prisoners, 103 note.

Leicester, Earl of, 37 note. 54. 281.

Leighton, Dr. relieved by Members' Fines, 249.

Lenthal, William (Woodstock), Speaker of the House of Commons, 22. His apprehensions of the results of his continuing Speaker, 23. Clarendon's portraiture of him, ibid. note. His obsequious Letter to Secretary Nicholas, 24, 25. His second thoughts on same subject, 28. His second Letter to Nicholas, ibid. note †. His memorable reply to Charles's demand for the Five Members, 191, 192. Amenities between him and D'Ewes, 229. 231. Impressions of his character as indicated in D'Ewes's Journal, 232. His conduct at the Restoration contrasted with Northumberland's, 234 and note. Always a time-server, 235. His conflicts with Members of the House, 236. 238. 241. Violates precedent by voting in a division, 237. Instances in which D'Ewes sets him right, 238. 239. 247. His deficiencies as Speaker, ibid. Rebuked for coming late to the House, 248. Effect of his example on another Member, 248, 249. See also 178. 219. 252.

Lords.

Lewis, Lady Theresa; her "Clarendon Gallery", 55 note.

Lichfield, Bishop of, at door of House, 102 note.

Lilly, William, on outbreak of Westminster tumults, 64 note. Puritans and Courtiers, 64, 65 notes. On the tumults, and on King and Queen's doings, 65 note. On Charles's manner of Speech, 192 note. On arrest of Members, King's conduct, &c. 217 note. Aspect of London on Sunday, 9th Jan. (1641-2), 338.

Lincoln, Earl of, 37 note.

Lincoln's Inn Reply to Common's Message, 176. See Inns of Court.

Lindsay, Robert Earl of, chosen Commander of Guard to Parliament, 116 note.

Lisle, Lord (Yarmouth, Hants), moves resolution on Irish affairs, 281.

Littleton, Sir Edward (Staffordshire), Lord Keeper, receives Bishops' Protestation from the King, 95. His share in impeachment of Five Members, 112, 113. Attorney-General Herbert's request to him, 312.

Liturgy, City Petition against enforcement of, 32 note.

London, City of, mulcted of its Plantation of Derry, 217 note. See City.

Long, Mr. Walter (Ludgershall), named on Committee of Safety, 280.

Lords, House of, refuse to join in Petition for Lunsford's removal, 36 note, 65 and note*. Protesting Peers in this and D. of Richmond's case, 36 note. 37 note. Their prompt action on impeachment of Bishops, 100. Vote come to by them, 100, 101. Bishop Hackett on their "anti-episcopal sourness", 101 note. Aspect of House after

Index. 407

Ludlow.

Bishops' Committal, 104. Impeachment of Five Members delivered to House, 112. Join with Commons in demand for Guard, 115. Copy of King's reply, 116 *note*.

Ludlow, Edmund, anecdote related by, 161 *note*. On number and equipment of Charles's Guards when he entered the House, 180. Anecdote of Lord Northumberland, 235 *note*.

Ludlow, Sir Henry (Wiltshire), moves Vote against Killegrew and Fleming, 341. Result of Discussion thereon, 342.

Lumley, Walter, scurrilities heard by, 362 *note*.

Lunsford Sir Thomas, appointed Governor of the Tower, 34. His character and antecedents, 34, 35. Object in appointing him, 35, 36. Clarendon's version of his appointment, 35 *note*. Commons solicit his removal, 37. Day on which his Warrant was signed, 61. His appointment cancelled, 62. Lords decline to petition for his dismissal, 36. 65. and *note*. Sidney Bere's report thereon, 69. Superseded, knighted, and pensioned, 70 and *note*. Effect of his dismissal on the people, 71. Captain Slingsby on same subject, 77. Led assault in Westminster Hall, 82. 185 *note*. Willing to help in any desperate affair, 205. 322. Stapelton's sarcastic allusion to him, 322 *note*. Excites fears in the City, 366, 367. His name and Digby's coupled, 367 *note*.

Lytton, Sir William (Herts), compliments Sir Simonds D'Ewes, 219. D'Ewes's services to him, *ibid. note*. His Suggestion to House, 276. Nominated on Committee of Safety, 280.

Milton.

MACAULAY, Lord, authority cited in Essays of, 312.

Majorities and Minorities, their respective rights, &c. 9. 18. 20.

Manchester, Earl of, 16. 34 *note*. 94.

Mandeville, Lord, puts in his claim for office, 54. Withdraws in favour of Hollis, 55. Impeached with Five Members, 182 *note*, 311 *note*. See *Kimbolton*.

MANUSCRIPT Authorities cited or referred to: See *Bere. Carterett. Dering. D'Ewes. Dowse. Latche. Marston. Nicholas. Porter. Slingsby. Smith (Thos.). Windebank. Wiseman (Thomas).*

Markham, John (Chief Justice temp. Edw. IV.) on King's right of arrest, 312.

Marston, John, warns Lord Kimbolton, 87. 117. Copy of his Letter, *ibid. note*. His sources of information, 88.

Marten, Harry (Berkshire), carries House's Message to Lord Newport, 37. How D'Ewes characterised him, 220.

Mary, Queen, 305.

Masham, Sir W. (Essex), opposes Lunsford's appointment, 36.

Maxwell, James, Usher of Black Rod and his Episcopal prisoners, 105 and *note*. Sent by the King for Rushworth, 251.

May, Thomas, on King's Visit to City, 130, 131 *notes*. On King's right to withhold names of his advisers, 141 *note*. On number and equipment of King's Guards on entering House, 180, 181. Mistakes made by him, 198 *note*.

Maynard, John (Totness), active in debate, 309. Able Speech by, 344—347. His baseness at the Restoration, 344.

Merchants of London in Charles's time, 253, 254.

Milton, John, vituperated by Bishop Hacket, 90, 91 *notes*.

E E 2

Mildmay.

Mildmay, Sir Henry (Malden), complains of Mr. Jesson's fierce look, 239, 240. Rebukes Speaker Lenthal, 248.

Montreuil, French Ambassador, warns popular Leaders, 86. 131. 328.

Montrose, James Graham, Lord, made a Marquis, 17. His offer to kill Argyle and Hamilton, 284, 285, 286 notes.

Moore, Mr. and the Clerk's Journals, 232.

Morton, Father, has a great mind to accuse Secretary Windebank, 224, 225 notes.

Motteville, Madame de, a suspected Betrayer of Court Secrets, 86. Incidents stated in her Memoirs, 130. 138. 139. 146.

Murray, William, suspected of betraying Court Secrets, 15 note. Closeted with the King and Queen, 139. Queen's designation of him, ibid. note.

Murrayes, the, 27 note.

NALSON, JOHN, on the cause of the Westminster tumults, 65 note.*

Nelson, Rev. Mr. sneers at Pym's Scholarship, 358 note.

Napier, Mr. on Montrose's murderous offer, 284, 285, 286 notes.

Newburgh, Lord, 34, note. To be Master of the Wards, 58.

Newgate, attacked by the Citizens, 32 and note.

Newport, Lord, 36 note. 37 note. Requested to take Command of Tower, 37. Dismissed by the King, ibid. Nature of Charge against him: Charles's demeanour towards him, 37—39. His dismissal debated in the Commons, 82.

Nicholas, Sir Edward, Secretary of State; appoints Sidney Bere Under-Secretary, 5. Communicates Lord Kimbolton's doings to the King, 15, 16. Vengeful purport of the King's letters, 17, 18. Speaker Lenthal's obsequiousness, 24, 25. 28 note †. Sidney Bere's testimony to his worth, 26, 27 note †. "Sworne Secretary of State and knighted", 28 note. 49. Communicates Court Gossip to Admiral Pennington, 54, 55. King's letters to him from Scotland, 57. Further news on Official changes, ibid. Why he objects to Ecclesiastical Reform, 58. His list of Popular Leaders designated for office, ibid. Premature in his anticipations of Dismissal, 59. Issues new Proclamation against *Five Members*, 269. His Instructions, 269, 270. His precaution in taking King's Orders, 271. 271 note. His connexion with Order relative to Trained Bands, 324 note. Griefs of self and wife, 362, 363. See also 49 note. 140. 155. 257 note.

North, Lord, 36 note, 37 note.

Northcote, Sir John (Ashburton), bold avowal by, 242, 243. Occasion on which same was made, 243 note.

Northumberland, Algernon Percy, Earl of, Lord Admiral: Intended successor to, 4. Joins in Protest relative to Lunsford's appointment, 36 note. 65. Dowse's Visits to him on Pennington's behalf, 51 note. Leads the Lords in the Bishops' case, 100. His change to the popular side, 135. His conduct contrasted with Lenthal's, 234, 235 notes. Retorts on the King, 382. See also 37 note. 76 note. 100. 297.

Note-taking, D'Ewes's comment on proposal for preventing, 233.

O'CONNEL, Captain Owen, Cromwell's complaint relative to, 85 note.

Ogle.

Ogle, Captain, depoſes to hoſtile intention of King's Guard, 327.
Oudart, Mr. 204 *note*.
Owen, Captain, 76 *note*.

PAGET, Lord, 37 *note*.
Palmer's, Geoffrey (Stamford), Proteſt againſt the Remonſtrance, and its Reſult, 7, 8. Effect on Charles of courſe taken by him and his aſſociates, 18.
Palmes, Sir Guy (Rutland), on propoſal to alter a meſſage, 232. Awed into a Vote, 241.
Paris, fierce froſt in Paris (1641-2), 67 *note*.
Parliament, Firſt great Diviſions in, 7. Reſult of firſt Party Struggle, 10. The People's only hope, 65 *note*. Foreign aid againſt it ſolicited for Charles I. 224. Expoſition of its powers, 273. See *Commons*. *Lords*.
Parry's Treaſon, temp. Q. Eliz. 305.
Party. See *Parliament*.
Peard, George (Barnſtable), nature of errand confided to, 174. Reproves members for interrupting D'Ewes, 222.
Pemberton, Subſtance of Examination of, 79 *note*.
Pembroke, Earl of, joins in the Lunſford Proteſt, 36 *note*. 65. How he bore his loſs of Office, 57.
Penningman. See *Pennyman*.
Pennington, Admiral Sir John. Value, for purpoſes of this Narrative, of Letters addreſſed to, 3. Services rendered by him to the King and his party, 3, 4. Clarendon's character of him, 3 *note*. Fate of his appointment as Lord Admiral, 4. Declines to act on Bere's hint, 30 *note*. Further on ſame topic, from Captain Dowſe, 51 *note*. Makes Secretary Nicholas's Wife a

Prieſts.

"Proude Woman", 57. Secret ſervice undertaken by him, 361. His Correſpondents: See *Bere. Carterett. Dowſe. Nicholas. Slingſby. Smith (Thomas). Wiſeman (Thomas)*.
Pennington, Alderman Iſaac (London), charged with important duty by the Commons, 124—155. 157. 174. Prominent in debate under Glyn, 309. Suſpects tamperings with Town Guards, 340, 341.
Pennyman, Sir William (Richmond), deſignated Succeſſor to Vane the younger, 30 *note*. 51 *note*. 52
Pepys's glee over Glyn's accident, 344 *note*. His tribute to Slingſby's memory, 365 *note*.
Percy, Henry (Northumberland), object of Conſpiracy of, with Goring, 246.
Pierrepoint, Francis (Nottingham), endeavours to exculpate Attorney-General Herbert, 128 *note*, 312, 313.
Pierrepoint, William (Great Wenlock), named on Committee of Safety, 280.
Pope, Foreign aid ſolicited by the, for Charles I. 224.
Porter, Endymion (Droitwich), why abſent from Parliamentary duties, 364 *note*. His characteriſtic Letter to his wife, 364, 365 *notes*.
Poulton, Ferdinando, repeats a Scurrilous Couplet, 358 *note*.
Prentices of London attacked by the Soldiers, 68. Exaſperation of the people thereat, 69.
Price, Charles (Radnorſhire), duty aſſigned to by Commons in expectation of Second Viſit from the King, 338.
Price, Herbert (Brecon), Teller in Diviſions, 279 and *note*. Named on Committee of Safety, 215, 280.
Prieſts condemned, commotion

Index.

Prince Elector.
caufed by Reprieve of, 31. 32. and *note*.
Prince Elector. See *Charles, Elector Palatine*.
Privilege not claimed by Commons to bar a juft Charge, 320. See *Commons*.
Pye, Sir Robert (Woodstock), duty impofed upon, 110. Wifhes for fome way of accommodation with the King, 201 *note*.
Pye, Sir Walter: Subject of his difcourfe with the Pope's nephew, 225 *note*.
Pym, John (Taviftock: one of the Five Accufed), refult of Court Offers of Place to, 9. Clarendon's infinuations refpecting him, 12. Offence intended to be charged on him by Charles, 12. 14. 15. Clarendon's regret at his non-acceptance of office, 13 *note*. 42. Object of Confultations at his Chelfea Lodgings, 16. His practical reply to parallel between him and Strafford, 19. Suggefts exiftence of Confpiracy to get up charges of treafon, *ibid*. Caufes of his great popularity; his earlier fervices and endurances, 39, 40. His rife to the Leaderfhip, and qualifications for fame, 41. Clarendon's tribute to his popularity, *ibid*. Why Charles's efforts to win him over failed, 42 *note*. Specimens of Royalift Lampoons on him, 43—46 *notes*. 199 *note*. His fecret influence over the King, 45—46. Ufe made of his Speeches by the King after his death, 46. His laft Refting-place, *ibid*, *note*. Renewed offers of Place made to him, 47. Points wherein he was lefs extreme than Hampden, *ibid*. Clarendon's teftimony on this head, *ibid*. *note*. Why Charles's Offers came too late: Sir Edward Dering's

Pym.
Minute on the fubject, 48. 152. Proximate date of the King's Offer to him, 49. His reception of old Vane on the latter's difmiffal, 52. Former offers of place to him and his party further difcuffed, 53—58. Charles's poffible motive in his later offer of Place to Pym alone, 59, 60. Had timely Information of King's Intent againft him, 88. Paffage on this topic from one of his Speeches, *ibid. note*. Members alarmed by a fuggeftion of his, 106. Character and object of his Speech, 107. His fources of information, 108. His Plan: how received by the Houfe, 108, 109. On King's refufal of Guard: fragments of his Speech, 118, 119. Seizure of his Papers by King's Warrant, 119, 120. 302. His connection with Lady Carlifle, 133. Scandal and Libels to which this Connection gave rife, 135, 136 *notes*. Queen's Queftion about "that roundheaded man", 136, 137 *notes*. Defends himfelf againft the Impeachment, 161—165. Away to the City by Water, 179. Looked for in the Houfe by Charles, 186. 189 *note*. 190. 191. His rejoinder to King's Complaint againft him, 210. Communicates to the Houfe anonymous warning of Treachery received by him, 210, 211. Tolerant feeling between him and D'Ewes, 220. Objection taken to Anfwer to Royal Meffage drawn by him, 221. His "difcretion and modefty" commended by D'Ewes, 222. His heavieft charge againft the King proved, 299, 300. Thoufands of Petitioners for him, 338. 357. Juftificatory paragraphs from Petition, 357 *note*. Sample of attacks upon

Reformadoes.

him, 358 *note.* Thanks City for protection, 371. Dering's characteristic expression, 372. Avowal made in his "Vindication", 379, 380. See also 13 *note.* 37. 177. 178. 182 *note.* 198. 213. 225 *note.* 233. 245. 246. 267. 269. 271 *note.* 272. 295. 311 *note.* 320. 328. 348.

REFORMADOES, what they were, 180 *note.*
Remonstrance, Debates on the, 4, 5. 6, 7. Palmer's Protest, 8. Tactics of the Minority, 9, 10. Its publication, 60. Its object, 377. Referred to, 113, 154, 163, 253, 274.
Richardson, junior, and John Walker find anonymous letter addressed to Pym, 210.
Richmond, James Stuart, Duke of, appointed Lord Steward, 30 *note.* His sally: Protest of Peers on the occasion, 36 *note.* 279 *note.* Windebank's liking for him, 50 *note**.
Rigby, Alexander (Wigan), purport of Motion made in Commons House by, 160, 161.
Robartes, Lord, 36 *note.*
Rochester, Earl of. See *Clarendon, Henry, Earl of.*
Rolle, Sir Samuel (Devon), named on Committee of Safety, 280.
Rome, letter on English politics at, 224, 225 *notes.*
Romilly, Sir John, Master of the Rolls: Services rendered to English History by, 3 *note.*
Roundheads and Cavaliers, first use of the epithets, 62, 63. Hampshire Vicar's antipathy, how expressed, 63 *note.* William Lilly on this topic, 64 *note.* Clarendon on origin of the two epithets, 74. Baxter's anecdote of the " roundheaded man", 136—7 *notes.* Rushworth

Sandford.

on the "first miniting" of "Roundheads", 185 *note.*
Rous, F. (Truro), moves presentation of Members' Fines to Dr. Leighton, 249.
Rowley's Evidence as to threats of French interference, 85.
Roxborough, Earl of, keeps the Commons' door open, 185.
Rudyard, Sir B. (Wilton), named on Committee of Safety, 280.
Rupert, Prince, 136 *note.* 185.
Rushworth, John, as to Guard accompanying King to House, 180. On the term Roundhead, 185 *note.* Takes down Charles's Speech, 187, 188. Charles's corrections and erasures therein *verbatim*, 188, 189. Sent for by the King, 251. King's rejoinder to his excuses, 252. What took place after he quitted the King, 253. His account of Charles's reception in Guildhall, 258, 259 *notes.* His statement of House's Proceedings on 5*th January*, 290 *note.* Extent of his notes of Guildhall Sitting on 6*th January*, 300. On number of Bucks Petitioners, 353 *note.* 347 *note.* 351 *note.* See also 289. 290. 292. 293.
Russell, Lord John, quoted, 40 *note* †.
Russell, Sir William, Joint Treasurer of the Navy, 51. Made Sole Treasurer, 52.

SAILOR VOLUNTEERS, Services of accepted by Commons, 347 and *note.* 348. Epithets bestowed on them by the King, 348. 359.
Saint John, Lord, 36 *note.*
Saint John, Oliver (Totnes); Clarendon's Speculations on possible result of offer of place to, 13 *note.* Not on Committee of Safety, 280.
Sandford, Mr. J. L. argument of,

Savile.

as to Strode's identity canvassed, 198 *note*.
Savile, Thomas, Lord, appointed Treasurer of Household, 30 *note*. 50.
Saye and Seale, William, Lord (Old Subtlety), 36 *note*. 37 *note*. 38. Office proposed to be given to him, 55. 58.
Scot the Regicide and Speaker Lenthal, 234.
Scottish Covenant and City of London, 256.
Selden, John (Oxford University), 40 *note*. 147 *note*.
Shakespeare, William, unnoticed and unknown, 91 *note*.
Shawberie, Thomas, asperses Pym, 358 *note*.
Shepherd, one Mr. in the wrong place, 251.
Simmons, S. Publisher of Paradise Lost, 91 *note*.
Skippon, Major, and his Trained Bands, 256. Invested with Command of Tower, 335. His character and subsequent eminence, *ibid*. Anecdote told by Whitelock, 334, 335 *notes*. Office created for him: its necessity, 336. Made Sergeant-Major-General of City forces, 351. Duties assigned to him, 351, 352.
Slingsby, Captain Robert (Correspondent of Admiral Pennington), presumed design of, in coming to London, 4. Letters on the Remonstrance Debate, 4, 7. Anticipates great things from King's Visit, 21, 22. Change wrought in his views, 25, 26. News of the King, the Houses, and the Citizens, 26 *note*. On altered aspect of affairs, 27. 28. On Commotion excited by reprieve of condemned Priests, 32 *note*. Animus of "some of the Parliament" towards himself, 76 *note*. His account of

Songs.

the Westminster tumults, 77. On charge against Earl of Bristol, 78. Issue predicted if the King yield not, 80. His account confirmed by D'Ewes, 81. His apprehensions as to the Bishops' Protestation, 97, 98. "Extreame tempestuous weather", 99 *note*. On number and equipment of King's Guard, 181—183. Describes Impeachment of Five Members, 182 *note*. How the King came into the House, 184. What the King did and said, 194 *note*. Charles' reception at Guildhall and how he fared by the way, 260—263. Curious incident related by him, 268 *note*. Further on position of Affairs between King and Parliament, 298, 299. His words a confirmation of Pym's Charge, 300. On Return of Five Members and King's flight, 366, 367. Close of his letter, 367 *note*. His after career: Pepys' tribute to his memory, 365, 366 *notes*.
Smith, Mr. Philip (Marlborough), brings up Middle Temple Reply, 177.
Smith, Thomas (Correspondent of Admiral Pennington): On differences between King and Commons, 61, 62. Attack of Soldiers on 'Prentices, 68, 69. On "the last plott of the Bishopps", 99. Compares Archbishop Williams to Achitophel, 100. Troubles consequent on the King's Attempt, 206—208. How matters stand between King and City, 297, 298. His View of King's Stretch of power, 311, 312 *notes*.
Soame, Alderman Sir Thomas (London) joined with Venn and Pennington in deputation to City, 174.
Songs and Libels on the Popular Leaders, and their friends, no-

Index. 413

Southampton.

ticed, 17. 43—46. 199. 256 *note*. 306 *note*. 355 *note*. 362 *note*.
Southampton, Earl of, made Privy Councillor, 267.
Southwark Trained Bands, 349. 359. 369.
Spencer, Lord, 36 *note*.
Spenser, Edmund, Bishop Hacket's esteem for, 91 *note*.
Stamford, Earl of, 36 *note*.
Stapleton, Sir Philip (Boroughbridge), appointed a manager in Conference with the Lords, 121. Nominated on Committee of Safety, 280. Moves resolution on Irish Affairs, 281. His sarcastic allusion to Lunsford, 322 *note*. See also 126. 309. 316.
Strafford, Thomas Wentworth, Earl of, 2. 4. 13. 19. 39. 41. 51. 51 *note*. 52. 54. 55. 76 *note*. 77. 134. 135 *note*. 136 *note*. 137. 162. 251. 256. 355 *note*. 357.
Strafford, young Earl of, Generosity of House of Commons to, 227 *note*.
Strode, William (Beeralston, one of the Five Accused), incredulous as to Herbert and Littleton's assertion, 128 and *note*. 313. Clarendon's uncivil allusion to him, 149 *note*, His declaration as to real object of Impeachment. 165. Dragged out of the House by his friend, 179. 198—200. On his identity with the Strode of James's Parliament, 198 *note*. Contempt of the Royalists for him, 199 *note*. Epithets bestowed upon him by D'Ewes, 220. Gets the worst in an altercation with D'Ewes, 222, 223. See also 177, 178. 182 *note*. 198. 270. 271 *note*. 311 *note*. 320. 348. 371. See *Five Members*.
Suffolk, Earl of, 36 *note*.
Sunday in London, *9th Jan.* (1641—2), described 338, 339.

Vane.

Swift's reminder, to a high-flying secretary, 382 *note*.

TORY and Whig, 62.
Tower; name bestowed by Courtiers on the, 33. Qualifications required in its Governor, *ibid*. Steps taken by Commons for its security, 334. Clarendon's admission, 334 *note*. Skippon invested with its command, 325. Pym's later reference to this subject, 325 *note*. Suspicions communicated by Alderman Pennington, 340, 341. Its Lieutenants and Governing Officers. See *Balfour. Biron. Coniers. Lunsford. Newport. Skippon.*
Temple, Inner and Middle, Replies of, to Commons' Message, 176, 177. See *Inns of Court*.
Trained Bands of London, 254. 323. 336. See *City. Southwark*.

VALENTINE. Mr. 27 *note*.
Vane, Sir Henry the elder (Wilton), superseded, 27 *note*, 30 *note*. 50. His Treasurership of the Household given to Lord Savile. Windebank's fellow feeling towards him, 50 *note**. Welcomed back by Pym, 52. Takes up extreme position in debate, 242, 243.
Vane, Sir Henry, the younger (Hull), dismissed from Office, 30 *note*. 51. Believed to be for " root and branch ", 47 *note*. Candidates for his post, 51 *note*. His position in the Opinion of the Commons, 52. Their displeasure at his dismissal, 53. Conference and committee on which he was named, 173. 316. Exception to Harry Killegrew's Speech, 244. His addition to Guildhall Resolution, 315, 316.

Vaughan.

319. Baseness of his former friends, 344. See 173. 316.
Vaughan, Mr. John (Cardigan Town), Supported by D'Ewes, 221.
Venn, Captain John (London), duty imposed by Commons on, 124. 155. 157. 174.
Verney, Sir Ralph (Aylesbury): Notes of proceedings of Long Parliament (Camden Society Book) by, quoted or referred to, 20 *note**. 37 *note*. 84. 180. 183. 184. 185. 193. 289. 290. 292. 343. 347. 347 *note*. His Statement of what took place 5*th January*, 290 *note*. His notes of Guildhall Sitting on the 6th Jan, 300. His mistakes, 351 *note*.

WALKER, John. See *Richardson, Simon*.
Waller's parallel between Pym and Strafford, 19.
Walsingham, Sir Thomas, Kt. (Rochester) named on Committee of Safety, 280.
War. See *Civil War*.
Warburton, Bishop, on Lunsford's appointment, 36.
Warrants, Royal, Debates and Resolutions on, 303—308. 313 —315. 330—332. 343. See *Charles. Commons*.
Warwick, Earl of, 36 *note*. Scurrilous Couplet on, 358 *note*.
Warwick, Sir Philip (Radnor Town); Scandal against Lady Carlisle, 135, 136 and *notes*. His opinion as to Hampden's death, 168 *note*. Suggests that Commons are guilty of Treason, 350. Anecdote told by him, 382 *note*.
"Water Rats", 348. 359.
Wentworth, Sir Peter (Tamworth), 241. Horror of Culpeper at his "folly", 242.
Westminster Tumults; William

Williams.

Lilly on, 64 *note*. Their real cause, 65 and *note**. Prologue to the Civil war, 66. Object aimed at, 66, 67. Soldiers' attack on Prentices, 68, 69. Cause of King's acceptance of Volunteer Guard, 76. Slingsby's Version of these Tumults, 77, 78. Action taken by Commons to prevent their recurrence, 85. Course adopted by Bishops, 89, 90.
Wharton, Lord (Beverley), 36 *note*. 38.
Wheeler, Mr. (Westbury), Watch duty imposed upon, 110. Named on Committee of Safety, 280.
Whig and Tory, 62.
Whitelock, Bulstrode (Marlow), on Queen's influence in King's Counsels, 129, 130. His View of Lady Carlisle's Warning, 145 *note*. Named on Committee of Safety, 280. His questionable assertion, 383. See 354, 354 *note*. 382.
Wich, Sir Peter, breaks open the Arms Chest, 217 *note*.
Wilde, Serjeant (Worcestershire), sits as Chairman of Committee, 309, 310. Wrong issue suggested by him, 314. Set right by D'Ewes, 314, 315. See 330.
Williams, John, Archbishop of York, roughly handled by the Prentices, 71 and *note* †. Slingsby's account of his treatment, 77. His part in the affray next day, 78. A fighting Archbishop, 79. Bramston's, Hyde's, and Hacket's Accounts compared, 89 *note*. Real Author of Bishops' Protestation, 91, 92. Proceedings had on the matter at his Lodgings, 94. Bishops surprised by him into concurrence, 95. Dubbed Achitophel, 100. How his Intrigue was baffled, *ibid*. He and Laud in prison together, 102. Caricatures

Index.

Willoughby.

upon him: Laud's enjoyment of fame, 102, 103, 103 *note*. Apprentices provoked by him, 185 *note*.

Willoughby de Parham, Lord, 37 *note*.

Windebank, Sir Francis, Clarendon on flight of, 32, 33 *notes*. His secret understanding with the Queen and grief at loss of Office, 49, 50 *notes*. His fellow feeling for a cast Courtier, 50 *note* *. Desires to return to England, 67, 68 *notes*. Concerning his connection with the Roman Catholics, 224, 225 *notes*.

Wiseman, Sir Richard, slain in the Westminster Tumults, 64. Further references to the occurrence, 70. 78. 80 *note*. 185 *note*.

Wiseman, Thomas (Correspondent of Admiral Pennington), cha-

Young Man.

racter and position of, 7. On Palmer's committal to the Tower, 8. On close of Remonstrance Debate, and state of Houses, 8, 9. On the King's reception in the City, 22. On Changes of offices, 29, 30. *notes*. On King's Second Visit to the City, 264—267. 268. His despairing View of affairs, 287. 295.

Wray, Sir C. (Great Grimsby),

Wray, Sir John (Lincolnshire), both named on Committee of Safety, 280.

Wright, Edward, Alderman, Substance of Pemberton's Examination before, 79 *note*.

Wright, Thomas, Political Ballads (Percy Society Book) edited by, 358 *note*.

YOUNG Man, Question raised by D'Ewes's use of the term, 198 and *note*. 279 *note*.

I HAVE to thank Mr. HENRY CAMPKIN for the great care and skill with which this Index has been compiled.

J. F.

THE END.

BRADBURY AND EVANS, PRINTERS, WHITEFRIARS.

ERRATA.

PAGE.
- 91. 5 from bottom (*note*): for "*B.* Simmons" read "*S.* Simmons."
- 126. Laſt line ⎱
- 137. Laſt line ⎰ for "A*r*chetil" read "A*n*chetil."
- 147. 4th marginal note, for "1828" read "1628."
- 280. Line 12, for "Cocker*worth*" read "Cocker*mouth*."
- 370. Laſt line but one (*note*), for "*poſt* 364" read "*poſt* 374."
- 371. Line 8 from bottom (*note*), for "title" read "letter."
- 382. Laſt line but one (*note*), for "worſhip" read "lordſhip."
- 389. (*Index*) under "Authorities cited": MS. after *Dering* inſert *D'Ewes*. PRINTED, after *Lilly* inſert *Ludlow*.
- 403. (*Index*) under "Herbert, Sir Edward," for "348. 371," read "378. 381," and *dele* 379.

www.ingramcontent.com/pod-product-compliance
Lightning Source LLC
Chambersburg PA
CBHW022147300426
44115CB00006B/382